Wounded Innocents
and Fallen Angels

Wounded Innocents and Fallen Angels

Child Abuse and Child Aggression

GREGORY K. MOFFATT

Westport, Connecticut
London

Library of Congress Cataloging-in-Publication Data

Moffatt, Gregory K., 1961–
    Wounded innocents and fallen angels : child abuse and child aggression / Gregory K.
    Moffatt.
        p. cm.
    Includes bibliographical references and index.
    ISBN 0–275–97848–6 (alk. paper)
    1. Child abuse. 2. Violence in children. I. Title.
HV6626.5.M64 2003
362.76—dc21   2002044986

British Library Cataloguing in Publication Data is available.

Library of Congress Catalog Card Number: 2002044986
ISBN: 0–275–97848–6

First published in 2003

Praeger Publishers, 88 Post Road West, Westport, CT 06881
An imprint of Greenwood Publishing Group, Inc.
www.praeger.com

Printed in the United States of America

The paper used in this book complies with the
Permanent Paper Standard issued by the National
Information Standards Organization (Z39.48–1984).

10 9 8 7 6 5 4 3 2 1

Contents

Tables

Acknowledgments

To Megan, Kara, and Benjamin. I have invested all of myself in being your father.

To Stacey, my best friend and most dependable supporter, for your patience while I write, study, interview, and edit. But more importantly, thank you for being a wonderful mother to our children.

I also extend my appreciation to Mrs. Jayne Flinn, former Director of Resource Development, The Center for Children's Services in Danville, Illinois, for providing the information and much of the text for the case study involving Mary in Chapter 3.

To all the children who have passed through my office doors—for the distinct honor and privilege of being entrusted with your secrets, your sorrows, and your dreams.

PART I

Wounded Innocents

Often and often afterwards, the beloved Aunt would ask me why I never told anyone how I was being treated. Children tell little more than animals, for what comes to them they accept as eternally established.
—Rudyard Kipling

My first two books focused on violent behavior—hate crimes, serial killers, domestic violence, and workplace homicide. My passion, however, has always been children. As a graduate student in the mid-1980s, I was preparing to do my residency. At that time in history, graduate programs did not routinely have coursework for therapy with children with the exception of developmental courses. I told my advisor that my plan was to do my residency and internship as a school counselor with grade school–age children. She agreed to this residency site, but she told me that she knew little about children and she wasn't sure how much help she would be to me. My residency and internship lasted a year and my advisor was some help, but her self-analysis proved correct. Often I was on my own. In retrospect, those were the dark ages of graduate education in terms of child advocacy. In those days, the study of psychology and counseling had come a long way in terms of research and theory, and yet it totally neglected this most critical area of counseling. Fortunately, many graduate programs today offer at least one course in counseling with children and many offer specializations for those who are interested in focusing their clinical practices on children.

In many ways, a dichotomy exists in children. Given their various development stages, they are capable of doing some things while other cognitive or behavioral tasks are impossible. In some ways, children are amazingly resilient, able to overcome many painful experiences, and yet in other ways they are incredibly fragile. Cognitive limitations during the grade school years make it impossible for them to understand the full nature of traumatic events. This limitation protects them in one way, but it also puts them at risk because they are unable to formulate effective copings strategies on their own. Adults also have difficulty putting traumas into perspective, but they have the cognitive ability to formulate ways to deal with the trauma. For example, when someone we care about dies, our minds are tormented by thoughts, hopes, and dreams that we know we will never see because the person we love is gone. Yet at the same time, we have the cognitive ability to understand that everyone dies sometime, tragedy strikes all families eventually, and we know that we can overcome. Children have no such ability; therefore, they experience emotional pain and yet they have no strategies to deal with it.

One of my graduate professors, a child psychologist, told me that a child's future is determined in the first two or three years of life. After many years of clinical experience, I am not sure that I totally agree with him, but generally, I think he was correct. The first two or three years of life set the course for the child's future. Although the course can be altered, after age three it is much harder to change than it is prior to that age. Those early years, as my professor told me, are crucial. On the other hand, something I learned not from my textbooks, but through experience, is that children are incredibly resilient. Many times I have been working with a child in my practice who has experienced some form of trauma. Even though the child may be the youngest family member and may have been the sole victim of the trauma, the child often is the most adjusted and healthy person in the family system.

Some years ago I worked with a couple who had divorced. They initially brought their daughter in to see me because they feared she had been sexually abused. During the first meeting, both biological parents were present, even though they were divorced and seeing other people at the time. I saw the child for several years and, because of a court order, at one time or another I worked with every member of the family. During those years, the child experienced a car accident in which she was nearly killed, she was separated from both biological parents for three months after an allegation of sexual abuse (that was never proven) came to the attention of Family and Children's Services. During that time she was in foster care. Both biological parents remarried. Her father married a woman who already had three children and then the two of them had two others, making for a very crowded home. The biological mother, who had numerous boyfriends, also had other children by a man she eventually married. Drugs were present in one of the homes and a constant state of animosity existed between all parties. In the midst of all of this confusion and turmoil, this little six-year-old girl was by far the most healthy member of the family. She amazed me as I watched her internal instincts assist her in coping with very difficult circumstances.

After the tragedy of September 11, 2001, in New York, Pennsylvania, and Washington, D.C., I had conversations with many children about the events and what they thought of them. One child was thirteen years old at the time. She was very bright and clearly moving into formal cognitive operations—the ability to think abstractly as identified by theorist Jean Piaget. We had a very productive conversation, but one thing she said provided a clue that she had not fully grasped the meaning of the events. She said, "In a way, it is kind of exciting being alive when something like this happens. I know that people will never forget it and I'll be able to say I was there." This child was able to think about the future and hypothesize about what people would be thinking at that time (a formal operational skill). Yet she was still not fully developed because even though she recognized that people had died and that the episode was a tragedy, she distanced the event from herself (they were people she did not know in a place she had never been). In the process, she formulated an egocentric meaning—that it was "neat." Most adults would never have used those words because the worldwide meaning of the events—terrorism on our home soil, our vulnerability, the possibility of war, empathizing with those who suffered loss even though we didn't know them, and the mass death of innocent lives—was so momentous that being able to say you were there paled in comparison.

As a therapist, it is my job to recognize the dichotomy in children. I need to be able to recognize their strengths, how their immature thinking works to their advantage or disadvantage, and to help foster an environment that promotes their resiliency. I cannot overlook how their development works against them—how their lack of experience, their inability to think abstractly, and their minimal coping skills can turn even minor incidents into insurmountable obstacles. This book presents two sides of children: children as victims and children as perpetrators. We most often think of children as victims, but they are also perpetrators. In the second half of this book I will address violence committed by children and I will show why children engage in violent acts such as rape, murder, vandalism, and assault. I will also address violence against self, specifically self-mutilation and suicide. It may come as no surprise to you, as you will see in the second half of this book, that many child perpetrators were at some point in their lives also victims of abuse or neglect.

VICTIMIZATION OF CHILDREN

Children are always the first to suffer in any time of hardship or crisis. Even though parents may do their best to provide for them, putting the children's needs before their own, their efforts are thwarted by social systems beyond their control. In countries where poverty and famine are widespread, aid in the form of food, clothing, and other supplies is provided by relief groups from around the world. Yet many of these supplies never reach their intended recipients. Corrupt military and government leaders commandeer these supplies either for their own personal use or to sell for personal profit. In the United States, state and federal legislators pay lip service to helping children, to education, and to child protection. Candidates running for public office give long campaign speeches about their interests in children, yet when they get in office, they spend billions of dollars on pork-barrel projects that serve either their own personal interests or their constituency with a single primary goal in mind—to get reelected. Children do not vote; therefore, they are only of tangential importance to legislators—a means to an end. Even when their authors' motives are pure, many laws intended to protect children are toothless and some actually cause more problems than they solve. For example, the concept behind welfare reform during the Clinton administration was noble. The idea was to prevent welfare recipients from becoming dependent on government aid. It is true that reliance on government support perpetuates itself from generation to generation. Children grow up in homes where their parents and their grandparents, aunts, uncles, sisters, and brothers received welfare. They know no other way of life and welfare reform attempted to stop this cycle of poverty and dependence. However, when government checks stop coming, recipients who have either no income or minimal income are forced to make very difficult choices. Rent and power bills must be paid, food must be purchased and supplies for work (i.e., uniforms, clothing, shoes, etc.) must be acquired in order to hold a job. Therefore, even in homes where parents are responsible, children's needs are forced into second, third, or fourth place behind these needs. In homes where children are being raised by irresponsible parents, the problem is even worse. Drugs, alcohol, cigarettes, and other adult pleasures and pursuits push children's needs even further down the line, often leaving them hungry and uncared for. In states where lotteries are legalized, far more lottery sales occur in areas of low income. Many have called the lottery a "tax on the poor" because desperate people are more likely to play the lottery as a means of resolving their financial problems, yet their chances of winning are so slight that they are basically throwing their money away—only perpetuating their problems and the problems of their children.

Judges overseeing court battles over child custody cases are often uninterested in the developmental and emotional needs of the children involved. Many judges believe that children are too young and too easily manipulated by one party or the other to play any active part in custody decisions. When I am involved on behalf of a child in the legal wrangling over child custody, some judges give only limited attention to my testimony. They carefully examine the legal rights of the biological parents, stepparents, guardians, and other adults who have some claim to visitation, but give only cursory attention to the interests and emotional needs of the children involved. I will examine just such a case in depth in Chapter 2. I used to fear telephone calls from lawyers. My heart used to skip a beat when a caller identified himself or herself as an attorney. I knew that anytime I was called to court as an expert witness, part of the opposition's job, as with any expert witness, was to discredit me and do everything possible to make me look incompetent. Now, however, I am ready and willing to go to court. I realized that I could be a voice for the child whose interests I represented. Unfortunately, the court often pays only cursory attention to the child's desires and interests and often does not hear from the child at all. Family court judges are not developmental psychologists and, therefore, they do not know the social, emotional, cognitive, and physical issues related to a child's development and how custody or visitation may affect those issues. Even though I would rather a judge hear a child's wishes directly from the child, I know that I may be the only voice that child has as decisions are made that will affect his or her future.

Years ago when I first started my work as a researcher in the area of violent behavior, my sister, who knew of my interest in children and children's issues, asked me what I was doing in the area of violence by children. At the time, I had no plans to pursue this area. I was quite busy polishing my theory on violence by adults and I was developing an assessment tool for use both by clinicians and the general public. I had a very difficult time getting cooperation from law enforcement agencies and other sources on adult cases and I was not interested in the added difficulties of pursuing juvenile court records. However, as time went on, I have found the study of violent children inescapable. Following the spring attack in 1999 on Columbine High School in Colorado, I turned a corner in my research and began testing the application of my theories with adults on children. Even though I have found some substantial differences between children and adults when it comes to the assessment and treatment of aggressive individuals, there are many more similarities than differences.

Since that time I have published articles, lectured many times on aggression and children, and consulted with school systems, law enforcement officials, and clinicians. This book is the culmination of my professional work in two areas: my years as a therapist with children and my work as an expert in violent behavior. In the first half of this book, I have detailed the various forms of aggression perpetrated against children. Unfortunately, throughout my years in clinical practice I have seen crimes against children that I never would have dreamed, in my worst nightmare, that any human being with a conscience could commit. However, these days almost nothing surprises me. Parents, brothers, sisters, aunts, uncles, neighbors, babysitters, ministers, and teachers—all individuals one would expect to seek only the best for a child—have raped, molested, neglected, beaten, and tortured the children in their homes or under their care. Here are just a few samples of how children have been mistreated:

- One of my clients, a girl sixteen years of age, was removed from her home by social services two years prior to our first contact because she had been shot while in her father's care. Upon investigation, social workers discovered that her father, a divorced, gambling, alcoholic man in his forties, was not only sexually abusing this lovely young girl, but he and his perverted gambling and drinking buddies would use her as the prize for their poker games. The winner got to take the tiny child, only twelve years old at the time, to bed for the night. She was shot in the groin when an argument ensued during a poker game over who would sleep with the girl and the two men drew weapons and fired at each other. Even after she was removed from this horrendous environment, men would write disgusting sexual letters to her when she was in foster care.

- Eighteen-year-old Melissa Drexler delivered a baby while at the prom and threw the tiny six-pound child in the trash before returning to the dance. She was convicted of aggravated manslaughter and served three years of her twenty-five-year prison term before being released on parole in 2002.[1]

- In Wheaton, Illinois, a mother distraught over her crumbling marriage drugged her three children, smothered them with her bare hands, and then attempted to kill herself by cutting her wrists. She survived and was convicted of murder.[2]

- One of my clients was a fourteen-year-old male. When he was brought into the facility where I was working as an intern, he was so filthy that we had to burn all of his clothing. At his home, he was one of nine children who lived in a cramped, three-room house with only one bedroom. His parents did not worry if he was out all night because it made for less arguing between siblings and provided more space for those who were there. He had severe skin rashes due to poor hygiene and his hair and clothes were infested with lice. It took my colleagues and me weeks to teach him how to properly use a toothbrush, shampoo, and soap.

- In 1997 in Macon, Georgia, a twenty-eight-year-old man, angered over his domestic relationship, stabbed to death his wife, their fifteen-month-old child, his wife's cousin, and her unborn child. He also stabbed his twelve-year-old stepdaughter, but she pretended to be dead for several hours until he was gone and then she stumbled to a neighbor's home for help. The man was convicted of murder and sentenced to three life terms without parole.

- My fifteen-year-old former client had been tested in childhood and diagnosed as mentally retarded. He was developmentally slow, but I was certain he was not retarded. His parents, however, were convinced that he was mentally retarded and had treated him like an animal for many years. They dressed him haphazardly, invested minimal effort in his grooming, and talked in front of him as if he could not hear or understand them. They rationalized these behaviors by saying, "He is retarded. He doesn't know any different." Once while talking with this boy in the kitchen of the foster home where he lived, he attacked me with a kitchen knife. I quickly restrained him and I asked him what he was thinking. He said, "I'm retarded. I don't know any better." Sadly, this client left the facility where I was seeing him and was later arrested for molesting a child. He was sentenced to prison.

- In 1999, an allegedly loving family man shot his wife as she was sleeping and then chased his daughter down the hallway as she ran in fear. He shot her in the chest and then shot her five more times in the back as she struggled to survive. The fourteen-year-old girl died as a result of her wounds. She reportedly had told a classmate the day before the killings that she was afraid of her father and she wanted to go home with a friend.[3]

- In Escondido, California, a man was charged with child endangerment when he left his four-month-old son locked in a car while he went shopping. A passerby found the child and called police. The father returned as police were trying to open the car. The temperature inside the car was 110 degrees. Fortunately, the child survived.

- In Michigan in 2002, a twenty-five-year-old Detroit woman left her ten-month-old daughter and three-year-old son in her hot car for more than three hours. The woman first told police she had been abducted and raped, but later admitted that she was having her hair done. Both children died in the car, where temperatures were estimated to have reached 120 degrees. The woman was charged with first-degree murder.

- A three-year-old child died when social workers in a city near Washington, D.C., failed to properly monitor her case. She had been taken into foster care, but returned to her parents. Babysitters noted visible bruises on the child afterward and reported their suspicions, but social services failed to intervene in a manner that would save the child's life. Not long after regaining custody of the child, the little girl was fatally injured by blunt trauma.

- Michael Sulsona, a forty-year-old gas station worker, was arrested and charged with manslaughter for the death of his two-month-old daughter. He took the child to the hospital, claiming that she had fallen while he was playing with her, tossing her in the air. The child was unconscious and died the next day. At Sulsona's trial, the attending physician testified that the child had classic symptoms of shaken baby syndrome.

- A twenty-one-year-old mother admitted in court to neglecting her children when she left them alone and they died in a house fire while she was gone. Two of her three children died and a third was taken into protective custody.

- In Salisbury, Massachusetts, a thirty-seven-year-old male was arrested on multiple charges, including rape, assault and battery, and assault with a dangerous weapon. The man allegedly held his six children and his spouse as virtual hostages in his home. The children, ranging in age from eight to seventeen, never received any public education and had never been to a doctor. The children were kept so isolated that neighbors were not even aware that the children lived in the home. The mother, who was also abused by the man, broke her silence and left the home with the children, prompting the charges. She alleged that the man repeatedly beat, raped, kicked, and assaulted the children with a belt, his fists, a flashlight, and rocks. At least one of the female children had been sexually abused as many as three times a week since she was four years old.[4]

- In February 1999, a man entered a kindergarten classroom in an elementary school with a machete and attacked six children and several teachers before being subdued. He was angry about personal life problems and apparently decided to take it out on the children. Fortunately, none of the children were seriously hurt and the teachers also survived.

These are but a few of the hundreds of cases that I could list where children were abused, neglected, or otherwise maltreated. Incidents of child abuse are always heartbreaking and difficult to understand, but perhaps the most difficult case to process is one where a mother kills her children. Our experience teaches us that mothers, above all others, protect their children at all costs. It seems incomprehensible that a mother could perpetrate any crime against her children. Susan Smith stunned the nation in 1994 when it was revealed that she had deliberately drowned her two boys in a lake in South Carolina, but, unfortunately, hers was not an isolated case. Here are three cases that gained national attention.

Lauren Calhoun

Barbara Calhoun Atkinson was born to a prostitute and drug addict. Her first three years of life were difficult until she was adopted into a loving home. However, she began having noticeable difficulties in her teens when friends claimed that she began to show signs of a personality disorder.[5] She quit school after the tenth grade and by age seventeen, she was married to a much older man and had become pregnant. Just months after their marriage, her husband, Jimmy Wayne Jenkins, moved out, leaving the young girl alone with no means of support. She moved in with sympathetic friends and bore a child named Lauren. Knowing that she could not care for the child, she surrendered her rights to the child to acquaintances named Bill and Sabrina Kavanaugh. After Barbara delivered her baby at the hospital, the Kavanaughs took the child home, intending to adopt Lauren. However, when Barbara's parents learned about her decision to give Lauren up for adoption, they forced her to reclaim Lauren. For nine months the Kavanaughs and Barbara Atkinson wrestled in court over the child. Included in the legal wrangling was the testimony of a court-appointed guardian who told the judge that Barbara Atkinson was unfit to be a parent and that Lauren would be better off in the custody of the Kavanaughs.[6] In the end, however, the judge determined that Barbara Kavanaugh had the legal right to the child and Lauren was returned to her custody. For the next year and a half, the Kavanaughs maintained periodic contact with the child until Lauren turned two. At that time, Barbara Atkinson stopped returning phone calls. Apparently, she had moved and her phone had been disconnected. The Kavanaughs would not see Lauren for six more years.

In June 2001, a concerned neighbor called police in Hutchins, Texas, a town just south of Dallas. In the home they found Lauren in deplorable conditions. The mobile home was occupied by Barbara Atkinson, Kenneth Ray Atkinson (Lauren's stepfather), and five other children. Lauren, nine years old by this time, was a foot smaller than most children her age and she weighed only twenty-five pounds—half the normal weight of a child her age. Authorities say that the child had been locked in a closet in the master bedroom of the trailer for four months. Her eyes were sunken, her skin was peeling, and her bloated stomach revealed clear signs of malnutrition. The child, who communicated on the level of a three year old, told police she was two years of age. Not only was she malnourished and neglected, but there was also evidence that she had been repeatedly sexually abused. The medical examiner discovered injuries to her genital area that were consistent with sexual intercourse or intercourse "by a blunt or sharp object."[7]

The Atkinsons eventually admitted their neglect when they told authorities that Lauren was left alone locked in a 4-by-8-foot closet while the "rest of the family went on trips out of town."[8] Lauren not only was locked away in the filthy, lice-infested closet for weeks, but she was forced to sleep on a urine-soaked blanket and was often covered in her own waste. Siblings reportedly told authorities that Lauren had been "locked away for being bad and for eating too much."[9] Relatives and friends said that they had not seen the child in weeks and when they inquired as to her whereabouts, they were told that the child had an eating disorder and was staying with a babysitter.[10] Even though it appears that none of Lauren's siblings attended school during the 2000–2001 school year, there was no indication that they were abused and neglected to the extent that Lauren was.

Barbara and Kenneth Atkinson were arrested on felony charges. Both of them expressed remorse for their behavior and it was clear that they knew what they had done was wrong. The other five children, ranging in age from twenty-three months to ten years, were placed in foster care. Protective services had visited the Atkinson home before in other places where they had lived, but no intervention involving Lauren occurred in those cases.

The Kavanaughs found out about Lauren after Barbara's arrest and made it clear that they were still interested in adopting the child. Barbara Atkinson's parents initially said that they would pursue custody of the child, but after Barbara voluntarily gave up her parental rights in favor of the Kavanaughs, they backed down. As of this writing, the Kavanaughs are on track to adopt Lauren. Lauren required several surgeries and extensive medical treatment. She most likely will have permanent cognitive limitations due to her maltreatment during the formative years that she was in the custody of her mother. In January 2002, after pleading guilty to the charge of bodily injury to a child, Barbara Atkinson was sentenced to life in prison. She will be eligible for parole in thirty years. Kenneth Atkinson was convicted of causing bodily injury to a child in December 2002. His sentence hearing is pending, but he faces from five years to life in prison.

Darlie Routier

At its extreme, child abuse leads to the death of a child. As I mentioned earlier, Susan Smith watched as her children drowned right before her eyes. Yet Susan Smith was a passive participant in her children's deaths. She did not have to look at their faces as they drowned. According to a jury, in June of 1996, Darlie Routier brutally stabbed her two sons to death while they slept in their own home.

At 2:30 in the morning on June 6, 1996, a 911 operator in the small town of Rowlett, Texas, received a frantic call from a mother saying that she and her children had been attacked by an intruder. Police responded to the scene and almost immediately began to suspect that Darlie Routier was not the innocent victim that she seemed to be. Routier, twenty-six at the time, claimed that she and her two sons had fallen asleep in the family room of their home while watching TV. Damon, age five, and Devon, age six, were sleeping on the floor while she occupied the couch. Upstairs, her husband, Darin, was sleeping with their six-month-old son, Drake. Darlie told police that she woke up to find a man dressed in dark clothing and a baseball cap on top of her, attacking her with a knife. After a brief struggle, she continued, the attacker ran through the kitchen. It was then that she noticed that her boys had been stabbed. She said that she chased the attacker through the kitchen and he fled through the garage and out through a window.

As she went through the kitchen, she said she found the knife on the floor and picked it up, placing it near the sink, and then pursued the man outside and down an alley, where she lost him. She then claimed that while she was outside she suddenly realized her boys needed her so she returned to the house, yet there is no indication that she did anything to help them. Her screams awakened her husband and he came downstairs to find the bloody scene. He found no pulse when he checked Devon, but he heard Damon's labored breathing. Her husband Darin decided to attempt resuscitation of Devon. By the time rescue workers and police arrived, Devon was dead and Damon was clinging to life. Despite efforts by rescue personnel, he died before he reached the hospital. Darlie was also taken to the hospital with knife wounds to her neck and shoulder.

Police descended upon the home, carefully searching for the intruder that they feared might still be in the house. Quickly, though, it became evident that pieces of Routier's story conflicted with the evidence in and around the home. The window where the intruder allegedly entered and exited had dust on the sill that was undisturbed. No blood was found on the window as would have been expected when the intruder fled, and the moist ground beneath the window showed no signs of disturbance. The bloody knife on the kitchen counter was taken from a knife rack in the Routier kitchen. The screen to the window had been cut, but if the intruder had a knife to cut the window, why would he have taken another knife from the kitchen? Upon further investigation, detectives using Luminol, a chemical that detects blood even after it has been washed away, realized that the kitchen sink had been cleaned of blood and a bloody handprint from one of the boys had been washed from the sofa in the den. There was no evidence of any kind outside that there had been an intruder—not a single drop of blood, no footprints, nothing. Likewise, no fingerprints were found in the home, except those belonging to the Routiers, and K-9 units found no trace of any intruder. Detectives were also at a loss to determine any motive for the alleged break-in and attack. The tiny family dog attacked a police officer, nipping at his heels, but apparently in no way reacted to the alleged attack. The minimal disturbance in the home was inconsistent with two struggling adults, and Routier's injuries, according to medical professionals, appeared self-inflicted. Darlie's behavior also troubled many who treated her injuries. Detectives, nurses, and others noticed an almost emotionless Routier as she discussed her children and even when she was taken to the same trauma room at the hospital occupied by her blood-covered deceased son, she simply turned away.

Both boys had deep penetrating wounds to the chest, puncturing their lungs. A former FBI special agent analyzed the murders and determined that the attacker knew the boys and that the wounds were personal—wounds of anger. Even though Darlie's neck wound narrowly missed her jugular vein, medical experts described Routier's wounds as superficial. She said that she woke up when she heard her son call her name and she felt the man get off of her.[11] Why would the attacker deliver fatal blows to the allegedly sleeping children and yet inflict such superficial wounds to the mother? Darlie said that after she fought off her attacker she saw him stabbing her son, yet she also said she fought him off and he ran through the kitchen. How did the alleged assailant complete the attack on the children, yet flee to the kitchen as she claimed? Why did she chase him, leaving her injured children in the house unattended? Why did she not check on her husband and infant child who were asleep upstairs? Why didn't she call her husband for help?

Perhaps confirming investigators' suspicions was Routier's behavior a few days after the murders. On what would have been Devon's fifth birthday, Darlie and others, in front of news cameras, celebrated the birthday at his grave. Images of Routier laughing, chewing gum, and spraying Silly String over the grave, were broadcast nationwide. Days later she was arrested and charged with murder.

She was tried only for the death of Damon. Prosecutors withheld the possibility of trying her for Devon's death in case of problems in the prosecution for the murder of Damon. The trial lasted four weeks and during that time prosecutors painted a painful picture of a cruel woman who coldheartedly slaughtered her children. Prosecutors argued that Routier was a woman of excess and materialism, indifferent and resentful of her sons, and prone to mood swings. The motive, they claimed, was her egocentric and extravagant lifestyle, her resentment of the boys, her inability to lose weight from her pregnancies, and financial stress. Having been denied a loan for $5,000 to cover their growing debt, the Routiers were in serious financial trouble. Later, Darlie told a friend that she would get $5,000 for each boy.[12] Routier's diary demonstrated the depth of her unhappiness when she allegedly wrote that she was desperate and suicidal the month before the killings.

Routier took the stand in her own defense, tearfully denying that she had anything to do with her sons' murders. Her pleas went unheeded as the jury took only ten hours to convict her. They recommended death for Routier just days later. Even though there is a possibility of a retrial because of court errors, today Darlie Routier awaits execution by lethal injection.

Darin Routier adamantly defended his wife, as did her friends. Even though Routier was convicted, there is evidence of her innocence. Just as the defense provided a weak motive for the break-in, prosecutors provided a weak motive for Routier's killing of the boys. Evidence discovered after the trial indicated the possibility of a latent print on the kitchen counter not belonging to the Routiers, and in June 2002 a fingerprint expert hired by Routier's attorneys said that a bloody fingerprint found on a coffee table did not belong to anyone in the Routier home. But other experts deny that this finding has any bearing on the case or a decision for a retrial. With regard to her behavior at her son's grave, people deal with grief and loss in a variety of ways and there is little evidence from this event alone that Darlie did not love her sons. The preponderance of the evidence, in my opinion, however, points to Routier as the assailant.

Andrea Yates

Andrea Yates, thirty-six, was from a small Texas suburb of Houston. There is no question that Yates killed her children. She admitted to drowning all five of her children, one at a time, in the bathtub. Afterward, she called her husband and said there was a problem at home and then she called police. When police arrived, she confessed. What makes the Yates case confusing is her motive. Yates allegedly killed her children due to insanity brought on by postpartum psychosis.

Andrea Pia Yates in many ways is atypical of mothers who kill their children. She was valedictorian of her high school class, captain of the swim team and a record holder, a registered nurse for several years, and a woman who seemed to have life together to those who knew her from a distance. Raised in a Catholic family, Yates married Russell Yates, a Methodist who worked as a NASA computer engineer at the Johnson Space Center, after living with him for a year. They planned to have as many children as "God wanted." Children followed one after another. Life was difficult for Yates, but it wasn't until the birth of her fourth child that Andrea began to exhibit symptoms of mental disturbance. She experienced postpartum depression, a common occurrence in women after they deliver children. However, for Andrea, the depression was not short-lived, as is usually the case. Not only that, her deep depression also led to symptoms of psychosis. Postpartum psychosis is very rare, occurring in one in five hundred to one in a thousand women.[13] It was this psychosis, her legal team alleged, that caused Andrea on June 20, 2001, to kill six-month-old Mary, two-year-old Luke, three-year-old Paul, five-year-old John, and seven-year-old Noah.

That morning, around 9:30 A.M., just after her husband had left for work and an hour before she expected her mother-in-law to arrive to help her around the house, Andrea Yates fixed breakfast for her children. Then she locked all of the doors in the house, filled a bathtub with water, and methodically took her five children into the bathroom, one at a time, held them under water for several minutes each, and drowned them. She began with Luke, then Paul, and then John. After drowning each one, she carried them to the master bedroom, laid them side by side in the bed, and covered them with a sheet. Next she drowned her infant daughter, Mary. As the child lay lifeless in the bathwater, seven-year-old Noah came into the room and asked, "What's wrong with Mary?" She told Noah to get into the tub, but he ran, asking his mother, "Have I been a bad boy?" Yates chased him down and drowned him beside his baby sister.

Yates removed Mary's limp body from the bathtub, bruised from struggling against her mother, but for some reason left Noah face down in the tub. When children are murdered, the position of the body provides clues to possible suspects. Whether the victim was known by the perpetrator or not, for example, can be hypothesized by body position. When parents kill their children, they do things to "comfort" the dead child, such as placing stuffed animals or special blankets with their bodies. Placing the children in the bed and covering them up was a way for Andrea to "care" for and comfort her dead children. So why did she leave Noah in the bathtub? I believe that the pain of chasing her eldest son and drowning him beside the infant child was too much to bear. Leaving him face down in the water was her subconscious way of not having to face him and a way to remove his frightened face from her memory. Adding credibility to my theory is the fact that when the first officer arrived on the scene, she told him about the four children, but never mentioned Noah in the bathtub. Again, I think she was trying to remove him from her mind.

After placing Mary's body beside those of her siblings in the bed, Andrea called her husband. She told him that he needed to come home. When he asked if anyone was hurt, she said "Yes." "Who?" he asked. "The children. All of them," she said.[14] Next she phoned 911 and told the operator her name. She calmly said that she needed someone to come to her home, but was hesitant to say why. When asked if she was ill, Andrea said "Yes," but that she did not need an ambulance. The operator pressured her further for information as to why Andrea needed the police, but she still would not say. The first officer on the scene, Officer Frank Stumpo, knocked on the door. Andrea opened the door and said, "I killed my children." She led him to the bedroom where he found the lifeless bodies, some still warm to the touch. Andrea sat calmly on the couch and did not mention the body in the bathtub, but Officer Stumpo discovered his body later. In the meantime, Russell arrived at home to find officers blocking his way into the home. "Andrea, how could you do this?" he screamed to her.[15]

Andrea Yates spent her life trying to please other people. She worked to please her parents when she was younger, taking care of her father as he suffered from a terminal illness. She was "always trying to be such a good girl [and] always thinking of other people," her mother said of her.[16] She even chose nursing as a career—a job that involved making life easier for others. She worked hard to maintain the appearance of a happy home, tending to her husband and children, despite clear symptoms of major depression and psychosis. Motherhood is difficult enough without the added stress of mental illness, which impairs one's ability to cope. She home-schooled her children and continued to bear children to please her husband, even when it was clear that her emotional life was in tatters.

It appears that her husband did not help to relieve her stress. He did not want her to work and was described as controlling by at least one therapist.[17] It also appears that even though she was suffering from depression after her fourth child was born, her husband may have pressured her to have yet another. Russell was described by Andrew Kennedy, a relative of Andrea's, as a self-centered person whose "communication skills are an F-minus."[18] He allegedly failed to take Andrea to her therapy appointments following one of her hospitalizations. His unrealistic expectations for the children may have added pressure on Andrea to perform as the perfect mother. Russell told a therapist that one of his main goals was to "teach his sons how to be quiet for longer periods of time."[19] Imagine trying to keep five children quiet for "long periods of time" even in the best of health, let alone when one is stressed, suffering depression, hearing voices, and unable to please those around you.

As if earthly pressures were not enough, after being told that she would go to hell because of her faith, she also endured spiritual pressure to convert from her Catholic faith to the Methodist faith.[20] She thought she was possessed. "How long do you think the devil has been in me?" she asked her brother some time after her arrest.[21] She believed that by killing her children, she was saving them from Satan and she believed they would be tormented the rest of their lives and wanted to spare them from that misery. Killing them, she believed, sent them on to heaven.

Perhaps the thread that held her life together was her medication. She had been prescribed several medications following a suicide attempt, but she was taken off her antipsychotic medications prior to the murders. In fact, Russell Yates said that two days before the drownings he talked with Andrea's psychiatrist and said that he thought she needed to start taking her antipsychotic medication again, but the psychiatrist said "No."[22] But the burden of responsibility for her medications must also be shared with Andrea. During her trial, a psychiatrist who interviewed her in prison said that she had secretly avoided taking her medications even when they were available.

Andrea was bright and people around her expected great things from her. Given all of these pressures, compounded by major depression and psychosis that brought uncontrolled voices and images into her world, it is no wonder that she believed she was a "bad mother who had permanently damaged" her children.[23]

The pressure became unbearable in June 1999, and she tried to take her own life by taking forty to fifty of her father's Alzheimer's pills. She was hospitalized for thirteen days. But only weeks after her release, she again was suicidal, this time cutting her neck with a steak knife. Again she was hospitalized. Andrea feared what she might do. One report from Andrea's medical records indicated that after this suicide attempt she told a doctor that she "tried to kill herself because she was afraid she might hurt somebody."[24]

Andrea had contemplated killing the children for several weeks. In fact, her mother-in-law saw that Andrea had filled the bathtub one day in May, just four weeks before she drowned her children, and when she asked Andrea why, she got no answer.[25] Later, she told investigators that she had contemplated killing them before, as recently as the night before she committed the murders, but she just wasn't ready.

Her doctors were concerned about her. They were aware of her depression and psychosis, as well as her husband's controlling behavior. Even though her depression began after the birth of her fourth child, she indicated that she began hearing voices after the birth of her first child.[26] Then, a year before the murders, she told her doctors that she was seeing visions. "There was a voice, then an image of the knife … I had a vision in my mind, get a knife, get a knife," she said.[27] She was prescribed Haldol, a powerful antipsychotic medication, but later was taken off that medication. Doctors were concerned about Andrea, and when they learned that she and Russell were planning to have another child, they wrote, "This will surely guarantee further psychotic depression."[28] Some critics have noted that Andrea was placed in group therapy for alcoholism and drug addiction, even though she suffered from neither of these, but that is not unusual. I have also placed clients in similar group therapy because of the many benefits of group accountability, even when alcoholism is not the presenting issue.

She was charged with capital murder in the deaths of Noah, John, and Mary. In Texas a person must commit two murders to get the death penalty. Andrea could have received the death penalty, but prosecutors offered to waive the death penalty and seek life in prison if Andrea would plead guilty. Instead, Andrea entered a plea of not guilty by reason of insanity. *Insanity* means that she did not know that what she did was wrong, and this defense rarely is successful. Clearly, Andrea knew what she was doing and I believe that at least she had an idea that it was wrong. When Officer Stumpo asked her if she realized what she had done, she said, "Yes I do. I killed my children."[29] However, I propose that the legal definition of *insanity* may not be broad enough for a case like Andrea Yates's. I believe it is possible that even though she knew that what she was doing was wrong, her mental dysfunction was so severe that she had no control over her behavior. Some have interpreted the calmness that she exhibited while on the phone with the 911 operator and later with police as cold-blooded cruelty, but her calmness could just as easily have been the result of dissociation, a common response to trauma.

In September 2002, after eight hours of deliberation, a jury decided that she was competent to stand trial. Her trial jury did not accept her insanity defense and after finding her guilty of capital murder, she was sentenced to life in prison. She could be paroled in forty years. Since her arrest, Andrea is back on medication and her psychological condition is reportedly improving.

I know it sounds cold, but in some cases of severe abuse, a part of me is almost relieved when I hear that the child died. Even though I would never wish death upon children and I know that those who survive severe abuse can eventually recover, to some degree, I also know that their lives will never be what they could have been. They very likely will never have normal relationships, they will never trust in a way they could have if they had not experienced such cruelty in their past, and I know that the specter of their abuse will always lurk in the shadows. We can know that Lauren Calhoun, at the very least, will have lifelong cognitive deficits that can be directly attributed to her abuse. Further, her emotional scars will be evident in all of her relationships as long as she lives. Part I of this book addresses these types of cases of sexual and physical abuse and neglect, and other cases of maltreatment. However, despite this depressing prognosis, there is hope for healing. Chapter 5 provides a look at treatment and hope for recovery for the child victims of abuse.

Writing about the causes of behavior is a touchy issue. On the one hand, as a psychologist, I can't help but see the social influences in a child's life and how those influences clearly affect his or her actions. Yet, on the other hand, it would be easy to dismiss personal responsibility and lay all of the blame for one's behavior at the feet of parents or the larger culture. What I hope I have accomplished in the pages of this book is to strike a balance between the two. One's environment clearly has a significant impact on the friends one chooses, the activities one undertakes, and the habits that become an everyday part of one's life. Yet it is equally clear that many children overcome the deficits in their environments and, rather than allowing their surroundings to mold them, they rise above them. For example, the research on serial killers has demonstrated a clear link between male children who are sexually humiliated by their parents and future sexual predatory behavior. Yet thousands of children are mistreated by their parents, many of them are sexually humiliated, and yet they turn out to be productive adults. What variable causes one person to act out in a dysfunctional way and prompts others to be something better?

This question is actually misleading. It would be convenient if we could say that the difference lay in a single variable, but it clearly does not. More likely, the differences include a number of variables and even more difficult to identify are the interactions between variables. When a physician prescribes a medication, let's say a painkiller, the dosage is based on the patient's age, weight, and relative health. Even though there may be standard dosages, the standard comes from these three variables, among others. Likewise, the same patient may choose to drink alcohol. Among the variables that will determine how much alcohol a person can drink before becoming intoxicated are the person's weight, diet, health, gender, and how much the person has eaten. Therefore, a twenty-one-year-old, 110-pound female who had nothing to eat for several hours could not drink as much without becoming intoxicated as a 225-pound male who just finished a large meal. In both of these cases—the prescription for a painkiller and the consumption of alcohol—several variables are involved in determining their respective effects. However, if the patient chooses to take the prescribed painkiller *and* drink alcohol, the two chemicals have a compounding interaction effect. Since painkillers and alcohol are both sedatives (this is not exactly pharmaceutically correct but, for the sake of simplicity, allow me some leeway), they compound the effects of each other. Therefore, while a patient could take either chemical with minimal risk of injury, the two combined could cause serious side effects or even death. Likewise, two common household cleansers are ammonia and Clorox. Using either of these chemicals is potentially hazardous, but when they are combined, they create chlorine gas, a noxious vapor that could be fatal if inhaled in large enough quantities. Again, even though both chemicals have individual effects, when combined they create a new chemical with its own effects.

Even though the effects of social and psychological variables are less precise than those of chemical ones, the analogy sheds light on this issue. Social factors tend to lead to given outcomes. For example, it is no surprise that children in prosperous school systems tend to be more likely to attend college than children from poorer school systems. Even though there is variability among individuals, there generally appears to be a cause-and-effect relationship. Yet we also know that an individual student can *choose* to succeed or fail. If we have an average or below-average student who chooses to fail, she would most likely do poorly regardless of the quality of the school system she was attending. On the other hand, a highly motivated student can overcome the weaknesses of a mediocre school system and excel despite those weaknesses. These two variables, social and personal, are independent of each other. How much better would a highly motivated student do in a prosperous school system? We can assume the highly motivated student would perform even better in this condition. However, we cannot stop our analysis with just these two variables. There are many other variables interacting in this example. Race, socioeconomic status of the parents, gender, motivation, personality, parental encouragement, intelligence, development, social emphasis on education, and many other variables interact to produce the final outcome—a successful or unsuccessful student.

This discourse serves to demonstrate that all of the causes of aggression that I will address in this book are variables that need to be considered in context. These variables interact to produce either a greater or lesser likelihood of aggression. If we can isolate these variables, their individual outcomes, and their interaction effects, we can assess the probability of a given child behaving aggressively or not.

As is always true with statistics and research, there are exceptions. Every semester, students in my psychology courses argue with me about the validity of a statement I make or the accuracy of a given theory. They tell me a personal story that appears to discredit my statement or theory. I have to remind them that there are always exceptions and many variables to consider. I would always expect some variation that statisticians call "error." Therefore, one should not suppose that in the few pages of this book I could address all the possible permutations of variables and how they interact. What I do provide is a basis for further study.

Cultural Diversity

America is a diverse country. Many of us believe that there is no better place to live in the world and certainly there are few countries that are more prosperous. Therefore, immigration to the United States has been continuous since its inception. In Atlanta, where I live, a person can sit in a downtown restaurant and hear conversations in Spanish, German, French, Arabic, Thai, Korean, Japanese, Cambodian, or a number of other languages. The diversity in language is indicative of the diversity of culture in our country. When working with families, especially when trying to determine the presence of abuse, it is imperative that psychologists and social workers be familiar with the many cultural variations that might affect the determination of abuse. In some cultures, a father, mother, and child might all sleep in the same bed and even bathe together. In an American culture, however, this is not usually appropriate. The use of corporal punishment varies by culture as well. Many cultures around the world use harsh corporal punishment in child rearing. An immigrant family that moves to the United States will not immediately be familiar with laws governing abuse, and even if the family is aware of those laws, it will take time for the family to learn and implement new forms of discipline. There is even variation within the United States from one region to another. For example, a friend once told me that when he first came to the South he was appalled that female children kissed their parents on the lips. In the North, where he was from, that was never done, yet in the South it is not uncommon for a father or mother to kiss a young child on the lips when saying "Good-bye" or "Good night."

It is hard for an American to relate to the difficulties faced by immigrants. Immigrants may not know anything about American culture. My family traveled to Europe for the Christmas holidays in 2001. None of us spoke much French. We struggled in a restaurant the very first day we were there, trying to read the menu, place our order, and get a refill for our drinks. We didn't know how to read the bill correctly or exactly how much we were spending, and I wasn't sure whether or not the tip was included on our bill. In this one situation, I realized what it must be like for an immigrant. Americans expect people to speak their language and understand their culture even when they are overseas. Immigrants, however, come to our country knowing that they are leaving behind a way of life they are familiar with, and they may have few, if any, family members or friends in the States to help them adjust. They bring their culture with them, and when that culture violates the law in American culture, it must be petrifying for them as they try to understand what they did wrong.

Traffic laws in Mexico are very different than those in the United States. In Mexico, stop signs, one-way signs, lane divisions, and so forth are merely suggestions in many places. A Mexican national told me once that the basic rule is that the biggest vehicle makes the rules. Driving the wrong way on a one-way street presents little risk of a ticket. If the vehicle were large enough, everyone would simply get out of its way.

In the Atlanta area, where the Latino population is growing ever larger, it is not uncommon to read about traffic accidents where a Latino is charged. In once case, a Mexican immigrant passed a school bus in an Atlanta suburb. He was speeding, passing a school bus illegally, and also passing in a no-passing zone. Most American drivers would never pass a school bus while it was stopped to load or unload children, but in his culture it isn't uncommon at all to disregard traffic regulations. He was on his way to work and he was driving as he would drive in his home country. Suddenly, as he passed the bus, he ran head-on into another vehicle, killing the driver. The Latino was charged with vehicular manslaughter. I watched him in court with a dazed expression on his face as he tried to understand the judge, the proceedings, and even his own attorney. He spoke no English and clearly had absolutely no idea what was going on. He must have been saying to himself, "What did I do?" I am not excusing him for breaking the law or for taking a life in the process. However, what I think was missing at his trial was an understanding of cultural difference. His mistake was the failure to understand the meaning of traffic laws rather than self-centeredness or thoughtlessness, as portrayed by the prosecutor.

Cultural differences also impede treatment. In Nashville, Tennessee, a ten-year-old girl had suffered ongoing sexual abuse. When she was brought to the attention of social services, she failed to receive any psychological help because there were no Spanish-speaking therapists available for the Chilean-born child, who spoke no English. Abusers use cultural difference to their advantage as well. Some abusers tell victims that they will be deported if they report the abuse.[30]

It is imperative that any analysis of behavior include an examination of cultural variations. Even though this volume does not include a chapter on cultural issues, it is important for the reader to understand the significant issues in analysis that cultural variables present. Responsible caseworkers, psychologists, judges, and police officers can avoid misunderstandings and errant charges by learning the cultural variations that exist within the populations that they serve.

CONCLUDING REMARKS

In many of the cases you will read about in this book, especially those concerning my own clients, I have changed some details in order to protect their identities. In cases where public information is available, I have done my best to present the facts as I know them. Any mistakes in fact that may exist are unintentional and in no way are meant to cause pain or harm, even to the perpetrators. I use these cases only to illustrate the issues that I address in each chapter.

Many times people have asked me how I can do the work that I do. How can I bear the emotional pain of seeing children victimized day in and day out? I can endure the tragedy of abuse and neglect because I understand it. I understand why it happens, how children deal with it, and how to help them overcome it, and I readily accept the opportunity to go to court to speak on a child's behalf. I understand perpetrators. I rarely feel hate or malice toward them—only pity. I have even seen great changes effected in evil perpetrators who truly sought to better themselves. Perhaps most exciting and rewarding of all is seeing a child move from helpless victim to mature, responsible, and healthy adult. To have former clients call me or mail a wedding invitation or birth announcement to me is worth the many hours I have spent laboring over their cases. I do the work that I do because I have always wanted to do more than simply feel sorry for the innocent. I can do the work that I do because I know I can make a difference. By reading this book, I hope you can see how you can make a difference, too.

NOTES

1. "Prom mom to be released from prison," *CNN On-Line*, www.cnn.com /2001/LAW/11/24/prom.mom.ap/index.html, November 24, 2001.

2. "Mother convicted of murdering her 3 children," *CNN On-Line*, www.cnn .com/2001/LAW/12/19/mother.convicted.ap/index.html, December 19, 2001.

3. Brad Schrade, "Slain Cobb teen told friend she feared father, police say," *Atlanta Journal/Constitution* (December 19, 1999): G1.

4. Ed Hayward and Franci Richardson, "Police: Abusive dad ruled house of horrors," *Boston Herald*, www2.bostonherald.com/news/local_regional/Sali 06152001.htm, June 15, 2001.

5. "Mother's life shadowed by resentment," *Texas News*, www.reporternews .com/2001/texas/life0618.html, January 23, 2002.

6. "Court guardian argued that closet girl's mother was unfit eight years ago," *Fathers Canada*, www.fathers.ca/child_lock_up.htm, June 15, 2001.

7. "Possible evidence seized from abused child's home," *Houston Chronicle*, www.chron.com/cs/CDA/story.hts/metropolitan/947960, June 19, 2001.

8. Ibid.

9. "Horrifying abuse of girl locked in closet," *NewsMax.com*, www.newsmax .com/archives/articles/2001/6/13/193724.shtml, June 14, 2001.

10. "Mother's life shadowed."

11. Joseph Geringer, "Darlie Routier: Doting mother/deadly mother," *Crime Library*, www.crimelibrary.com/fillicide/routier/4.htm, January 2000.

12. Ibid.

13. American Psychiatric Association, *Diagnostic and statistical manual of mental disorders, 4th ed., text revision* (Washington, DC: American Psychiatric Press, 2000), p. 422.

14. Evan Thomas, Dirk Johnson, Anne Gesalman, Vern E. Smith, Ellise Pierce, Devin Peraino, and Andrew Murr, "Motherhood and murder," *Newsweek* (Internet Edition), July 2, 2001.

15. Ibid.

16. Susan Schindehette, Gabrielle Cosgriff, Bob Stewart, Fannie Weinstein, Melody Simmons, Don Sider, Beverly Keel, and Nina Biddle, "Nightmare," *People* (July 9, 2001): 60.

17. Anne Belli Gesalman, "In medical records, hints of a tragedy," *Newsweek* (Internet Edition), September 17, 2001.

18. Anne Belli Gesalman, "Signs of a family feud," *Newsweek* (Internet Edition), January 21, 2002.

19. Laura Parker, "'Psychotic,' but is Andrea Yates legally insane?," *USA Today* (September 11, 2001): 2A.

20. Gesalman, "Signs of a family feud."

21. "Texas mom believes 'devil' is in her, brother says," *CNN On-Line,* www.cnn.com/, July 1, 2001.

22. "Confession, 911 call allowed as evidence against Yates," *CNN On-Line,* www.cnn.com/2001/LAW/12/05/childrenslain.ap/index.html, December 5, 2001.

23. Amanda Ripley, Deborah Fowler, and Alice Park, "A mother no more," *Time* (July 2, 2001): 30.

24. "Why mother accused of drowning kids attempted suicide," *CNN On-Line,* www.cnn.com/2001/LAW/08/31/children.slain.ap/index.html, August 31, 2001.

25. Gesalman, "In medical records."

26. Parker.

27. "Why mother accused of drowning kids attempted suicide."

28. Parker.

29. Thomas et al. "Motherhood and murder."

30. Sheila Burke, "Counselors help Latino abuse victims 'lost in the system,'" *The Tennessean,* www.tennessean.com/local/archives/01/04/05898709 .shtml?Element_ID55898709, June 18, 2001.

CHAPTER 1

Munchausen Syndrome by Proxy

Selfishness is not living as one wishes to live,
It is forcing others to live as one wishes to live.

—Oscar Wilde

Julie was only three when her mother first began taking her to physicians seeking "treatment" for disorders that were actually only fabricated by her mother. By the time Julie was nine, her mother had graduated from visiting physicians to requesting surgery. This defenseless child was subjected to a painful iodine catheter used to introduce the dye into the body. Unknown to well-intentioned medical personnel, the only purpose this painful procedure served was to sate her mother's morbid need for attention from doctors. Her mother fabricated symptoms, such as headaches and sore throats that Julie never had, and she starved Julie to keep her weak and underweight, providing visible evidence to perplexed specialists that something was wrong with the child. Julie was prescribed medications for nonexistent symptoms, and all the while her mother threatened Julie to keep her mouth shut. Julie points out that her mother deliberately selected male doctors to ensure that she would always be in the examining room with her and how her mother covered her tracks by making sure medical records were not forwarded from one doctor to another.

As further evidence of her selfish motives, before office visits she would spend "hours" primping, changing clothes, and asking Julie "how she looked."[1] Julie's father intervened only when Julie's mother tried to induce symptoms in her brother, sparing him the decade-long pain and agony his sister would endure.

Julie asked for help, telling at least one nurse that her mother was making the symptoms up, but who listens to a child? The procedures continued. Her mother tried to force doctors to perform open-heart surgery on Julie, but when there were no physical indications of a need for such an invasive procedure, they refused. Julie's mother wasn't defeated. She continued her hunt for a doctor who would operate on the child and eventually found one who agreed to perform an exploratory heart catheterization. By the time she was eighteen, Julie had seen numerous doctors, undergone countless invasive procedures, and had been starved, forced to consume unnecessary medication, and had numerous needle pricks and vials of blood drawn. She finally confided what her mother was doing to her to a group of friends. Like the nurse in whom she had confided, her friends refused to believe her and severed their friendship with her for making "false" allegations against her loving mother.[2]

The only happy ending to Julie's story is that she survived. She finally got old enough to escape her mother's cruel manipulations. Her mother was never caught, prosecuted, or forced in any way to answer for her unconscionable behavior. Unbelievably, ten years after the abuse stopped, Julie's mother asked her to be a character reference. She was trying to become a foster parent. Julie contacted the agency and warned them about her predilection to perpetrate abuse.[3]

Waneta Hoyt became pregnant with her first child when she was only fourteen years old. In 1965, only three months after her son was born, he died at home. Waneta was alone with the child when he died. Again, she became pregnant and delivered a second son. This child lived for two years, but then he too died of no apparent cause while alone at home with his mother. A third time Waneta gave birth to a child, this time a daughter. However, after just forty-eight short days, the baby allegedly choked to death while Waneta was breast-feeding her. Once again there were no witnesses and it was assumed that the child had died of the same mysterious illness that had killed her siblings. Around this same time, a doctor named Alfred Steinschneider was pursuing a theory that babies who died suddenly, like the Hoyt children, were victims of sleep apnea. The Hoyts were encouraged to seek Steinschneider's help, which they did when Waneta had her fourth and fifth children. After they were delivered, the babies were observed at Steinschneider's clinic and were subjected to numerous tests. Eventually, he released them. The children were among the first to use the sleep monitors advocated by Dr. Steinschneider; nevertheless, both of them died before they reached their fourth month of life. Few people seemed to question the coincidence that these last two children, like the three previous ones, had all died while under Waneta's care and when no other witnesses were present. As with the previous children, sudden infant death syndrome (SIDS) was determined to be the cause of death. That was 1971.

Waneta and her husband later adopted a child. This son was the only Hoyt child to survive. Twenty years after the death of the fifth Hoyt baby, an assistant district attorney named Bill Fitzpatrick, as a part of a homicide investigation, was reading a paper on SIDS written by Dr. Steinschneider in 1972. In the document was the case of a family identified as "H" and it chronicled the death of five children in that family. He was certain the "H" children had been murdered. Along with an investigator, Fitzpatrick was able to convince the current district attorney in Hoyt's home county to prosecute her for murder.

In 1994, police questioned Waneta and she confessed to killing all five children. She detailed her frustration and how she had killed each one. Regarding the death of one of her sons, she said, "I was getting dressed in the bathroom, and he wanted to come in, and I didn't want him to. I told him to wait out in the hall until I was done, and he kept yelling, 'Mommy, mommy,' and screaming. And I took the towel and went out in the living room, and I put the towel over his face to get him to quiet down, and he struggled. And once he finally got quiet, he was gone."[4] She later recanted her confession, but was convicted of the murders in 1995 and sentenced to life in prison.

HISTORY, DEFINITION, AND PERPETRATORS

The two cases at the beginning of this chapter are examples of the disorder known as Munchausen syndrome by proxy (MSBP). MSBP is a controversial disorder in which someone causes illness in another person, usually a child under the perpetrator's care, in order to gain attention for rescuing or caring for the victim. The name for the disorder comes from an eighteenth-century German named Baron Karl Friedrich von Munchausen who was known for the fantastic and elaborate tales he spun of his military and hunting experiences. His fabrications were so well known that his name became synonymous with lying or exaggerated tales and deceptions. In the 1950s the term Munchausen syndrome (MS) was first used to describe patients who made themselves sick and seemed to thrive on the attention from doctors and others that their sicknesses generated. Munchausen syndrome by proxy was first identified in the 1970s by a British physician. By the 1980s, numerous articles about MSBP had begun to appear in research journals in the areas of mental health, law enforcement, and medicine. In 1993, just ten short years ago, Schreier and Libow published one of the first full-length volumes on MSBP for clinicians entitled, *Hurting for Love: Munchausen by Proxy Syndrome.*

Critics of the MSBP diagnosis argue that the American Psychiatric Association does not recognize the disorder. In a sense, that is true. There is no MSBP diagnosis in the current edition of the *Diagnostic and Statistical Manual (DSM IV-TR)*. The term Munchausen syndrome appeared in an earlier edition of the *DSM*, the *DSM III-R*, but it was not included as a diagnostic term. It was only mentioned as a common name for what we now call *fac-titious disorders*. In the *DSM III-R*, there was no diagnosis of factitious dis-order by proxy—factitious disorders by proxy are those in which physical symptoms are induced in another person. Therefore, there was no men-tion of MSBP at that time, either. Factitious disorders include one of two types of disorders that involve deception or lying. (The other diagnosis is called *malingering*, which I will address in the case of Kathy Bush, later in this chapter.)

Starting with the *DSM IV*, factitious disorders by proxy, the clinical term for MSBP, were included as a possible diagnosis. The current edi-tion of the *DSM*, the *DSM IV-TR*, clearly includes a discussion of what is otherwise called MSBP. This discussion in the *DSM IV-TR*, as with that in the *DSM IV*, falls under factitious disorders by proxy. It should be noted, however, that the *DSM IV-TR* refers to factitious disorder by proxy as a "proposed disorder."[5] Technically, MSBP would be classified as "Facti-tious Disorder Not Otherwise Specified." Not otherwise specified (NOS) diagnoses exist in every category of mental health diagnostics and are catchall categories for disorders that approach the diagnosis, but do not meet the criteria. Therefore, despite the fact that the colloquial name for the disorder does not appear in the *DSM IV-TR*, mental health, law enforcement, social services, and the medical community all recognize this disorder by its clinical name and have ever since it was first identi-fied.

Giving critics of the diagnosis their due, unlike many other mental health diagnoses there is no set of diagnostic criteria associated with the disorder. Therefore, even though mental health professionals recognize its existence, there currently is no clear standard for making the diagnosis. However, a similar issue was raised during the government's study on pornography in the 1980s. One observer was noted as saying, even though there is no formal definition, "I know it when I see it." That is the current status for MSBP in the mental health field.

The disorder is almost always identified first by the physical symptoms of the victim. Pediatricians or other medical personnel pass their suspi-cions along to law enforcement or social services personnel who then investigate. Perpetrators of MSBP are most often female, usually mothers, but they can be fathers, brothers, grandmothers, babysitters, or even doc-tors or nurses. Any caregiver who has access to the child victim could be a perpetrator. Perpetrators usually act alone, but there are some cases in which parents have colluded. The purpose the disorder serves for the per-son with MSBP is to fulfill his or her need to gain attention as a caring indi-vidual or to gain attention specifically from health care workers.

Perpetrators may exaggerate or even concoct false symptoms and force the victim to take prescribed medication for the nonexistent illnesses. Other perpetrators use an even more invasive approach to induce illness in their victims. Perpetrators have been known to inject fecal material into the child's feeding tube or to blow into feeding tubes to cause pain. They may put blood in urine specimens, scrub the skin of the victim with abrasive chemicals (like oven cleaners) to cause rashes, adjust feeding tubes to restrict intake, tamper with medication or medical instructions, and some have laced food with laxatives to induce diarrhea.

According to the *DSM IV-TR*, the most common symptoms of MSBP in the victim include vomiting, diarrhea, respiratory arrest, asthma, central nervous system dysfunctions, fever, infection, bleeding, failure to thrive, hypoglycemia, and rash.[6] Perpetrators rarely prey on more than one victim at a time and they most often smother their victims or in some way restrict their breathing. Therefore, many victims are thought to have sleep disorders like apnea or they are thought to be at risk for SIDS. Victims most often are children younger than age five—an age when they are too young to effectively verbalize their thoughts and feelings or to explain what a caregiver is doing to them. Victims are equally likely to be male or female. Other common symptoms include prolonged illness with no clear medical cause, symptoms that disappear in the absence of the suspected perpetrator, illnesses incongruent with each other, siblings with SIDS diagnoses, a parent who is exceedingly interested in medical jargon and procedures, and an overly attentive parent. Children who are victims of MSBP perpetrators may be forced to endure hundreds of doctor visits, hospital stays, invasive exploratory procedures, surgeries, and painful examinations. Perpetrators thrive on the attention they receive while attending to a child who is going through painful procedures. Some victims endure only temporary discomfort while others suffer permanent brain damage, psychological damage, limps, mental retardation, skeletal changes, coma, or even death. It is estimated that as many as 30 percent of the victims of MSBP perpetrators die.[7]

Schreier and Libow identify two common forms of MSBP.[8] *Doctor addicts* derive satisfaction from manufacturing nonexistent symptoms or exaggerating symptoms in order to gain attention from physicians. *Active inducers* are those MSBP perpetrators who actually cause illnesses in their children. It is suggested that MSBP develops from some traumatic loss in mother's life.

Even though there is variability in the profile of perpetrators, Kathryn Artingstall, a detective with the Orlando (Florida) Police Department, summarized the general profile of the MSBP perpetrator in a 1995 article for the *FBI Law Enforcement Bulletin*.[9] According to Artingstall, 80 percent of MSBP perpetrators have a professional health care background and 80 percent engage in Munchausen syndrome prior to inducing symptoms in others. The majority, again 80 percent, have some history of psychiatric treatment; 50 percent are suicidal at some point in their past, and the perpetrator is usually the mother. They almost always deny allegations of

Table 1.1
Issues Correlated with MSBP

❑   History of MSBP or Munchausen Syndrome in the suspected perpetrator.
❑   Suspected perpetrator has a history of suicide attempts and/or psychiatric treatment.
❑   History of SIDS in the family of the victim.
❑   Suspected perpetrator is a married woman between 25 and 35.
❑   Suspected perpetrator has history as health care worker.
❑   Prior MSBP behavior.
❑   Suspected perpetrator has history of psychiatric treatment.
❑   Suspected perpetrator has suicidal behavior in past.
❑   All classes are represented by those who have MSBP, but some studies indicate that many
     perpetrators are on welfare. [I suggest that wealthier mothers/fathers may simply be less likely
     suspects.]
❑   Illness cannot be explained through normal testing.
❑   Symptoms contradict each other.
❑   Victim's condition worsens when perpetrator is present and improves in the absence of the
     perpetrator.
❑   Covert video provides evidence of manipulation of medical equipment.
❑   Parent seems excited or happy about painful procedures.
❑   Parent is knowledgeable about the illness or shows excessive interest in medical terms, medical
     environments, and seeks attention from doctors and nurses.
❑   Suspected perpetrator is overly attentive to the child.
❑   Victim tells medical staff that perpetrator gave injections or medications that were not part of the
     prescribed regimen.

---

their involvement. Table 1.1 identifies issues that are correlated with the
existence of MSBP.

SIDS AND MSBP

Sudden infant death syndrome (SIDS) was first labeled in a paper published in the journal *Pediatrics* in 1972. Children were dying in their sleep
for no apparent reason and it appeared that a sleep disorder called *sleep
apnea* was to blame for many of the deaths. SIDS has also been called "crib
death" in the United States and "cot death" in Great Britain. With this disorder, as the child sleeps, he or she stops breathing periodically. If the
child's breathing pauses for an extended period of time, the child suffocates. In the human body, the nervous system is divided into two major
categories—the somatic system and the autonomic system. The somatic
system rules our voluntary functions such as walking, sitting, or standing.
The autonomic system controls all of our functions that are reflexive or
automatic. Heart rate, liver and kidney functions, and respiration are all
controlled by the autonomic system. Fortunately, these functions operate
on their own and we do not have to think about them. It is the autonomic
nervous system that makes it impossible for you to hold your breath until
you die. I have had many child clients over the years who would hold
their breath during tantrums until they passed out. Mothers and even

pediatricians have called me, concerned that the child might suffocate during these tantrums. I have assured them that it is quite impossible. The biggest risk for such a child is that he will injure himself in a fall after he passes out. As far as breathing is concerned, as soon as he loses consciousness, his autonomic system will override the somatic system that was allowing him to hold his breath and he will start breathing again. In some neonates, however, the autonomic system does not function properly. As the infant sleeps, his or her respiration slows and periodically stops. In many children, even though breathing may become very slow or even stop, it eventually starts again and the child is fine. In some neonates, however, the child does not start breathing again. He literally suffocates because his body forgot to breathe.

Since 1972, many physicians have questioned apnea as the cause of SIDS and its actual cause remains controversial. Hence, the label "sudden infant death" continues to be used because physicians are still unsure in some cases why the child died. Regardless, babies at risk for SIDS are easily treated either with a sleep monitor or more likely by having them sleep on their backs or sides rather than on the stomach. This adjustment in sleep position reduced SIDS deaths by 30 percent between 1992 and 1996.[10]

Risk for SIDS dramatically declines after the child reaches six months of age and it is statistically improbable after the child reaches twelve months of age. Any time I am asked by law enforcement officials about a SIDS death and I discover that the child was over twelve months of age, I am suspicious and suggest that homicide be considered as a viable possibility. Yet the cause of SIDS as well as its frequency continue to be debated. Even more controversial is the role of MSBP or other forms of homicide in cases of SIDS. For example, in an article in the *Journal of the American Medical Association*, Pennsylvania coroner Cyril Wecht argues that homicide accounts for less than 3 percent of all SIDS deaths.[11] Other researchers suggest that as many as 5 percent of SIDS cases are misdiagnoses. Whatever the case, even though the incidence of homicide among SIDS deaths is very small, they clearly exist and should be considered possible by law enforcement officers when investigating such deaths.

CONTROVERSIAL DIAGNOSIS

Some people doubt the existence of MSBP, but there are numerous well-documented cases of the disorder. For example, one twenty-two-year-old woman was convicted of injury to a child and sentenced to twenty-four years in prison for causing the death of her twenty-one-month-old daughter. She suffocated the child in order to gain "sympathy and attention."[12] The child survived on life support for three months after the incident before she died. Likewise, between 1977 and 1990, six of Diane Lumbrera's own children, as well as her niece, died while under her care. In each case, she would rush to the hospital with the dead child and then blame hospital staff for not reviving the child.[13] She claimed that her mother-in-law had cursed her. She was eventually convicted of two of the deaths, one in Kansas and one in Texas, and received life sentences for each murder. In another case, a woman who was a victim of MSBP as a child tells of her mother torturing her for eight years. She recalled her mother rubbing coffee grounds into infected wounds and even tying her to a chair and hitting her in the foot with a hammer. "I'm doing this for your own good. The doctor wants me to do this treatment to make you better," she told her daughter.[14]

A well-known case of MSBP involved a woman named Marybeth Tinning. She killed eight of her nine children between 1972 and 1985. Her first child died of meningitis when the baby was only eight days old. Perhaps that event pushed her over some mental threshold because three weeks after that death her two-year-old died. Six weeks later her four-year-old also died. One after another, her children died of unexplained causes at three months, five months, two years, and three years of age. Tinning had a reputation as a good mother and it seems that this, along with the tragic loss of her child to meningitis, kept investigators from probing too deeply into the deaths of her other children; SIDS was repeatedly listed as the cause of death. The last child to die was her three-month-old daughter Tami in 1985. With this last death, police finally decided to thoroughly investigate the death and they subsequently had enough evidence to charge Tinning with murder. She eventually confessed to killing three of her children, smothering them each with a pillow, but denied that she had killed the others. In 1987, she was convicted of Tami's murder.

For every documented case of MSBP, dissenters present cases of mothers who believe they have been falsely accused of having the disorder. For example, in British Columbia, a mother of a child with severe medical problems was taught by her physician to perform a procedure that would prevent her daughter from choking. The procedure involved adjusting the child's jaw while holding her neck. While in the hospital, another woman witnessed the mother performing this procedure and mistakenly thought the woman was choking her daughter. The woman reported what she had seen to authorities and an investigation led to allegations that the mother was abusing her daughter. Even after explaining that she was following the orders of her physician, the doctor in the hospital did not follow up with the child's original physician. The child was taken away from the mother and placed in protective foster care. It took more than seven months and thousands of dollars in legal bills to eventually resolve the issue and exonerate the mother of wrongdoing.

Certainly, a court verdict that a caregiver is guilty of killing one or more of his/her children does not prove the existence of MSBP. No perpetrator is ever charged with having the disorder. In fact, many times the courts won't allow testimony regarding the disorder because of the vague diagnostic criteria. Instead, perpetrators are charged with child abuse, maltreatment, or murder. It is only by examining court records that researchers, like myself, can conclude that it was possible that the perpetrator suffered from MSBP. One of the most vocal self-proclaimed "victims" of a false diagnosis of MSBP is Yvonne Eldridge.

Eldridge and her husband were foster parents. In 1987 they agreed to participate in a program that placed medically ill infants in foster homes. Their first medically ill foster child was one who had AIDS and who only lived a few months. Later, they took in two girls with serious medical problems. Even though these children already had special medical needs when they came into the Eldridge home, a physician began to suspect that Yvonne was inducing some of their symptoms. He claimed that Eldridge caused illnesses in the two foster children and later in her own granddaughter. Social services threatened to remove both of her foster children—and eventually did—even taking her granddaughter away from Eldridge's daughter for fear that Eldridge would harm her as well. Social workers argued that the baby was at risk because they believed Eldridge had MSBP. Even after the Eldridges, their daughter, and their granddaughter (who was returned after Eldridge met certain court stipulations) moved to another state, Yvonne came under scrutiny again. In the end, Eldridge was convicted of two counts of child endangerment and sentenced to forty months in prison.

Eldridge argued that the whole misunderstanding stemmed from one physician. She said that the accusations were the result of a vendetta because Yvonne and her daughter had shunned his physical advances. She also argued that her public defender did not present pertinent medical information at her trial; he called no witnesses during her trial; and she had great difficulty gaining access to medical records necessary to prove her innocence. Despite her denials—and her accusations against social workers, doctors, medical personnel, the legal system, and her lawyer— she was convicted. Her sentence has been stayed for the moment as she pursues a retrial. She continues to maintain her innocence in both the legal and public opinion arenas.

Eldridge's case presents both the good and the bad of the MSBP diagnosis. If, as the court asserted, she was guilty of child abuse, the two girls in her care and perhaps her own granddaughter were spared months or years of pain and maltreatment. In fact, one might suppose that a person with MSBP might be eager to participate in a foster care program for medically ill infants. One would be provided with victims to feed one's need for attention from medical personnel. Yet, on the other hand, it is possible that mistakes were made. A vindictive doctor could create the very scenario that the Eldridges claim; social services personnel tend to believe physicians over suspects. In fact, one prosecutor investigated charges against Yvonne and refused to prosecute, saying the charges were unfounded. The Eldridges were known to be good parents and were recognized by First Lady Nancy Reagan and presented with the Great American Families award in 1988. Unfortunately, as is often true with perpetrators, Yvonne Eldridge's account of her ordeal is somewhat believable and the jury, as well as the general public, has been left with a decision to believe either her or the professionals who presented testimony in the case. The very fact that MSBP perpetrators are convincing liars complicates the search for truth. In Yvonne's case, the jury chose not to believe her. She is pursuing a retrial and if one is granted, perhaps the outcome will be different.

Further evidence of the problems inherent with the MSBP diagnosis involves the principal study cited by almost all experts in the field. The 1980 study by Rosenberg, one that pioneered the diagnosis, included 117 cases—a relatively small sample. According to forensic specialist Eric Mart, this amounts to mere "preliminary data" rather than confirmation of the existence of the disorder. Likewise, Mart concedes that MSBP lacks clear diagnostic criteria.[15] Also complicating the accurate diagnosis of MSBP is the fact that there are a few rare diseases that physicians can easily misdiagnose as physical abuse or MSBP. A *vitamin K deficiency* can cause brain hemorrhaging due to coagulation problems leading to bleeding through the nose, in the gastrointestinal tract, or from needle punctures. Babies normally get vitamin K from shots or formula, but breast-fed babies don't get the vitamin unless it is supplemented. A physician unaware of this disorder or one who is unprepared to diagnose this disorder could easily mistake it for physical abuse. Likewise, *osteogenesis imperfecta,* a disorder more commonly known as *brittle bone disease,* results in skeletal pain, bone fractures, tooth abnormalities, and deformities. There are four types of this disorder, three of which are easily misdiagnosed as child abuse.[16] Children with this disorder frequently have broken bones. Infants and toddlers normally have soft, flexible bones that are not easily broken. This protects them from the many falls and tumbles they take while learning to walk, climb, and get around on their own. A well-intentioned pediatrician could mistake broken bones as abuse when in fact they are the result of this disorder. Another rare disorder is called *aciduria type 1.* This is a disorder that results from a buildup of glutaric acid in the body. Children with this disorder could experience neurological problems, vomiting, movement disorders (dyskinesia), and seizures. Coma, retardation, and irreversible brain damage are all possible outcomes if this disorder is left untreated. In short, a physician could easily mistake all of these disorders for abuse or MSBP if he or she does not test for the disorders.

Despite the controversy over the existence of the disorder and problems with its diagnosis, it seems clear that the disorder exists and is a very real threat to children. Consider the following cases.

Brenda Snyder

Brenda Snyder was the mother of four children, including a two-year-old named Lisa. On January 12, 1996, Lisa died. Two years later in 1998, the twenty-nine-year-old woman was arrested for the child's murder and also charged with trying to kill her six-year-old son. Her trial began in May 2001. Snyder maintained that she was a caring mother who was trying to protect her children and find out what was wrong with them. Yet even if that were so, in the process they were subjected to numerous doctor visits, "fifteen hospital visits, more than forty rescue calls and thirty emergency-room visits."[17] The frustrated woman addressed this issue by saying, "If you don't seek medical attention for your kids, you get neglect. If you do, you get endangerment and assault."[18]

Prosecutors, however, said that the real problem all along was that she repeatedly smothered her children, but on January 12, 1996, Lisa could not be resuscitated. They claim that Snyder confessed she had tried to smother Lisa when she was only a few weeks old. As is true with nearly all MSBP assaults, Snyder was alone with the children at the times of their distress. This uncaring mother, they argued, subjected her children to numerous unnecessary tests, including painful procedures like spinal taps.

During her trial, Snyder's family stood by her and denied her involvement in Lisa's death and her son's illness. Her mother said that during hospitalizations, Snyder "rarely left the bedside" of her children and "had to be coaxed into eating by family members."[19] This fact neither convicts nor exonerates Snyder. One might expect similar behavior from a parent who had nothing to do with the child's illness. However, the behavior is also consistent with MSBP. The whole point of the disorder is to gain attention. Therefore, one would expect the perpetrator to rarely leave the bedside of the victim.

Despite Snyder's character references and her proclamations of innocence, the jury convicted her of second-degree murder in June 2001 and sentenced her to fifty years in prison. She was also convicted of assault on her son.

Kathy Bush

Kathy Bush was the mother of three—a daughter named Jennifer and two sons, Jason and Matthew. Neither son had any serious health problems, but Jennifer exhibited a host of symptoms for which no clear cause could be identified. In an attempt to find the cause of her symptoms, her mother kept taking her for medical care: By age eight she endured numerous doctor visits, procedures, medications, more than 200 hospital visits, and forty surgeries. In a two-year period between 1993 and 1995 alone, Jennifer was taken to the hospital 130 times by her mother. She constantly suffered from intestinal problems, she had a feeding tube inserted at one point, and she had part of her intestine, her gall bladder, and her appendix removed. Jennifer had catheters and tubes implanted throughout her body, she suffered infections, diarrhea, vomiting, and seizures. By the time she was eight years old, Jennifer had spent 640 days in the hospital. The most likely diagnosis that doctors could come up with was gastrointestinal pseudo obstruction—a disorder where the stomach does not digest food. This situation was frustrating and financially draining. The Bush family sought media attention and public funds. Baseball players from the Florida Marlins baseball team visited Jennifer, and her case became so well known that Hillary Clinton visited Kathy Bush in 1994 as the First Lady championed her health care reform program.

Behind the scenes, however, health care workers began to see a disturbing pattern—Jennifer's condition would get worse after visits with her mother. Jennifer's symptoms appeared to directly coincide with the presence of just one person—Kathy Bush. Not only did this unusual pattern persist, but there were other behaviors that troubled the medical staff. She would "draw the curtains and close the door and then Jennifer would be sick," said one witness.[20] During her trial, both nurses and doctors testified that they suspected that Kathy Bush "tampered with her daughter's feeding pump, and gave her unprescribed medication. One nurse testified that she once heard Jennifer yelling, "No, Mommy. No."[21] Prosecutors also claimed that Kathy Bush tampered with doctor's orders, modifying their written instructions so that her child would receive toxic levels of medications; they even charged that she put fecal material into Jennifer's feeding tube.

In 1996, Bush was arrested and charged with aggravated child abuse as well as welfare fraud for failing to report assets that would have made her ineligible for Medicaid. Jennifer was removed from the Bush home and placed in foster care. Almost immediately, her health began to improve, but the case against her mother was largely circumstantial. Witnesses for the prosecution said that Bush exaggerated her daughter's illnesses. Testimony from doctors and nurses confirmed the correlation of Jennifer's illnesses with Kathy Bush's presence. Testimony also was presented that it was rare for a child to have all the symptoms Jennifer had at the same time (i.e., seizures, vomiting, and diarrhea as well as gastrointestinal and immune-system problems). Perhaps most telling of all was the fact that Jennifer wasn't sick or hospitalized a single time after she was removed from Kathy Bush's custody.

The defense called to the stand Bush's twenty-year-old son, who was in the U.S. Marines. He testified that his mother had done everything she could for Jennifer. The defense also argued that Jennifer was outgrowing her ailments and that her health was improving even before Kathy's arrest. One nurse testified that the child had been improving and that feeding tubes were about to be removed just before Kathy's arrest. However, that testimony did not explain why Jennifer's condition worsened when Kathy visited and it doesn't fully explain the little girl's seemingly miraculous recovery once she was removed from Kathy's custody.

During her three-month trial, prosecutors never mentioned MSBP and there are two reasons why it is probably a good thing that they did not. First, the charges against Bush contradicted the disorder. As I mentioned at the beginning of the chapter, there are two mental health diagnoses that address deception—factitious disorders and malingering. With malingering, the purpose for the deception is some external gain, such as money. With factitious disorders, the benefit is something internal, as appears to be the case with MSBP. Financial gain would not be the motive with MSBP. Yet Bush was not only charged with child abuse, but she was also charged with fraud. The prosecution alleged that she sought to defraud health care and charitable organizations for money. This is inconsistent with a diagnosis of a factitious disorder. The state's charges against her do not discount the probability of MSBP, but the defense could easily have made it appear as if it were impossible for her to have MSBP because of this contradiction.

The second reason it would have been inappropriate to introduce MSBP in the case is that it is not a legal issue. As it currently stands, MSBP is only a profile, not a clinical diagnosis. As I mentioned earlier, when discussing MSBP and the *DSM*, Bush would have technically been diagnosed with factitious disorders not otherwise specified (NOS)—not MSBP. Even if diagnostic criteria for MSBP did exist, to address the disorder in the courtroom would only have assisted the prosecution in providing motive. The diagnosis could help the jury understand that something exists where people harm others for attention. However, it would not have been evidence for conviction. To convict someone based on a profile or even a diagnosis would be analogous to convicting someone of robbery because she fits the profile of a thief.

Prosecutors were embarrassed during the trial when somehow Joe DiMaggio's medical records ended up in the three thousand pages of documents related to Jennifer's case. Even with this gaffe, and despite no testimony regarding MSBP, it took a jury only eight hours to find her guilty. In October 1999, forty-two-year-old Kathy Bush was convicted and sentenced to five years in prison. She was also sentenced to five years' probation and she can have no contact with her daughter until she has served out her sentence. Bush appealed her conviction. In the meantime, her husband, Craig, sought custody of Jennifer, who was still in foster care. However, the state of Florida sought to terminate his parental rights as well.

As she awaited her appeal on the child abuse conviction, Bush pleaded guilty to welfare fraud. As I write these pages, it has been three and a half years since Jennifer was removed from Kathy's custody. During that time Jennifer has appeared to be happy and healthy, is playing sports, and has only had a few colds and a broken bone from a sports injury. Her gastrointestinal symptoms have vanished.

DANGERS OF MISDIAGNOSIS

Julie Patrick was a caring mother whose eleven-month-old son died in 1996. He was born with multiple birth defects, but doctors apparently ignored that when they cataloged the child's unusual symptoms. That, along with the fact that Julie fit the profile of a MSBP mother, led them to accuse her of causing her son's illness. During the final days of her son's life, the state took custody of him. Julie was subjected to scrutiny by social services, and she was only allowed limited visitation with her dying son. The child died of his illness despite Julie Patrick being restricted from any opportunity to further aggravate his symptoms. More than four years after his death, a review of the case by a different medical examiner concluded that Julie Patrick had not harmed her child and that the boy had died of a gastrointestinal illness brought on by multiple birth defects. The second medical examiner concluded that the original diagnosis of MSBP was incorrect and Patrick was exonerated.[22] Because of this false charge, Patrick had to endure public embarrassment, expensive legal fees, and an emotionally trying ordeal. Perhaps worst of all, because of the false accusation she was deprived of the final hours with her son, and her dying son was deprived of the love and comfort of his mother.

What Is at Risk with Accusations of MSBP?

Any parent who has a sick child, especially if that illness is unidentified, has a host of pragmatic and emotional issues with which to contend. First of all, the parent must deal with the helplessness of the unknown and the agony of knowing that one cannot make the child's pain go away. At only twelve months of age, my own daughter spent a full week in the hospital, near death, as physicians tried to determine what was wrong. The cause was never identified, but I can assure the reader that I never felt more helpless. Parents of sick children, especially if those children are very young, must also deal with the child's inability to understand that painful procedures they are forced to undergo are not meant to be cruel. One of my children was diagnosed with asthma when she was just three years old. During her first (and thankfully only) hospitalization, I held her down while a nurse inserted an IV. Her face was only inches from mine as she looked at me with pleading eyes and begged, "Daddy, don't let them hurt me!" Of course, I had to allow them to insert the needle. It crushed me and even hurts to think about it these many years later. Lastly, caregivers must also contend with the ever-rising costs of medical tests, hospital visits, doctor's fees, and other associated expenses. Even with health insurance, personal financial liability can be overwhelming. Time away from work while tending to a sick child can result in lost wages or even loss of one's job, leading to missed credit-card payments, repossession of automobiles, eviction, and possibly foreclosure and per- sonal bankruptcy. All these possibilities further increase one's anxiety and stress.

If a caregiver is accused of abusing the child, he or she not only has to cope with the overwhelming issues mentioned above, but also the added fear of being falsely charged with a crime and the embarrassment and humiliation of being suspected of harming the very object of one's devo- tion. Likewise, added to the medical costs they have incurred, they also may have attorney's fees, court fees, bail, and other costs associated with being arrested and charged with a crime. If the child is removed from the parent's custody, the pain of being prohibited from visiting the sick child at a time when the child needs parental comfort the most is unbearable. Finally, potential emotional damage to the child, who may learn that par- ent was suspected of harming him or her, must also be considered. In short, when caregivers are attempting to cope with a seriously ill child, law enforcement, physicians, and social workers who falsely accuse them of abuse compound their grief and despair. For all these reasons, one must be exceptionally cautious in investigating and charging potential suspects with abuse.

If the suspicion of MSBP exists, the appropriate response is to seek con- crete evidence. The profile of an abuser is not enough to arrest or remove children. With any type of perpetrator profiling, the responsible agency should consider the profile only the starting point for the investigation. Unfortunately, in their well-intentioned but zealous attempts to protect children, many social workers, health care providers, and law enforce- ment personnel more readily accept the profile as the conclusion rather than the starting point, despite the lack of robust evidence even when an attempt to gain such evidence (i.e., videotaping) has been unfruitful. Imagine walking into a convenience store just after it had been robbed in the middle of the night. You find the attendant on the floor behind the counter so you rush to his aid only to find him dead. Just as you rise from the floor to call for help, the police arrive and see you standing over the dead man. Even though the circumstances look bad, you are completely ignorant as to the identity of the real perpetrator. You might be detained, but minimal investigation would quickly show that you had nothing to do with the robbery and murder. On the other hand, imagine this same scenario, yet instead of investigating your alibi, the police arrest you simply because you are assumed to be guilty based on a profile of perpetrators of such crimes. Based on that assumption, no further investigation takes place. This is in essence what can happen when social services removes a child from the home based on a false allegation of MSBP. The circumstances may look bad and you might not be able to identify the real perpetrator (illness), but since you are assumed to be guilty, social services does not look any further.

There are ways to ensure the safety of the child while investigating the possibility of MSBP. Those responsible for investigating allegations of abuse should take the following precautions. Don't make any assumptions. Look for evidence that MSBP may exist, but also look for evidence that it is *not* the cause. Covert video surveillance has proven to be a very effective tool in proving MSBP cases. A parent does not have to know that officials suspect her of MSBP. If MSBP is present, eventually evidence on the video will demonstrate that it is. If the child's illness continues while in the hospital under constant medical supervision and video surveillance does not provide any evidence of interference by the caregiver, one can more easily suppose that the parent is innocent and that some biological cause is at the root of the problem.

Look for a pattern in bouts with the illness. If it is only occurring in the presence of one person, MSBP is a distinct possibility. Seek and rule out all other possible medical explanations. Don't read too much into the behavior of a mother or caregiver during a child's serious illness. What may seem cold or distant to an observer may simply be the parent's attempt to cope with unbearable pain. Law enforcement and social services agencies that suspect MSBP should check with all the victim's previous physicians. This cross-check can assist in either establishing a pattern of abuse or minimizing the likelihood of a false charge of MSBP.

It should also be noted that physicians could falsely diagnose MSBP deliberately. When a physician is having trouble diagnosing a child's illness, or he fears that the family is considering filing a charge of medical malpractice against him, that might lead him to accuse the parent of abuse. A malpractice lawsuit can be seriously damaging to a physician's practice and potentially career-ending. The physician might choose to allege MSBP to divert attention from himself. Parents in heated custody battles might also deliberately allege MSBP or a similar form of abuse. In my practice with children I have dealt with several cases of alleged abuse that were nothing more than innuendo presented by one parent to skew the court's decision for custody.

Alternative Explanations

Alternative explanations for the child's illness, the behavior of the mother, and other issues related to the profile of a MSBP caregiver should be examined. Again, not only should the investigator look for evidence of abuse, but he or she should also seek alternative explanations. There are a number of reasonable alternative explanations for many of the MSBP symptoms.

Parent Highly Attentive to the Victim

Most caring parents will appear highly attentive to their children while hospitalized. They may refuse to go home, sleep, or leave for meals. This is not unusual. Even if the child is comatose or sleeping, the parent may fear that the child will wake up and want "mommy" while the mother is out of the room. The helpless feeling of having a sick child and the irrational belief that one has somehow failed the sick child only strengthens the need for self-denial and causes one to remain at the child's beside for days.

Response of Caregiver

When children are critically ill, their caregivers respond in a number of ways. They may be calm, hysterical, or somewhere in between. There is no "normal" response. Certainly we would expect mothers and fathers to express interest in the diagnosis and treatment that their children are receiving. In the case of illnesses that elude diagnosis, one should not be surprised that a parent would do some research on his or her own. In fact, we would expect that people in the health care industry (nurses, paramedics, etc.) would be even more likely to do such research, offer possible explanations to physicians, and to take a more active role in the diagnosis and treatment of their child.

Unidentifiable Illnesses

There are disorders that mimic symptoms of abuse. Before supposing that abuse is a certainty, experts in the diagnosis of rare disorders should be consulted.

Denial of Responsibility

The accused almost always deny their role, but this proves nothing. One who is falsely accused would also deny any role in causing symptoms. Therefore, one would expect a denial in either case. MSBP perpetrators will deny their role even when confronted with videotapes or other convincing evidence. It is the evidence, however, not the denial, that is persuasive.

Mother Seems Exceptionally Interested in Medical Issues, Terminology, or Treatments

Many caregivers, especially in this day and age of the Internet and accessibility to the latest information, study diligently to learn about the child's illness, symptoms, and possible causes. An informed parent can be an ally to the medical team.

There are numerous risks associated with allegations of child abuse. Social services does not need proof that a parent is abusing a child in order to remove the child from the parent's custody. Suspicion that the parent is abusing coupled with imminent risk to the child is enough for at least a temporary removal of the child from the home. The department of family services is ordinarily reluctant to remove children from the custody of their parents or guardians unless evidence suggests that the child is in imminent danger. In fact, I have often had more difficulty convincing social workers that a child *should* be removed from the home than the other way around. However, when children are removed from a home, the guardian never has to be charged with any crime and has limited legal recourse to fight false allegations. Many of the rights that American citizens take for granted with regard to criminal charges do not apply in cases of suspected abuse. While the mere suspicion of MSBP is not enough to justify a public investigation, neither is it sufficient evidence to remove a child from the parent's custody. Pursuit of alternative explanations for the alleged illness should be the first step.

TREATMENT

Kathryn Artingstall notes that abuse associated with MSBP ends in one of three ways. Abuse for a given victim ends if the child dies. A second possibility is that the perpetrator moves on to a new victim once the initial victim grows up or is no longer available. The third possibility is that the perpetrator is apprehended.[23] Catching the victim, as the previous pages have described, can be very difficult. Victims make poor witnesses because they may not be aware that the perpetrator is actually causing the illness and pain they are experiencing. Young victims trust their caregivers even when they are subjected to painful procedures. They will take any "medicine" that the caregiver requires, allow injections, and let the caregiver to lace food or beverages with substances that cause their symptoms. They do not know any different; even when they do, they are often powerless to help themselves. Therefore, children are not very good witnesses to exonerate the caregiver. Older children, however, like Julie in the opening story of this chapter, can provide helpful evidence against a per-petrator from the perspective of time and distance.

Once they are identified, treating perpetrators is very difficult. The risk of recidivism is so great that some courts refuse the perpetrator the right to ever see or have contact with the child again. That is extreme, but the prognosis for MSBP is poor, especially if the perpetrator maintains inno-cence, as most perpetrators do. If a client is unwilling to accept any responsibility, progress is nearly impossible. Schreier and Libow state that for the patient with MSBP, the child is seen as an object to be used rather than a person to be loved and cared for.[24] In order to treat the MSBP patient, the therapist must alter this perspective. Some treatments have included medications, such as antianxiolitics and antidepressants. Group therapy, nurturing therapy, family therapy, confrontational therapy, psy-chodynamic therapy, and behavioral therapy have all been suggested as possible treatments. The research with regard to treatment, however, is weak and there is little evidence testifying to the effectiveness of these therapies or medications.

Therapists must be cautious of the manipulative MSBP client. Perpetra-tors with factitious disorders are accomplished and convincing liars. They polish their acting abilities and by the time they reach the therapy room, they have fooled doctors, nurses, EMTs, and potentially even social work-ers and law enforcement personnel. The normal empathetic approach to therapy only sets the therapist up to be manipulated and to perpetuate the client's self-deceptions. The victims of MSBP also need psychotherapy to deal with their pain, trauma, confusion, and sense of betrayal.

Reunification

Younger children must be protected from perpetrators; this is usually done by ordering supervised visitations with the perpetrator. Children are less likely to be victims as they get older and are able to take some initia-tive to protect themselves, but even then strict supervision of the perpe-trator is necessary. Perpetrators who refuse to admit their role should not be reunified with the child. In their minds, it only provides evidence to others of their innocence. They can then say, "See, I have my child back. They didn't have any evidence allowing them to keep the child so I must continue seeking the 'real' cause of the illness." Hence, the abuse can con-tinue. Because treatment for MSBP is unproven, some argue that offenders should never be allowed custody of the victim again.

Both the child and the perpetrator should be in therapy with separate therapists. Schreier and Libow suggest that the child's therapist is a more objective judge of the situation and the risk to the child than the perpetra-tor's therapist. It should be noted, however, that the offender seeks to con-trol every aspect of the child's life, especially as it pertains to the abuse.

Therefore, the parent will usually attempt to force his or her involvement in the child's therapy. Consequently, the child's therapist can potentially be manipulated by partial truths, misinformation, or flat-out lies concocted by the perpetrator for personal gain. As a child therapist, I encourage parental involvement in therapy. I also recognize that what I learn from therapy cannot always be verified. Therefore, I must draw conclusions based on my experience, the facts as I know them, and what seems most believable. When dealing with MSBP perpetrators, the perpetrators cannot be directly involved in the child's therapy.

CONCLUDING REMARKS

MSBP is one of the most controversial issues in mental health. The lack of clear diagnostic criteria, errors in the application of the diagnosis, and questions as to whether or not the disorder even exists all contribute to the debate. I do not doubt the existence of the disorder. Clearly, however, future versions of the *DSM* must formalize criteria. Two paragraphs in the nine-hundred-plus-page diagnostic manual regarding factitious disorders by proxy are without question inadequate.

Mental health experts, law enforcement officials, social services personnel, doctors, and all health care providers should all be cautious when MSBP is suspected. False accusations of MSBP can leave a painful wake in the alleged victim, the alleged perpetrator, and the family. Yet when the facts support investigation, protection of the child takes top priority, even if the investigation exonerates the accused.

NOTES

1. "Munchausen syndrome by proxy," www.faculty.rsu.edu/~felwell/Probweb/Presentations/munchausen.htm, February 2002.

2. Ibid.

3. Ibid.

4. Richard Firstman and Jamie Talan, *The death of innocents* (New York: Bantam Books, 1997), p. 513.

5. American Psychiatric Association, *Diagnostic and statistical manual of mental disorders, 4th ed., text revision* (Washington, DC: American Psychiatric Press, 2000), p. 782.

6. Ibid.

7. Kathryn A. Artingstall, "Munchausen syndrome by proxy," *FBI Law Enforcement Bulletin*, 198.252.9.108/govper/fbi.law.enforcement.bulletin/www.fbi.gov/library/leb/1995/Aug/95AUG002.TXT, August 1995.

8. Herbert A. Schreier and Judith A. Libow, *Hurting for love: Munchausen by proxy syndrome* (New York: Guilford Press, 1993), p. 10.

9. Artingstall.

10. Cyril H. Wecht, "Sudden infant death," *Journal of the American Medical Association, 279* (January 7, 1998): 85.

11. Wecht, p. 86.

12. Jennifer Liebrum, "Mother who killed tot is sentenced," *Houston Chronicle,* www.chron.com/content/chronicle/metropolitan/96/01/05/padron.html, January 4, 1996.

13. "Not without precedent," *Houston Chronicle,* www.chron.com/cs/CDA /story.hts/special/drownings/957431, July 1, 2001.

14. "Victim of MSP tells of her experiences," *Associated Press,* www.ashermeadow .com/caseaccct5.htm, July 7, 1997.

15. Eric G. Mart, "Problems with the diagnosis of factitious disorder by proxy in forensic settings," *American Journal of Forensic Psychology* (Internet edition), www.msbp.com/ericmart.htm, 1999.

16. Kristin Kimmel, "'Brittle bone disease' or child abuse," www.law.umich .edu/centersandprograms/childlaw/resourcecenter/research/BRITTLE.html, February 2002.

17. Denise A. Raymo, "Setback for Snyder murder defense," *Press Republican,* www.pressrepublican.com/Archive/2000/09_2000/091320005.htm, September 13, 2000.

18. Denise A. Raymo, "Angry Snyder gets 50 years," *Press Republican,* www.pressrepublican.com/Archive/2001/07_2001/073120011.htm, July 31, 2001.

19. Ibid.

20. "Bush convicted of child abuse in alleged Fla. Munchausen case," *Court TV,* www.courttv.com/trials/munchausen/100799_verdict_ctv.html, October 7, 1999.

21. "Mother found guilty of child abuse, fraud for making daughter sick," *CNN On-Line,* www.cnn.com/US/9910/07/munchausen.verdict/, October 7, 1999.

22. Bill Snyder, "Review vindicates mother," *The Tennessean,* www.tennessean .com/local/archives/01/02/02663457.shtml, February 20, 2001.

23. Artingstall, "Munchausen syndrome by proxy."

24. Schreier and Libow, p. 11.

CHAPTER 2

Physical/Emotional Abuse and Neglect

If you bungle raising your children, I don't think whatever else you do well matters much.

—Jacqueline Kennedy Onassis

Violence of any kind is hard for us to understand, but crimes against children are perhaps the hardest to comprehend. In my book, *A Violent Heart*, I addressed a number of crimes against children that stagger the imagination. Richard Allen Davis broke into a home in California and kidnapped twelve-year-old Polly Klaas while her mother slept in another room. He later killed her. For no clear reason, Jonathon David Bruce broke into the home of John Carpenter and killed two of his five children with a pitchfork. Jon Venables and Robert Thompson, just children themselves, kidnapped two-year-old James Bulger from a shopping mall in England, tortured him, and then beat him to death, violating his corpse afterward. It is heartbreaking to read stories like these, but every day children are physically abused and tortured, not by strangers who break into their homes or by delinquent adolescents, but by family members and trusted family friends. Far more children suffer at the hands of their caregivers than at the hands of strangers. In nearly two decades of work with children, I've seen such a wide variety of abuse against children that almost nothing surprises me anymore. The problem of child maltreatment is pervasive.

Abusers can be any person with access to the child—a parent, a guardian, a stepparent, a boyfriend, a babysitter, a nanny or a child-care worker, a minister, a teacher, or a sibling or other relative. For the sake of simplicity I will refer to abusers as parents or caregivers, but it easily could be someone other than the parent. About half the children I see in my practice are abused or neglected, and most of the cases where I am asked to consult involve abuse. According to the United States Department of Health and Human Services (HHS), there were approximately 900,000 reported cases of abuse in 2000.[1] Of those 900,000 cases, 54 percent involved neglect, 23 percent involved physical abuse, and 12 percent involved sexual abuse.[2] These percentages have changed little over the last few years. Though these numbers are staggering, they actually represent a reduction in reported cases of abuse. The number of reported cases of abuse in 1995 was over 1 million cases and in 1996 it had fallen to just under 1 million. The number of incidents may actually have declined more than the numbers represent. Because of increased awareness of abuse, mandatory reporting laws, and other variables, we would suppose that the numbers of reported cases would increase. Yet total reported cases are declining. Therefore, one may assume that the total number of abuse cases has actually declined more than the number of reported cases reflects. This is not the first time this observation has been made. For example, Straus and Gelles reported in 1985 that even though incidents of abuse increased between 1975 and 1985, they argued that the true incidence of abuse was actually declining for the same reasons I listed above.[3]

Regardless of the actual number of cases of abuse, even one case is too many. Sadly, the Department of HHS reported in 1998 that almost 1,100 children died in 1996 as a result of abuse or neglect.[4] Most children who are abused are younger than eight years of age and the younger the child, the more likely the child is to suffer fatal injury. Even though people of all races abuse their children, the Department of HHS reported in 1998 that African American and Native American children were "abused and neglected at a rate almost twice their proportions in the national child population."[5] These cases are not directly related to race, but are more likely the result of poverty, lack of education, substance abuse, and other sociocultural factors. A little over half of all victims of abuse are Caucasian (53%) while victims of abuse are approximately equally divided by gender (52% female, 48% male).[6]

One must ask why parents or other caregivers would ever harm their children. Animals will neglect or even kill their own young. For example, runts in many species are tormented by parents, especially fathers, and are ignored by mothers as they tend to healthier cubs and kits. In some species, mothers even kill some of their young, thus providing more nourishment and attention for the ones that remain. Yet this serves an evolutionary purpose that ensures the survival of the species. Maltreatment by humans, however, has nothing to do with survival of the species. The behavior results from both personal factors in perpetrators as well as interaction between the personal factors of perpetrators and those of their victims.

DEFINITIONS OF ABUSE

Alice Flanagan, a researcher, provides a clear, concise, and comprehensive definition of abuse. According to Flanagan, child abuse is "any non-accidental injury or an act of omission by the child's parent, caretaker, or guardian which results in some injury or an imminent risk of serious harm or substantial risk of death, impairment of health, or loss of impairment of function to the child."[7] Maltreatment, the generic term for the many forms of child abuse or neglect, can be divided into several categories. Flanagan distinguishes between active abuse, which includes sexual or physical abuse (non-accidental injury), and passive abuse, which includes neglect (acts of omission). Child endangerment is yet another form of abuse. In such cases, a person responsible for a child's safety in some way exposes that child to danger. Allowing a child to ride in a vehicle without a child safety seat or allowing a dangerous animal access to a toddler would be examples of endangerment. The most common divisions of abuse, and the ones that I will refer to in this chapter, are physical abuse, emotional abuse, and neglect. Sexual abuse is another form of child abuse, but I will discuss this subject at length in Chapter 3.

Physical Abuse

Physical abuse may result in either temporary or permanent damage to organs, bones, and brain tissue, and it may also be fatal. Flanagan identifies physical abuse as follows: bruises/welts, burns, fractures, abdominal injuries, lacerations or abrasions, damage to the central nervous system.[8] Parents may physically abuse their children unintentionally while disciplining them or they may do it intentionally out of thoughtlessness, cruelty, rage, or while intoxicated. Physically abused children may endure beatings, burns from cigarettes, blows to the head and body, internal bleeding, and a host of other injuries. Physical abuse may continue for many months or even years if the injuries are not visible and/or if the child is not frequently around other children or adults who witness and report abuse symptoms. Pediatricians, teachers, or child-care workers are the most likely adults who would recognize physical abuse and take action to intervene on behalf of the child.

Emotional Abuse

In her description of emotional abuse, Flanagan includes verbal abuse, inadequate nurturance/affection (a behavior that I prefer to classify as "emotional neglect"), witnessing domestic violence, and substance and/or alcohol abuse.[9] *Emotional abuse* is a term that is sometimes misused when referring to normal relationship frustrations. For example, a husband and wife who argue over issues related to their marriage are not necessarily abusing each other or their children. Likewise, a parent who, in the process of appropriately disciplining a child, causes that child to cry or become upset, is not emotionally abusing the child. These are isolated, normal situations in human interaction and parenting. On the other hand, emotional abuse is ongoing, often deliberate, and abnormal in human interaction. Also called "psychological maltreatment," emotional abuse is perhaps the most difficult to prove. It does not involve visible, physical injury to the child, but it causes deep emotional damage that may last for decades.

A physician can look at an x-ray and determine that a bone was broken some time in the past. She can tell us how long ago it was broken and how effectively it healed. In a similar way, a dermatologist can look at a scar and make a reasonable guess as to how old it is and what caused it. However, even though emotional damage becomes evident in therapy, it is difficult to communicate the extent of the damage to one who does not understand the way the mind works because damage from emotional abuse, unlike that from physical abuse, leaves no visible trace. It only leaves footprints. In court, for example, a physician can show a jury of laypersons the x-ray and the damage can be seen. Because psychologists, therapists, and counselors cannot show anything tangible to laypersons, it is much more difficult to convince them of the severity of the emotional damage. The footprints of abuse are seen in lowered self-esteem, dysfunctional relationships, ineffective coping skills, and skewed world view—all difficult things to assess and even more difficult to demonstrate for a judge or jury. As you will see in the case of Michael Jones at the end of this chapter, the damage he suffered because of his biological mother's behavior was clear to me, but difficult to demonstrate in court.

Emotional damage may, in fact, be the hardest to overcome and emotional abuse usually accompanies physical abuse. For example, many years ago, a man attempted to kill his son by burning him alive. The man poured gasoline on his son in a hotel room and set him on fire. Miraculously the child survived, but he was horribly deformed. His ears, nose, and lips were completely missing and only random strands of hair would grow on his head. Even after numerous reconstructive surgeries, the boy still looked horrifying to one who was not prepared to see the results of his injuries. Even though this young man had many physical obstacles to overcome, including being reminded of his ghastly appearance every day as he looked in the mirror, the more difficult damage to heal was the knowledge of what had been done to him—grappling for an answer to why his father would do this to him.

Neglect

Neglect is the failure to meet the basic needs of a child. Flanagan includes refusal or delay of psychological care, permitted chronic truancy, failure to enroll in school, and failure to access special education services in her list of issues related to neglect.[10] This definition is inadequate by itself because it fails to delineate between physical and emotional neglect. Physical neglect is the failure of a caregiver to provide shelter, food, clothing, supervision, education, medical attention, and so forth. Emotional neglect is the failure of a caregiver to provide warmth, nurturance, and emotional security. Emotional neglect differs from emotional abuse in that the parent is withholding nurturance and affection rather than actively doing something to interrupt bonding and nurturance with the child. Caregivers may be emotionally neglectful because of thoughtlessness (they are too busy) or because of intrapsychic forces within themselves that cause them to withhold affection and nurturance. These intrapsychic forces are often related to their own upbringings and emotional and/or physical abuse they suffered as well. For example, I once counseled a married couple who were having significant marital problems. The woman was not interested in sex with her husband and often withheld affection from him when she was angry. She also withheld her motherly affections from her children as a way of punishing them. As therapy progressed, the husband told me that his wife's mother had explained to her in her childhood years that sex was a dirty thing and that men used women only as sexual objects. Her mother was cold and aloof to all her children, but especially to her girls. As I got to know more about the woman's upbringing, it became obvious to me that her mother had very likely been sexually abused as a child. Therefore, the mother's own abuse in childhood had led her to raise her daughter with a skewed view of affection and sexuality that was then played out a generation later in her daughter's family—my clients.

It is important to note that neglect must also be considered in light of one's culture. What is neglectful in one part of the United States is not necessarily neglectful in another. Likewise, what is neglectful in the United States may not be neglectful in another country. For example, in 1997, a thirty-year-old Danish actress named Anette Sorensen left her fourteen-month-old daughter in a baby carriage outside a New York café while she and her husband had a drink inside. Customers and employees alike were troubled by what they saw and one customer called police. Despite the protests of her parents, the child was taken into protective custody and both the mother and father were arrested and charged with child endangerment. Sorensen was strip-searched and held in custody for two days. Four days later, the child was returned to Sorensen's care following a judge's order, and the charges against Sorensen were eventually dropped. In America, and especially in New York City, the Sorensens' behavior was dangerous and neglectful, but in their home country of Denmark, it is common practice to leave a child unattended outside a restaurant while the parents dine inside and it poses no risk to the child at all. Sorensen had only been in the United States for two days when this episode took place. Danes were just as shocked by the reaction of New York City authorities as Americans were by the incident itself. The difference in culture was adequately summarized by one writer who said, "In Denmark, parents often leave children unattended while they shop or dine. In New York, people chain up outdoor garbage cans and flower pots if they want to keep them."[11] Sorensen sued the City of New York and won a $66,000 judgment based on the fact that the city did not advise her that she had the right to contact her consulate after her arrest. When assessing for possible abuse or neglect, social workers, counselors, and others who work with children need to be aware of cultural differences that might mitigate neglect.

WHY DO CAREGIVERS ABUSE/NEGLECT?

It seems inconceivable that a parent or guardian could deliberately harm a child or neglect a child's needs, yet perusal of the national news reveals the unmistakable truth that such thoughtlessness and cruelty exist. Psychologically, we can look to a number of reasons why parents abuse their children. Three of these reasons are termed *defense mechanisms* because they are ways in which people psychologically defend themselves from their self-perceived weaknesses. Denial, rationalization, and justification are these three. Other psychological reasons that contribute to abuse are ignorance, poor problem-solving skills, poor coping skills, substance abuse, and cruelty.

Denial

Denial is a defense mechanism where one refuses to believe the obvious. Abusing parents may deny that they are abusing a child by pretending that their behavior is not abusive or by denying that they are doing anything to the child at all. When officials intervene on a child's behalf, the denying abuser is obvious because no matter what evidence of abuse social workers provide—broken bones, scars, burns, and so forth—the abuser excuses that evidence, dismisses it, or discounts its seriousness.

As I noted earlier in the discussion on neglect, abuse can also be partially culture-bound. Prior to the mid-1960s, it was not uncommon for parents to use corporal punishment. In even earlier decades, severe use of corporal punishment was not uncommon, even if it left marks such as bruises. Parents were not being cruel or abusive by the standards of the day. They were simply using the method of discipline that the culture at that time accepted as appropriate. Now, in a new millennium, any punishment that leaves marks of any kind is cause for suspicion of abuse. The culture has changed and methods of punishment that were once acceptable are no longer acceptable. Therefore, an accused abuser from an earlier generation may truly not understand his or her abuse in this new age. Officials involved in intervention should be sensitive to this possibility when charging an individual with a crime or when providing intervention or treatment.

Rationalization

A second defense mechanism that contributes to abuse is rationalization. With this defense, one uses false logic to explain away seemingly inappropriate behavior, making it appear acceptable. Most of us use this defense at one time or another. We might argue on the one hand that it is wrong to exceed the speed limit when we drive, yet when we get behind the wheel, we exceed the speed limit. We "reason" that we aren't really speeding as long as we are within a certain number of miles per hour over the speed limit. Or we may argue that everyone else is speeding; therefore, our behavior is acceptable. On a fast-moving interstate, we might argue that it is dangerous to drive the speed limit because everyone else is driving so fast that they might run over us. All these excuses are rationalizations and are based on false logic. In other words, we have to juxtapose two opposing truths—our belief that speeding is wrong and yet we speed.

Abusers rationalize in the same way—excusing their behavior by using false logic. They might say they don't "ordinarily" lose their temper and strike a child, as if it is acceptable to do that once in a while. Or they might argue that they were "disciplined" like that when they were children and they "turned out all right." With these rationalized explanations, the abuser is ignoring the primary issue—what is best for the child.

Justification

Justification, a third defense mechanism, is a defense where one excuses behaviors based on some perceived "permission." In World War II, for example, guards in the Nazi death camps justified their inhumane treatment of inmates by arguing that they were simply "following orders." The fact that they were following orders gave them permission to be cruel. Likewise, as I discussed in my book *A Violent Heart*, members of hate groups justify their hatred by contending that they have been called by god to maim or destroy other humans. The most egregious example of justification in recent history came in September 2001—the terrorist attacks on the Pentagon and the World Trade Center's twin towers. The perpetrators believed they were justified in killing thousands of people and causing billions of dollars in damage because they perceived themselves to be engaged in a holy war—a jihad—commissioned by god to rid the earth of infidels.

Abusers justify their behavior by these same means. They may argue that they are only disciplining the child, hence giving themselves permission to harm a child. Or they may believe that a child "asked for" the abuse because of deliberate misbehavior. Abusers, like terrorists, may even believe that god has called them to beat or neglect a child. In 2000 in Atlanta, Georgia, an entire church congregation came under the scrutiny of the Department of Family and Children's Services (DFACS) because of abuse that had been alleged. These members were publicly flogging one another's children. Even after social services removed more than forty of these children, the families refused to agree to stop the behaviors that the state had determined to be abusive, arguing that they could not deny what they believed to be a religious command. Obviously, there is flawed logic operating in all of these examples, but the abuser either does not see it or chooses to ignore it.

Ignorance

Some caregivers abuse or neglect their children simply because they aren't very bright, they are immature, or they do not know any better. Especially among the poor and uneducated, parents may neglect or abuse their children because they have never been taught effective ways to discipline and care for their children. Very young parents are more likely to be abusive than older parents because younger parents may only have found yelling, hitting, or ignoring as effective ways of disciplining their children. Older parents, on the other hand, have learned a number of ways to gain compliance from their children. I have worked with many parents over the years who have abused or neglected their children and when they realized what they were doing, they were more than willing to try something new. Education and training often resolved the problems.

Poor Problem-Solving Skills

Problem-solving skills are those cognitive activities that we use to achieve our goals. When we run out of ideas for solving a problem, we experience frustration, and frustration leads to anger. Caregivers who have minimal problem-solving skills quickly become frustrated with children when they do not cooperate. Many infants have been injured or killed by something called "shaken baby syndrome." A baby's head is heavy in proportion to its body and infants do not have strength enough in the neck to support that weight. Shaking the infant causes the head to jerk back and forth, and can easily injure the base of the brain. Frustrated caregivers run out of ways to deal with a crying child and, in their frustration, they shake the child. This is obviously an ineffective strategy for solving the problem of a crying infant, but in the midst of crisis, the abusing parent does not recognize that fact or does not know what else to do.

Several years ago I was forced to call the county Department of Family and Children's Services (DFACS) because a family I was working with was clearly neglecting their four children. The youngest child was just over one year of age and the eldest was eight. The father worked long hours and, therefore, was gone much of the time. The mother was very young and she was easily stressed. Daily, she would lock herself in her bedroom, leaving the children unattended for hours at a time. One day, I was driving near their home and saw a child sitting literally in the middle of the roadway, cars passing on either side. Just by chance it was the youngest child of this family that I knew. I stopped my vehicle, removed the child from the roadway, and took her home. The mother was locked in her bedroom asleep, completely unaware that the child had even left the house, not to mention sitting in the middle of a busy roadway. Clearly, the mother's problem-solving strategy of hiding in her room was both ineffective and inappropriate. Part of her treatment involved learning more effective ways to cope with her stress, depression, loneliness, and frustrations with her children.

Poor Coping Skills

In all three of my books, coping skills have shown up as a topic. I cannot see how anyone in mental health could address any dysfunction without considering this most important issue. Coping skills are the strategies and tools that we use to help us deal with the stress we face in life. In early years, children have very few coping skills. They scream, whine, or cry if they are uncomfortable or if their immediate needs are not being met. As children age, they learn some coping skills through direct instructions. That is, they are given specific directions by parents, teachers, or other adults as to how they can learn to cope with their difficulties. For example, a parent who intervenes in a fight between children and says, "Next time you are angry you should first ... " is teaching the child a coping skill. Other coping skills are acquired through trial and error. Often, adults may find themselves in their thirties or forties before they develop coping strategies that are fully functional in helping them deal with their rage, depression, or frustrations.

When coping skills are absent or ineffective, the individual becomes frustrated. When the parent runs out of coping skills, he or she is most likely to strike a child. Some parents think they have effective coping skills, but they do not. They make the mistake of assuming that just because they use a given coping strategy regularly, that it is an effective one. For example, one parent I worked with who had anger-management problems told me, "I always spank when I'm angry." To him, that seemed like a perfectly reasonable justification for his physical aggression toward his children, even though it was both ineffective and inappropriate.

Baby temperament may also contribute to abuse in infants. Research has demonstrated that there are three major temperaments in infants— easy, slow-to-warm, and difficult. Most babies are easy or slow-to-warm and like to be snuggled, and even though they will cry with some frequency, they are quickly calmed if their needs are met. Researchers, however, identified a small percentage of babies as "difficult" babies. These children do not like to be held, snuggled, or coddled. They cry most of their waking hours and, regardless of a parent's good intentions, they are not easily calmed. Anyone who has ever walked a fussy baby at two o'clock in the morning can relate to how frustrating it is when the baby cannot be mollified. Parents who have poor problem-solving skills and/or poor coping skills will become frustrated more quickly and are more likely to strike or shake a child, thereby causing injury.

Single parents are also at a disadvantage. In a two-parent home, part of the coping strategy is to pass responsibility to the other parent when one's stress level rises. This is not an option for single parents. This, combined with the fact that many very young parents are unmarried, increases the likelihood of abuse by young parents.

Substance Abuse

The probability for child abuse increases significantly if substance abuse is present in the home. Nearly half of all substantiated cases of abuse involve some form of parental substance abuse.[12] The risk of child maltreatment is even greater in single-parent homes. Chemical addictions reduce one's ability to function, think rationally, and engage in the normal business of life. Addicted individuals will neglect all responsibilities in the pursuit of their drug. Alcohol reduces inhibitions and increases the likelihood of uncontrolled rage. When that rage is directed at a defenseless child, the results are devastating. While no abuse is acceptable, children of alcoholics or other substance abusers are more likely to suffer injuries than children who are maltreated in homes where alcohol is not an issue.[13]

Cruelty

Some people are cruel. They are heartless, selfish, and egocentric, pursuing their own pleasures even at the expense of their own children. These sadistic people delight in controlling and manipulating other people and they have no remorse for their behavior when they are caught. Cruel people will abuse children "just because they feel like it" or even for entertainment. For example, a man in Missouri was arrested for burning a kitten on his outdoor grill just for the fun of it while nearly a dozen friends watched and laughed at the helpless kitten. To me, people like this are as frightening as any serial killer and anyone who finds pleasure in this kind of cruelty is seriously disturbed. Fortunately, most abusers do not fall exclusively into this category.

WHY DOESN'T THE OTHER PARENT PROTECT THE CHILD?

I have seen cases where a parent or guardian is truly unaware that the other parent is abusing one or more children in the home. Some parents are so totally disengaged from their children and households, either by choice or because of work or other obligations, that they truly don't know that the spouse is physically abusing one or more children in the home. In cases like these, when the non-abusive parent discovers the abuse, he or she is often responsive to intervention, painful as it may be. Many times, however, a parent or guardian either suspects abuse or is fully aware of the abuse that is taking place in the home, but fails to intervene. It seems incredible that a loving parent, as many of them are, would not do something to protect their children. Among the reasons they do not intervene are the same three defense mechanisms that I discussed above: denial, rationalization, and justification. Other reasons include fear of the perpetrator, poor problem-solving skills, fear of government intervention, and abuse in their own childhood.

Denial

As I discussed earlier in this chapter, a person denies the truth because it is easier to deny the existence of abuse by the spouse, lover, or relative than to address it with all of its consequences. An abusive parent may repeatedly explain a child's cuts, bruises, or burns with vague explanations like these: "She fell off her bike" or "He burned his arm on the stove." Even though these explanations for the injuries clearly do not match the form of the injury, the denying parent accepts the explanation. It is easier to pretend that one's child has had a normal childhood accident than to admit to oneself that one's spouse is an abuser.

While in graduate school, I became good friends with a man who was working on his degree as a therapist. Toward the end of his program, he told me about a conversation he had had with his academic advisor. During a private consultation with his advisor, she asked him about the abuse he had suffered in his childhood. My friend was indignant and defended his parents, proclaiming their virtue and insisting that he had not been abused as a child.

"But didn't you tell me that your mother told you she beat you?" she asked my friend.

"Yes, but she was disciplining me. I was a very difficult child."

"But didn't you also tell me that your father beat you many times until your buttocks and legs were black with bruises?" she asked again.

"Yes," he explained again, "but my father was not being mean. He was trying to teach me."

"Didn't you tell me that they refused to take you to the hospital when you were seriously injured because they were too busy?" she probed.

"Yes, but they just didn't understand the seriousness of my injuries at the time. How could they be responsible for something they didn't understand?"

The conversation continued like this until it suddenly dawned on my friend that, indeed, he had been abused as a child. This man, nearly finished with a graduate degree in psychology, could not see a classic case of denial operating in his own mind.

Rationalization

A parent may rationalize a partner's aggression against a child by discounting the significance of the abuse or by noting that the abuser "just gets a little out of control when he drinks." A parent might also rationalize abuse by pretending that the abuse isn't as bad as the child makes it out to be or even by blaming the child for the abuse, arguing that if the child were better behaved, the abuser would not get so angry.

Justification

People can use almost anything to justify their behavior, but a common justification for abusing a child is religion. In my book *A Violent Heart*, I addressed hate crimes and terrorism and how perpetrators of these crimes justified their behavior using religious teachings. I have spoken to several hundred groups over the past many years on parenting issues, and many times churches or religious groups have invited me to give a lecture or series of seminars. In this environment, more than any other, people will attempt to justify striking their children regardless of the alternative disciplinary options that I present. Once I was speaking on the subject of discipline to a group of about two hundred parents. The host organization was a Protestant church. When the question came up regarding whether or not I thought children should be spanked, I gave the same answer I always give: "If you can achieve the same goal with your children—compliance, obedience, respect, or whatever—without hitting them, why would you want to hit?" I did not say that one should never spank, I only suggested that if we can achieve the same end without hitting, it seems reasonable that we should try. A man in the audience became furious with me, refusing to let me either answer his questions or continue my seminar. He was so disruptive that my host had to terminate the seminar.

The man argued that the Bible instructed parents to spank their children. He told me that his father had beaten him and he had "turned out fine" and he had "beaten his three boys," who were now adults, and they had turned out fine. This is clearly a case of justification. Regardless of one's interpretation of holy writings, the man used a form of punishment that he wanted to impose and regardless of any evidence that contradicted his approach, he was going to find a way to justify his perspective. After the meeting ended that night, I was told that two of the man's boys were in prison and the third would not speak to him. One might question whether or not they really had "turned out fine." The man's wife was in the audience and she never said a word to me or to her husband. Even though I can only guess, I suspect that she believed his interpretation of "god's instructions for discipline" and, therefore, made no attempt to protect her children when they were young.

Fear of Perpetrator

The non-abusing parent may fear antagonizing the abuser by addressing the issue or by calling social services or the police. In the mind of the non-abusing parent, antagonizing the abuser could eventually lead to abuse of other children or even him/herself. The unfortunate truth is that in some states, even when abuse is evident, the perpetrator may very likely be free on bail within days or even hours after being arrested, assuming he or she is even taken into custody. Even if convicted, sentences for child abuse and neglect are generally short. Hence, it is possible that within hours of filing a complaint against an abusing spouse, the individual could be out of jail and free to terrorize his family. Even though a court order might require him to stay away from his family, there is almost nothing to keep him from violating a restraining order if he or she chooses. Fear of the perpetrator, therefore, is not an unrealistic fear.

Poor Problem-Solving Skills

Although this is by no means always the case, many children who are abused are raised by very young parents. Because of their youth, teenagers have fewer problem-solving skills than more mature parents. What may seem like an obvious solution to someone who has reasonably mature problem-solving skills is not always obvious to a young parent, especially one who is under stress. For example, one of my clients, a seventeen-year-old high school girl, came to therapy and confessed to me that she feared she was pregnant. I was the first person to whom she had confided her fears except for a classmate who had suggested to her that she come to see me. When I asked her why she thought she was pregnant, she said she hadn't had a normal menstrual cycle for two months. I asked if that was unusual for her, knowing that some women are irregular because of stress, eating disorders, or even athletic activity. She told me that she was usually regular and when she missed the first month she became very concerned.

I asked her if she had taken a home pregnancy test or made any plans to see a physician and she said that she had not. She was clearly very worried and for the past six weeks she had been sleeping irregularly, eating only minimally, and having tremendous difficulty concentrating on her schoolwork. Instead of simply finding out for sure if she was pregnant, she worried herself sick those many weeks with no plan other than hoping she wasn't pregnant. Her age, in part, contributed to her difficulty in solving the problem. We made arrangements for her to meet with her physician, to talk to her mother, and to work on the problems that made her believe she could not take her troubles to her parents—both of whom were very devoted and caring people. As it turned out, she was not pregnant and most likely her fears and stress contributed to her missed periods. If she had taken a home pregnancy test as soon as she missed her first period, she would have saved herself several weeks of stress, but poor problem-solving skills do not always allow one to do what seems obvious to others.

In the case of abuse, a parent may see the abuse, realize it is wrong, but simply not know what to do about it. Like my client, they may be doing the best they can, but they have no reasonable plan for addressing the issue.

Fear of Government Intervention

A parent may know that abuse is occurring, but the fear of having children removed from the home by social services or potentially having a spouse arrested creates cognitive dissonance. Many parents who have discovered abuse perpetrated by their partners have immediately called police or social services, more concerned about the safety of the child than the welfare of the spouse or future of the family unit, but many parents do not reach such a decision so quickly. Their loyalties are divided between their love for the abuser, their love for their children, the need for support and shelter, and other pragmatic concerns. A woman may deeply love her spouse or be so dependent on him emotionally and/or financially that the thought of losing him or the children is unbearable. The woman may rationalize that the abuse is the trade-off for a warm bed at night for her children, food on the table, and a complete family unit.

This may indeed be a realistic fear. Every state and county social services program is different. Some are very reluctant to remove children from the home, while others will do so if there is even suspicion of abuse. The National Clearinghouse on Child Abuse and Neglect Information contends that a child should be removed from the home in specific situations. These include situations where life-threatening conditions exist, abuse is premeditated, there have been previous reports of abuse, instruments are used in abuse, there is an increase in the intensity and frequency of abuse, the child is under six, the child is fearful of the caregiver, the child is suicidal, the parent's behavior is bizarre, there is substance abuse by the parent, the parent's view of the child is bizarre (i.e., the parent believes the child is possessed by the devil), the parent hides the child, the parent threatens the child, or there is spousal abuse.[14]

When children are removed from the home, they stay in foster care until the court determines an appropriate interim situation; that is, until charges can be addressed in court. Even though a child may stay in foster care for only a few days and he may be released to a temporary guardian such as a grandparent or other relative until trial, the parents in question may be allowed no contact with that child until their case goes to court. One of my clients, a five-year-old girl, was placed in the custody of her grandmother for four months, during which time her parents could have no contact with her. Allegations of abuse that had been made against her parents were false, but it took four months for the case to come before a judge and receive a ruling. As one can see, the fear of government intervention is not an idle one.

Abuse in One's Own History

One final factor that keeps parents from intervening to save their children from abuse is the normalizing of abuse. I have had many clients over the years who, because they were raised in abusive homes, supposed that all homes were that way; hence, they saw no need for intervention. One woman told me about her revelation that abuse was not the norm. She had grown up in a home with mean-spirited parents who frequently lobbed insults at their children and physically abused them in the process of disciplining them. My client married a very fine gentleman and eventually became a mother. It was not until she began to see her husband interacting in a loving way with her daughter that she realized that what she endured as a child was abnormal.

IDENTIFYING ABUSE AND ABUSERS

Pediatricians, teachers, counselors, youth pastors, and child-care workers are usually trained to identify child abuse, since people in these fields are regularly in direct contact with children. Pediatricians are concerned about children who frequently show up in their clinics with unexplained injuries or cases where the explanation does not fit the injury. They also look for situations where parents are nervous or agitated when asked about their child's injuries. Nonphysicians who work with children are concerned about visible bruising, cuts, burns, emaciation, or a child's comments alleging or implying abuse or neglect. Most states have mandatory reporting laws that state that poeple who work with children, such as those listed above, are required to contact social services if they suspect that a child is being maltreated. In many states callers may make reports anonymously. When social services is contacted, a caseworker is assigned and the suspicion of abuse is investigated, usually within forty-eight hours.

Among the signs of abuse that social workers look for are caregivers who deny responsibility for their actions or who blame victims, those who do the opposite of what they advocate, those who have a history of abuse, and those who obsess about their own needs rather than the needs of their children.[15] There are also a number of objective checklists available to social workers that help them identify potential abuse. The "Child Abuse Potential Inventory," the "Child Maltreatment Interview Schedule," and the "Family Assessment Form" assist in identifying potential abuse and aid in determining appropriate intervention.[16]

Abusers come in all shapes and sizes, from all races, and from all socio-economic classes, but according to HHS, parents are the perpetrators of abuse and neglect more than 80 percent of the time.[17] Statistically, perpetrators tend to have a personal history of abuse as a child; be lacking in parenting skills; have a history of depression; have poor coping skills; and be emotionally immature, young (teenage), and single.[18] Also, in homes where spuosal abuse is present, children are fifteen times more likely to be abused.[19]

Sadly, abusers are numbered among those who might appear altruistic on the surface. People who work in foster care or who adopt children sometimes abuse the children under their care. People work in foster care and adopt for a variety of reasons, many of which are pure and selfless. However, some couples adopt children to fulfill their own personal needs and insecurities, which stem from their own immaturity. In circumstances like these, when the child fails to live up to the expectation of the guardian, the parent becomes disenchanted with the child. When this happens, these guardians can easily become abusive or neglectful.

EFFECTS OF ABUSE

There are a number of effects of abuse, some that are short term and some that are long lasting. These effects are physical, emotional, and social.

Physical

Short-term physical problems include infections, bruises, broken bones, brain damage, visual and auditory impairment, contusions, burns, exposure, and death. Long-term physical problems include bones weakened by breaks that do not heal properly, brain damage, and visual and auditory impairment. Physical effects can be long lasting, but emotional and social problems are perhaps the most devastating in the long term.

Emotional

The residual effects of abuse go far beyond scars on the skin and bones. Emotional problems run deep and are difficult to treat the longer they go without intervention. Maltreatment betrays the fundamental bond of trust between a caregiver and a child. From his earliest days, the infant seeks resolution for his physical and emotional needs. In normal parent-child relationships, not only does the child seek affection and connection with a primary caregiver, but the caregiver is equally willing to provide warmth and affection. In these cases, the child learns that the world is safe, people can be trusted, and his needs will be met. This is called *attachment*. When these needs are compromised, he begins to question the stability of the world and the trustworthiness of those who are closest to him.

Because of cruelty, ignorance, the confluence of drug abuse by the parent(s), or other factors in parents of children who are severely abused in infancy, they may be left in a crib for hours or days at a time. Social workers routinely find children in filthy apartments where bugs and rats roam freely. Children are found in cribs with soiled diapers, sores indicating they have not been changed in days, bottles of soured milk beside them, totally alone, and severely malnourished. It is not unusual for these children to be left on their backs in a crib for so long that the backs of their heads flatten to conform to the mattress. In cases of extreme abuse like these, these youngsters learn that the world is unsafe and that they should not trust others. This failure to trust leads to an inability to emotionally connect with other humans even when the child wants to. These detached children are cold in their affect, they do not like to receive the hugs, kisses, and snuggling that most children thrive on, and they are incapable of showing genuine care, love, or empathy for anyone else, even parents or siblings.

Not only are they incapable of giving or receiving normal loving affection, they resent those who try to give it to them as well as those around them who receive it. Their resentment for what they cannot receive and what others are receiving leads them to strike out in cruel ways. Even if they are removed from their abusive environments and placed in living situations where nurturing adults care for them, their resentment does not go away. They may torture animals because animals are easy targets for young children: They are vulnerable, available, and unable to seek help. These children may also strike out against their siblings, especially vulnerable younger siblings, and they may attack their guardians, even killing them. Children like these who suffer from attachment disorders are rare, but the process of violating trust operates even in older children. Their failure to trust causes them to question their own self-worth and directly effects their social relationships.

Children who are abused exhibit symptoms of post-traumatic stress disorder, depression, and anxiety. Flanagan also enumerates other emotional issues that one might expect in abused children, which include social isolation, self-loathing, self-criticism, guilt, and shame, as well as behavioral issues such as the risk of suicide, substance abuse, self-mutilation, and violence.[20] Some of these symptoms are temporary and some of them will last forever. At the very least, without treatment, many of these symptoms will endure for years.

Social

Not every child responds to abuse by failure to bond, as I described above, and even those who are severely abused may not react in such an extreme fashion. However, at the very least, the long-term effects of abuse can be easily seen in the individual's relationships in both adolescence and adulthood. These relationships may move in one of two directions. The child may abandon all hopes of normal relationships, becoming isolated or antisocial. Even if this person marries later in life, he or she is distant and has difficulty trusting a spouse or lover.

On the other hand, the abused child may be so hungry for affection, safety, and warmth that he or she is indiscriminant about relationships. The abused child may fall quickly into sexual relationships, misinterpreting sex as emotional commitment, or remain satisfied with sex as a shallow replacement for deeper emotional commitment. Adolescents may engage in relationships with partners who mistreat them both physically and emotionally. Their only model for relationships has been dysfunctional and they, therefore, do not recognize the abnormal nature of an abusive relationship. This lifestyle can easily carry over into adulthood and adult relationships. Both in dating relationships and in marriage, these adult victims of child abuse will remain committed to a partner who shows little interest in them or even with one who regularly and openly betrays the trust of the relationship. The fear of being alone and unloved overrides the logic that goads one to leave.

My client Marie was in her thirties when I first saw her. She had been married a dozen years or so and had two children by her spouse. He was a very cruel man who made fun of her on a regular basis, making very thoughtless jokes at her expense in front of their children and also in public. He called her names and even hit her on occasion. When she first came to see me, she said she was afraid her marriage was in trouble. I asked her why she thought that and she told me about an affair that her husband was having.

It became obvious within minutes that he had made no attempt to hide this affair, even bringing his girlfriend home for supper and going off with her for weekend getaways. He had also had several similar affairs over the years of their marriage. Yet my client sat across from me, tears in her eyes, trying to figure out what *she* was doing wrong. It doesn't take a psychiatrist to figure out that her problem was that she was married to a selfish, cruel loser who had no intentions of changing his behavior, but she couldn't see that. Instead, she blamed herself for his unconscionable behavior.

Over the course of therapy, as I suspected from the first day we met, I found out that as a child this woman had been physically mistreated by her parents. She had no memory of her parents ever hugging her, comforting her, or telling her she was pretty or that she had done something well. When she was only seven or eight years old, she was hit by a car while crossing the street in front of her house. Hearing the noise, her father stepped out of the front door of their home. His response as she lay bleeding in the middle of the street, the driver giving her aid, was to yell at her for disobeying him by going into the street. He then went back inside and continued watching TV. Fortunately, she was not seriously hurt, but this episode was characteristic of the way both of her parents treated her.

She tearfully described her father's alcohol abuse and her mother's absence as she worked, trying to make ends meet financially. Because of his chemical addiction, her father often hit her without warning. Because of her mother's exhaustion, frustration, and disappointment with life, she gave the child minimal attention and often used extreme corporal punishment to impose discipline. As a result, twenty years later this young woman, now a mother herself, had difficulty distinguishing a healthy relationship from an unhealthy one.

MICHAEL JONES—A CASE STUDY

I first met Michael clinically when his step-grandmother brought him to me with an unusual request. She wanted to evaluate whether or not Michael, a tiny seven-year-old boy, was mature enough to fly alone from Atlanta, Georgia, to Germany. Over the next several years I got to know Michael very well. He was a child who suffered physical abuse, neglect, and emotional abuse at the hands of his biological mother and her lovers.

Michael's mother, Ellie, was young and unmarried when she became pregnant with him. It was her first child and she never married the man with whom she conceived Michael. She and Michael moved in with Ellie's father and his new wife, Mr. and Mrs. Warren. Ellie's father had been divorced some years earlier and then remarried. After living there for six months, Ellie decided to allow her biological mother, who had not remarried, to take custody of Michael, and Ellie disappeared from his life as she pursued her personal interests. Michael lived in his grandmother's home for the next two years. During the two years he was living with his grandmother, Ellie briefly came back into his life. She and a boyfriend with whom she was living took charge of Michael for a two-week period during which time the boyfriend was physically abusive to Michael. After this episode, Michael returned to his grandmother's home.

Following that two-year period of his life, the Warrens took responsibility for raising Michael, again allowing Ellie to continue pursuing a life of her own. Michael remained in Ellie's legal custody during those years, but she did not exercise any of her parental rights, leaving all parenting responsibilities to the Warrens.

Five years later, when I first had contact with Michael, many things had changed. Ellie, after having a series of live-in boyfriends, eventually married a man with whom she had a daughter. She and her new husband indicated that they wanted to take charge of Michael and raise him in their home. At about that time, Michael's biological father, a military man named Sam who was stationed overseas, also indicated a desire to exercise his visitation rights. Because Ellie still retained legal custody, the Warrens had no legal right to refuse either of them. Suddenly, this seven-year-old child was forced by the court not only to visit his mother, but also to spend several weeks in Europe with his biological father—a man he barely knew—who was now married and had children. After seven years of disengagement from Michael, Sam had decided that he wanted to get to know his son. Sam said he wanted to be a responsible father, but he was unwilling to come to the States to meet his seven-year-old son and fly back to Germany with him. Rather, he expected Michael to make the eight-hour flight to Europe by himself. This prompted my first contact with Michael. During the first court hearing, Sam told the judge that he wanted to spend time with his son and that the Warrens were preventing him from being a good father. Sometimes, however, the loving thing to do would be to consider what the child wanted. Michael clearly did not want to be around him; he feared him as well. Michael was a small child for his age and his father was rough with him, teasing him for not being tough enough. The court, however, paid no attention to Michael's wishes and forced him to fly to Germany alone to spend several weeks with his biological father. Fortunately for Michael, Sam only pursued these visits twice and then he lost interest.

Even more disturbing to Michael was the fact that at any moment Ellie could legally take him from the only life he knew and it was possible he would never be allowed to return to the Warrens' home. Michael had never bonded with Ellie. His worldview was shaky and his sense of security had been greatly threatened. Above all, it was abundantly clear to me that the interest in Michael expressed by both of his biological parents, especially his mother, was very selfish. His mother broke promise after promise, missed events that she said she would attend, and left Michael waiting by the door, failing to show up when she promised to come pick him up for visits. Both Ellie and Sam popped in and out of his life based on their own whims and I believe they wanted him in much the same way as a one might want a puppy. Michael was a novelty that they wanted to have around, rather than a human being for whom they sought the best circumstances. The Warrens, the people Michael had always considered mother and father, fought desperately to gain legal guardianship, investing thousands of dollars and hundreds of hours, hiring lawyers and psychologists, and even lobbying for a new law in the state legislature. During this time the court allowed the Warrens to retain temporary custody of Michael, pending a permanent custody decision.

Deep down inside, Michael loved his mother and he wanted her to love him, but he resented what she had done to him. The emotional damage she had done to him was irreparable. Over the next several years and many trips to court, lawyers from both sides argued for the rights of their clients. In the many hearings regarding Michael's custody, Ellie's lawyer repeatedly noted that Ellie and Sam had attempted to repair their relationship and that Ellie had gotten her life back together and was effectively raising her youngest child, a three-year-old girl named Hailey. Ellie's attorney argued that Ellie had matured, changed her wild ways, and was a stable mother and capable of caring for Michael. Unfortunately, the law did not focus much attention on what was best for the child—the law only looked at the rights of the biological parents. A psychologist colleague of mine and I worked on this case together. Before our final trip to court for Michael, we discussed the significance of what it appeared that the court was about to do. It was possible that the judge would give legal custody to the mother with visitation rights to the Warrens and to Sam. I suggested to my colleague, who I was fairly certain would give testimony, that she explain the absurd nature of any such decision to the judge. My argument, which she eventually did present in court, was that Michael's sense of trust had been betrayed repeatedly by a mother who made promises she did not keep and who had shown only minimal interest in him throughout his entire life. Forcing him to move in with her would be analogous to forcing a couple who had experienced infidelity and subsequent divorce to move back into the same home with each other. Even though the unfaithful party may be truly changed, the damage from the betrayal would potentially be irreparable. No judge would force an adult to live with a partner who had betrayed him or her nor would a judge expect the betrayed adult to "learn to adjust to living with the betrayer," yet the court was about to force this child into a very similar situation. Even if Ellie had matured and changed, the damage she had done to the relationship between her and her son was so extensive, so deeply rooted, that he would never, without a will to do so, be able to overcome his hurt, anger, and resentment. It would have been totally unrealistic to expect this ten-year-old boy to suddenly forgive and forget ten years of betrayal and emotional torture. I was confident that Michael would never be able to bond with his mother. The damage that had been done to their relationship over many years left him not only distrusting of her, but of others as well. The ever-present threat that he would be displaced left him nervous and angry. If Ellie had been granted full custody of Michael, I am confident that he would have been an extremely unhappy child and would almost certainly have rebelled in his adolescence.

Michael's hurt, frustration, emotional turmoil, and lack of control over his circumstances exhibited themselves in two ways in therapy. First, he was very impatient with himself. He was a very bright child and he accepted nothing but perfection from himself. This unrealistic expectation derives from a desire to be "good enough" that can be directly connected to emotional abuse and neglect. Second, Michael exhibited symptoms of aggression both against himself and against others. With regard to aggression against himself, when he would get frustrated with himself in therapy, he would slap himself in the head and he said there were times when he had considered shooting himself. With regard to his aggression toward others, many times he talked about wishing that his biological parents were dead and choking his half-sister; he even fantasized about killing his biological parents. In one fantasy, he told me about inventing a killing machine made up of "lots of hammers" that would "beat his mother's brains out." Another fantasy involved setting up a machine gun to kill her. At his age it was unlikely that he was a threat to her, but my fear for him as he got older was that he would generate more plausible fantasies; thus, putting his biological parents at risk.

I did not think that Ellie was a risk to Michael. I had seen no evidence that she had physically harmed him. However, I did fear for his emotional well-being if Ellie were awarded custody. What Michael needed was a permanent sense of security. He could cope with short visits with Ellie and he somehow managed to survive the long weeks in faraway lands with his biological father. He needed to know, though, that he would eventually be going home—to the only stable home he had ever known—with the Warrens.

This story has a happy ending. After four years of court hearings, testimony, social service investigation, and therapy, the judge finally awarded permanent custody to the Warrens. Sam reentered Michael's life once again. This time, however, he molded his schedule around Michael's and by all appearances, he truly wanted to be a good father to Michael. I have never spoken to Sam, but reports of his behavior make it apparent to me that he realizes he has missed his opportunity to be a father and the best he can hope for is a friendly relationship with the boy he fathered.

Even though Michael's situation has been resolved legally, he will always deal with relationship issues and I think it is likely that he will have feelings of distrust, fear, and anxiety in his personal relationships for a long time to come.

CONCLUDING REMARKS

Maltreatment is damaging in both the short term and the long term. It leaves visible scars, but the emotional damage is deep and sometimes difficult to see. Caring for our nation's children begins with responsible parenting, but it does not end there. All of us have a role to play in protecting these defenseless children by holding parents accountable and by watching for signs of abuse. A teacher, a neighbor, a member of the clergy, or a therapist might be the one person to whom the abused child will go to find refuge and help. It is a responsibility we cannot afford to take lightly.

NOTES

1. "HHS reports new child abuse and neglect statistics," Press release, *Department of Health and Human Services*, www.hhs.gov/news/press/2000pres/20000410.html, Washington, DC, April 10, 2000.

2. Ibid.

3. M. A. Straus, and R. J. Gelles, "Societal change and change in family violence from 1975 to 1985 as revealed by two national surveys," *Journal of Marriage and the Family, 48* (1986), www.jimhopper.com/abstats.

4. "HHS report shows continued record high child abuse and neglect levels," Press release, *Department of Health and Human Services*, www.hhs.gov/news/press/1998pres/980417a.html, Washington, DC, April 17, 1998.

5. "HHS reports new child abuse and neglect statistics."

6. Ibid.

7. Alice Yick Flanagan, "Child abuse and neglect: What healthcare professionals need to know," www.nursingceu.com/NCEU/courses/childabuse, June 26, 1998.

8. Ibid.

9. Ibid.

10. Ibid.

11. "Mother and child reunion: Stroller mix-up illustrates culture clash," *CNN On-Line*, http://www8.cnn.com/US/9705/14/denmark.parents/index.html, May 14, 1997.

12. "Child abuse statistics," *Child Abuse.com,* www.childabuse.com/newsletter/stat0301.htm, March 2001.

13. Ibid.

14. "Factors necessitating an immediate response," National Clearinghouse on Child Abuse and Neglect Information, www.calib.com/nccanch/pubs/usermanuals/cpswork/table2.cfm, Washington, DC, April 6, 2001.

15. "Crisis intervention assessment," National Clearinghouse on Child Abuse and Neglect Information, April 6, 2001. www.calib.com/nccanch/pubs/usermanuals/crisis/assess.cfm, Washington, DC, April 6, 2001.

16. Ibid.

17. "HHS report shows continued record high child abuse and neglect levels."

18. Alice Yick Flanagan, "Child abuse and neglect: What healthcare professionals need to know," www.nursingceu.com/NCEU/courses/childabuse, June 26, 1998.

19. Ibid.

20. Ibid.

CHAPTER 3

Sexual Abuse

Look now how mortals are blaming the gods,
for they say that evils come from us, but in fact
they themselves have woes beyond their share
because of their own follies.

—Homer, *The Odyssey*

The devil hath power to assume a pleasing shape.
—William Shakespeare, *Hamlet*

Mary had been an active student involved in extracurricular activities until the beginning of her freshman year in high school. During that year she began to dress in the "Goth" look and also began experimenting with drugs and alcohol. She dropped out of sports and other activities and, according to a school counselor, she appeared to work very hard at being a nonconformist.

While still in elementary school, Mary had developed a positive relationship with Cynthia, the school's home-school liaison. Cynthia's job was to develop programs to help parents, teachers, and students work together on various academic and personal issues. Mary and Cynthia both enjoyed the time they spent together in that context.

At fourteen years of age, when Mary started high school and her behavior became deviant, a high school teacher who knew of Cynthia's prior work with Mary notified her about Mary's behavior change. Cynthia made contact with Mary, but the child seemed uninterested in talking to her. Mary told her that "things were cool" and that she just wanted to be left alone. Cynthia respected her wishes, but asked Mary if she would be willing to help her with some clerical work during her free period at the high school. Mary agreed to help.

For the next two months, Mary showed up for this volunteer position without fail. Even though she was quiet during her working hours, she seemed to enjoy the time she spent with Cynthia and then one day Mary asked Cynthia if they could talk in private.

"Would you have to report it if I told you that I have been having sex, and giving oral sex to a policeman for the past three years?" she calmly asked Cynthia.

Cynthia said that she was a mandated reporter and that she would have no choice but to report that kind of behavior to authorities. For several minutes, Mary sat in silence, but then she began to cry. "I just want it to end," she said. She then opened up to Cynthia and related the following story.

When she was eleven years old, a policeman named Paul stopped Mary on the street and struck up a conversation with her. Mary's community was very small and she knew Paul from seeing him around town. Paul was forty years old, married, and he had three children. After that first meeting, Paul invited Mary to come visit him in the mornings on her way to school at the F.O.P. house, a facility run by the Fraternal Order of Police. This facility served as a rest and recreation facility for police officers and was also used for meetings. It was used mainly in the evenings, but ordinarily was unoccupied in the mornings. Mary made her first visit to Paul at the F.O.P. house the next morning. He was very kind to her and he told her how mature she was for an eleven-year-old. At one point he said that she didn't look eleven years old, but that she looked old enough to be his girlfriend. His words and attention were flattering to Mary. During this time, Mary's parents were going through a difficult divorce and Mary spent much of her time without supervision due to her parents' work schedules. Mary was bitter about her parents' divorce and she felt that Paul was the only adult giving her attention. Unfortunately for Mary, this predator was taking advantage of her home-life difficulties and was gently manipulating her for his own perverse pleasures.

After several visits with Paul, their conversations grew more intimate and he eventually told her that he wanted to show her how to "be with boys" so that she could be prepared when she was older. For several days Paul and Mary engaged in kissing sessions where he supposedly was teaching her how to kiss. Eventually, they began to engage in oral sex until finally they began to have sexual intercourse. Mary told Cynthia that Paul always wore his holstered weapon and many times it was all he would have on.

After a year of intimacy with Paul, Mary wanted to disengage from him and she began to pull away, but Paul wasn't about to let her go. He told her that he loved her and he said that when she was old enough, he would divorce his wife and they would be together forever. Mary believed that she might actually love him, but she felt a "pit" in her stomach that kept getting bigger every time she went to see him. Her guilt and discomfort with the relationship led her to change her looks, hoping that this would turn him off. When that failed to drive him away, she stopped visiting the F.O.P. house, but this only angered him. He threatened to tell her parents what she had been doing. He became increasingly aggressive and Mary told Cynthia that during their last meeting together at the F.O.P. house, their sexual encounter felt like rape because she did not want to be with him anymore.

When Mary finished telling her story to Cynthia, Cynthia told Mary that she was proud of her for having the courage to tell her story and promised to help keep her safe. Unfortunately, it was not a promise that she could fully keep. After meeting with the school principal, Cynthia reported the situation to authorities. When Cynthia talked to the sheriff about Paul's behavior, he was receptive and he promised to take action. The sheriff's office met with Mary's mother and related all that had happened to her daughter. That same day, the police placed a wiretap on Mary's home phone, hoping to document any conversation between Paul and Mary that would assist in prosecuting the case. It appeared they got the evidence they were after when Mary talked to Paul on the phone and told him that she had disclosed their secret. Paul became loud and upset.

"Oh my God, Mary, why did you do this?" he exclaimed. "You have to go talk to her again and say you deny it! Deny it! Deny it! How could you do this? What were you thinking? You have ruined my life.... After all we've been through how could turn on me?!"

To Cynthia, it seemed clear that Paul's words had convicted him. The state attorney's office filed charges against Paul, the media picked up the story, and Mary entered the Victims Assistance Program offered through the state attorney's office. She also began professional counseling. It looked like the beginning of the end for Paul and a new start for Mary.

While the sexual abuse had stopped for Mary, the ordeal had really only begun. Seemingly respectable individuals in her community tormented Mary, saying she had asked for it. She looked older than her years, they argued, so it wasn't the perpetrator's fault. Mary sank deep into depression. Over the period of a year and a half, the trial was continued three times. During all these continuances, Mary continued with counseling and slowly began to heal. By the time the actual trial began, she had a renewed sense of strength and her relationship with her parents had improved. The community, however, was still very much against her and supportive of their local "son."

When Cynthia was called to testify, the attorney for the defense attempted to discredit her. He tried to convince the jury that Cynthia was unqualified to assist the victim and even laughed out loud at the fact that Cynthia's bachelor's degree was in therapeutic recreation. Cynthia was not swayed and reminded the defense attorney that everyone at school is a mandated reporter of abuse, including the custodians. When she tried to read from a segment of the Mandated Reporters Act, the defense attorney abruptly cut her off. The judge admonished her and told her to answer the questions concisely and not give commentary. Fortunately, the prosecution allowed Cynthia to give a full and complete account of Mary's disclosure.

Although Mary had received instructions on what to expect during her testimony, she left the stand feeling very disheartened. As harsh as the defense attorney was on Cynthia, he was ruthless with the victim. The defense placed the blame squarely on her shoulders and painted a picture of Mary as a tramp and a liar. During the prosecution's presentation, they played the taped conversation of Paul's reaction to Mary's disclosure. Gasps and murmurs were heard throughout the courtroom and it seemed that Mary would be vindicated, but as the trial drew to a close and the verdict was read, the jury did not convict Paul. When interviewed after the trial, jurors said their reason for not convicting Paul was that because he never actually confessed to having sex with Mary, the tape was meaningless. Some jurors believed that Paul did have sex with Mary, but since Mary was unusually mature for her age, they argued, it was consensual sex and, therefore, it was Mary's fault.

Mary is now twenty-four years old. She is married and has moved away from her hometown. She has continued with counseling and, at this point in her life, she does not regret disclosing her abuse. Even though the end result was not favorable, she says that she knows she did everything she could to prevent this from happening to another little girl. Paul quit his job as a police officer and began work as a security guard. He was later arrested and convicted of sexual harassment.

Sexual abuse is a pervasive problem. One 1990 study found that 27 percent of women and 16 percent of men had been sexually abused as children.[1] A more recent study of 722 college students conducted in South Africa in 2001, found similar results showing 21.7 percent of males and 23.7 percent for females.[2] In my own private practice, I have found that over the past twenty years, nearly all of my adult female clients have some history of sexual abuse, rape, or other molestation in their pasts. Of the children I've worked with in my practice over these same years, about half of them have been sexually abused. One psychologist and internationally recognized expert on child sexual abuse once told me that during the early years of his practice he looked for signs of sexual abuse in his clients, but as time wore on and he realized how widespread the problem was, he began to assume it was a likely issue even before the client came through the door for the first time.

Our sexuality is the most personal thing to us. About once a year I teach a class over the Internet for suspense writers. The class has around a hundred students from all over the world and topics cover a wide range of issues related to violent behavior like serial killers, stalkers, and child molestation. The course runs for a month and participants interact via e-mail. About two-thirds of the way through the course one year, I was addressing a question about adult relationships. I made a passing comment about sexual behavior in the process of answering the question. I said that if a woman were sexually active with her boyfriend before there was some emotional commitment on his side, she should not expect him to be motivated to go much deeper in the relationship. My reasoning was that if men were getting what they wanted, they wouldn't necessarily be motivated to work harder at a deeper, more committed relationship. For two days, I received shocked responses from participants about my comment. Many of them adamantly disagreed with my opinion. I was surprised that so many of them disagreed as well as how much they had focused on this passing comment to the exclusion of the actual point of my statements. Then the irony struck me. For three weeks we had been discussing some of the most horrible behaviors imaginable—pedophilia, sexual torture, serial sexual crime, murder, and the like. Yet the thing that generated the most emotional reaction was a passing comment about sexuality. We cannot escape our sexuality and it is an inseparable part of who we are.

Rapists are not primarily interested in sex. They are interested in controlling and often in humiliating their victims. There are several types of rape, but most of them involve some form of control or humiliation. Sex is obviously involved, but it is only a medium by which the perpetrator can achieve his goal of control and humiliation. It is for this reason that a man might rape a ninety-year-old woman. There is no sexual attraction to the victim. The perpetrator's goal is to dominate and humiliate; therefore, the victim doesn't have to be sexually attractive. It can be anyone. There is little that would humiliate us more than being sexually exposed in public. Likewise, to be forced to engage in sex compounds our embarrassment and humiliation. In fact, I venture to guess that most people would be humiliated if the general public knew about their *voluntary* sexual exploits. Sex is personal, both for adults and for children.

VICTIMS

Sexual abuse occurs when the age difference between the perpetrator and the victim is at least five or more years.[3] Victims of sexual abuse are equally likely to be male or female. Sexual abuse includes inappropriate sexual conversations with a child, voyeurism, child prostitution, pornography, exhibitionism, molestation, sexual penetration, and rape.[4] Even if a child like Mary is a consensual partner in sex with an adult, it is still considered sexual abuse because the child's developmental limitations make it impossible for a child to fully comprehend the significance and ramifi-cations of any sexual act.

Sexual abuse has lifelong effects on one's self-image and in relation-ships. Children who have been sexually abused may exhibit a host of other symptoms as well. Anxiety, sleep disturbance, bed-wetting, insom-nia, nightmares, and somatic complaints are not uncommon. Children might also experience symptoms of post-traumatic stress disorder (PTSD), have memory problems, or create imaginary friends. Depression, suicidal behaviors, eating disorders, and promiscuity or other sexual acting out are not unlikely. Excessive masturbation, even in toddlerhood, is also com-mon. Anger, self-blame and self-doubt, guilt, repression, and apathy are all possible emotional reactions. Abused children do not easily trust others and they may engage in aggressive behaviors, even sexually abusing other children. A sexually abused child may change his or her habits of dress, as demonstrated in Mary's story, as well as show a change in school performance. Changes in school performance might include improve-ments in academic work as well as poorer grades. Some children improve in their schoolwork because they believe that if they perform better on some task, such as their grades, the abuse will stop.

One consistent symptom of abuse in children is something called *abre-action*. Abreaction is the replaying of the traumatic event through play or other activities. For example, children who have experienced a car acci-dent will draw pictures of car wrecks, play with toy cars and crash them together, and perform other such behaviors through which they can relive the event. They will abreact until they resolve the traumatic experience. Abreaction is prominent in the child's drawings, clay creations, and other forms of play. It is the analysis of abreaction in play that assists therapists in assessing and treating sexual abuse.

SEXUAL PREDATORS

According to the *DSM IV-TR*, a pedophile is one who has recurrent or intense sexually arousing fantasies, urges, or behaviors involving sexual behavior with children, usually under the age of thirteen. The perpetrator must be at least sixteen years of age and be at least five years older than the victim.[5] It is believed that pedophilia results when a person is abused as a child and then becomes an abuser himself. The process repeats itself in a vicious cycle. Fathers who sexually abuse one child in the home may also prey on other children at home as well. They may abuse siblings con-currently or, as one victim ages, the perpetrator may stop abusing that child only to prey on a younger sibling. Most pedophiles are male, but it is suspected that many more women sexually fondle children than the sta-tistics reflect. This is hypothesized because in our culture women are expected to bathe, change, and care for children. Their inappropriate fondling of a child could easily be disguised by one of these routine behaviors.

Researcher Ron O'Grady writes that there are three characteristics of pedophiles. According to O'Grady, first of all, they are obsessed with child victims and they structure their lives, jobs, and hobbies around the pursuit of their obsession. Second, they are predatory, stalking their victims for weeks or months. Finally, O'Grady concludes that they are collectors who keep pictures and videotapes of their abuse of victims.[6]

Sexual predators statistically are most likely to abuse their own children or children of acquaintances. According to one expert on child sexual abuse, between 80 percent and 90 percent of prison inmates arrested for sexual crimes committed their sex crimes against their own children.[7] This same research study indicated that 12 percent of prison inmates preyed on children of friends. Even though sexual abuse in day care settings makes national headlines, only 3 percent of all sexual abuse happens at day care centers and in foster homes.[8]

The National Clearinghouse on Child Abuse lists a number of variables that increase the risk for sexual abuse. Among these variables are having a stepfather in the home, the victim living without a mother at some point, mothers who did not finish high school, mothers who are sexually punitive toward the child (meaning hostile about any of the child's sexual impulses), and an income of less than $10,000 per year.[9] One of the biggest variables that increases the likelihood of sexual abuse is the presence of one stepparent and one biological parent. In this condition, a child is forty times more likely to be sexually abused than children who live in a home with two biological parents.[10] One should not suppose, however, that abuse doesn't happen in two-parent homes, single-parent homes, upper-class homes, or homes where mothers are college graduates.

Pedophiles love to volunteer. In Illinois in 2002, two foster parents who had been cited as "Foster Family of the Year" were charged with child abuse and child sexual abuse. The family was caring for six foster children at the time the charges were filed. Church youth work, scouting, and babysitting are all mediums that allow perpetrators access to potential victims. They perfect the ability to gain the parent's confidence. For example, in South Carolina, a man who was a part-time babysitter was charged with eight counts of first-degree criminal sexual conduct as well as other charges when he was accused of fondling and sexually assaulting a six-year-old boy and he was also accused of sexually assaulting an eleven-year-old boy.[11] I never have trusted my children with anyone I did not know personally. I never hired a sitter without knowing the person and following up on references. I've always been a little surprised at how readily parents will leave their children with strangers at child-care centers at resorts, hotels, or convention halls. Parents want to believe their children are safe when they leave them with another adult, such as a scout troop leader or a youth minister. In fact, one therapeutic issue with parents whose children have been molested by a teacher, babysitter, or other trusted individual is the feeling of guilt for having trusted the person. These parents cannot believe that they would willingly hand their children over to a perpetrator. Of course, this is false logic because they could not have known that the person was a perpetrator. Pedophiles take advantage of this trust.

When parents discover that their children have been molested by a family member, friend, or other trusted individual, they cannot believe that such a "nice" individual could ever do such a thing. They are, in part, coping with the more personal question—"How could I have let this happen?"—and the accompanying guilt. Pedophiles don't walk around with signs on their shirts identifying themselves as such. Likewise, observant parents would not give their children over to the care of someone who looked like a perpetrator. Therefore, perpetrators work very hard to appear trustworthy. In fact, they may cultivate a parent's trust for weeks or months before they begin their abuse of a child.

Pedophiles use a number of techniques to keep children from talking about the abuse. Some pedophiles murder their victims to ensure that their secret is kept, but most pedophiles do not murder their victims. More likely, they threaten to harm the child, the child's pet, or the child's parents or siblings, or they threaten the child with jail, saying if they tell, the police will arrest them. These children are too developmentally immature to realize how absurd this threat is. Perpetrators ensure silence by making the child feel responsible for the event, as if the child had done something wrong and they would get in trouble if they told. They may convince their victims that they have a secret that is just between them and they will emphasize that "good friends" don't tell secrets. They make the child feel emotionally responsible for the ongoing abuse by saying, "I need this," or "You have always done this before," or "What's the matter with *you*?" Just like with Mary in the opening story, the molester makes the victim feel responsible—as if she owed something to the perpetrator. All these threats and mechanisms involve placing responsibility on the child.

Sexual predators have found it easier to collect child pornography, to meet one another, and to acquire victims with the explosive use of the Internet. The Internet provides anonymity, plus quick and easy access to pornographic images of children, and chat rooms offer a private place to meet and lure victims.[12] Using the Internet, a perpetrator doesn't even have to leave his home to prey on children.

THE SECRECY OF ABUSE

Almost everyone who works with children in social or psychological services agrees that the data underestimates actual incidents of abuse. Victims are often afraid to tell and many incidents go unreported because the victim remains silent. Just like with rape, the fear, embarrassment, and shame that accompany sexual molestation prevent many victims from discussing their experience. When the relationship between the child and the perpetrator is a trusted one, such as that between a child and a parent or a child and a teacher, the child may not believe that she can say "No."[13] Yet if the child tells someone about the abuse, she erroneously believes that telling may get her in trouble. Therefore, she doesn't tell anyone.

Some victims fear they will not be believed—a realistic fear. Children are too young and do not have the physical, cognitive, or financial resources to pursue resolution of a molestation incident on their own. Therefore, they must first tell an adult. Even when children do tell an adult, many cases of abuse go unreported because adults either do not believe the child's story or they don't want to believe the child's story. Several times I have worked on cases where I was positive a child was being sexually abused, but the parent did not want to believe abuse had occurred. To acknowledge that the child had been abused meant that the parent had failed to protect his child. That choice was just too painful to accept and it was easier to pretend that there had been no abuse at all.

In other cases, adults who learn of abuse believe that the abuse has occurred, but they are unwilling to report it. Some parents erroneously believe that they can protect the child from a family member or neighbor and they don't want to go through all that would be required if the case became public. Unfortunately, even if the parent is successful at protecting the child from the perpetrator, that parent has little or no ability to protect *other* children. Perpetrators are manipulators. They not only manipulate their victims, but they can be very convincing liars when they are caught. They will promise never to do it again and swear all sorts of oaths. Yet when they have the chance, they will abuse again.

Finally, some adults who learn of abuse are afraid or unwilling to report it because of divided loyalties between people that they care about. They love their children and want to protect them, but when the perpetrator is a husband, father, uncle, son, or other close family member, the decision to call social services or the police is a difficult one. I have worked with parents who have courageously left spouses they loved very much for the sole purpose of protecting a child who was sexually abused. Likewise, a parent may rationalize that the embarrassment from public arrest and trial of a family member may not offset their desire to protect the child. Finally, some parents blame their children for the abuse they experience and have absolutely no intentions of involving social services or law enforcement. I will share just such a case before I close this chapter.

Public agencies like schools and churches, as well as private businesses, may fear that reporting a case of abuse will be damaging to the child—or damaging to the organization's reputation—by making the incident public.

They may fear lawsuits or they may have personal allegiances to the abuser. These very allegations have been lodged against the Catholic church. In 2002, the incidence of sexual abuse by priests seemed to reach epidemic proportions to the point that the Vatican itself has had to wrestle with the issue. For example, in Louisiana, a jury awarded $1 million to the family of an abused child because "The bishop knew the priest had problems and moved him to another parish where he abused more children."[14] On February 19, 2002, the "president of the U.S. Conference of Catholic Bishops expressed 'profound sorrow' for the sexual abuse of children by priests," also saying that abuse by priests is "a reality against which we must be ceaselessly on guard."[15] Discussions at the conference that year resulted in policies to address sexual abuse and to protect children by recognizing ways in which abusive priests protect their reputations (i.e., moving from parish to parish).

As a sidenote, some people have argued that the church's policy on celibacy creates the problem of pedophilia among priests, but there is no data that supports such a conclusion. More likely, men who struggle with sexual issues may pursue the priesthood either in hopes of some divine cure for their sexual urges or specifically to gain access to children.

VARIABLE RESPONSES TO SEXUAL ABUSE

Sexual abuse is not always a traumatic experience for the child. In fact, unless the molestation is painful, children may not even know they have been fondled and some children may actually find the experience pleasurable. Abuse for these children does not become a problem until their behavior is discovered or when they reach puberty and realize that the behavior is inappropriate. In both cases, they will suffer guilt, shame, and feelings of responsibility. One of my adult female clients was sexually active with her father for nearly a decade. The two of them engaged in fondling, oral stimulation, and autoerotic behavior from the time she was three years old until she reached puberty, around age thirteen. These experiences were pleasant for the child and made her feel closer to her father. It wasn't until she reached puberty that she began to realize that all children did not do what she was doing and that it was abnormal behavior. She realized that her father's actions were wrong and she decided to talk to her mother about it. Unfortunately, when she explained to her mother what had been happening, her mother blamed her, saying she behaved seductively and she deserved it. I suspect the mother may have known about the abuse all along and resented her daughter's beauty and the sexual attention she received from her father. All of my client's future relationships were sexualized until we began therapy. It took us more than five years of therapy for her to begin to significantly change the way she viewed men and relationships.

It may sound odd to one who has been sensitized to the plague of sexual abuse that a child might find "abuse" pleasurable, but children have to be taught that some behaviors are sexually inappropriate. As I mentioned earlier, women may sexually fondle a child during routine caretaking tasks like changing or bathing the child. If the child is not hurt or traumatized by the sexual behavior, it is possible the child may not even know that he or she has been sexually fondled. Likewise, in Mary's case, it is very likely that Mary enjoyed some of her sexual experiences with Paul. Sexual stimulation ordinarily is pleasurable. Unfortunately, it is this pleasure that compounds one's sense of guilt. The victim believes that since she enjoyed the experience, she was to blame for it. This, of course, is absurd.

Many times I have talked with parents whose children were fondled by neighbors, babysitters, or playmates. They are beside themselves with guilt, fear, grief, and other emotions because they fear their child will be permanently scarred by the experience. I assure them that the occurrence of the abuse by itself does not mean that the child even knows that he has been fondled. If the event was not painful or invasive, and especially if the child is young, the child may simply need to be informed that the behavior is inappropriate. It is possible in cases like this that the child will have no long-term symptoms related to the abuse. A parent may actually create more trauma by his or her response than the abuse itself may have caused. A hysterical parent may generate fear, guilt, and shame in the child who may not fully understand what has happened. An informed evaluation of the child is necessary. In this evaluation, the therapist or social worker needs to be made aware of as many of the known details of the event as possible and be provided information on the child's reactions. Based on this information I may ask the parent to bring the child in to my office for evaluation or I may provide some suggestions on how to talk to the child about the event. Likewise, I may tell the parents to wait, providing them with a list of symptoms to watch for, and suggest that they call me if any of the symptoms show up. No therapy may be necessary.

Of course there are many times, however, when sexual abuse not only puts children at risk for long-term problems and emotional trauma, but it may be a threat to life and limb. This was the case for Richard and Maureen Kanka. Little did they know that all three of the men who shared a rental house diagonally across the street from them in Hamilton, New Jersey, were convicted pedophiles. One of them would change their lives forever.

JESSE TIMMENDEQUAS

It was a sunny summer afternoon on July 29, 1994. Megan Nicole Kanka, seven years old, had spent most of the afternoon riding her bicycle with her eight-year-old friend who lived directly across the street from her and next door to thirty-three-year-old Jesse Timmendequas. Megan's friend left her sometime in the late afternoon, but her friend's sister, seventeen-year-old Chrissy Foster, saw Megan talking to Timmendequas in his driveway. She was the last person to see Megan alive.

Around 5 P.M., Megan's mother realized she was not in the house and began looking for her. She went house to house, places where her daughter played, asking neighbors if they had seen Megan. One of her stops was at Timmendequas's house. He told Maureen Kanka that he had seen Megan earlier in the day while he was working on his car. He offered to make and distribute missing-person fliers using a picture of the blonde-haired child. By 8 P.M., the Kankas notified police and a formal search was under way. Three hundred volunteers turned out to canvass the area. Police went door to door interviewing potential witnesses.

Only a few hours after Megan turned up missing, investigators began to focus their attention on the house across the street, which they had learned was occupied by Brian Jenin, a convicted pedophile who was on parole. Also living in the house with Jenin and Timmendequas was Joseph Cifelli, another convicted pedophile. The three men had met in prison. Police initially suspected Jenin, but Timmendequas's nervous behavior, combined with his sexual history and the fact that he was the last one to see her alive, attracted their attention and he quickly became the prime suspect. Timmendequas voluntarily went to police headquarters for questioning. Night passed and by the next day hope of finding the missing child had dimmed. Scarcely twenty-four hours after her disappearance, Timmendequas confessed to killing the child. Using information he provided, police quickly discovered Megan's body in a park not far from her home, plastic bags covering her head.

During interrogation, Timmendequas told police he had been "getting those feelings again" for little girls when Megan came by as he was cleaning his boat (not working on his car as he had told Maureen Kanka).[16] He told her he had a puppy inside and asked her if she wanted to see it. He said the puppy was too young to come outside.

Once inside, he grabbed her by the back of her pants and attempted to molest her, but the child fought back fiercely. She screamed and bit Timmendequas on the hand hard enough to leave a mark. During their struggle, Timmendequas tore the child's pants and she fell and hit her head on a dresser. Timmendequas reached for a belt that was on the back of a door and wrapped it around her neck. With it, he strangled her to death. Fearing that bloodstains would provide evidence of his involvement in her death, he wrapped two plastic bags over her head. He then put the child's body in an old toy box and loaded it into the back of his pickup truck. He later said that he heard noises like coughing from the toy box as he carried it out of the house, so it is possible that Megan was still alive at that point.

He drove a few miles away to the Mercer County Park, where he dumped her fragile body in the weeds. Before he left, though, he sexually assaulted her a second time.[17] Returning home, he scrubbed the house thoroughly to removed any traces of evidence.[18]

Sadly, this wasn't his first experience with sexually assaulting a child. In 1979, Timmendequas attacked a five-year-old girl who, like Megan, lived across the street from him. He lured her into a wooded area and tried to fondle her, but when she screamed, a passing teenager rescued her. Timmendequas was arrested the next day. After pleading guilty to sexual assault, he was sentenced to five years—suspended.[19] Just two years later, in 1981, Timmendequas grabbed seven-year-old Leanna Guido off her bicycle and dragged her to a wooded area behind a school where he raped and attempted to murder her. He choked her until she lost consciousness. Thinking she was dead, he left her body in the woods, but she survived. Timmendequas was arrested again and this time, following his conviction, he was sentenced to ten years in prison. The sentence, however, was reduced to six years for good behavior.

At his trial for Megan's murder, the defense attempted to show that Timmendequas was the victim of a cruel father and a disengaged mother, a woman who conceived ten children by seven different men. It was argued that Timmendequas was the result of "three generations of sexual abuse, mental instability, broken homes, alcoholism, poverty, crime and neglect."[20] His brother, Paul Timmendequas, testified about physical and sexual abuse that he and his brother suffered as children at the hands of their father, Charles Hall. He said that when he was around age five and Jesse was around age seven, their father began sexually assaulting them weekly and the assaults continued for four years.[21] These assaults always occurred while their mother, Doris Unangst, was out of the house. But their own abuse was not the limit of their father's cruelty. According to Paul, he and his brother were forced to watch their father rape an eight-year-old neighbor girl in his pickup truck, an allegation that Hall denied.[22] Many child molesters threaten to kill a child's pet to ensure their silence. Hall, however, didn't threaten. He drowned their pet dog, cut off the head of the family cat, and killed their pet rabbit in front of the boys to keep them from talking about his abuse.[23]

The psychiatrist who examined Timmendequas said that he was borderline mentally retarded and that the reason he killed Megan was that he was afraid she would tell and he would go back to jail. His attempt to cover up his crime made it clear that he knew what he was doing and any insanity defense would have been pointless. By the close of the trial, the prosecution had presented a solid case and a guilty verdict was likely.

In May 1997, the jury spent ten hours in deliberation before they convicted him of kidnapping, rape, and murder and they later voted unanimously for a death sentence. Jurors were torn between the horror of his past and the horror of his actions against Megan, but the heartless and selfish crime swayed their votes. After his conviction, but before sentencing, Timmendequas apologized, saying, "OK. I am sorry for what I've done to Megan. I ask you to let me live, so I, some day, I can understand and have an understanding why something like this could happen."[24] Timmendequas remains on death row. In the twenty years that the state has had capital punishment, no prisoner has yet been executed. Maybe Timmendequas will be the first. Richard and Maureen Kanka started the Megan Nicole Kanka Foundation to educate parents and children about the danger of sexual attacks, and legislators eventually passed Megan's Law requiring registration of sexual offenders.

This was a tragic case, as all murders are, but the development of the animal that Timmendequas became did not occur overnight. His upbringing surely contributed and for that, in my opinion, some blame for Megan's death falls on his parents. His father was abusive and cruel and his mother was somehow so disengaged from the lives of her children that she was never aware of the abuse or never intervened when abuse was occurring. Following the trial, Doris Unangst said of her son, "I guess if I was more in tune with my kids, this would not have happened."[25] You think?

GEORGE FRANKLIN—SEXUAL ABUSE AND REPRESSED MEMORIES

One of the ways our minds keep information from our consciousness is through repression. Once in a while, an event in one's life is so terrible, so overwhelming, that one's mind blocks it from consciousness, making voluntary recall of the event nearly impossible. The memory of the event may surface days, months, or even years later in life or it may remain repressed forever. Author and psychiatrist Dr. Lenore Terr chronicles a highly controversial case of sexual assault, trauma, repressed memories, and the legal system in her 1994 work *Unchained Memories*. This was the case of George Franklin and Eileen Franklin Lipsker, his daughter.

Eileen Franklin Lipsker was twenty-eight years old, married, and a mother herself when she first began to recall events that had occurred twenty years earlier. The look of her eight-year-old daughter as she played on the living room floor with friends paralleled a pleading look from a playmate in 1969. That day the image of her daughter sparked a memory that caused her to recall the rape and murder of her playmate, Susan Nason.

It was September 22, 1969. Eileen and her father, a fireman and real estate agent, were driving in his VW van. They saw Susan Nason playing in her yard and Eileen suggested that they let her ride along with them. Franklin agreed and picked up the child. They drove around for a while and ended up in a secluded area at Crystal Springs Reservoir near San Francisco, California. The girls were playing on a mattress in the back of the van and George Franklin came back to play with them, but Franklin wasn't interested in childhood games. Franklin ordered his daughter to the front seat of the van. From there, she watched helplessly as her father raped her screaming playmate. Then, Franklin took a rock and struck the child. Susan tried to protect herself by raising her hand. The rock struck her finger and bent a ring she was wearing. Eileen said that as her father was about to smash Susan's head with the rock, she made eye contact with her friend and it was a similar look that she saw in her own daughter's eyes twenty years later that triggered the memory.[26]

Again Franklin brought the rock down on the child, this time connecting with her skull and killing her. Franklin allegedly dumped the dead child's body in the weeds, where it would be found two months later. After seeing her playmate murdered, Eileen tried to run, but her father caught her and allegedly threatened to kill her too if she told anyone.[27] He told his daughter that the murder was her fault because she had invited Susan to come along with them.[28] Initially, Eileen forced the memory of the event into the shadows of her mind and over time her subconscious mind took control of it. The memory remained unavailable to Eileen for two decades.

One who does not understand repression can't help but wonder how anyone could forget such a terrible event. The answer lies in an examination of how repression works during a trauma. For isolated traumatic events, memory is ordinarily very precise. People may remember the most minute details—the smells in the air, subtle facial expressions, the sound of a bird chirping. For example, for the soldier who experiences the horror of battle for the first time, the acrid smell of gunpowder or the last words of a dying comrade may be indelibly etched into his mind. Sometimes, the event is so overwhelming for the person that the mind recognizes the inability to cope with the trauma of the event and shuts it out, even if it is an isolated event, making recall impossible. More likely, however, when a person is repeatedly exposed to traumatic events, repression pushes those details to the back of one's mind. Continuing my battlefield example, after six months engaged in heavy combat, this same soldier may have minimal memory or no memory at all of who did what, when things happened, or whether it was day or night. In order to cope with the gruesomeness of battle, the soldier's mind blocks out details. The process works the same way with ongoing physical or sexual abuse. Children may "practice" forgetting the pain and humiliation of abuse to the point that they condition their minds not to remember the abuse. In some cases, much of one's childhood is forgotten in this way, as well. It always concerns me when an adult client tells me, "I really don't remember much before about age twelve." This is a significant symptom of abuse.

In Eileen's case, she had allegedly been physically abused many times by her alcoholic father, giving her ample practice at repression. Eileen herself said that she learned to deal with her abuse by "forgetting" what was happening.[29] Twenty years after the fact, when she was older and better able to cope with the memory of Susan's death, the look of her own daughter was enough of a cue to trigger the memory. Her mind no longer needed to repress it, since she was able to cope with the horror of the event.

Eileen kept her new memory to herself for many months. She sought counseling to deal with her memories, wondering if she were going crazy or if it was possible that her father had actually committed this crime. Eventually, she shared her secret with her husband. Over time he was able to convince her to talk anonymously with the prosecutor. After many weeks of covert conversations, the prosecutor was able to convince Eileen to provide a formal statement so that prosecution of the murder could begin. Finally in 1989, Franklin was arrested for Susan Nason's murder, but Eileen's ordeal was far from over.

The trial was a landmark case. The defendant was charged and tried for a crime based almost exclusively on the testimony of an eyewitness who had a "recovered memory" although there was evidence presented other than Eileen's memory. For example, prosecutors painted a picture of Franklin as a pedophile and even presented a witness who told the court that Franklin had asked her if he could have sex with her eight-year-old daughter.[30] The defense attacked the validity of Eileen's recovered memory. Allegations were made that Eileen made up the story because she wanted revenge against her father for the abuse she had suffered in her childhood. The defense said her motive may have been financial because she signed a $500,000 book and movie deal. However, I find it unlikely that someone would plan such an elaborate hoax solely on the remote chance of obtaining a movie or book deal.

The Franklin family was divided with regard to his guilt. Eileen's brother (George, Jr.) took the stand in support of his father while Eileen's sister Janice and her mother Leah, who divorced Franklin in 1975, supported Eileen.[31] A persuasive part of this case for me is the fact that Eileen was not the only person to suspect Franklin of murdering Susan. Five years before Eileen brought her story to prosecutors, Janice had gone to authorities and conveyed her own suspicions about her father's involvement in the child's death, but police had no evidence beyond her suspicions so no investigation was pursued.[32] Leah Franklin, at the time of the murder, also wondered about her husband's involvement in Susan's death. She asked him point-blank if he had murdered Susan. Both Janice and Leah said Eileen had never told them what she had seen or discussed their own suspicions with her.[33]

Ultimately, Eileen's testimony was convincing and in 1990 the jury convicted Franklin of the murder. In 1991, Franklin was sentenced to life in prison, but the story still wasn't over. After spending six and a half years in prison, Franklin was released by a federal judge who overturned the conviction on a technicality. The judge said that jurors were "improperly told that, by staying silent in the face of his daughter's accusation during a prison visit, he had admitted his crime."[34]

In the meantime, both Eileen and Janice continued with therapy. More importantly, both had allowed themselves to be hypnotized. Hypnosis is a highly controversial treatment technique with regard to memories. The research on the use of hypnosis seems clear. Anything can be implanted as a memory in a subject's mind while he or she is under hypnosis and the subject will then believe it to be true. Studies known as "the mall" studies provide evidence for this fact. In these studies, college students were asked to participate in a study of hypnosis and memory. Prior to the study, the researchers checked the backgrounds on all subjects to ensure that they had never been abducted from a shopping mall. Then, while under hypnosis, subjects were exposed to a variety of false experiences ("memories") involving everything from talking to a stranger at a shopping mall to being abducted from the mall. After the hypnosis sessions, these subjects were convinced that these memories were real. This same phenomenon addresses why hypnosis often yields "memories" of past lives, abduction by UFOs, and other such extreme experiences. In short, hypnosis is not only a highly unreliable tool for gathering factual information, but once hypnosis is involved, all future "memories" are open to question.

Eileen accused her father of murdering two other people, but Franklin could not possibly have committed these other two murders because in one case he had an alibi and DNA evidence did not match his DNA. In the other case, there was no murder police could find that matched Eileen's memory.[35] It is possible that these murders were false memories stemming from Eileen's imagination or an implanted hypnotic suggestion. However, with regard to the Susan Nason murder, Eileen was not hypnotized until *after* she had memories of her father's involvement in Susan's death—not before. The validity of the first accusation is not compromised even if the two other murder accusations were the result of unintended hypnotic suggestion by her therapist.

Some have cited the overturned conviction and the decision not to retry Franklin as "proof" that Eileen made up her allegations or that her memories were distorted. Regardless of a district attorney's opinion regarding the guilt or innocence of a perpetrator, the DA has to be able to prove guilt to a jury. If the case lacks evidence or credible testimony, a perpetrator may never even be charged with the crime. Franklin was not retried for the murder of Susan Nason because Eileen's testimony, the primary evidence against him, was so tainted by the two false allegations and by hypnosis, that she would not have been a believable witness. Even if the retrial had taken place, the case would not have resulted in a conviction. The decision not to retry Franklin does not exonerate him. It is only reflective of a case that was not winnable. The law and mental health operate in two very different arenas. The law is concerned with what can be concretely demonstrated. Memories—complex chemical activities in the synapses of the brain—cannot be proven as factual even when they are. The courts have determined that Franklin was wrongfully convicted, and, therefore, was innocent of any wrongdoing. It is not impossible, however, that Eileen was right all along.

A THERAPEUTIC RESPONSE TO REPRESSION/SUPPRESSION

Therapists must be very careful about how they approach the possibility of repressed memories, especially with regard to sexual or physical abuse. A client came to my office for the first time as a grown woman. She was eighteen and her presenting problem was difficulty in relationships and an eating disorder. She said that she was having trouble getting along with boyfriends and that she had been in physically abusive relationships with several older men, beginning at age fourteen. She had been sexually active since puberty as well and she also said she had bulimia, an eating disorder where one binges for several days and then engages in varied behaviors such as self-induced vomiting or the use of laxatives to avoid weight gain. Almost immediately I suspected sexual abuse in her past. About half my clients have sexual abuse in their past in one form or another—either in childhood or some sexual assault or rape in adulthood. Therefore, there is about a 50/50 probability that anyone walking through my office door has been a victim of sexual abuse. This client showed many symptoms of sexual abuse in her past. Being sexually active from such an early age, having boyfriends who were controlling and physically abusive toward her, and her nearly nonexistent self-esteem and overly eager-to-please personality were all symptomatic of past sexual abuse. Likewise, despite her sexual relationships, she was outwardly very conservative in her dress and she found almost no pleasure in her sexual encounters, another symptom of abuse.

More convincing than these symptoms, however, was the fact that my client would occasionally directly refer to her father's behavior. The statements stood in isolation and almost never fit the context of our conversation. She never said specifically what his behavior was, but almost subconsciously she would drop lines in our conversation such as, "Can you believe an elder in the church would behave that way?" Other times she would make statements like, "He should never have done that to me" or "If people only knew how he really was, they wouldn't believe it." It was as if some part of her subconscious wanted to talk about something, but she was doing everything she could to keep it beneath the surface.

Sigmund Freud suggested that our personalities are like icebergs—only a tiny portion is exposed (our consciousness) and the rest lies deep below the surface. The part of our personality just beneath the surface of the water is what he termed the *preconscious.* This part of the personality is outside of one's awareness, but with some introspection it is accessible to our conscious minds. For example, have you ever found yourself saying something or doing something and asked yourself, "Now why did I say that?" only to think about it more deeply and realize you know why? That is how the preconscious operates. Motives are accessible with introspection. Yet, according to Freud, the vast majority of our personality lies far below the surface and well out of our reach in the area Freud called the *subconscious.* This part of our personality can only be accessed (according to Freud, anyway) through psychoanalysis. Freud said that the majority of what we say or do is driven by the preconscious and the subconscious, although our minds work very hard to keep those drives out of sight. This process of forcing our drives down below the surface is known as *suppression.* (*Repression* is similar, but it is involuntary while suppression is a voluntary process. The result of both suppression and repression is the same—inaccessible memories.) Sometimes, however, our drives are forced to the surface. Slips of the tongue, for example, are demonstrative of what is "really" on our minds slipping out of our mouths.

I believed that my client's comments about her father were, in part, her preconscious trying to force the topic of her past abuse to the surface, but she had suppressed those images for so long that she couldn't allow it to be a conscious act. Therefore, the words popped to the surface randomly through weaknesses in her conscious attempt to suppress them.

I would never tell a client that he or she had been sexually or physically abused in the past, even if I was certain that abuse existed. These clients must first bring it up themselves. I will, however, ask questions or open the door for discussion of such issues and I did so with this woman. I asked her early in our therapeutic relationship if she had any history of abuse of any kind. The question was in the context of our intake interview that included questions about many areas of her life. She had answered or discussed every question quite openly until I came to that question. With this question, however, she stopped and looked directly at me.

"Why would you ask that?" she said.

"It is a routine question," I responded, "especially with female clients who have some of the symptoms you are presenting."

I went on to explain that there were many causes of various symptoms, but I would be remiss if I did not explore all options. She seemed satisfied with the explanation and said there was no abuse in her past, although I was almost certain even then that she was hiding something from me, either deliberately or subconsciously. As therapy progressed and she made comments about her father as I described above, I would occasionally mention them to her. For example, I once said:

"You know, more than once you have made comments about your father as if there is something painful or embarrassing there. What is that about?"

Usually, she would brush me off or just ignore the question altogether. I did not believe she was capable of facing it so I did not push her too hard and I would let it go until the next time she brought it up. We made progress in therapy, her eating disorder went into remission, and her relationships improved slightly, but I was still concerned about her past and how that would affect her future relationships once we terminated therapy. As time went by, she eventually stopped attending therapy. Then some months later, I received a phone call from a psychiatrist. He was treating her for depression and she had gone into a tantrum in his office. He knew about my prior work with her and as he tried to calm her, she said she wanted to talk to me. The psychiatrist asked me if I would talk to her and see if I could calm her down. I agreed, of course, and when she came to the phone she was hysterical. Apparently, the psychiatrist had in some way or another concluded the same thing that I had about her past, but instead of working slowly through it, he had simply said, "Of course, you know you have been sexually abused by your father, don't you?" an approach I wouldn't have used myself. Regardless of his methodology, however, her hysteria and adamant denial of his statement further convinced me that the psychiatrist and I were both correct in our conclusions. I was able to calm her down by reassuring her that his assessment did not prove anything and there could be other reasons for the symptoms that had led him to that conclusion. I reminded her that I, too, had asked her about the possibility of sexual abuse many months before.

After this episode, she decided to reengage in therapy with me. For several more months we worked on relationships as well as her self-image and, as before, symptoms of sexual abuse were pervasive in her words and behavior. As before, she refused to talk about it and, as with our first round of therapy, she eventually stopped keeping her appointments. I didn't see her for several weeks until one day she came to my office with no appointment. Fortunately, I had no one with me and I had time to see her. She was hysterical and almost completely incoherent.

"I know he did it, but he couldn't have. How could he do that to me? What kind of man would do that to a child?" she ranted. Her hysteria continued like this for several minutes, tears streaming down her cheeks. I tried to calm her, but she only became more upset. Finally, I told her that she was scaring me and that if she couldn't calm down I was going to have to call for help. She settled down enough to talk to me and we spent an hour working through the issues that had brought her to my office that day.

She told me about a sexual relationship with her father that had gone on since early in her childhood and even now he would still occasionally pressure her to "play" with him. I listened patiently as she told me that she felt like she had known it all along, but couldn't admit it because no one would believe her and she was so ashamed. Note how her words are indicative of suppressed memory, as I had described earlier. We scheduled several more sessions and made tremendous progress in those subsequent weeks. Then one day she appeared at my door, again without an appointment. She was very calm—almost detached.

"I made it all up," she said. "It never happened and I don't want to talk about it anymore."

I was very disappointed. I realized she was slipping backward, coping with her pain through suppression. The pain of dealing with the issue was too much for her to bear and it was easier to be dysfunctional than to endure the pain of healing. We talked about how she had brought this to me and, for the first time, I pressed her, suggesting that suppression may be at work. She refused to acknowledge it. After that appointment I never saw her again.

The therapist has to be extremely careful that he or she does not "present" a history for the client. The client must bring up the information from his or her past when ready. The therapist who moves too aggressively risks, at the very least, frightening the client—as happened when the psychiatrist pushed my client too far. At its worst, presenting a history that is unfounded creates turmoil for the client, on top of what he or she is already dealing with, and it also destroys families.

FALSE ACCUSATIONS OF ABUSE

Erroneous accusations of abuse are inevitable. Because of mandated reporting laws in many states, people who work with children are required to report "suspicions" of abuse. They do not have to be certain that abuse has occurred. False or erroneous accusations come from several sources. Social workers, therapists, physicians, teachers, and other mandated reporters might mistakenly report abuse when the symptoms are present, but these symptoms are actually the result of some other cause. These false accusations come from misperceptions, misinterpretation of symptoms, personal agendas, or incompetence.

Couples involved in custody disputes may accuse the spouse/former spouse of sexual or physical abuse in order to increase the likelihood of a favorable custody ruling. I have suspected this motive in many of the parents of my own clients. Research suggests that as many as 60 percent of all allegations of abuse are made during custody disputes and that of those allegations, 66 percent were unsubstantiated.[36] This doesn't mean abuse *didn't* occur—only that abuse was not shown to be the definitive cause of the symptoms that led to the allegations.

Some accusations of abuse come directly from the victims themselves. The motives for these false allegations are varied. Some of these children have been indoctrinated by unethical or incompetent therapists, parents who have personal agendas, or others who may believe that the child has been abused. After hearing from these adults repeatedly about the "abuse" they have suffered, these children begin to believe it. This coercion often comes in the form of poor interview techniques.[37] Adults coerce the child, either intentionally or unintentionally, into believing that the abuse has occurred. Childhood memory is readily open to distortions because of developmental age prior to around age six. Children remember selectively and recall events that are significant to them—not necessarily those that are significant to parents, prosecutors, or therapists. The interviewer has to be extremely cautious so that he or she does not lead the child and present a "memory" that wasn't there to begin with. When parents call me suspecting that their children have been abused, I always caution them about how they address the issue with the child. Innocent, but inappropriate, comments by the parent could compromise the prosecution of a perpetrator or result in the false accusation of an innocent person.

In my experience, young children almost never deliberately falsely accuse an adult of sexual abuse. There is no clear research on the percentages of accusations that result from deliberate false accusations by children, but the consensus is that such false accusations are rare. However, there are some circumstances where they do occur. Children who have been sexually abused are more likely to make additional false accusations of abuse, especially to get their way in foster care custody or to exact revenge on foster parents. This creates a huge risk to people who work with this population. Teenagers are more likely to deliberately make false accusations than younger children. Some researchers suggest that deliberate false accusations from children could be the result of their own sexual fantasies.[38] These accusations are rooted in the adolescent's sexual interests in an adult. In a related issue, children may make false allegations of abuse to exact revenge against an adult. For example, one researcher tells the story of a child who accused a parent of incest to exact revenge against her mother who was about to remarry.[39] The falsely accused adult may be a parent who has angered the child in some way, or it could easily be an adult who has appropriately shunned the sexual advances of the minor. In order to pressure the adult into a sexual relationship, or to get retribution for one's unrequited advances, the adolescent then accuses the object of her affection of sexual misconduct.

Another reason children might allege abuse is to protect themselves. Children who have been sexually active and either fear or know for certain that they have a sexually transmitted disease or are pregnant may allege abuse to avoid having to face the punitive consequences of voluntary sexual activity. For example, one child alleged abuse in order to cover up her own masturbation.[40] These children would rather be seen as victims than admit their sexual behaviors.

When false accusations are made, there are numerous problems that affect the accused and their families. The accused often experience suicidal thoughts, anxiety, and depression. They may incur huge debts in the process of paying lawyers, bail, and other legal fees. They may be fired from their jobs, simply based on the allegation of sexual abuse. In my field, just the allegation of abuse could so seriously damage my reputation that I would have trouble finding work. What parent would bring her child to a therapist who has been accused of sexually molesting children? Losing one's job, of course, only compounds the financial pressures of defending oneself against an accusation of sexual abuse. Some marriages cannot bear the strain of investigation and the possibility of the truth of the accusation and, even if the allegation is shown to be false, marriages sometimes crumble. At the very least, an investigation by social services or law enforcement is humiliating and embarrassing.

The primary dilemma facing those of us in the mental health and social services fields is "how to protect children from abuse while protecting the rights of families."[41] This is a task that requires experience, education, and training. I will address some of the therapeutic techniques used to investigate allegations of abuse in Chapter 5.

PROSECUTION OF PERPETRATORS

The legal system is not friendly to a child who has been abused. Prosecutors need the child's testimony in order to prosecute the case. I can testify about what a child has told me in therapy or about what I have learned through the child's behavior in therapy, but the child is potentially a stronger witness. Likewise, no prosecutor would pursue a case if he or she did not believe that abuse had occurred. Therefore, exposing the child to the perpetrator in court and cross-examination by defense attorneys may retraumatize the child. This is sometimes an unfounded fear, however. Many children are actually empowered by confronting their perpetrator, and going to court to stand up for their rights may be an important step in the healing process. Defense attorneys must also tread lightly. They believe their clients are innocent, but they cannot verbally assault the character and story of a child witness in the same way they might approach an adult witness. Doing so would potentially alienate the jury if they believed the attorney were being cruel to the child in his/her cross-examination.

Children must deal with a host of emotions with regard to courtroom testimony. Courts are sterile, scary places, even for adults, and even though testifying can be empowering to the child, facing the accused in court can be frightening. Some courts have used protective screens and closed-circuit TV, but there are questions about the effect of such devices on juries. In one supreme court decision (*Coy v. Iowa*, 1988), one justice argued that the use of such devices could create an impression that the accused was guilty.[42]

Recidivism is high among sexual offenders.[43] If I had my choice, I would almost prefer to see pedophiles receive life sentences than murderers. Judges are faced with difficult decisions regarding sentencing. They may want a perpetrator to stay behind bars indefinitely, but they are limited in sentencing by the letter of the law. Other judges are not sensitive to the huge risk pedophiles pose to the general public and hand down very light sentences, allowing these predators to walk the streets within a few months or years of their convictions.

APOLOGISTS FOR PEDOPHILIA

People with extreme ideas are nothing new. Even today, in the twenty-first century, for example, there are some who contend that the world is flat. They argue that moon landings, space exploration, and so forth are all a part of a government hoax. This marginal segment of society usually attracts attention only as comic relief, but it is disturbing to note that such extremist views have infiltrated the mental health field. For years there have been marginal individuals who have advocated sexual relationships between adults and children, yet those people had always remained on the fringe of society and certainly had not been accepted by the academic/ therapeutic world. Yet in 1998, *Psychological Bulletin,* the journal published by the American Psychological Association, published a meta-analysis by Bruce Rind et al., which basically downplayed the negative effects of child sexual abuse, claimed it could even be beneficial, and appeared to present a case for the normalization of pedophilia.[44] I fear that this view, which since 1998 has gained some acceptance in the field, will be mainstream thinking in coming years. It has happened before. In the early 1970s, homosexuality was removed from the *DSM* in large part due to political correctness, not because of empirical data that supported such a change. One's opinion of the normalcy of homosexuality, a highly controversial topic, is not the issue here. The issue is that the organization that identifies mental disorders has demonstrated through this issue that it is willing to change diagnostic criteria based on lobbying efforts by its members rather than on empirical data. I withdrew my membership from the American Psychological Association after more than fifteen years of membership because of this article.

Space does not allow me to outline the flaws in the paper by Rind et al., but there were many methodological flaws (questionable data analysis, misleading statements, questionable sample, etc.) as well as ridiculous assumptions regarding a child's cognitive ability to make "consenting" decisions about such behaviors. Advocacy for such an extreme position, I fear, will lead to its acceptance and, consequently, legitimize the victimization of children simply because adults wished to normalize their own personal desires at the expense of children.

CONCLUDING REMARKS

The Federal Child Abuse Prevention and Treatment Act (CAPTA) of 1974 authorized mandated reporting of the suspicion of child abuse.[45] This led to an increase in false accusations, but also an increased number of children being protected from perpetrators. Failure to report not only leaves children vulnerable to their perpetrators, but it opens the door to civil litigation. For example, in 2001, two female adult survivors of sexual abuse sued the Jehovah's Witnesses because elders in the church failed to report abuse of the minors when the facts were presented to them. The father of the two women was eventually convicted of sexual assault.

Megan's Law, the New Jersey legislation that was a response to the abduction and murder of Megan Kanka, is another governmental step toward curbing child sexual abuse. The law requires individuals convicted of sexual crimes to register in their communities. There are three types of registration—low risk, medium risk, and high risk. The requirements for registration vary depending on risk, but with high-risk perpetrators, police then must notify anyone the offender is likely to encounter, including going door to door notifying neighbors of a predator's presence. Some form of Megan's Law exists in all fifty states. In some jurisdictions, along with registration, maps with street names and general locations are available on the Internet. However, the law is not without problems. Even though the law has withstood court challenges that have argued that registration in essence forces offenders to be punished twice for the same crime, some prosecutors are actually opposed to the law. They argue that most sexual offenders are convicted by confession. They worry that if accused pedophiles fear being branded as pedophiles because of lifelong registration, they will be reluctant to confess.

Short of a child telling what has happened or the perpetrator being caught in the act, physicians are the most likely people regularly interacting with children who would be able to identify sexual abuse. Pediatricians are trained to recognize the signs of sexual abuse and also how to report it. A May 2001 article in the journal *Contemporary Pediatrics* focused on identification of sexual abuse and also discussed how to report abuse and communicate with the family.[46] Well-written and thoroughly researched articles like this one address the social and psychological dynamics of abuse and provide detailed ways for pediatricians to identify abuse.

I have presented lectures to medical students several times on the behavioral signs of sexual abuse. These behavioral indicators include eating disorders, behavioral problems, depression, guilt, excessive masturbation, phobias, promiscuity, sexual activity toward other children or adults, sexualized play, sleep disturbances, statements about sexual activity, substance abuse, suicidal behavior, and aggressive behavior.[47] Abuse will continue as long as it is allowed to continue. Active intervention, prevention, and prosecution of perpetrators will assist in the protection of the most vulnerable members of our society.

NOTES

1. D. Finkelhor, G. Hotaling, I. A. Lewis, and C. Smith, "Sexual abuse in a national survey of adult men and women: Prevalence, characteristics, and risk factors," *Child Abuse and Neglect, 14* (Internet Edition), 1990.

2. S. N. Madu, "The prevalence and patterns of childhood sexual abuse and victim-perpetrator relationship among a sample of college students," *South African Journal of Psychology, 31* (2001): 32–38.

3. Alice Yick Flanagan, "Child abuse and neglect: What healthcare professionals need to know," www.nursingceu.com/NCEU/courses/childabuse, June 26, 2000.

4. Ibid.

5. American Psychiatric Association, *Diagnostic and statistical manual of mental disorders, 4th edition, text revision* (Washington, DC: American Psychiatric Press, 2000), p. 572.

6. Ron O'Grady, "Eradicating pedophilia: Toward the humanization of society," *Journal of International Affairs, 55* (Internet Edition), 2001.

7. F. Felicia Ferrara, *Childhood sexual abuse* (Pacific Grove, CA: Brooks/Cole, 2002), p. 43.

8. Ibid.

9. "Crisis intervention assessment," National Clearinghouse on Child Abuse and Neglect Information, Washington, DC, www.calib.com/nccanch/pubs/usermanuals/crisis/assess.cfm, April 6, 2001.

10. Martin Daly and Margo Wilson, "Child abuse and other risks of not living with both parents," *Ethnology and Sociobiology, 6*, (1985), 197–210.

11. Katie Throne, "Sitter charged in sex crimes," *Augusta Chronicle,* augustachronicle.com/stories/060901/met_110–5185.000.shtml, June 9, 2001.

12. O'Grady, "Eradicating pedophila."

13. Flanagan, "Child abuse and neglect."

14. "Sexual abuse by priests," *America* (February 18, 2002): 3.

15. "Signs of the times," *America* (March 4, 2002): 4–5.

16. Seamus McGraw, "Suffer the children: The story of Megan's Law/Behind closed doors," www.crimelibrary.com/serial_killers/predators/megans_law/4.htm, March 2002.

17. Ibid.

18. Ibid.

19. "Former Timmendequas victim awaits retribution 16 years later," *New Jersey On-Line,* www.nj.com/news/stories/0611megan.html, June 11, 1997.

20. Tom Hester, "Megan Killer's kin maps boyhood horrors," *New Jersey On-Line,* www.nj.com/news/stories/meganboyhood.html, June 11, 1997.

21. Ibid.

22. Ibid.

23. Ibid.

24. McGraw, "Suffer the children: The story of Megan's Law/Behind closed doors."

25. Hester, "Megan Killer's kin maps boyhood horrors."

26. Margaret Carlson, "Daddy's little girl," *Time* (June 4, 1990): 2C.

27. Lenore Terr, *Unchained memories: True stories of traumatic memories, lost and found* (New York: Basic Books, 1994), p. 6.

28. Carlson, p. 2C.

29. Barbara Kantrowitz and Nadine Joseph, "Forgetting to remember," *Newsweek* (Internet Edition), February 11, 1991.

30. Ibid.

31. Carlson, "Daddy's little girl." p. 2C.

32. Ibid.

33. Terr, *Unchained memories,* p. 14.

34. Diana Brahams, " 'Repressed memories' and the law," *Lancet, 356* (July 29, 2000): 358.

35. "Man jailed in repressed memory case is finally free," *Skeptic* (1996): 14.

36. Aaron R. Lawson, "False accusations of abuse," *Expert Law,* www.expertlaw.com/larson/articles/false.html, March 2002.

37. John C. Yuille, Robin Hunter, Risha Joffe, and Judy Zaparniuk, "Interviewing children in sexual abuse cases." In Gail S. Goodman and Bette L. Bottoms, eds., *Child victims, child witnesses: Understanding and improving testimony,* pp. 95–115 (New York: Guilford Press, 1993), p. 96.

38. Darrell W. Richardson, "The effects of a false allegation of child sexual abuse on an intact middle class family," *Institute for Psychological Theories Journal,* www.ipt-forensics.com/journal/volume2/j2_4_7.htm, March 8, 2001.

39. Ibid.

40. Ibid.

41. Ibid.

42. Jennifer Marie Batterman-Faunce and Gail S. Goodman, "Effects of context on the accuracy and suggestibility of child witnesses." In Gail S. Goodman and Bette L. Bottoms, eds., *Child victims, child witnesses: Understanding and improving testimony,* pp. 301–330 (New York: Guilford Press, 1993), p. 317.

43. Ferrara, p. 37.

44. Bruce Rind, Philip Tromovitch, and Robert Bauserman, "A meta-analysis examination of assumed properties of child sexual abuse using college samples," *Psychological Bulletin, 124* (July 1998): 22–53.

45. Ferrara, *Childhood sexual abuse,* p. 19.

46. Ranee M. Leder, John R. Knight, and Jean S. Emans, "Sexual abuse: Management strategies and legal issues, part 2," *Contemporary Pediatrics, 18* (Internet Edition), May 2001.

47. Ibid.

CHAPTER 4

Child Abduction

We laugh at honor and yet are shocked to find traitors in our midst.
—C. S. Lewis

Perhaps nothing frightens parents as much as the possibility of someone taking their children. Imagining the fear, pain, and horror that their children may experience is beyond comprehension. Faces on milk cartons and road-side billboards remind parents of the ever-present dangers that lurk on street corners and bus stops, in alleyways and shopping centers, and in parking lots. Alton Coleman and his girlfriend Debra Denise Brown were a real part of that threat. They toured the Midwest in 1984, terrorizing children and adults, kidnapping, raping, and murdering their victims. The pair were implicated in or convicted of numerous murders, kidnappings, rapes, and robberies. One victim was a nine-year-old girl named Vernita Wheat.

Coleman and Brown did not have to attack or threaten their victims in order to abduct them. Most of their victims voluntarily went along with the couple in their car or invited them into their homes. The pair had a way of earning the trust of their many victims—elderly women, teenagers, and children. Vernita was no exception. Vernita lived in the town of Kenosha, Wisconsin, a suburb just south of Milwaukee on Lake Michigan. It was there that Coleman, using the alias Robert Knight, and Brown befriended Vernita. On May 29, 1984, Vernita begged her mother to let her go with "Robert Knight" and his girlfriend to their apartment fifteen miles away in Waukegan. The couple had promised the child a stereo. Vernita's mother had met the couple and they had earned her trust as well so she gave in to Vernita's pleas and allowed her to go, a decision she soon regretted. When Vernita and the couple did not return by the next day, Vernita's mother called police. Approximately three weeks later, on June 19, Vernita's body was discovered in an abandoned building in Waukegan. The child had been strangled. Vernita's mother quickly identified Coleman from a police photo lineup. Before police could apprehend the couple, however, they killed, raped, tortured, and attempted to kill several other children and adults in three different states. When they were eventually caught and tried, Coleman was convicted and sentenced to death in three different states for his crimes, including the murder of Vernita. He was executed by lethal injection on April 26, 2002. Debra Brown was convicted of several crimes and received the death penalty, which was later commuted to a life sentence, for a murder in Ohio and she received the death penalty for another murder in Indiana.

A five-year-old child named Rilya Wilson was removed from the custody of her mother by social services in 1999 because of drug problems. The child was placed in the custody of her grandmother, but she was required to attend weekly meetings with a caseworker. However, those monthly meetings did not occur. In January 2001, a person claiming to be a caseworker showed up at the grandmother's home and said it was necessary to take Rilya in for evaluations. A week later, the "caseworker" returned to pick up Rilya's clothes, saying the tests were taking longer than expected.[1] Rilya's grandmother claimed that she called repeatedly over the next several months to check on the child, but social services had no record of those calls. Over a year later, in April 2002, a caseworker called Rilya's grandmother to set up a meeting to check on the child. It was only then that it was discovered that the child had apparently been abducted fifteen months earlier. The child's father claimed that he had not seen her for more than two years. Rilya's whereabouts are still unknown and no significant leads as to the identity of the "caseworker" have been reported.

Abductions are not limited to individuals. Several times in recent history, one or more perpetrators have abducted groups of children. In January 2002, Otto Nuss, a sixty-three-year-old bus driver, kidnapped the thirteen children on his school bus, ages six to fifteen. That morning on the way to school in Oley, Pennsylvania, instead of a six-mile, fifteen-minute trip to school, Nuss turned the bus toward Washington, D.C. For the next several hours and over a distance of more than a hundred miles, Nuss ignored calls over his radio to return the children and he told the thirteen children he was taking them on a field trip. The children were aware that something was wrong and they waved to passing motorists, signaling for help. One child wrote "Call 911" on a sign and put it in the bus window while another wrote "911" in the moisture on the window. Nuss finally ended the trip when he pulled into a parking lot. He told the children he was going into the store to ask for directions. In reality, he had seen the police car of an off-duty officer who was working security in the store. He went inside and surrendered to the officer. Nuss, who was charged with kidnapping, told authorities he just wanted to show the children Washington, D.C. Although he never threatened the children, investigators found an M-1A rifle and seventy-five rounds of ammunition on the bus. At his home, they discovered forty-eight other firearms. None of the children, grades 1 through 9, were injured and Nuss stopped the bus several times during the trip so children could use the bathroom and even bought their lunch at a Burger King. A psychiatric evaluation suggested that Nuss was suffering from schizophrenia.

Nuss was not the first to abduct a bus full of children. On July 15, 1976, three men abducted twenty-six children and their driver from a school bus as they returned from a swim outing. Unlike Nuss, these perpetrators were not interested in taking the children on a field trip. Ransom was their motive. Around 4:00 P.M., just a few miles outside of Chowchilla, California, the men stopped the bus and forced the nineteen girls and seven boys ranging in age from five to fifteen, and their fifty-five-year-old bus driver named Ed Ray into two vans. The men drove the children around well into the night and eventually stopped at a rock quarry about a hundred miles from Chowchilla. There, the captors shuttled the children and Ray into an underground room that was later discovered to be a buried moving van. In the meantime, the abandoned bus was found empty and covered with brush. A massive search was launched to find the missing children, but almost no clues were available to investigators.

Back in their underground tomb, Ray and two of the older boys decided to try to free themselves. They located a break in the roof of their tomb and then dug their way to the surface. Sixteen hours after they were buried, the children and Ray crawled out of the crypt to safety. Once investigators interviewed the victims, they discovered that the van had been buried in the quarry about seven months earlier. The son of the quarry's owner, Fred Newhall Woods IV, age twenty-four, was missing. A draft of a $5 million ransom note was found on the Woods estate and quickly Woods and two of his friends became suspects. Arrest warrants were issued for Woods as well as James Schoenfeld, age twenty-four, and his brother Richard Schoenfeld, age twenty-two. Richard Schoenfeld turned himself in and the other two were quickly captured. All three pled guilty to kidnapping and were sentenced to life in prison. They all have been denied parole several times. Woods later sued the producers of a 1993 TV drama about the kidnapping for allegedly distorting his role in the kidnapping, but the California Supreme Court refused to hear the case. A detailed account of this kidnapping and its long-term effects on the victims is provided in an outstanding 1990 book by Dr. Lenore Terr titled *Too Scared to Cry: How Trauma Affects Children ... and Ultimately Us All.*

TYPES OF ABDUCTIONS

The motives for abductions vary. Perpetrators like Otto Nuss abduct children because they are confused or suffering from mental illnesses. Some perpetrators abduct children during the commission of other crimes, like a carjacking. Some, like Coleman and Brown, abduct victims to feed their insatiable lust for sex, abuse, and torture. Still others abduct children not for their own personal sexual pleasure, but rather to provide victims for child prostitution rings or the global child sex industry. Even though it is rare, some perpetrators abduct children because they want to have a child and either don't qualify for adoption or they are unwilling to go through the trouble of legally adopting a child. These perpetrators either cannot have children of their own or they want more children than they already have. Even though these are frightening motives for kidnapping, most often abductions are committed by relatives, usually parents, who either are unhappy with custody decisions or who believe they are protecting their children from abuse by the other parent.

Abduction during Commission of Other Crimes

One of the most common forms of child abduction during the commission of another crime occurs during carjackings or stealing of cars. Perpetrators want the vehicle and, in the case of a carjacking, force the driver out of the car and drive away unaware that a child is in the vehicle. The child may be sleeping or sitting quietly in a car seat of the vehicle. Carjackers do not realize the child is in the car until after they have already stolen the vehicle. Usually, perpetrators in cases like this will either abandon the vehicle with the child still in the car seat, or drop the child off at a store, gas station, or some other populated area, and then leave in the stolen vehicle. Mothers often panic when they have been carjacked and their infants are sleeping in the back seat, but the good news is that they almost always get these children back unharmed and usually within minutes or hours.

Some sexual predators who seek adult female victims are more ruthless. They purposefully prey on adult women with children. It may seem unlikely that a rapist would choose a woman with children as a victim, but he can use the children to manipulate the woman. Many adults would be willing to endure pain or injury to save their own lives, but few of us would allow our children to be harmed. A perpetrator may accost a woman and her children in a parking lot. If he put a knife to the woman's throat, she would most likely scream for her children to run despite any risk to her own life, but if he put a knife to her child's throat, threatening to kill the child if the woman didn't cooperate, she would do whatever he said to protect the child. Ironically, the woman's best hope for her own safety and the safety of her children in this situation is to refuse to cooperate. This type of perpetrator is gambling that the woman will not allow her child to be harmed. He is counting on the woman acceding to his wishes because he knows that if she screams or yells, or if the child screams or yells, it will be unlikely that he would be able to control both mother and child and still complete his abduction. He is hoping that her fear will override her better judgment. The chances of survival for both mother and child are much better in a crowded parking lot than if the perpetrator is allowed to drive them off to some secluded spot.

Abduction to Become a Parent

Some perpetrators just want to have a new baby. There have been cases all across the United States where perpetrators kidnap children from neonatal units in hospitals with the intention of raising these children as their own. Usually these children are infants. Perpetrators tell relatives and friends that they adopted the child or they may even plan the abduction months in advance, feigning pregnancy in the interim. In some cases perpetrators have killed pregnant mothers, cut them open, and removed their nearly full-term fetuses. Babies rarely survive this gruesome act.

Child Prostitution/Pornography

The problem of child prostitution has grown in recent years. Experts claim that the globalization of child pornography and child prostitution can be traced in large part to two sources—the world tourism industry and the Internet.[2] Low airfares and favorable economies make it possible for pedophiles to travel to countries where child prostitution is either legal or, more likely, where child prostitution laws are loosely enforced. The "sex tourism" industry organizes tour groups just as a group might organize around any other common interest, like snorkeling, except that these groups are organized for pedophiles. Instead of structuring the tour around snorkeling, golf, or bird-watching, these trips center around child prostitution. It is estimated that more than a million children are enslaved in child prostitution rings in Asia alone, serving the interests of these groups and individuals.[3]

The Internet contributes to child pornography by making it possible for pedophiles to easily find places to engage in their perverse habits through chat rooms and Internet sites that specialize in pedophilia. Many children who are filmed or photographed for the child pornography industry are the children or stepchildren of the photographers or children of their girlfriends or boyfriends. Others are runaways or destitute children who are paid for their participation; still others are abducted and forced to engage in sexual activities that are then photographed or filmed. The availability of inexpensive, high-quality digital photography equipment and software for editing photographs has only made the problem worse. Chat rooms and Internet sites provide amateur pornographers with easy distribution channels for their filthy product. Law enforcement agencies have scarcely scratched the surface in policing this new medium for pedophiles. Current definitions of child pornography do not take into account the ever-changing digital age. Even though it is illegal to photograph or distribute pictures of nude models who are under age, digitally produced "children" in pornographic movies or adult actors who are digitally altered to appear to be children are legal under current laws. New definitions as well as new methods of locating and catching pornographers who perpetuate the child sex industry in what is literally a worldwide market will be necessary before any significant impact can be made on the industry.

Parents have been known to sell their children into the child sex industry. Worldwide, this is a common practice, but in the United States, it is less common. When this happens, these parents will file missing-persons reports with police in order to explain their missing child to friends and relatives. In Atlanta a few years ago, a woman claimed that her infant was abducted from her arms while she was waiting for a doctor's appointment at a local hospital. The story sounded questionable to me from the first media report and, in fact, a few weeks later authorities discovered that the woman had sold her infant to an acquaintance for a few hundred dollars.

Custody Abductions

Most of the children who are abducted in the United States each year are taken by relatives. In most of these cases, custody is the issue. Some children are labeled "abducted" even though they may only have violated a custody order for a few hours or days. A parent who is late bringing the child home after a visitation might find himself accused of abducting the child. In heated, antagonistic relationships, the accusing parent may either wish simply to cause trouble for the ex-spouse or he/she may be establishing a paper trail for future custody hearings. Having a kidnapping charge on one's record is not helpful in custody hearings. In other cases, custodial parents file kidnapping complaints against their former spouses because of a legitimate fear that the child will not be returned; there certainly are times when parents flee with a child with no intentions of returning. Some of these abductors are unhappy with the custody decisions of the courts while others believe that they are protecting the children from the custodial parent (i.e., the other parent is molesting them). Organizations exist that specialize in helping these parents hide their children from their former spouses and from the law. Unfortunately, some parents fabricate stories of child molestation or abuse in order to gain the help of these organizations. Therefore, these underground organizations end up abetting a parent in circumventing the law as well as depriving the legal custodial parent of the right of access to the child. Statistically, most parents amicably resolve custody issues during divorce. Only about 20 percent involve heated custody debates and only about 2 percent of those cases involve allegations of sexual abuse.[4] Yet even though the majority of these custody situations are resolved peacefully, it is estimated that 100,000 women go into hiding each year and that as many as 90 percent of the missing children whose faces appear on milk cartons are abducted by their parents.[5]

Faye Yager was a mother and wife in the 1970s when she discovered that her husband, Roger Jones, had been sexually abusing their two-year-old daughter, Michelle. She tried to protect Michelle from her husband, but he was able to convince authorities that he was innocent. He eventually had Yager committed to mental institutions where she received electroshock therapy. She was medicated and "treated" for mental disorders when the entire time she had been trying to protect her daughter from her husband, who was perpetrating sexual abuse. Eventually, it was discovered that Jones was indeed molesting Michelle, but much more than that, he was a serial pedophile who became one of the FBI's most wanted. He was eventually arrested and convicted of abusing a thirteen-year-old girl, but it was believed that he had molested over sixty children. Jones is now in prison. As a result of her experiences, Yager started Children of the Underground, an organization that helps abused women and children hide from the law and, more importantly, from their abusers. Yager ran the organization for ten years, often enduring severe pressure from the press, spouses seeking their children, and the law, who argued that she was merely helping women who had fabricated stories to serve their own interests to avoid prosecution. She left the organization in 1998.

In the best-case scenario, parents who abduct their children seek to protect them, but still maintain as normal a life as possible. They attempt to create a normal school, home, and social life for the child without demonizing the other parent. In the worst cases, parents who abduct their children vilify their former partners, thus alienating the children from the other parent. According to one expert, the goal of the alienator is to "deprive the lost parent, not only of the child's time but of the time of childhood."[6] These children suffer from anger, depression, and other disorders that affect their adjustment into adulthood. If and when these children are ever reunited with their custodial parents, they are angry with them and often want nothing to do with them, even if the allegations of abuse turn out to be false.

Underground organizations create false identities for both child and mother and assist them while they are in hiding; these children and their parents may stay on the run for years. Even when the allegations of abuse are true, these mothers risk permanent loss of their children as well as jail sentences for kidnapping if they are caught, limiting their ability to protect their children. In such cases, the law is on the side of the custodial parent, even though law enforcement and other governmental resources may actually be working on behalf of a perpetrator (i.e., a child abuser). Consequently, when a parent abducts a child in order to protect him or her, the FBI and other law enforcement agencies may in fact help return kidnapped children to their abusers. There have been cases, though, where mothers were caught, only to be exonerated by the court. Even though they were clearly guilty of kidnapping, juries decided that they were justified in their actions.

Mothers are not the only ones who abduct their children. There are numerous cases where fathers have taken their children. To explain why the children could not see their mothers any longer, these men have concocted stories about the mothers being killed in accidents or by disease. In 1979, Stephen Fagan fled the Boston area for Florida with his two daughters, five-year-old Rachael and two-year-old Wendy. He and his ex-wife, Barbara Kurth, were in the midst of a custody dispute over the children. Fagan told his children that their mother had been killed in an automobile accident and that they were starting life anew. He changed his name to William Martin, remarried, and created a new identity that included stories of nonexistent degrees in psychology and psychiatry, a former career as a Harvard Law School and Cornell University student, CIA agent, and presidential advisor. For eighteen years, he maintained this façade until his arrest in 1998 on kidnapping charges. By this time, the girls had grown up never knowing their mother. Fagan claimed that he fled to protect the girls from Kurth, whom he claimed was an unfit mother because she was an alcoholic. Two DUI arrests on Kurth's record provided some evidence that he was telling the truth, but it was never proven that Kurth was an unfit mother or an alcoholic. Fagan was sentenced to five years' probation, community service, and a $100,000 fine. Wendy and Rachael supported their father, despite the fact that they had no memory of their mother, alcoholism, or neglect.

International Abductions

The U.S. State Department has handled seven thousand claims of international child abduction since the 1970s.[7] This number includes children who were prevented from reentering the United States even though these children had not technically been abducted. When a child is prevented from returning from a foreign country it is termed *wrongful retention*. However, this number does not represent all the parents who have elected not to use the State Department in their quests to retrieve an abducted child. Therefore, the actual number of international abductions is unknown, but clearly numbers in the thousands.

As I have already noted, some international abductions involve the child prostitution or child pornography industry. Other international abductions have their roots in cultural or religious teachings. For example, if a man from an Islamic culture believes he is responsible not only for raising his child, but also for ensuring that the child is raised in an Islamic home, losing custody following a divorce from a non-Islamic woman preys on his mind. If the man fears that his American ex-wife will gain custody and, consequently, fail to raise the child following Islamic traditions, he may believe it is his religious duty to protect that child by abducting the child and returning to his home country to raise the child.

"The *Convention on the Civil Aspects of International Child Abduction*, done at The Hague on October 25, 1980, establishes legal rights and procedures for the prompt return of children who have been wrongfully removed or retained."[8] Membership in the Hague Convention is supposed to make it easier for parents to regain custody of those children if they were seized illegally, but membership in the Hague Convention does not guarantee that the child will be returned. Membership appears to demonstrate good intentions by participating countries rather than actual assistance. In fact, the U.S. Department of State, Bureau of Consular Affairs, makes it clear in their publications that the responsibility for retrieving a child who has been abducted across international borders lies solely on the shoulders of the parent seeking the child's return. "You, as the deprived parent," they write, "must direct the search and recovery operation yourself."[9] The Bureau of Consular Affairs can help parents by providing information, documents, forms, and direction, but the bureau cannot enforce American custody agreements nor can it force a foreign country to decide a case in a particular way.[10]

The Department of State lists a number of circumstances that increase the probability of an international abduction: when the relationship with the other parent is dissolved or troubled, especially if it is a cross-cultural marriage; when the other parent has close ties to another country; and when the other country has traditions or laws that may be prejudicial to a parent of your gender or to aliens in general.[11] If a parent suspects his or her children might be abducted to a foreign country, several precautions are advisable. The Department of State advises that a custody decree, especially one that prohibits the child from crossing international borders without the parent's consent, should be obtained. Some countries will not recognize the parent's right to the child without such a decree, even if they are members of the Hague Convention.[12] In order to make it easier to regain custody of one's child, the Department of State recommends that parents do the following:

1. Keep a list of addresses and telephone numbers of the other parent's relatives, friends, and business associates both here and abroad.

2. Keep records of important numbers: passport, social security, bank account(s), driver's license, and vehicle registration, on the other parent

3. Keep a written description of your child, including hair and eye color, height, weight, and any special physical characteristics.

4. Take color photographs of your child every six months.

5. Teach your child to use the telephone—including how to make international and collect calls.[13]

These precautions may seem extreme and, indeed, for most marriages they are unnecessary, but for some they are prudent precautions. Prenuptial financial agreements are unnecessary in relationships where neither partner has substantial financial holdings. However, in cases where one or the other partner has exceptional financial holdings, a prenuptial agreement is advisable. Likewise, in cross-cultural marriages, especially if those marriages begin to spiral toward dissolution, these precautions provide insurance in case they are needed.

DAVID WESTERFIELD

Abductions by strangers, especially strangers who abduct children from their own homes, are very rare. In San Diego County, California, for example, only two of the more than 6,300 children abducted in 2000 were abducted by strangers.[14] Of the hundreds of child abductions that I am aware of, I only know of a handful where children were taken from their own beds by strangers. On February 2, 2002, sometime in the early morning hours, a seven-year-old girl was snatched from her own bed by a monster who would later take her life. Danielle van Dam was the daughter of reportedly loving parents. The family lived in the upscale neighborhood of Sabre Springs, a San Diego suburb where they had moved from Dallas four years earlier.[15] Brenda van Dam was a stay-at-home mom and her thirty-six-year-old husband of thirteen years, Damon, worked as an engineer for a cell phone manufacturer. Friday night, February 1, was to be girls' night out for Brenda van Dam. Early in the evening, Brenda, along with some friends and Damon, had been drinking beer and had then smoked a marijuana joint at home, opening a sliding door to let the smoke escape. This door would be found still ajar at 2:30 A.M. on February 2. Around 8:00 P.M. on February 1, Brenda left the house with a group of her girlfriends for Dad's Café, a restaurant and bar just a few minutes from the van Dams' home. Damon stayed home with their three children, two boys, ages five and nine, and Danielle. Around 10:00 P.M., Damon tucked Danielle into her white canopy bed and soon after went to bed himself. It was the last time he would see his daughter alive. At 1:30 A.M. on February 2, the van Dams' barking dog awakened Damon so he got up and let the dog out for a few minutes. He then sat up and watched TV as he waited for Brenda to return from her night out.

Brenda had enjoyed a night of dancing, playing pool, drinking, and visiting with her friends. She had imbibed several mixed drinks and smoked pot with a friend in her truck.[16] While at Dad's Café, she had run into a neighbor, David Westerfield. The two had chatted briefly. Later, Westerfield, as well as other witnesses, said that they had danced together and that Brenda was "rubbing herself all over Westerfield," but Brenda denied that—testifying that he only asked to be introduced to her friend. Brenda returned home after 2:00 A.M. with several male and female friends. When she came home, she noticed the security light blinking.[17] She found the sliding door still open from earlier in the evening and she closed it. The adults stayed up chatting until 3:30 A.M. At that time, the friends left and the van Dams went to bed.

The next morning Brenda went to Danielle's room to wake her at 9:00 A.M. Finding Danielle's bed empty, Brenda and Damon searched the house, inspecting all the places where Danielle was known to hide while playing hide-and-seek. When they could not locate her, they called police. The van Dams were questioned, but almost immediately a neighbor became the primary suspect. David Westerfield, forty-nine, who lived two doors away, had disappeared that night and police were seeking him for questioning.

Investigators caught up with Westerfield on Monday morning, three days after Danielle's disappearance. Twice divorced, he was an engineer with three patents for prosthetic-related devices to his name. He was a quiet neighbor, known to work on cars for friends or on the motor home in his driveway. People who knew him described him as a "puppy dog" and a "lovable guy."[18] He had lived in the Sabre Springs neighborhood since 1997, but had only interacted with the van Dams a few times. The week before Danielle's disappearance, Danielle, her brother Dylan, and Brenda had visited Westerfield's home when Danielle was selling Girl Scout cookies. The children explored Westerfield's home while Brenda and Westerfield got acquainted. Westerfield reportedly invited Brenda and her husband to a party and gave Brenda his telephone number.[19] Other than a drunk-driving conviction in 1996, the same year he divorced his second wife, Westerfield had no criminal history.

Investigators asked Westerfield if he would be willing to come in for questioning and he agreed, but he asked if he needed an attorney. He was told that he was not under arrest, but it was his right to have an attorney.[20] This conversation and its meaning became a point of dispute between the prosecutor and the defense after Westerfield was charged and arrested. From 2:30 P.M. until nearly midnight, February 4, police questioned Wester-field about his whereabouts, his knowledge of the van Dams and of Danielle. His defense attorney later argued that during this time, investigators badgered Westerfield and they ignored him when he repeatedly asked for an attorney. "All that was missing were the bright lights and a rubber hose," his attorney claimed, describing the hours of interrogation.[21]

Westerfield's account of his whereabouts from Friday to Monday is confusing. He told police he ate supper alone at home on Friday evening and then met some friends at Dad's Café where he ran into Brenda van Dam. He said the two talked about Danielle. Brenda told him that Danielle was going to a father-daughter dance the next week and that she was growing up fast.[22] After coming home late that night, he said he went to bed and then rose early the next morning. He drove his motor home several hundred miles during the next three days, driving between a state park, his home, and the desert. Twice during the weekend his motor home became stuck, once to the point that he required a tow truck. He claimed that after driving to the Silver Strand State Beach on Saturday morning, he realized he had forgotten his wallet and he returned home for it later that day. However, a park ranger says that he saw Westerfield and that Westerfield had his wallet with him.

When Westerfield returned to his neighborhood around 3:30 P.M. on Saturday, he found the roads blocked off as officials were conducting their investigation into the missing child. He told police that he feared that the child had fallen in his pool or gotten inside his house.[23] This statement provides evidence of deception. When people have something to hide, they tend to provide extra details. I find it interesting that Westerfield immediately created a reason for his involvement. Why would he assume the child had gotten into *his* house? This seems to be an unusual reaction when, after all, he barely knew the van Dams.

After retrieving his wallet that Saturday, he said he drove back and forth between the desert and the beach several times. The tow truck driver who helped him one of the times he became stuck, confirmed that Westerfield's vehicle had been stuck in the sand in a location 150 miles from Sabre Springs. He eventually returned home on Monday morning around 8:30 A.M.

Westerfield's story did not convince officials that he was uninvolved in Danielle's disappearance. While he was being questioned, investigators were searching his house and motor home. The motor home had a strong smell of bleach, as if it had been recently cleaned.[24] Fingerprints were found on a cabinet in the motor home next to the bed. These prints were later found to match Danielle's. Also found in the motor home was blood on the carpeting that was found via DNA testing to be Danielle's. Investigators also confiscated materials that Westerfield had taken to a dry cleaners and asked to have "rush service" on. Among these items was a jacket on which Danielle's blood was found. Search dogs seeking Danielle's scent signaled that her scent was both in Westerfield's house and also on a storage area of the exterior of the motor home.[25]

After Westerfield left the police station and returned home, detectives would not allow him inside. Instead, two detectives sat in his car with him and questioned him further. Westerfield's lawyer later argued that the interrogations were abusive and that Westerfield was given the impression he was under arrest even though police say they made it clear he was free to leave any time he wanted.[26] This is an important distinction because investigators have more leeway to question a suspect and they can continue to question that suspect even after he asks for a lawyer if the suspect is not under arrest. Yet if "a reasonable person in his position wouldn't have felt free to get up and leave," then the law would hold the investigators accountable as if the suspect were under arrest.[27] If Westerfield's lawyers could demonstrate that he believed he was under arrest, the court might throw out all evidence related to his questioning.

In the first days following Danielle's disappearance, detectives described Westerfield as extremely cooperative and they alleged that he consented to having his home searched. His lawyers, however, later contested this claim, saying he was coerced. Investigators searched his home, his computers, and his motor home. Among the things they took from his home were Zip disks and CD-ROMs that were later searched, along with the data from a handheld computer and his desktop computer hard drive, for any evidence that might pertain to Danielle's disappearance. That search of computer data turned up thousands of images that computer experts then had to cull through. Their search resulted in around a hundred pornographic images. These images depicted bestiality, children in sexual poses, children engaged in sexual acts, and cartoon images with sexual bondage themes involving young girls bound with ropes being sexually assaulted.[28]

Even though the focus of the investigation centered around Westerfield, the van Dams took and passed a lie detector test. In the days following the abduction, nearly three hundred volunteers from around the community pitched in to help search for Danielle. Teams of ten each spread out over an area twenty-five miles in radius and searched the rocky, brush-covered terrain for clues to the child's whereabouts. Posters of Danielle wearing a plastic necklace were printed, as were three thousand lapel buttons with her picture. Thousands of dollars were promised as a reward for information leading to the recovery of her body.

On February 22, police arrested Westerfield. Just five days later, on Wednesday, February 27, three and a half weeks after Danielle's abduction, a thirty-two-year-old man who was part of a volunteer search team spotted the nude, badly decomposed body of a child about thirty feet off a two-lane road just outside El Cajon, twenty-five miles from San Diego. The body appeared to have been laid out, not dumped, buried, or hidden. Facial features were indistinguishable, but the plastic necklace and one Mickey Mouse earring matched the description of jewelry Danielle was

wearing the night of her disappearance. Because of the level of decompo-
sition, the medical examiner was neither able to determine the cause of
death nor could it be determined if Danielle had been sexually assaulted.
With the discovery of her body, the circumstantial evidence against Westerfield got even stronger. In addition to all the other evidence they had
gathered against him, the body was discovered only two miles from a
Native American reservation where Westerfield was a member of a gambling club.

The van Dams' lifestyle was an important part of this case. If I had been
investigating the case, I most definitely would have wanted to talk to the
men who came home with Brenda in the early morning hours of February
2. They were invited into the home, all of the adults there at the time had
been drinking, and at least some of them, including Brenda van Dam, had
been smoking marijuana. These two men had the opportunity to abduct
Danielle because they were in the house and drugs and alcohol had potentially compromised the van Dams' cognitive abilities. A search of the vehicles and homes of these men for any sign of the child would be necessary.
Also, as an investigator, I would have been suspicious of the parents. As I
have said, most children are abducted by people they know, usually relatives. As investigators discovered that the mother had been out all evening
carousing with girlfriends and other men, they would certainly have suspected the parents as potential perpetrators. There were also rumors that
the van Dams practiced "swinging"—a term referring to wife swapping.
Once the alleged sexual "swinging" of the couple became known, investigators might also wonder if their liberal sexual games might have included
children. Fortunately, with the identification of Westerfield as a suspect, it
was unnecessary to consume precious man-hours following up on these
potential suspects.

Their lifestyle also became an issue in court. Damon van Dam admitted
that he had smoked marijuana with and had sexual relationships with the
women who were with Brenda the night of the kidnapping and Brenda
also admitted in court that she had had extramarital sexual relationships.
The defense, using a tactic that has been common in rape trials for years,
attempted to paint a dismal picture of the van Dams, as if that made them
any less victims. Perhaps the defense was hoping that jurors would look at
the van Dams as partially to blame, distracting them from the real perpetrator. Unfortunately, jurors often are swayed by these tactics, regardless
of the evidence against a perpetrator.

Westerfield was charged with murder, kidnapping, and possession of
child pornography, and he pleaded not guilty at his arraignment. As the
defense prepared their strategy, the evidence against Westerfield was challenging to refute. They could most easily explain the fingerprints in his
motor home. Because children from the neighborhood played outside, it is
conceivable that Danielle and others had played inside the motor home

prior to her disappearance. The dogs that signaled the presence of her scent in his home and trailer could have been picking up a scent left from the child's visit to the home days earlier. The pornography on his computer, the defense argued, could have been downloaded by anyone who had access to that computer, which included Westerfield's son. Even though the material was on his computer, there was no proof that Westerfield was the one who had put it there or that he had any knowledge that it was even on his computer. Since Westerfield had not been arrested or convicted of sex crimes of any kind, if it could be shown that Westerfield had no knowledge of the pornography on his computer, or if he did have knowledge of it but it could be shown that it someone else had downloaded it, the only circumstantial evidence that indicated that Westerfield was a pedophile would be lost.

More difficult to explain, however, was the blood on his jacket and in the motor home. It was genetically identified as belonging to Danielle. Juries have become accustomed to accepting genetic evidence as readily as they accept fingerprint evidence. Also, Westerfield's jumbled stories concerning his whereabouts the day of Danielle's disappearance and the following days was shaky. The best the defense could do was to demonstrate incompetence in the investigation and interrogation of Westerfield. If the defense team could show that there was reason to suspect the validity of the DNA evidence (i.e., that it was planted or tainted), the strongest link to Danielle's murder would be called into question. In a similar vein, if they could portray the investigative officers as rebel detectives who ignored the rules of law and legal interrogation practices, the prosecution's final link between Westerfield and the murder would be destroyed. Indeed, in initial hearings, the defense began their case by seeking access to the personnel records of two of the investigative officers. In their records were allegations of planted evidence and physical abuse of a handcuffed inmate.

Robert Boyce, Westerfield's attorney, argued in court that detectives were so aggressive in their questioning of Westerfield that "he started to unravel."[29] While it may seem rude or unnecessary to the untrained observer, interrogations are often forceful. Even though perpetrators occasionally walk into police stations and confess their crimes, such behavior is the exception rather than the rule. The art of interrogation requires a careful balance between what is legal and what is necessary to pressure the guilty party into making incriminating statements or confessing. Detectives would certainly prefer to simply ask the perpetrator nicely to tell the truth and save themselves the time and energy required to conduct carefully crafted interrogations. Unfortunately, it doesn't work that way. Like a crafty poker player, the investigator must know what to say, when and how to say it, and what not to say during the interrogation, all the while staying *within* the bounds of the law and upholding the rights of the accused. Knowing when to leave the room for a cup of coffee, and when to soothe a suspect by offering cigarettes, coffee, or a soft drink, are all part of the skill of interrogation. Interrogation is an art that requires training, experience, and patience to conduct effectively without compromising the prosecution of the case.

Westerfield pled innocent of the charges in the trial that began in the spring of 2002. On August 21, after a two-month trial, 100 witnesses, 200 exhibits, and 9 days of deliberations, jurors found Westerfield guilty of kidnapping, murder, and possession of child pornography. Jurors rejected the defense position that the van Dams' lifestyle contributed to Danielle's death and three months after Westerfield's conviction the same jury returned a sentencing decision of death by lethal injection. Westerfield did not speak on his own behalf in court. Following the trial, the judge released portions of the interrogation videotape that previously had been unavailable to jurors. In one segment, Westerfield told detectives that his life was over and he asked to be left alone with one of their service weapons. The request was denied.

FOUR ENEMIES TO A CHILD'S SAFETY

There are several normal developmental issues in children that actually work against them and to the advantage of perpetrators who wish to abduct children. Knowing these issues and training children with these in mind can help protect them.

Trust and Obedience

Children are trusting. Children's lives are flooded by people telling them what to do. Adults may not realize how many people give their children orders during a week and parents expect their children to obey these strangers. For example, there are numerous teachers and administrators at a child's school, most of whom the children do not know. Their school day is spent in the company of their own teachers, and yet when they walk the halls, go to the rest room, eat in the cafeteria, or play on the playground, "strangers" come around and tell them to be quiet, to stand here or there, or to go to the library or the gymnasium. If they do not obey these adults, they get in trouble—yet we tell them not to talk to or obey strangers. It is easy for adults to forget that just because they know most of the teachers and office workers at the child's school, it does not mean that the child knows these people. At churches, day cares, amusement parks, and other public places, adults give children orders and children trust that these adults have the authority to give those commands. An adult can distinguish who has authority to give them commands based on manner of dress, location, or prior knowledge of the individual, but children cannot make such distinctions. For example, children overgeneralize rules, making it easy for them to mistake the uniform of a washing machine repairman for that of a policeman. From a child's perspective, the uniforms look the same.

A child needs to be taught how to distinguish a "stranger" from an adult who has authority over them. One difference is that an adult who has authority over them will never ask them to go alone with them into an apartment, a house, or an automobile. A responsible adult will almost never cause a child to be alone with him or her in an unpopulated place like a closet, a bedroom, or an office. Adults who have authority over children in one environment will not give them orders on the street or in a shopping mall. Abductors take advantage of a child's trust and use that trust to lure children to their cars, secluded places, their apartments, or their houses. They use trickery to make it appear that they should be trusted. For example, a perpetrator might see a child on a playground and say that his mother told him to come get the child and take him to the hospital because she had been in an accident. A child needs to know that the parent would never send a stranger to take him anywhere for any reason.

Some parents teach their children a code word. Anyone who has the parent's permission to take the child somewhere would need to tell the child the memorized code word before the child would trust the stranger. Code words can be helpful, but someone who has an understanding of a child's thinking can easily bypass them. I cannot ethically tell you how to do this without presenting a how-to for perpetrators. However, if I wanted, I could get almost any child to get into my car with me or to follow me out of a shopping mall—easily bypassing code words. I have bypassed code words in demonstrations for law enforcement officers, teachers, and therapists who happened to have brought their children with them to seminars that I have conducted. They believed that they had effectively trained their children to beware of strangers and they had code words that the children knew. I was able to bypass their code words with ease. This was, as you could imagine, disconcerting for these parents. It is for this reason that no code words, no training, and no videos on how to stay safe are better than supervision of one's children.

In 1981, six-year-old Adam Walsh and his mother were shopping at a mall in Hollywood, Florida. Mrs. Walsh momentarily left Adam alone in a toy store. When she returned, the child was gone. Less than a month later, Adam's head was discovered in a drainage ditch. His body has never been recovered. John Walsh, Adam's father, has made a living since that time helping catch perpetrators of crime. He has been an advocate for children's safety and often provides the public with information that leads to the rescue of abducted children. He and his wife started the Adam Walsh Child Resource Center and that organization later merged with the National Center for Missing and Exploited Children. This organization, as well as John Walsh's television program, *America's Most Wanted,* provides education on how children can stay safe. This is all good information and I have, myself, often taught safety to groups of children. However, none of this information is as critical as a parent maintaining visual contact with the child. I have no intentions of compounding the grief the Walshes have experienced by the loss of their son, but we can learn from their mistake. It is doubtful that Adam would have been abducted if he had not been left alone in the toy store. One of the brochures produced by the National Center for Missing and Exploited Children addresses after-school safety tips for children who are home alone. Even though children are left alone every day, I fear our culture has come to accept this as a reasonable way of life when it is not. I would encourage the production of a brochure that might be titled, "Parents—Why You Should Be Home with Your Children Rather Than Leaving Them Alone." Whenever I address groups of children, I always address the adults in the room as well. Whether they are teachers, scout leaders, members of the clergy, or parents, I try to impress upon them the importance of supervising their children. We cannot expect children to make rational, adult-like decisions when they are six or seven years of age.

Children's names should not appear in plain view on their clothing or possessions. When the child's name is visible, it makes it easy for a perpetrator to open a conversation using the child's name. When a child hears her name, she supposes that the speaker knows her. In her mind, someone who knows her name cannot be a stranger. Telemarketers and salesmen use this same technique with adults. They attempt to gain our trust by using our name. (Ironically, as I was writing this very sentence a telemarketer called me saying, "Hello, Greg . . . ?") Occasionally, adults are at least initially fooled into thinking the person on the telephone (the salesman) is someone known to them. If identifying labels are necessary on a child's clothes, write the child's name on the inside.

Solution

Teach your children to ask another grown-up if it is OK to go along with an adult unknown to them. If the adult has bad intentions, he will most likely leave the scene. Teach your children to run to another adult if they are afraid or uncomfortable, and if a stranger tries to force the child, he should *never* let the stranger take him anywhere. Your child's chances of survival are best at the point of the attempted abduction. A child should be taught that he will never get in trouble for being safe and careful.

To avoid being pulled into an apartment, house, or vehicle, teach your child never to get close enough to be touched. If a child is abducted, a perpetrator will command her to sit quietly and not to move. Teach your children that they do not have to obey this order, especially if an opportunity to flee arises. Even adults make the mistake of obeying a perpetrator's orders when escape is possible. One of the many victims of violent crime I have interviewed was a woman who was abducted in her own automobile from a parking lot. The perpetrator pretended to need a jump-start. As she opened the hood of her car to help him, he drew a knife and forced her onto the floor of the front seat, ordering her to stay put. He left the front seat and went around to the front of the car to close the hood. Instead of seizing the opportunity to flee, she obediently waited for him in the car. He then took her to a remote area, raped her, and nearly killed her. She may have been injured if she had tried to escape from the car while her attacker was shutting the hood, but at least she would have had a fighting chance.

Curiosity

Perpetrators take advantage of children's curiosity and their inability to delay gratification until later. For example, Megan Kanka, as discussed in Chapter 3, was abducted by a neighbor who lured her with promises to see a newborn puppy. There are numerous other stories of perpetrators luring children with promises to see puppies, other animals, computer games, or toys. Perpetrators might also say they need help with an injured animal or ask the child to come sit with the injured animal while they go for help. Others have promised children candy or money if they tag along to the perpetrator's car or apartment. Children are not mature enough to ask themselves why some stranger would want to show them a puppy or give them candy or money. Again, even adults fall into this same trap. Telemarketers call offering something that sounds too good to be true. Rather than developmental issues, it is greed that overshadows an adult's reasoning to the point that the victim never stops to ask the question, "Why is this stranger calling me?" Obviously, the answer is that the telemarketer has something to gain. A perpetrator has something to gain as well.

Solution

Teach your child to use good judgment and practice setting aside personal desires. This is part of self-discipline that can help your children in many ways as they mature. Role-playing a perpetrator trying to stage an abduction using a lure tactic can also be helpful. Children can play the role of both the perpetrator and the victim. Both roles will help them learn how to be safe.

Silence

The biggest risk to a perpetrator in the process of an abduction is attention from bystanders. Bystanders can intervene and they are also potential witnesses to the crime. Anything that draws attention to the perpetrator can lead to his undoing. Yet there have been occasions when children have missed the opportunity to get help. In 1993, Polly Klaas was abducted from her bedroom by Richard Allen Davis, a man with no apparent connection to the child. Just a few hours after her abduction, Davis ran his car off the road in a remote area in a neighboring county. Two sheriff's deputies stopped to investigate the situation and after checking for warrants, they actually helped Davis push his car back onto the road. The entire time, Polly was in the trunk. After his arrest, Davis admitted that Polly was alive at the time and he expressed surprise that she did not yell out. Likewise, in Great Britain, also in 1993, two ten-year-old boys named Robert Thompson and Jon Venables led two-year-old James Bulger out of a busy shopping mall. For several hours they led him through the streets of Liverpool. During this time dozens of people saw them and several people actually talked to the boys. Bulger remained silent several times in the presence of these potential rescuers even when Jon Venables said that James was their little brother.

Solution

Teach your child to scream. When I do safety seminars with children, we have screaming practice. The children love it and it teaches them an important lesson. Much of their day they are told to be quiet. Rarely, if ever, are they allowed to make unrestrained noise, yet a noisy, screaming child is the very last thing a perpetrator wants. People will walk through parking lots ignoring car alarms, but almost any adult will pay attention to a child who screams in distress. If confronted by another adult, the perpetrator will try to keep the child silent by monopolizing the conversation, thereby making it difficult for the child to "politely" wait his turn to talk. Teach your children that when they are in trouble, especially if they have been abducted, that it is OK to interrupt the perpetrator when he is talking and that it is OK to make noise.

Perceived Appearances

What does a bad guy look like? In the 1960s when I was a grade school student, local police officers came to our school and taught us how to stay safe. I still recall a pamphlet that we were given telling us not to talk to strangers. In the multipage document, a "bad" man in a big black car approached children. The children in the story made the correct choice and ran away from the perpetrator. This tool was used to teach us that we should never talk to strangers, but what stands out in my mind about this brochure was the bad man's appearance. Well-intentioned as it was, this was a very unrealistic teaching tool. Even as a grade school child, I could tell who the bad man was simply by looking at him. He looked evil, he drove an ominous-looking car, and on his partially shadowed face he wore an evil expression. Unfortunately, in real life the bad man does not always look the part. In fact, many women found Ted Bundy both charming and very handsome. Fortunately, the material used in this type of education these days is much better and it is harder to tell who the perpetrator is by appearances alone.

Sometimes perpetrators do look the part. My children and I stopped at a convenience store one afternoon. A patron of the store came out as we approached. My first impression of him was one of caution. I've spent years working with people from all walks of life—some who were perpetrators and some who were not. I could list a number of objective things that told me this was someone to avoid—it wasn't just a gut feeling. Yet my children all commented on the "scary-looking" man. I doubt that any child would have to be taught to be leery of this particular person, but perpetrators can easily look like anybody else walking down the street.

Solution

Teach your child to think about rules rather than looks. The rules are these: Never talk to strangers; never get in a car with a stranger; never follow a stranger out of a building; never be lured by candy, money, or promises. *Rules overrule looks.*

EFFECTS OF ABDUCTION ON CHILDREN

Once children are returned to their rightful guardians, an assessment of physical and emotional distress is essential. Clinical treatment begins with analysis of the abduction. The child's age, the nature of the abduction, and any injury to the child are important issues to consider. For example, a nine-year-old child abducted from a bus stop by a stranger, molested, and saved by police will have a different response than a four-year-old child abducted by a parent and told that the other parent is deceased. In cases such as the Fagan abduction, where the father told the children that their mother was dead, treatment would have to address the child's sense of betrayal by the father for telling the lie, grief over the belief that the mother had died as well as grief for lost time, resentment and anger for being displaced as well as for the severed relationship that led to the abduction in the first place. With an older child, a broader set of therapeutic tools can be used than for a younger child. The child who is abducted by a stranger, molested, and saved by police will struggle with issues of trust, vulnerability, irrational and/or exaggerated fears (the "boogeyman" really does exist for these children), generalization of fears, and anxiety. PTSD symptoms would be expected, not to mention the issues related to molestation of any kind. At four years of age, the therapeutic approach would be very different than if the child were nine or ten.

With most forms of abduction, one would expect to see trauma-related symptoms, including PTSD, as well as issues involving trust of self and others, grief, worry, anxiety, vulnerability, and both rational and irrational fears. If the child was physically injured, sexually abused, malnourished, or threatened while captive, issues related to those experiences would also be expected. Physical symptoms related to malnourishment, exposure, abuse, sleep deprivation, excessive anxiety, or missed medications would also be a concern with these children.

If the child was missing for several months or years, reacclimation to one's family and culture may be necessary, especially in the case of an international abduction. The Stockholm syndrome, in which the captive individual begins to grow emotionally close to his or her captor, is possible, especially in long-term abductions. In an international abduction, the child may have acclimated to the foreign culture and adopted those habits and traditions. Readjustment to an American culture will take time. The child may experience divided loyalties both between the abductor and the child's parents as well as divided loyalties between cultures.

Personality changes are to be expected, especially in long-term abductions. In the normal course of development, children change quickly. The parent who sees a child for the first time after a year or more following an abduction will see a very different person from the one who left. Changes create resentment, loss, and grief in the parent. The issues facing the child are then compounded as he tries to understand the reaction of the parent. As parents attempt to deal with their emotions, they will mourn the lost days, weeks, or months that can never be recovered. They will experience resentment, rage, and depression as they wish that things could be "like they were before." They may even experience resentment toward the child, somehow blaming the child for being a different person after the abduction. Counseling for the entire family system may be necessary. Many of the therapeutic tools addressed in Chapter 5 will be a part of the treatment of both child and parents.

CONCLUDING REMARKS

The stories of child abductions run into the thousands and most of these children are abducted by relatives. Whether the abductor's reasons stem from vindictiveness, anger, poor judgment, religious/cultural reasons, or desire to protect their children, these parents or other relatives elect to circumvent the law for their own purposes or out of concern for their children. Fortunately, many children are eventually reunited with their parents. Some are rescued by law enforcement, while others are returned by their abductors. Most exciting to me are the victims who save themselves—cases where quick thinking and survival instincts have proved effective. In March 2002, a seven-year-old was abducted from her bedroom. Her parents heard a muffled scream from her room, but when they went to investigate, the child was gone. As her captor fled with her, he realized he had lost his wallet. When he stopped to look for it, the girl escaped from his car. He not only lost his wallet and let his victim escape, but he had dropped his wallet in the child's home and police used the information in the wallet to identify and arrest him. The child was only gone for a few hours before she was reunited with her parents.

In Nebraska in April 2001, seventeen-year-old Anne Sluti was walking across a parking lot when a twenty-nine-year-old man struck her in the head, dragged her into his vehicle, and drove away. He drove her to a rural cabin near Yellowstone National Park and held her captive for six days. Sluti was able to make a quick 911 telephone call several days into her captivity. Even though her call was cut off, presumably by her captor, law enforcement officials were able to trace the call to the cabin. Police surrounded the cabin and during a ten-hour standoff, police said that Sluti cleverly negotiated with her captor and eventually convinced him to surrender. She was freed with minor injuries.

In Brooklyn, New York, in April 2001, an eleven-year-old boy freed himself from his abductor when the man stopped his van at an intersection in Manhattan. The boy took advantage of the opportunity and jumped from the van. He ran to a nearby police officer and said that he had been kidnapped. The van was stopped and the driver was arrested. Links between the driver and another kidnapping the previous month were investigated.

These stories encourage me because I know children can make good decisions when they think and seize opportunities when they arise. By far, the most effective intervention is prevention—protecting children from abduction in the first place. Nothing replaces adult supervision in preventing abductions. Parents mistakenly believe their children will be safe riding their bikes on the road in front of their homes or playing in parks, playgrounds, and other areas designed for children. The facts, however, doesn't support this belief. If one needs groceries, one goes to the grocery store because that is where the food is. If one wants to prey on children, one goes where the children are—places designed to attract them (parks and playgrounds)—locations where parents are easily distracted or lulled into a false sense of security. As I was writing this chapter, I took a break and went for an afternoon run. I ran through a local park in our rural community. It was the middle of the week and only 11:30 in the morning. Most children were in school and the park was largely deserted except for two children who were playing in the back of a pickup truck. I looked around expecting to see an adult at the baseball diamond pitching balls or playing catch with a Little Leaguer, but I saw no adult. As I rounded the back of the park a quarter of a mile away, I saw who I believed was the parent of the two children. He was working on a baseball field. From where he was he could not see his children. His back was to the area where they were playing and he did not even look up as I ran by. Even if he could have seen his children, because he was so far away, a perpetrator could easily have taken his children right out from under his nose. By the time he could have run across several ball fields to reach his truck, the perpetrator and his children would have been long gone—no witnesses and no one to help the children. On a regular basis I see parents who allow their children to play in one area of a park while they are watching another child play soccer or baseball. Within minutes, they could lose their unsupervised child even though the child is only a hundred yards away because their attention is focused elsewhere.

Supervision is imperative because children cannot be expected to protect themselves. They are trusting and very easily deceived or confused. When my son was five years old and playing in his very first league soccer game, he scored two goals. Unfortunately, both goals were for the other team. At the beginning of the game, the coaches explained to the team which direction they were supposed to run and asked the boys if they understood. They all said they did. Minutes later my son ran the wrong way down the field and scored a beautiful goal for the opposing team. Again, the coaches gathered the team together and showed them the direction they were supposed to run and at which goal they were supposed to shoot. They asked my son specifically if he understood. He said he did. Minutes later he again ran the wrong way down the field and scored another goal—again for the other team. The point is that even under the close supervision of adults, children can easily get confused, forget the rules, or forget what they have been taught. It is unrealistic to expect children to protect themselves. Part of being a parent or guardian is investing the time and energy necessary to protect one's children.

NOTES

1. "Florida girl lost a year before reported missing," *CNN On-Line*, www.cnn.com/2002/US/05/01/missing.florida.girl/index.html, May 2, 2002.

2. Ron O'Grady, "Eradicating pedophilia: Toward the humanization of society," *Journal of International Affairs* (Internet Edition), *55*, 2001.

3. Ibid.

4. Miriam Raftery, "Desperate moms taking abused children underground," *Womensenews.org*, www.womensenews.org/article.cfm/dyn/aid/676, October 7, 2001.

5. Ibid.

6. Dean Tong, "Child abductions and the abuse excuse," *Patriot.net*, patriot .net/~crouch/tong.html, April 18, 2002.

7. "International Child Abductions," *U.S. Department of State, Bureau of Consular Affairs*, dosfan.lib.uic.edu/ERC/population/children/9501.html, January 1995.

8. "International Child Abduction Remedies Act (ICARA)," Section 11601a.4., travel.state.gov/icara.html, April 18, 2002.

9. "International Child Abductions."

10. Ibid.

11. Ibid.

12. Ibid.

13. Ibid.

14. Anne Krueger, "Rarity of abductions outside family raises interest in such cases," *Union Tribune,* www.uniontrib.com/news/metro/danielle/20020210-9999 _1n10rare.html, February 10, 2002.

15. Bill Hewitt, Maureen Harrington, Michelle Bowers, and Jill Movshin, "Taken in the night," *People* (Internet Edition), February 25, 2002.

16. "Slain girl's mother describes 'girls night'," *CNN On-Line,* www.cnn.com /2002/US/03/14/van.dam.girl/index.html, March 15, 2002.

17. Ibid.

18. Michael Stetz and Kristen Green, "Van Dam neighbor had been focus for investigators almost from start," *Union Tribune,* www.uniontrib.com/news /metro/danielle/20020223-9999_1n23wester.html, February 23, 2002.

19. Kristen Green, "Suspect said weekend was spent mostly on the road," *Union Tribune,* www.uniontrib.com/news/metro/danielle/20020312-9999_1n12 wester.html, March 12, 2002.

20. Alex Roth, "Prosecutors respond to defense claims of rights violations," *Union Tribune,* www.uniontrib.com/news/metro/danielle/20020412-9999_6m12 wester.html, April 12, 2002.

21. Alex Roth, "Attorney says police ignored client's requests for a lawyer," *Union Tribune,* www.uniontrib.com/news/metro/danielle/20020404-9999_m4 feldman.html, April 4, 2002.

22. Green.

23. Ibid.

24. David Wright, "Identify confirmed," *ABC News,* abcnews.go.com/sections /us/DailyNews/missinggirl020228.html, February 28, 2002.

25. Roth, "Prosecutors respond to defense claims of rights violations."

26. Roth, "Attorney says police ignored client's requests for a lawyer."

27. Ibid.

28. Alex Roth, "Experts agree defense team for Westerfield has hard task," *Union Tribune,* www.uniontrib.com/news/metro/danielle/20020314-9999_1n14 feldman.html, March 14, 2002.

29. Roth, "Attorney says police ignored client's requests for a lawyer."

CHAPTER 5

Treating Victimized Children

While there's life, there's hope.

—Marcus Tullius Cicero

Light streams in through the crack in the door. From the bed I hear voices on the other side, and I desperately want it to be my mother or father...But it's not Mommy. It's the woman who lives in this house. I have no idea who she is. Sometimes there are other children here. I play with them during the day, but when darkness sets in, they disappear, and the feeling of loneliness is deeper. Where is my mother, and why won't she come to get me? I cry myself to sleep believing that I will wake up in her arms. But in the morning I'm still alone ... I drop out of bed and trudge into the kitchen...I turn to the woman and ask her, "When is Mommy coming to get me?" She looks at me and smiles gently. Her voice is not unkind. "Maybe today, dear." But quickly it is night again and the fear comes over me like a fever. I don't want to go back to that room. The woman reaches out with a dark, worn hand, glistening and oily to the touch. She walks me to the room and guides me into bed. I don't want to be here! I lie there, staring at the column of light through the crack in the door. "Where is Mommy?" I cry out, but no one answers. I'm afraid I will be here forever. My mother will never come for me and I will never go home.[1]

These are the heart-wrenching memories of a four-year-old boy. This child, Bernard Kerik, grew up without his mother and went on to become police commissioner of New York City. His mother was a drug addict and prostitute who left her son to be raised by near strangers while she pursued her own selfish lifestyle. His mother never did come for him and even though he never really knew her, he loved her deeply and wished for her return. Kerik's memory of endless waiting for his mother, for something safe and familiar, is a response shared by many children who are in foster care. His words demonstrate that despite the neglect he suffered, his longing for his mother was even more powerful. The need to find her followed him far into his adult years. A child may be deeply devoted to the very person who is responsible for his abuse.

Even in the very best circumstances, abused and neglected children have multiple issues to deal with. Kerik's story demonstrates the added trauma of being removed from one's home. A therapist has to be aware of the many emotions and issues involved when evaluating and treating abused and neglected children. The child may suffer from broken bones, burns, contusions, cuts, and internal injuries that present emotional problems on their own, even if they were received through accidents. When a child has any injury, inconvenience, or difficulties in movement, fear of pain, doctors, hospitals, and the fear of dying are all potential problems. The emotional issues related to such injuries are exacerbated when they have been deliberately inflicted. With deliberately inflicted injuries, dissonant emotions with regard to the perpetrator are almost guaranteed. The child may love the perpetrator deeply, but at the same time fear and resent him or her.

Intervention by social workers, doctors, or therapists is confusing to a child. He understands little about what is going on or what the outcome of such intervention will be. All he knows is that strange people are asking scary questions that he does not understand. He may then be whisked away, maybe to a strange place as in the foster care illustration above. Fear of the unknown is to be expected at any age, but increases the younger the victim is. All children are egocentric, causing them to wonder what they did to deserve the "punishment" that they are experiencing. Because of this fear and anxiety, even severely abused children will tell authorities that they want to go home—a place where familiarity provides comfort.

If the child has been sexually abused, interviews by therapists, law enforcement officers, and attorneys force them to relive an embarrassing and painful experience. Guilt, embarrassment, and shame are common emotional reactions. Abuse compromises the child's ability to trust and her belief that the world is a safe place because, in fact, it has not been a safe place for that child. If the child was abducted, issues of trust are only compounded.

In this chapter I will address how a therapist begins initial consultations with a traumatized child, treating these children through play therapy, and issues that complicate court testimony as well as therapeutic progress. Examples of the resiliency of children, memory issues, case studies, and stories of survival follow.

INITIAL INTERVIEWS

Initial interviews with a traumatized child require skill and training. Untrained interviewers can easily retraumatize children, generating even more mistrust than the children already are experiencing, or they can ask leading questions or suggest ideas that complicate future prosecution of perpetrators. A child's memory can be distorted by suggestions or ideas that the interviewer presents. Therefore, the therapist, police officer, social worker, or parent must be careful not to put any ideas in the child's head. I once was involved in a case where a father was accused of molesting his daughter. In the initial investigation, the investigating social worker asked the child, "Where did your father touch you?" When a child is asked a leading question like this, she assumes that her father *did* touch her, even if he didn't. Therefore, she will answer the question as if he had touched her. In this interview, the child said, "On my body." Again, the social worker asked an inappropriate and leading question when she probed further. "Where on your body? Did he touch you here or here?" she said, pointing to her buttocks and breasts. Again, children assume that adults know that something has happened, even if it hasn't. Therefore, the child can assume from a question like this that the *correct* answer is that the father must have touched her in one of these two places. In this case, the child answered, "Here," pointing to her buttocks.

The social worker continued asking leading questions and mangled the interview so badly that prosecution of the father was impossible. I believe that the father did, in fact, molest the child, but because the interview was so tainted, the district attorney believed a conviction would be impossible to obtain. Therefore, no case was brought against the father. Once a child's idea of what has occurred is skewed by an interview, it is almost impossible to discover what really happened. After an interview like the one conducted by this social worker, another therapist, even using appropriate interview techniques, cannot be 100 percent confident that any indication of abuse resulted from actual abuse or from ideas presented to the child during the initial interview.

Inappropriate interview techniques can lead to the perpetrator being exonerated in court. Equally troubling is the fact that inappropriate interview techniques can also lead to innocent men and women landing in jail, their careers, reputations, and lives destroyed. The McMartin Preschool in California and the Little Rascals Day Care Center in Edenton, North Carolina, are cases where it appears this very thing occurred. In 1983, parents accused Raymond Buckey, his grandmother, and several other family members, of ritualistically abusing children at the McMartin Preschool, even though there was little evidence that anything untoward had occurred. Eventually, panic led to more than 400 interviews with children from the preschool and an alleged 369 cases of satanic ritual abuse. Accusations included children being forced to eat fecal material and human flesh, the dismemberment of corpses, and infant sacrifice. Several defendants were acquitted, others had charges eventually either dropped or reduced, or juries became deadlocked. In the Little Rascals case, seven defendants were accused of conspiring to molest almost thirty children. One child claimed to have been cooked in a microwave oven, another said the day care owner regularly shot babies, and another said a child was fed to a shark. Two defendants were convicted, but an appeals court later overturned those convictions. Charges against other defendants were either reduced or dropped altogether. What seems clear in both of these cases is that the children's testimony was so tainted by well-intentioned parents, prosecutors, and overzealous therapists that what, if anything, happened will probably never be known.

As an interviewer begins his or her first contact with the child, the most important goal is establishing a relationship with the child. If the child does not trust the interviewer, he will not engage in open discussion about the traumatic event. If the child fears that the interviewer is mad at him or that the child is in trouble, it will be much more difficult to elicit information from the child. A child who trusts his therapist will be more relaxed and information presented during the interview will be more credible.

In order to protect the possibility of prosecuting a child abuser, initial interviews should involve nondirective techniques. Closed-ended questions, those that can be answered with a single word like "yes" or "no," are problematic for three reasons. When an adult asks a child a closed-ended question, the child assumes that he is supposed to know the answer to the question. Therefore, he will select one of the two options. For example, suppose a child has *not* been inappropriately touched, but the interviewer asks the child, "Did the man touch you here or here?" pointing to the child's groin and bottom. The child may easily believe that the "correct" answer is one of those two choices rather than the correct answer, "neither." A second problem with a closed-ended question is that it gives the child an easy way out of the conversation. Answering with a simple "yes" or "no" is much easier than elaborating, which would provide more information to the interviewer. Finally, closed-ended questions are interrogative and give the child the impression that he is in trouble, making it less likely that the child will feel comfortable opening up to the interviewer.

Using open-ended interview techniques avoids these problems. They are not leading, they foster rapport, and they encourage the child to elaborate on her experience. When interviewing a child for the first time, I might not ask any questions at all. I use pencil, paper, and crayons and ask the child to draw a picture of a person or of the child's family. How a child draws herself and other family members, the juxtaposition of those members, and the colors the child uses tell me a great deal. Alternatively, I may ask the child to draw a picture of a house and of a tree. This simple technique is called the "tree/house/person" technique and is widely used in play therapy. I might let the child play with dolls, dollhouses, Play Dough, a sand tray and sand toys, or a host of other toys in my therapy room.

Even if I wanted to elicit information about something the child was drawing, I still would not have to ask any direct questions. If the child's drawing, for example, showed a child who was crying, I would say, "This child looks sad. I wonder why she is crying." Unlike the social worker's questions that I described above, my statement is only responding to what the child has already said through the drawing. My comment on the drawing invites the child to elaborate, but does not provide an answer to my question.

Also important in initial interviews is an evaluation of the child's language capacity and memory skills. Memory and language limitations will determine the interview approach as well as interpretation of information gleaned from the interview. Once rapport has been established with the child and an initial assessment has been completed, goals for therapy can then be established. Goals for therapy differ depending on the child's needs, level of and response to trauma, and the role, if any, that the child will play in the prosecution of a perpetrator. A child who will be testifying in court will have different therapeutic goals than a child who was traumatized and whose perpetrator is unidentified. Armed with this information, the therapist, the child, and the parent can begin the process of healing.

MEMORY, DECEPTION, AND DISTORTION

As a graduate student I was attending group supervision with my graduate professor. Each of the five students under her direction would play audiotapes from our sessions and she would critique, answer questions, and provide feedback. As I played a tape and discussed my client, a nine-year-old boy, I related a story he told me during the session. As I concluded my comments, I added that I didn't know if he was telling me the truth or not. "Why would he lie?" she asked me. My initial thought was, "Of course kids tell stories," but then I realized I was automatically assuming he was untrustworthy—a serious mistake. I've never forgotten her words as I have worked with children in my therapy room for these many years. Children do fabricate, elaborate, and exaggerate stories, but the lesson I learned from my professor is that we assume they are not telling us the truth when we hear something that doesn't match our predetermined assumptions of what could and could not be true. This is just what happened in December 1999 to Lydia Hanson, a seven-year-old child in the second grade. She told her teacher that her mother had died at home and that she was alone. Instead of investigating the story, her teacher reprimanded her for telling "stories" and sent her back to her seat.[2] Her failure to get help from an adult defeated her, so instead of telling her story to someone else, she finished the school day, quietly boarded the school bus, and rode home. There, she fixed herself leftover spaghetti and curled up on the couch next to her dead mother. Lydia held her hand, watched TV, and made popcorn because her mother always made popcorn in the evenings. At bedtime, she laid across her mother's lap and went to sleep. The next day, Lydia's grandfather came by to check on Lydia's mom, who was a diabetic, and discovered the child and her dead mother. The cause of her death was unknown. "Why would she lie?" is a question the teacher should have asked herself.

When a child is trying to communicate the facts of an event, he can easily misunderstand what he interprets as fact. This misunderstanding appears to some as deception, but the child is not necessarily lying. A child's ability to convey factual events is limited by lack of understanding of time, place, geography, and vocabulary. The child will provide the "facts" as best he can, given these limitations. Whether something happened here or there, yesterday or a year ago, at a friend's house or in the grocery store, are all details that may not necessarily be credible. The role of the therapist is to interpret the relevant data from an otherwise convoluted story. For example, a child may say something happened "last year." Whether it happened literally last year, a few days ago, or a few months ago is not the real issue and there is no way to know based only on the child's memory. The real issue is that from a child's perspective, the event happened in the past—maybe a long time ago. In a similar way, adults do the same thing. They might say they waited in line for a week at the Department of Motor Vehicles. They don't really mean they waited an entire week, but neither are they lying. They are communicating that they had to wait a long time; therefore, whether it was an hour, two hours, or five hours, the essence of the communication is the same. The only difference between this and what children do is that adults purposefully use exaggeration to emphasize the point (it was a long wait), while children do it because they only have a limited number of words that refer to time (day, week, year) and they do not have a full understanding of the meanings of those words.

Children will fabricate stories similar to ones they have seen in a movie, read in a book, or heard from someone else. For example, a kindergartner may hear a classmate tell a story about going to an amusement park. He may then volunteer a story about his own trip to an amusement park that might sound strangely similar to the previous child's story. Even though he is making up a story about going to an amusement park, he is actually trying to communicate something quite different. Depending on the context, he may be trying to express that he would have liked for this to have happened to him, or it may be that he has noticed the attention the other storyteller received and what he is really saying is "Notice me." Children rarely spontaneously make up the root of a story, such as a mother being dead at home, without something to prompt the fabrication. If I had been privy to Lydia's story, the first thing I would have wanted to know is whether or not someone else in the class may have described a death or if the class had read a book or seen a video about a relative dying. If not, I would have been very concerned that Lydia was trying to convey important information. Even though to Lydia, *dead* may have meant in a coma, extremely ill, or sedated, I would have checked on her story to see what else she knew. If the child was home alone, as in this case, it wouldn't matter if the mother was extremely ill, sedated, in a coma, or dead. The child needed help, regardless. Children often fear telling an adult about abuse because they do not think they will be believed. Unfortunately, just like Lydia, their fears are sometimes justified.

When an abuse case is presented to a court, the defense will attempt to discredit the testimony of the child. To directly attack the child's credibility would be unwise. Juries tend to empathize with children and an aggressive attorney could easily alienate herself from the jury. Instead, the attorney will attack the child's credibility through the back door, in a sense, by making it look as if the child were incapable of knowing what happened because of developmental limitations. One could develop a rather convincing argument that children's memories cannot be trusted. However, what the attorney would not address is the fact that young children do not have as much motivation to lie as adults. Even if they were motivated to lie, very young children lack the ability to manipulate multiple issues simultaneously in their minds. In order to tell a convincing lie, one must think about the motive for the lie, the story to be told, and how to present it in a given context so that it will be believed. Young children cannot effectively perform all these operations at one time. It is usually obvious when a child is lying because the story she tells is easily discredited by the facts, but she cannot think far enough ahead to realize that; therefore, she presents information that makes sense to her at the moment. For example, I once caught one of my children with her hand literally in the cookie jar. She explained that she was "returning" the cookies because they fell out of the cookie jar. What she did not consider was the fact that cookies were missing, crumbs were all over the counter and the floor, and she had chocolate on her face and lips. She was not cognitively mature enough to consider the impossible physics of cookies leaping from the cookie jar and falling to the counter. As her cognitive skills improved over the years, she would be able to formulate a much more believable story—her sister took the cookies. Learning from my graduate school professor, I tend to believe a child unless there is an obvious reason not to.

Some theorists argue that stressful events distort memories. It makes sense that traumatic events, such as a molestation or rape, could make it difficult to think clearly; hence, memories would be significantly distorted. Yet, recent research has shown that this is not true. Children's recall under simulated stressful events is equal to that of their nonstressed counterparts.[3] In fact, this study demonstrated that distortion was more likely due to ineffective or biased interviewers.[4]

The credibility of a child's testimony has been critical in a number of cases. For example, in 2000, a martial arts instructor in suburban Atlanta was accused of molesting several different boys, ages four to twelve, over a four-year period. The case began when one of the boys touched his sister inappropriately. When his mother asked him about his behavior, he told her that his karate teacher touched him that way. As in the McMartin and Little Rascals cases, one parent contacted other parents and eventually the list of allegedly abused children grew to twenty-two children. In court, some of the boys gave testimony that differed from that given in their initial interviews. The influence of the parents, therapists, and lawyers on the children's stories was difficult to determine. In the end, however, the perpetrator was convicted and sentenced to ninety years in prison. Unlike the McMartin and Little Rascals cases, however, the evidence against this perpetrator was more than circumstantial and it appears unlikely that an appeal will be successful.

PLAY THERAPY

Memory is generally an unreliable tool, even for adults. Memories are always distorted, both at the point of encoding as well as at the point of recall, by our expectations, biases, and beliefs. These distortions may have minimal effect on the memory or the memory may be significantly altered by these distortions, but either way, distortion is inevitable. Even as the event to be remembered is occurring, the encoding of that event into a memory is prone to error. As time goes on, our memories are modified by our experiences, perceptions, and misperceptions, further reducing the reliability of that memory. No one, regardless of age, is exempt from this process, but children have added limitations that complicate their ability to remember events. Children's ability to recall facts and events and their memory strategies are generally poorer than those of adults, but children are also limited in their ability to communicate the memories that they can recall. Limited vocabulary and ability to use language make it difficult for them to express through words the information that is accessible to them in their minds. In fact, some psychologists suggest that children are actually more limited by the ability to express their thoughts than they are limited in their ability to remember. Therefore, in order to more accurately interpret what a child is trying to communicate as he provides clues to his memories, one must rely on more than a child's words. Clues to one's memory appear in a child's expressions, activities, and play. Play therapy is a therapeutic method that uses toys, puppets, and other media through which a child can act out his memory, thus using a means of communication that comes more easily to him than language. The therapist then interprets these behaviors and conveys their meaning to parents, social workers, and the court system.

There are many methods in use today for treating abused children, but play therapy is currently one of the most common and widely accepted approaches. In play therapy, a child is provided with toys, games, pens, pencils, Play Dough, sand, or a variety of other media. By observing the child's play, the therapist can make evaluations, assessments, and diagnoses. She can also address issues as they arise and help the child move toward resolution. I am almost always an active participant with children in therapy if they want me to play with them, but some therapists prefer to remain as passive observers. I often allow the parents to sit in the therapy room during therapy and if they are interested, I encourage them to play with the child and me. Parental participation is important to me because it helps me to observe the interaction between the parent and the child and it tells me something about their relationship. In fact, *filial play therapy* is a form of play therapy specifically structured for parents to participate in the therapy with the child. In this therapy approach, the parent, in a way, is acting as the child's therapist under the direction of the play therapist.

Play therapy has been around for fifty years, but it wasn't until the 1980s that it became widely accepted as a therapeutic method. When I first began my career in 1985, there were few resources available on the subject, but today there are thousands of books, videotapes, and other materials on play therapy available to counselors, psychologists, and others who work with children.

Therapy Tools

My office is often the butt of jokes from the maintenance crew, secretaries, students, and even my colleagues. When they see toys, dolls, dollhouses, crayons, and other items strewn around, they wonder aloud what kind of "work" is going on when the door is closed. The truth is, these tools are as important to me in my work as a therapist as a hammer or saw is to a carpenter. I could not do my job without them. "I wish I got paid to play with sand," my colleagues have jokingly said. "Lucky me," is usually my succinct response, but despite its title, play therapy is work. It requires training, energy, and patience.

When a child enters my office, she does not know what to expect. If she has been traumatized, her ability to trust in the world is compromised. To her, I am just another grown-up that she is being forced to interact with. In those first few minutes when I tell her she can play with anything she wants, she won't believe me. She tentatively wanders toward the toy box, all the time watching me out of the corner of her eye. Cautiously, she reaches out and picks up a toy, but then looks at me to see my reaction.

"Go ahead," I encourage her as she checks to make sure I really mean that she can play with "anything." Within minutes, the child has every toy on the floor and is engrossed in some activity. I carefully move to the floor nearby and watch.

"Tell me about what you are making," I ask her as she stacks Lego blocks on top of one another. From there, she will open up. I am earning her trust and she sees that I am interested in her and what she is doing. She realizes that this "interview" is not going to be like all the others where she is seated at a table and bombarded with questions by some stranger, but it still may take many sessions before she fully trusts me and understands that I believe in her. Even more challenging is my task to reintroduce her to the idea that she is lovable and that she can believe in herself.

The toys in my office are varied. Every therapist has his or her own favorites. A staple among many play therapists is the sand tray. Sand trays are wooden boxes filled with sand. Using the sand and a variety of minia-ture items (people, animals, buildings, etc.), the child creates scenarios or stories that are then interpreted by the therapist. Once, while I was attend-ing a conference on sand play, I heard the presenter tell the audience that necessary items that should be available to the child while using the sand tray are "representations of everything that exists in real life, both natural and manufactured." The audience snickered, but she was completely seri-ous. Her office contained shelves full of hundreds of miniature people, bridges, animals, monsters, houses, cars, trucks, planes, hats, and so forth. Her office did, in fact, contain a representation of almost everything that exists in life. This broad selection of miniatures expands the child's "vocabulary" as she creates her story in the sand tray.

Other tools common in play therapy are creative toys, real-life toys, dolls, Legos, Tinkertoys, blocks, finger paints, and Play Dough—my per-sonal favorite. Play Dough is used in somewhat the same way as sand, but it can be molded into anything the child wishes to imagine. It is a versatile play therapy tool. I have found that even adults enjoy playing with Play Dough in therapy and it can be a very useful tool with them as well.

Puppets are sometimes used to allow children to act out scenes between characters. Using puppets, the child will act out traumatic events that are obvious reflections of their own experiences. However, the puppets allow the child to avoid saying "I" or "me" in reference to the events. There are several types of puppets, each with its own purpose. "Perpetrator" pup-pets are those that are aggressive, such as alligators, lions, or wolves. "Vic-tim" puppets are those that are helpless or passive, such as lambs or kittens. Other puppets may be "neutral." Animal puppets are useful because it is easier for a child to create a story where the "bad alligator" attacks the baby lamb rather than to create a story where the man puppet attacks the child puppet, but the message in both scenes is the same.

I prefer toys that are ambiguous because they actually make it easier to determine what is going on in a child's mind. A toy that has a known purpose already will more likely illicit the known purpose rather than a projection of the child's thoughts. There are very expensive puppets available on the market. These elaborate puppets have hair, eyes, nice clothing, and other details and they cost $100 or more each. Yet I have found that a tube sock with a painted face is actually more useful to me. It doesn't look as fancy—of course it isn't—but it encourages the child to use his imagination rather than letting the appearance of the toy determine the details.

Paper, pens, crayons, board games, clay, bubbles, baby bottles, toy animals, and a toy telephone are important toys to have in the playroom. A toy telephone, for example, allows children to "call" anyone they wish—a family member, a deceased person, police, or even a perpetrator. I will sometimes use the toy telephone to engage a resistant child in therapy. I will pick up the toy phone and begin a conversation, eventually working the child's name into the conversation. I will then pass the phone to him or her and the child will almost always engage with me in the play. Cameras, musical instruments, and even food can also be used. All these tools of therapy provide a means of communication for the child. Using these toys and tools, the child can tell me about his experience, take control of that experience, and eventually resolve the trauma.

Anatomically Correct Dolls

I doubt there is a therapist in the field who doesn't have an opinion about the use of anatomically correct dolls. These dolls come in various shapes, sizes, genders, and races and have various levels of anatomically correct details. Some have genitalia, but no pubic hair. Others are accurate to every detail. The theory behind the use of these dolls is that an investigator can allow a child to demonstrate what happened to him or her, thus circumventing language limitations.

The most obvious problem with these dolls is that their use sensitizes a child to anatomy issues that she may never have been exposed to. As a result, all future interviews are potentially tainted by the use of the doll. For example, suppose a three-year-old child has *not* been molested, but a social worker or police investigator uses an anatomically correct doll. The child is then exposed to a penis, pubic hair, and nudity that she had not before been exposed to. Now the knowledge of these body parts is in her mind and future interviewers will not be able to distinguish between exposure to real body parts and those of the anatomically correct doll.

Even though this is a good reason to avoid anatomically correct dolls, I do not favor their use for a much simpler reason. They are not necessary. A child will demonstrate her knowledge and experience without such dolls and a skilled therapist can easily see it without the risks posed by use of anatomically correct dolls. As an analogy, let me address a similar issue. Many parents do not like their children to play with toy guns of any kind. Yet even when manufactured toy weapons are not available, children will make them using sticks, other toys, or perhaps nothing more than their thumb and forefinger. These children have weapons on their minds, even if they don't have the artificial tools to assist them. Therefore, when they play they will create weapons to match the ones in their minds. Likewise, if a child has been molested, the event is in her head and she cannot help but demonstrate it through her play. Just as I prefer simple puppets, simple, ambiguous dolls are better than anatomically correct ones.

Parental Involvement in Therapy

Parental partnership with me in therapy can make or break therapy. Not only do I depend on parents to bring their children to sessions, but I also depend on them to follow up during the week with the child's homework assignments and sometimes assignments of their own. A divorced mother brought her son Andrew to see me. The child was seven years old and extremely aggressive. His mother worried that his aggression was the result of abuse or molestation. In my intake interview with the mother, it did not take long to realize that she was an emotionally needy woman and in her attempt to cope with her loneliness, a constant stream of men had passed through her home. They came into her home and stayed for a few weeks, just long enough for Andrew to get the impression that he had a "new dad," and then they would disappear. Initially, because of the number of men who had access to Andrew, I was concerned that abuse was likely, but after seeing him in therapy, it became apparent that his aggressive behavior was due to the unpredictability and instability of his home life rather than physical or sexual abuse. In private, I suggested to his mother that if she wanted to help her son, she had to set dating aside for a while and that she needed to reconcile enough with her ex-husband so that they could work together to raise Andrew. I explained that he needed a stable male role model and that it would be helpful if her husband could be available for him. I could tell by the look on her face and by her comments that she had no intentions of doing either thing I suggested. She left therapy and did not bring her son back for his next appointment. Unfortunately, as a therapist, I sometimes have to live with the fact that parents are either incapable of doing or unwilling to do what is best for their children.

A school principal called one day expressing concern about a child's drawings as well as some things she had said. Her language was full of explicit sexual content and after I examined the pictures, I concluded that they were textbook examples of those that are created by sexually abused children. For example, all the drawings by this child included pubic hair, exaggerated and explicit genitalia, teary faces of females, and objects being inserted into the vagina of the female characters. I try not to jump to conclusions about abuse, but this case was as clear as I had ever seen. I did not know who the abuser was, but I was positive the child had been sexually mistreated. Based on my analysis, the principal informed the parents that it was likely that the child had been abused. Naturally, the parents were devastated. By law, the administrators at the school were required to report their suspicions to social services. The caseworker reviewed the case and found no evidence that either parent was an abuser. I was called again after the caseworker had finished her evaluation and asked if I still believed abuse was present. I maintained my view. A week or so later, the father called me. He was a good man who wanted more than anything for me to be wrong. He and his wife had concluded that the child behaved as she did because she wanted to get attention and she had heard some other children at school talking about sex. That was their explanation for her behavior, but they were wrong. I cannot know who abused the child or whether the abuse was past or current, but I am certain it happened. I admit that if it were my child, I might grasp at any possibility other than sexual abuse. These parents found it easier to rationalize away the symptoms than to admit that their daughter had been sexually abused. I suspect that ten or twenty years from now, this child will be in a counselor's office weeping over this issue, resentful that her parents didn't help her.

Therapy is most effective when parents are willing participants in the process. I give homework to all my clients and it is up to the parent to help the child follow through with the assignments I give during the week. Usually, these homework assignments involve practicing some skill or working on a specific behavior. When parents engage in therapy with me as my partners and do what I ask them to do—even when it is hard—children can make great progress very quickly. If a parent is unwilling to help or participate, as was the case with Andrew's mother, therapy may have little effect on the child's behavior.

Goals, Length, and Scope of Therapy

Therapeutic goals are essential because goals direct therapy. I supervise therapists who are working on their state licenses. The most common problem that I encounter with them is that they lose their way in therapy and find themselves either wasting time or unsure about what to do next. I always refer them to their therapeutic goals. Once the therapist focuses on the goals of therapy, direction is usually clear. Goals, in part, make the difference between productive play and unproductive play in therapy. If the play, the play medium, or the conversation leads one toward the goals of therapy, then it is appropriate. If it does not, then the play, the play medium, or the conversation is a waste of time. With the participation of the child and his or her guardian, I set concrete, measurable goals that are clear to everyone involved. Nearly all the children that I see and absolutely all the adults that I work with can tell me at any time during our therapeutic relationship what our goals are, how we will know when we have achieved them, and where we are in the process. This measurable and overt process allows for the parent as well as the therapist to monitor progress and to avoid pointless, time-wasting, and money-wasting exercises during therapy.

There is no way any therapist can tell a parent ahead of time how long it will take to achieve the goals of therapy. I have worked with children where we have resolved issues and reached our goals in only a few weeks and at other times I have worked with children for over a year and still not reached all our goals. I usually recommend to parents that I will need at least two or three sessions to build rapport and to evaluate a child. Even when the issues that need attention are ones that I have worked with many times and I might be able to give the parent a general idea how long therapy will last (i.e., four to eight sessions), I am reluctant to do so. The child's level of maturity, level of development, response to trauma, and parental support greatly affect the child's response to therapy.

A stable home, loving parents, and parents who are willing to participate in therapy/homework with their children can speed up the process. Disengaged parents or an unstable home, like Andrew's, may actually undermine the work we do in therapy. The more areas of a child's life that I have access to and the larger the "team" working on the child's case, the more productive therapy can be. With the parent's (and sometimes the child's) consent, I often work in conjunction with siblings, teachers, pediatricians, social workers, and even members of the clergy on a child's case. When all these individuals join together as a team, the child's overall environment can be more carefully monitored, controlled, and stabilized.

Treatment of Sexual Abuse

As I said in Chapter 3, nothing is more personal than our sexuality. While attending a conference on child sexual abuse, I heard the child psychologist presenting that day tell the members of the audience to think about their most embarrassing sexual experience. The audience murmured and snickered as specific incidents came to their minds. "Now," he said, "turn to the person next to you and tell them about it." The group of three hundred therapists gasped and nobody complied. The speaker then explained that when therapists, social workers, police officers, and even parents try to coax information out of a child who has been molested or raped, they are asking her to tell them about her most embarrassing sexual experience. It is very awkward, to say the least.

When children are sexually abused, they experience a number of losses. They lose innocence, dignity, and control.[5] Sexual abuse treatment must address these losses; therefore, a therapist must provide a way for these children to regain their dignity and control and also to empower them as they face future discouragements and setbacks that are a natural part of life. Byron Norton, a psychologist and expert on play therapy, has identified four stages of therapy that achieve these goals.[6] First, children must be allowed to tell their story. Disclosure is the process of verbally telling about their experience or, more likely, reliving the experience through play—a process called *abreaction* (see Chapter 3). As the child "tells" about his experience, the therapist affirms that she or he understands what is being communicated, both affectively and factually.

Second, the child must be allowed to mourn his losses. Innocence, for example, can never be recovered. Grieving involves acknowledging the loss and learning how to cope with and overcome it. Third, the child must find a way to conquer the perpetrator. As you will see in the case study involving Cameron, burying his perpetrator (represented by a small doll) in Play Dough each week was part of the process of conquering him. Testifying in court can also empower children and promote their recovery because it gives them a sense of control over their own fate and over their perpetrator.

Finally, the child must regain control of his environment. This involves teaching the child to use his available skills or teaching the child new skills that are needed for recovery. Stories of survival and good decisions that one has made and books or videos about trauma and recovery are all tools that can empower a child, leading to the achievement of the goals of therapy.

Resilience

It is a common mistake to assume that children are so resilient that they will eventually "get over it" when they are sexually abused. Sometimes this is true, but a person without training and experience is unqualified to make such evaluations. Even with a Ph.D. and twenty years of experience, I cannot *know* whether or not a child will recover without therapy. I can only make a professional judgment. Unfortunately, parents use the belief in a child's resilience as an excuse not to pursue therapy when it is needed. When parents tell me their children are resilient and they will get over it, I suspect the proper translation of their comments is, "I don't want to be troubled by this," "I don't want to spend the money for therapy," or "I just want to put this behind me and therapy for my child will only remind *me* of a painful event in *my* life."

I briefly addressed resilience in the Part 1 introduction, but as I develop this issue here, it is important to note that my experience has been that parents are more likely to inappropriately assume resilience in their children than to bring their children to see me when they do not need to. With this caveat, it is true that some children are indeed capable of enduring in the midst of seemingly insurmountable odds and their ability to overcome these obstacles is amazing. Children like Leslie, whose case I describe at the end of this chapter, have taught me how amazingly resilient children can be. In Leslie's case, even though she was the youngest person in the family—only five years old—she was the most stable and mentally healthy person in her family.

Dallas psychologist Barbara Rila has noted three issues that contribute to resiliency in children.[7] First, when the victims of abuse are older children, they are more likely to recover than children who are abused when they are very young. Second, the more quickly intervention occurs, including removal of the child from the dysfunctional home and reestablishing healthy relationships elsewhere, the better the prognosis. Finally, children who have strong relationships outside the family are more likely to cope with their abuse in a healthy way. Big Brothers/Big Sisters programs, ministries in religious organizations, or mentoring programs can meet this need. With this resilience, children can develop resolve and problem-solving skills that actually help them later in life.

In both children and adults, coping skills vary, but the more resolved one is to survive, the better one functions in the face of trauma. Professional assessment can determine how healthy one's coping skills are, it can identify dysfunction that is difficult to see, and it can provide suggestions that may or may not involve therapy. On occasion, I have chosen to "treat" resilient children only through regular telephone consultation with parents. A weekly or monthly consultation over the phone can help me identify potential problems and this process saves the parents time and money, and keeps them actively involved in their child's recovery.

Risk of Abuse

As I evaluate a child who has been traumatized, I am looking for the symptoms of abuse and warning signs of problems that need to be addressed in therapy. Sometimes these symptoms are obvious. For example, a client once came to my office for an initial visit. She was sixteen years old and had been repeatedly molested by her father. When she sat down, even before she said hello, she pulled up one leg of her blue jeans to reveal her calf. There, she had carved the word "HELP" with a pocketknife. "Do you think this is a problem?" she asked me. Obviously, this was a serious problem. Other times, however, symptoms are more difficult to see.

When I suspect abuse or when I know for certain that abuse has occurred, my first responsibility is to ensure that the child is no longer in danger of repeated victimization. Some related issues that make it more likely that a child will be sexually and/or physically abused include situations where a child is living in a home with marital conflict, stepparenting conflict, or very young parents. Other correlated issues between abuse and the home are substance abuse, spouse abuse, mental illness, and poverty.[8] Even a history of dog bites at home indicates a higher likelihood of abuse for two reasons. First, researchers have discovered that adults who mistreat the family dog are more likely to abuse their children.[9] Mistreated animals are more likely to bite. Likewise, it has also been found that in homes where adults physically abuse children, dog bites are more likely. It is believed that the dog mimics the abusive behavior of its master.[10]

Parents with chronic coping problems are more likely to abuse.[11] Young, especially single, parents are statistically a greater threat to children. It is believed that these young parents are more likely to be poor, stressed, have minimal coping skills, and be unprepared for parenthood. They may be "adolescents who have little knowledge of children's needs (no prenatal care) and have unrealistic expectations of their children."[12] According to the National Clearinghouse on Child Abuse and Neglect Information, these young parents:

... need help in providing nutrition, preventative care, emotional nurturance, and discipline. They need to understand their own human growth and development, as well as that of their children. Mistakenly, many had thought that a child would meet their needs for love and admiration. They felt that a child would be all theirs, something that they could control, something that would help them gain status, never realizing that the child would interfere with dating and socializing.[13]

Awareness of situations where abuse is more likely keeps the therapist on guard and prepared to intervene on behalf of the child. Intervention may involve mandated reporting, coordinated efforts with social workers or the court system, or perhaps family or marital therapy as well as therapy with the child.

Controversial Therapies

There are a few therapeutic techniques with children that are highly controversial. *Holding therapy* and *rebirth therapies* are used most often with children with attachment disorders. Even though these are questionable methods, I mention them here because children who are victims of serious abuse, especially in infancy, are prime candidates for attachment issues. These techniques have resulted in lawsuits and, in the case of rebirth therapy, have even resulted in the death of the client. There is theoretical logic that supports both of these techniques, but I do not use either one in my practice. Use of these techniques requires extensive training in the appropriateness of their use. A parent who knows that the therapist uses one of these methods should be aware of the controversial nature of these therapies and make an informed decision about whether or not to allow the child to participate or whether to seek help from a different therapist.

CAMERON

Cameron first came to my office when he was six years old. He had been to a host of therapists before me and he had been hospitalized twice. His mental health history included an array of diagnoses by various clinicians, including attention deficit/hyperactivity disorder (ADHD) and obsessive-compulsive disorder (OCD). His behavior was out of control both at home and at school and he was exhibiting sexually inappropriate behaviors in a variety of contexts, including masturbation in public. In fact, Cameron masturbated so frequently that he had been treated for rashes and infections on his penis. Cameron was sexually aggressive and on one occasion he exposed himself to a female kindergartner while riding the school bus. In our first meeting, his mother informed me that she suspected that a babysitter had molested Cameron just prior to his third birthday.

Since the alleged perpetrator was no longer a danger to this child, my most immediate concern was Cameron's incorrigible behavior. Even though the sexual behaviors he exhibited were troubling, before they could be addressed, it was necessary to gain control of his behavior. Cameron was a very demanding child and after a lengthy discussion with his mother I realized that they catered to his every whim just to appease him. I did not doubt the ADHD diagnosis for which he was currently on medication, but I suspected that much of his impulsivity was simply a six-year-old's realization that he could get his way if he threw a loud enough tantrum.

Regaining control of a child like Cameron requires patience from both the therapist and, even more importantly, from parents. Parents must regain the power they have given up to the child. No child likes to lose power and I warn parents to expect the child's behavior to get worse before it improves. Like saddling a wild horse, the child will buck and scream, assuming that his tantrums will force the parent to cede, but it is absolutely imperative that parents not give in. If they do, they will only reinforce in the child's mind that a tantrum will eventually result in regaining control over the parents. Cameron's behavior was so incorrigible that an extreme response was necessary. He needed to know that he was not in charge and that he had to earn every privilege. I asked the parents to remove everything from his room. I wanted his room free of toys, posters, TVs, and radios. I didn't want anything in his room except his bed, his pillow, and his blanket. He would have to earn everything back. Prior to seeing me, his parents would send him to his room as "punishment." Yet in his room he had video games, a television, mountains of toys, and a telephone. Going to his room wasn't punishment. His parents complied with my request and over the next two weeks, Cameron gradually earned some of his toys back. His behavior improved dramatically both at home and at school.

Cameron stayed in therapy with me for several months, but as his behavior improved, his parents, who drove more than sixty miles each way to my office, withdrew him from therapy. Because we had only begun our work on his abuse, I knew his disruptive behavior would resurface. Sure enough, a few months later his mother called me requesting an appointment because Cameron had sexually fondled a seven-year-old relative. We reengaged in therapy and picked up where we had left off.

Cameron's sexual behaviors were the result of two things. First, masturbation and other sexual behaviors are pleasant feelings. Masturbation is a normal behavior in children and only a few of the many children who masturbate have been molested. Once they learn autoerotic behavior, either by random experimentation or through instruction from a sibling or abuser, they do not necessarily realize that there is anything socially unacceptable about it and since it feels pleasurable, they are apt to repeat the behavior. Second, Cameron's sexual behavior was a form of abreaction. Exposing himself to the kindergartner, masturbation, and fondling his relative were ways in which he could take control of his sexuality and relive the traumatic event.

Cameron was molested just prior to his third birthday. At this stage of life he was unable to form memories in the same way that adults form memories. When an older child or an adult is asked to recall an event from the past, he formulates a picture in his mind about the event. This type of memory, known as *iconic* memory, is one of the first types of memory to develop. For most people, their earliest memory in life is some event—a still picture in their minds. Yet prior to iconic memory, children have a *conditioned* memory. This memory, which is more primitive, creates an affective response in the individual. It is impossible for the child to "recall" these memories in the same way adults recall iconic memories. More likely, one's memory will appear as affect—pleasant or unpleasant—when confronted with people, places, or circumstances related to those memories. The memory is, in a way, exhibited by the response to the stimulus. Cameron never spoke about his molestation. I do not believe he remembered it in iconic form. Yet it was clear to me that he was aware of the molestation in a conditioned form. I am sure that Cameron was forced to engage in oral intercourse with the adult male who molested him because numerous times in his play, he created phallic symbols and forced dolls or stuffed animals to "eat" or "taste" the phallic symbol. Sometimes he would even force himself to put an object in his mouth, telling me the whole time how he didn't want it in there.

One of the toys in my therapy toy box is a little plastic doll with its head divided in half at the mouth and hinged at the back. The doll originally contained candy, but I keep it in my toy box because the hinged head allows children to hide things inside it—something many kids like to do. One day as Cameron and I were playing on the floor together, he had the plastic doll in one hand. In the other, he had taken a long Tinkertoy rod and he had slipped an orange ring over the end of it at the base. Even though I had seen him construct a number of phallic symbols, I was surprised at how much this simple toy looked like an erect penis. Cameron opened the hinged head of the toy in his left hand. The look on his face changed from a playful face to an angry, determined face. He took the Tinkertoy "penis" and crammed it inside the mouth of the plastic toy, making guttural sounds, almost a growl, as he did it. Several times he withdrew the object only to cram it into the toy's mouth again.

"He doesn't want it in his mouth," Cameron told me, "but he has to taste it."

This behavior was clearly abreaction. He was reliving the event and until we resolved this part of his past, he would not be finished with therapy.

Cameron also made regular use of a tiny plastic figure of a bridegroom that was in my toy box. The little man was no more than half of an inch tall. Every time Cameron came into my office he would go directly to the toy box and hunt for that little man. Once he found the man, he would completely bury it in Play Dough. He never played with the lump of Play Dough after the man was buried, rather he would set it aside, leaving the buried man alone during our session. At the end of our sessions, he always begged me to leave the man buried until he came back the next time, but one of my rules in therapy is that the playroom will be returned to normal after a session so that the next child will have access to all toys. Therefore, Cameron re-buried the man every session.

I believed that burying the man was Cameron's way of protecting himself. The man represented the perpetrator for Cameron. With the man safely hidden, incapacitated inside a sarcophagus of clay, Cameron knew where he was until he could figure out what else to do with him. Testing my theory, I asked Cameron if he thought the man could get out of the Play Dough. Considering this possibility troubled him, but only for a moment. "No way. He is stuck. I won't let him out!" Cameron said.

"What if someone lets him out?" I asked.

"I won't let them," Cameron said.

He would not allow for the possibility that the man could escape. I was certain that during treatment I would have to teach him to deal with the possibility that the man could get out. Cameron's perpetrator was never arrested or tried for the crime against him; therefore, he was free to roam around the world. Cameron's play showed me that he was aware that his perpetrator roamed freely, even if he could not describe his abuse in words. His therapy had to address the subconscious issues that drove his dysfunctional reaction to his molestation and his fear of being a victim again.

As we made progress in therapy, I occasionally suggested that we let the man out. Initially, he would agree to allow only the man's hat to be exposed. Eventually, he allowed the man's head to be exposed and later his torso, although he never let the man be fully free from the Play Dough. Once, as the toy's little plastic eyes watched us during our play, we talked about the man and what he was thinking.

"I wonder what the man is thinking as he watches us play," I said to Cameron.

Cameron stopped and thought for a moment. He looked at the man as a person might look at a dog one was not yet sure was friendly or not and told me that the man was "thinking mean thoughts."

At this point I was able to begin to help Cameron take control of his life. We worked on how to deal with men who were thinking "mean thoughts." We were able to talk about how men with "mean thoughts" made children feel and how to deal with those feelings.

After weeks of therapy, Cameron had made great progress. Cameron, like most of the kids I see, often asked if he could take a toy home that he had played with during therapy. I only allow that when our work is done; as a sort of graduation present, I let children pick one toy to keep. I felt like we had made progress one day when Cameron asked if he could take the man home.

"But what if he thinks mean thoughts?" I asked Cameron, feigning concern.

"I'm not afraid of the man. I can handle him," he told me.

I wish I could say that Cameron's story had a happy ending, but I cannot be certain that it does. When his symptoms began to disappear, his mother began missing appointments. Eventually, she stopped bringing him to therapy. About two years after our last appointment, I received a call from another parent who knew that I had seen Cameron. Cameron was her son's playmate and Cameron had attempted to fondle him. She was concerned both about her own son and about Cameron. That was the last time I had any information on this child. If his mother had not disengaged from therapy and allowed us to finish, I do not think Cameron would have been a risk to any child. As it is, I can only speculate about his future and, unfortunately, I fear further difficulties lay ahead for him.

LESLIE

The therapist has to be aware of how particular symptoms might mimic the symptoms of sexually or physically abused children, but may actually be a sign of something else altogether. A woman called and told me that she and her husband had divorced two years earlier and they were in the process of a court battle over custody of their five-year-old daughter, Leslie. "I'm hoping that my daughter hasn't been molested," Emily told me on the phone, "but she is doing some things that make me wonder." I asked Emily to describe some of the behaviors she had seen in her daughter. Among them were vocabulary words that most five-year-old children do not know. In the middle of other conversations, Leslie also had randomly brought up the need for "protecting her privates" with her mother. Even though a physical examination with a pediatrician had not provided any evidence of abuse, I conceded that sexual abuse was a possibility. I requested that Emily, her ex-husband, and Leslie—all three—come in for an appointment. After several telephone conversations and negotiation of an appointment time, they agreed.

During our first session, Leslie showed no aversion whatsoever to her father. She played freely with him on the floor and the two interacted with ease. I found it interesting that Emily chose not to participate in the child's play; rather she took an observer's role in a chair across the room.

During that first hour, I saw absolutely no symptoms of any sexual abuse. Toward the end of that hour, I looked at Emily and asked, "Has any adult that is a regular part of this child's life ever been molested or raped?" Emily's mouth dropped open and her eyes swelled with tears. Obviously, I had hit a nerve. I asked Leslie and her dad to continue playing in an adjacent room for a while so that I could talk with Emily. Over the next several minutes, Emily confessed that she had been molested as a child and twice in her adult life she had been raped. She asked me how I knew. During my evaluation of Leslie, I asked myself why a child who seemingly had not been molested might have presented the symptoms of molestation that Emily had observed at home. I concluded that either the mother was totally fabricating the conversations with her child or someone in the child's life had discussed sexual issues with her. When I asked myself why someone would sensitize such a young child about sexual issues, I concluded that it would be someone who had been sexually assaulted or mistreated. Her history might logically make her oversensitive to such issues and want to protect this defenseless five-year-old from the fate she herself had endured. My hunch was correct.

I saw Leslie two more times to ensure that my initial assessment was correct and subsequent sessions were mirror images of the first. Over time, the relationship between Emily and her ex-husband worsened and the custody battle over Leslie escalated. Despite the pediatrician's report and my evaluation, Emily lodged a formal accusation of sexual abuse with the Department of Family and Children's Services against her ex-husband. Leslie was removed from his home and for the next several months he was allowed no contact with her while the investigation was under way. During these months, Emily chose to take the child to another psychologist who told her the child *had* been molested. Yet consistent with the pediatrician's findings and my own, the investigation by family services produced no evidence of abuse. Leslie was returned to her father's custody and, as the custody dispute continued, the court ordered the family into family counseling. They all chose to return to my office and I worked with them over the next several months. Evidence of sexual abuse continued to be absent from Leslie's play and behavior.

After the court released the family from therapy, I continued to see one or more of the family members over the next several years. Fortunately, the relationship between Emily and her ex-husband improved dramatically and they established an amicable relationship with regard to their daughter. Leslie was provided with a safe home and the hard work that both her mother and father invested in their parenting skills paid off. During all these years, Leslie never showed any signs of abuse and Emily admitted to me that the psychologist who had diagnosed the alleged abuse was "flakey" (to use her term) in many ways and that is why she had elected to return to therapy with me. She openly questioned the woman's competence. Privately, so did I.

SURVIVAL STORIES

Stories of resilience and survival encourage me. They demonstrate the strength, resources, and resolve that some children have, despite the horrifying situations that they are sometimes forced to endure. Travis Butler and Midsi Sanchez are children whose fortitude is a model for the rest of us. Travis Butler was a nine-year-old fourth grader in 1999. He and his mother, Crystal Wells, age thirty, shared a small apartment in Memphis, Tennessee. They were very private people, keeping to themselves since Travis's father had died. Acquaintances even described Crystal as distrusting of people and a loner. On November 3, 1999, Crystal fell in the living room and died from what was later determined to be a tumor in her lungs. Travis had inherited her distrust of people, but also her sense of self-sufficiency. He feared he would be sent to an orphanage if his mother's death were discovered so he covered her body with a coat and covered her face with notebook paper. For the next thirty-three days, he lived on his own, his mother's body lying where it had fallen in the living room. He went to school on time, signed his mother's name to his papers and report cards, shopped with money he found in the house, cut his own hair, and washed and ironed his own clothes. When anyone inquired about his mother, he said she was unavailable. Crystal was unemployed so she was not missed at work and the rent was paid through the end of November, so no landlord came knocking.

Finally, at the first of December, Dorothy and Nathaniel Jeffries, friends of Crystal and Travis, came by to check on her. Travis told the Jeffries that his mother was at work and he wouldn't let them in, but they realized something was wrong. Pressuring him for more information, Travis finally allowed them in the apartment, saying his mother was sick and he thought she might be dead. They found her body on the floor in the living room, still covered with paper and a coat. Travis begged the Jeffries not to tell anyone and tried to convince them that he could take care of himself.[14] The Jeffries, in turn, convinced him that they had no choice but to call the authorities, which they did.

Travis spent that night in a shelter, but the next day he went to live with his maternal grandparents. "Grandmother, it feels so good being in your arms," Travis told his grandmother, undoubtedly relieved to know his fears of an orphanage were unjustified.[15] In August 2000, the court awarded temporary custody of Travis to the Jeffries. The reason for the court's decision to remove Travis from a blood relative and award temporary custody to a family friend was not made public. The Jeffries said that during the entire ordeal the only time Travis seemed frightened was when police arrived at the apartment, but even then he maintained his composure, telling Mrs. Jeffries, "Don't worry. It'll be all right."[16] As of the publication of this book, Travis continues to live with the Jeffries.

On Thursday, August 10, 2000, eight-year-old Midsi Sanchez was walking the five blocks home from school in Vallejo, California. Halfway home, a man pulled his car alongside her and dragged her inside. When she failed to return home, police were notified and within a day, missing child posters were printed and distributed. Volunteers arrived at the Sanchez home to help search for Midsi. One of them was a thirty-nine-year-old man named Curtis Dean Anderson. He told Mrs. Sanchez that he wanted to help. She had seen the same man the day of the kidnapping loitering on a street corner near her home smoking a cigarette. It was Anderson who would later be arrested and charged with Midsi's disappearance. In fact, Anderson had only been out of prison for a month after being convicted of kidnapping a woman in 1991.

Anderson kept Midsi shackled in the front seat of his car Thursday, Friday, and Saturday, allegedly assaulting her during this period of time. On Friday when she was left alone in the car, she tried to pick the lock on the shackles with a fingernail file, but was unsuccessful. Anderson drove to Santa Clara, a town seventy miles southwest of Vallejo, and parked his vehicle in the parking lot at American Networking, a luggage-delivery company where he had once worked. Around 11:00 A.M. on Saturday, Anderson went inside the business to talk with Thomas Flores, a friend who was working there at the time. He told Flores he needed some money and also asked him for a plastic bag. Flores looked around and came up with $2 to help Anderson.

While Anderson was inside, Midsi fumbled through the key ring that he had left in the car until she found the key that opened the locks that confined her. Freeing herself, she ran from the vehicle. Anderson saw her through the window of the business and scrambled after her. Midsi ran barefoot down the street screaming that she had been kidnapped as Anderson raced after her demanding that she come back. Flores saw the unfolding events and also gave chase to the child, but Midsi feared he was an accomplice. Just then, truck driver Carl Tafua was coming down the street. Midsi ran to the truck and launched herself through the window of the cab, landing in Tafua's lap. When she identified herself and said she had been kidnapped, Tafua recognized her from the media coverage.

Seeing that Midsi had reached safety, Anderson returned to American Networking, but before he could flee the scene, Tafua noted his license plate number, which he later gave to police. A few hours later, police arrested Anderson in a trailer park and charged him with kidnapping, aggravated sexual assault on a minor, rape, and two other related charges. Investigators also examined the possibility that Anderson was involved in other unsolved child disappearances in the area.

At home, her family was notified of her miraculous escape and joyfully they went up and down the street and wrote "FOUND" on the missing child posters.[17] On Saturday night, over a hundred friends and family members celebrated Midsi's return as well as her eighth birthday, a party that had already been scheduled.

Flores later told reporters that he believed that his delay in giving Anderson the $2 gave Midsi the needed minutes to escape.[18] Relatively unharmed, Midsi was reportedly doing fine and expected to return to school the following Monday.[19]

Children like Travis and Midsi are a testament to the survival instincts children possess. A therapist's job is to harness those instincts in the process of helping a child recover from trauma. Showing them how their courage, fortitude, and quick thinking saved their lives can be tools of encouragement that can prompt healing.

CONCLUDING REMARKS

I have loved working with children therapeutically since my very first experience with children in the early 1980s. Over the years it has become obvious to me that the sooner treatment begins, the better one's prognosis. Rarely have I treated adults who were traumatized as children who also were treated at that time. More often, my adult clients experienced abuse, rape, or some other trauma and never dealt with it effectively. Then, ten, twenty, thirty, or even more years later, they come to therapy having experienced lifelong difficulties in relationships and self-esteem that can be directly traced to their victimization in childhood. These many years later

I not only have to treat the results of the trauma, but also a lifelong dysfunctional pattern of behavior. Habits are hard to break and even dysfunctional behaviors are often preferred over functional ones simply because they are known and comfortable.

In Gwinnett County, Georgia, a county in the Atlanta metropolitan area, the solicitor's office has begun a program where therapists travel to a home with the police who are called on domestic violence calls. These therapists provide on-the-spot crisis intervention for children who are abused and/or who are being removed from the home. This frontline treatment can ease the transition for the children and begin the process of healing almost immediately.

Children need to be taught that if they are victimized, it is not their fault. They need to know that they will not be in trouble and that perpetrators count on children's fear of being in trouble to keep them quiet. The child's environment should be structured so that he or she knows that an adult will always be willing to listen and help. Exposure and training in situations that involve trust with police officers, social workers, teachers, and other adults in the child's environment can foster this belief. When a child sees that these people are on her side, she will be more likely to seek help from these adults. Adults also need to learn how to listen to children and to create an environment that fosters trust.

I will never run out of clients. Perpetrators abound. In fact, at the time of Midsi Sanchez's abduction there were two hundred registered sex offenders living in Vallejo alone.[20] Countless are the individuals who mistreat, sexually abuse, inappropriately discipline, neglect, and otherwise prey on children. The best that those of us who are therapists can hope for is to keep pace with the need. Educating the public on issues related to child maltreatment and protection is the first step in prevention.

NOTES

1. Bernard Kerik, *The lost son: A life in pursuit of justice* (New York: Regan Books, 2001), p. 3.

2. "Girl stays overnight with dead mother after teacher ignores her story," *CNN On-Line*, www.cnn.com/1999/US/12/14/dead.mother.ap/index.html, December 14, 1999.

3. Hunter Downing Alessi, "Memory development in children: Implications for children as witnesses in situations of possible abuse," *Journal of Counseling & Development* (Internet Edition), *79*, 2001.

4. Ibid.

5. This material is unpublished, but credited to Byron Norton, Greeley, Colorado.

6. Ibid.

7. Kendall Anderson and Mark Wrolstad, "Normal life within victims' grasp despite childhood trauma of abuse," *Dallas Morning News*, www.dallasnews.com /metro/stories/395128_nuresilient_16.html, January 28, 2002.

8. "Understanding special family situations," *National Clearinghouse on Child Abuse and Neglect Information,* Washington, DC, www.calib.com/nccanch/pubs /usermanuals/crisis/family.cfm, April 6, 2001.

9. Reuben Vaisman-Tzachor, "Could family dog bites raise suspicions of child abuse?" *The Forensic Examiner* (September/October 2001): 19.

10. Ibid.

11. "Understanding crisis," National Clearinghouse on Child Abuse and Neglect Information, Washington, DC, www.calib.com/nccanch/pubs/usermanuals /crisis/crisis.cfm, April 6, 2001.

12. "Understanding special family situations."

13. Ibid.

14. "9-year-old who lived with mother's corpse says final goodbyes to her," *CNN On-Line,* www.cnn.com/1999/US/12/14/boy.with.corpse.ap/, December 8, 1999.

15. Ibid.

16. Ibid.

17. Marsha Ginsburg, "Daring escape by stolen girl," *The San Francisco Examiner,* www.sfgate.com/cgi-bin/article.cgi?file=examiner/archive/2000/08/13 /NEWS1416.dtl, August 13, 2000.

18. Don Frances, "Witness to narrow escape: 'My eyes caught the girl right there,'" *InsideBayArea.com,* www.insidebayarea.com/news/abduction/ArticleTemp .asp?Name=abduct03, August 20, 2000.

19. Ginsburg, "Daring escape by stolen girl."

20. Ibid.

PART II

Fallen Angels

The first half of this book addressed violence against children, but it is an unfortunate reality that children are not always victims. In fact, children have perpetrated some of the coldest crimes I have ever seen. A few of these children were raised in good homes with loving parents, but a consistent theme in most cases is one of severe abuse or neglect. These children were sexually mistreated, even in infancy, or their most basic needs were unmet. They were forced to live in filth without the normal nurturance one usually receives from caregivers. As babies, some of these children were beaten when they cried or soiled a diaper. They learned that they could not trust other human beings and that the only way to survive was to care for oneself.

Other children I will describe in the coming chapters were mistreated in ways that were much more difficult for people outside the family to observe. They were emotionally abused, ignored, or mistreated. Their parents created dysfunctional egos in these children—they used words like "stupid," "ugly," and "idiot" as building blocks. Some of these children were rejected by parents, often for traits that were beyond their control or traits that the parents themselves created. For example, the father of one of my female clients was a man who used women and was sexually promiscuous. He regularly made sexual comments about women, even in sessions with me. Yet he accused his very attractive daughter of promiscuity and sensual behaviors. He modeled the value of female sexuality through his words and deeds and his daughter had learned the value of women from him, yet when she exhibited the behaviors that she thought he valued, he criticized and humiliated her.

Other parents fail to discipline their children appropriately, catering to their whims; as a result, they create selfish and self-absorbed children who believe they can do whatever they want with impunity and that the world is in some way indebted to them. Even after these children's arrests for violent crimes, parents stand behind these children, pointing fingers of blame in every direction except at themselves.

For some reason, cultures worldwide have assumed that the ability to procreate gives one the necessary qualifications to be a parent. Obviously, this is not the case. Even devoted and well-intentioned parents recognize the many difficulties in raising children and adequately meeting their needs. Western culture places great emphasis on the rights of parents to raise their children as they see fit, but invests little energy in forcing those parents to be accountable for their actions when it comes to child rearing. Most of the children you will read about in the coming chapters have been mistreated, neglected, and abused. Part of their abuse includes lack of structure and discipline. Their dysfunctional behaviors, both internalized and externalized, are the by-products of their environments. In short, you reap what you sow.

It is not my desire to excuse the actions of aggressive or troubled children. Rather, my intent is to demonstrate that these children are created, not born. They are the products of careless parents and a society that produces ample rhetoric, but minimal effort in the advocacy, protection, and development of children. When the monotone voice of news reporters fills our living rooms with ghastly stories of crimes committed by children, our mouths fall open and we shake our heads. "Some kids are just evil," we may mistakenly say. Yet careful inspection of the lives of these children makes it clear that behavior always—always—occurs in a context. These children should be held accountable for their crimes, but the system should recognize that the response to their actions must go beyond punishment. Their rehabilitation and treatment should include therapy that addresses the social contexts from which they come. Otherwise, if these children are ever released from hospitals or prison, they will continue to pose a threat to society and to themselves.

As you scan these paragraphs, I can almost hear heads shaking. "What about all the kids who are abused who turn out fine?" you may say aloud. You may wonder how I can make excuses for them, but I am not making excuses and I have addressed resilience in the previous chapter. I am only stating the obvious—that no behavior exists in a vacuum. The fact that children differentially respond to their environments should be of no surprise, but regardless of the debate, the fact is we have a culture of violent children who demand our attention. In the following chapters I will demonstrate how these behaviors develop and how they can be treated.

CHAPTER 6

Bullies

All cruelty springs from weakness.

—Seneca, 4 B.C.–A.D. 65

I believe there is no one principle which predominates in human nature so much in every stage of life, from the cradle to the grave, in males and females, old and young, black and white, rich and poor, high and low, as this passion for superiority.

—John Adams, *John Adams*, by David McCullough

I sit in the classroom at my desk. The teacher is talking about history, or math, or perhaps something else. I don't know because her words are foggy echoes in the background of my mind. Instead, my mind is focused on the large round wall clock, each revolution of its sweeping second hand draws ever nearer the close of the school day. Yet unlike most of the other students for whom the closing bell signals freedom, I fear it. I want the school day to last eternally, for it is here, in the classroom, that I am safe. When I step beyond the doorway of my classroom, even if just to the bathroom or the playground, I am defenseless and alone. I know that just beyond the schoolyard someone is waiting for me. In my mind I can hear his laughter from previous days as he teased, threatened, and tormented me. My face flushes and sweat beads on my forehead even at the memory of my humiliation before my friends. I am no match for him. He is far bigger, stronger, and meaner than I will ever be.

"Stand up to him," people have told me, but fear paralyzes me when I even think of taking a stand. I wish I could be invisible—on the playground, in the cafeteria, and especially on the walk home. I would gladly trade having friends for the safety of anonymity. I have to walk right past his house on my way home. My teacher once tried to protect me by asking me to stay a few minutes with her after school, but she unknowingly robbed me of my best defense—my speed. I could outrun him if I could see him coming, but on that day, he waited for me just one block away from the school. His smug expression let me know that no teacher could protect me from him and that I would never be beyond his reach.

It was a daily ritual these last few minutes of school as my mind raced trying to think of a way to protect myself and make it home safely. On a good day, I avoided him altogether. He picked on someone else or just wasn't interested in me. I hoped for that each day. On a bad day, it seemed like he looked for any reason to say that I provoked him. If I looked away, he said I was ignoring him, but if I looked at him he said I was staring—anything that gave him an excuse to challenge me to fight. If I tried to be nice, I was a "pansy," but I didn't dare act tough—it would only ensure he would take that as a challenge and he knew that in a fistfight, he could easily defeat me.

As the minute hand approaches 2:30 P.M., I realize that I don't remember how many days this has gone on, but to me, only eight years old, it seems like a lifetime and I can't imagine it ever ending. I think of running away, leaving my family that I love, just so that I can be free from him. The bell rings. I have to leave. I have to face him yet again.

These are the thoughts of a frightened third grader—a child who was victimized not only by this bully, but also by several others throughout most of his elementary, middle, and high school years. These words are very real to me because I was this child. From the third grade until the last semester of my senior year, I was bullied. In junior high school we had a piranha in a fish tank in our science classroom. Once a week we fed it a live fish. When the fish was dropped into the tank, it momentarily floated very still, its large round eyes roaming here and there. It looked to me as helpless as I felt every day at the close of school and I knew that this fish surely was aware that danger was near, but it also knew it was completely alone and no one was coming to its rescue. Even now, more than thirty years later, I can clearly remember how frightened I was and, illogical as it is to me now, how I feared for my life. I was small, unsure of myself, and vulnerable. Bullying sometimes leads to serious physical injury or death, but more often its scars are unseen—wounds that are indelibly etched in the minds and on the hearts of victims. This chapter addresses both the bully and the victim, why children bully other children, and how adults can intervene in the lives of children to protect them from fear, injury, and even death.

THE PSYCHOLOGY OF BULLYING

I have always been a fan of Sigmund Freud. Nearly every theory in contemporary psychology has borrowed from his work or in some cases practically plagiarized it, simply changing the jargon. Even though theoretically I tend to lean in an eclectic direction, Freud's work clearly permeates my theoretical approach to psychology and therapy. In this book I have addressed the significance of sexuality, an idea that began with Freud, and in previous books I have written extensively about his view of psychological defenses and how they contribute to dysfunctional behavior as well as to my own theories about aggression. His influence on me is obvious to anyone who knows psychology. In fact, one of my psychologist friends at the Behavioral Science Unit at the FBI Academy observed after hearing my lecture, "This is all so Freudian, but you never had to say it." When my students hear me talk about Freud, they mistakenly suppose that I agree with *everything* Freud said. Of course I don't. Freud's theory was based in large part on his own dysfunctions, his theory almost exclusively addresses males to the neglect of females, his theory says almost nothing about development after puberty, and I disagree with his sweeping views of religion as a dysfunctional coping strategy. Yet parts of his theory are helpful to me in many ways. Most pertinent to this chapter are Freud's ideas concerning egoism. I do not believe that there is any such thing as an egotist, at least as we commonly use the term, and I believe that true egoists, as Freud described them, are very rare.

In our everyday language, we use the term *egotist* to refer to someone who is arrogant, but that idea is not consistent with Freud's concept of the ego. Freud believed that personality is divided into three parts. The *id* is the basic, self-seeking, me-first part of our personality. The id operates on what Freud called the *pleasure principle*. In short, the pleasure principle says, "If it feels good, do it." A baby's personality is almost exclusively id. Babies are only interested in their own needs to the exclusion of anyone else's needs, feelings, or interests. They are incapable of feeling guilt because they have not yet developed that component of their personalities. The component that allows us to feel guilt is called the *superego*. This component begins to develop around age two. The superego is an antagonist to the id. Its message to the person is, "Don't do it, especially if it feels good." The term *conscience* is somewhat synonymous with the superego. It tells us what not to do and suppresses our desires. Therefore, in each of us, there is an id that is trying to force us to pursue our desires and a superego that is trying to force us to set our desires aside.

Fortunately, there is a moderator between these two warring factions. The *ego* is the parent that steps between these two other pieces of one's personality and, ideally, balances them. The ego operates on what Freud called the *reality principle*. Even though I could spend the next fifty pages discussing the meaning of reality, for the sake of argument, the reality principle sees the facts as they are. In other words, while the id is screaming, "Do it, do it!" and the superego in its puritanical self-righteousness is saying, "Stop, stop!," the ego looks at the pros and cons of a situation and makes a reasonable decision. For example, every day as I drive home from my office in Atlanta, I pass a Corvette store. They always have both new and classic Corvettes on display along the curb. As I drive by, my id nudges me and says, "Cool! Buy one!" My superego automatically responds by telling me, "Of course you can't buy a Corvette. Don't be irresponsible!" If it wasn't for the ego, whichever of these other two components was the loudest at any given time would win. My ego weighs all the facts. I am a family man, I have three children and financial obligations, yet I make a decent living and I could buy one if I wanted. As this subconscious process takes place each day, my ego convinces me that it would not be a good idea to spend $50,000 or more on a car that I don't really need now, but maybe I'll buy it some other time later in life. I can assure you that my wife is thankful for my ego's conclusion each day.

It is a balance of these three pieces of our personality that helps us function productively. Sometimes it is OK to play—to let the id win. Other times, such as when a married person eyes someone who is attractive and considers flirting, it is probably a good idea to let the superego win. Yet in our day-to-day lives, in order to maintain our obligations and keep our lives in order, the ego has to take a leading role. Dysfunction in personality occurs when any of these three components gains control to the exclusion of the others. An adolescent or adult whose id is out of control would be very selfish and self-seeking. Likewise, an adolescent or adult whose superego is out of control would be depressed and feel guilty all the time. At its extreme, an out-of-control superego would lead a person to punish himself either by withdrawal of all pleasure or by self-infliction of pain. I will address this issue in more detail in Chapter 8.

With this understanding, one can see that an ego that is out of control— an egoist—would create a very confident person. The egoist would not be swayed by guilt or primitive desires and would always pursue the logical conclusion. Mr. Spock from the *Star Trek* television series would be the most obvious example of someone without a functioning id or superego. Therefore, an egoist, or an egotist as we more often say, is not arrogant, but rather confident. My argument, I suppose, is not actually with Freud's concept, but with the way we use the term. I do not believe that most people whom we call egotists are confident at all. In fact, just the opposite is true. Let us consider the motive for an egotist's behavior. An egotist, as the term is commonly used, is one who is a braggart, but why would someone brag about himself? What purpose does bragging serve? If the person were truly an egoist by Freudian standards, the person would be confident; therefore, bragging would be unnecessary. You may have noticed that the most stable and confident people that you know rarely, if ever, have the need to garner recognition from others and they almost never talk about themselves or their accomplishments unless goaded to do so. Even then, they almost seem embarrassed to do so.

The braggart, on the other hand, is not confident, but insecure. In fact, she is so insecure that she won't wait for someone else to compliment her on what she does well. She does it herself. Someone once said that it isn't bragging if you can do it, but I disagree. The arrogant individual who says, "Look at what I can do," is, in a sense, saying, "Aren't I OK? I can do this or that." Her insecurity— not her confidence—drives her to brag. Children do this all the time and we usually recognize it for the insecurity that it is. For example, just as I did when I was a lad, when my son was younger he would say, "Dad, watch what I can do." He then would jump, do a cartwheel, or count to twenty. He sought to prove his value to me. Not only did he want to hear, "I'm impressed with what you did," but more importantly he wanted to hear, "I love you and I'm impressed with *you*."

This digression into basic Freudian theory has a purpose here. We must consider the motives of someone who derives pleasure from harming others. Taking Freudian theory even further than his three-part theory of personality, I believe that most dysfunctional behaviors that do not have a physiological cause (e.g., some forms of depression, ADHD, and other disorders that are based in neurophysiology) are defensive. Supposing this is true, the question then is from what is such a person defending himself? We must discover what it is that threatens him to such an extent that he believes that striking out at others will protect him. What bullies fear is intimacy. To allow oneself to be intimate is to be vulnerable and to be vulnerable means one must risk being hurt. Some theorists contend that bullies do not have weak egos. For example, one expert wrote, "Contrary to popular belief, bullies tend to have high self-esteem and report ease in making friends."[1] Yet this appears to be completely contradictory to the theory, not to mention the fact that many people with low self-esteem are well liked by others. A bully may be well liked, but still be insecure.

Ideally, a healthy individual has a few close friends and relationships. People with a strong ego care what other people think about them, but they are selective about who those people are—they give away power discriminatingly. If an acquaintance makes a rude or insulting remark to the person with the strong ego, assuming it is not someone with whom the person has a close relationship, the person will not allow the comment to hurt him. Instead of thinking how hurtful the comment was, this individual will wonder what the other person's problem was that would lead to such a comment. A true egoist would be unconcerned about the general opinions of others—yet another reason an egoist would not be a braggart. Because a person with a strong ego is confident, he is willing to risk vulnerability. He will engage in relationships and open himself up to others. A bully, on the other hand, cares about what *everyone* thinks. Any person is a threat that must be put in his or her place. Unlike the healthy person who has a few close friendships, a bully is indiscriminate when it comes to ceding power; thus, anyone who says something even unintentionally threatening or hurtful to the bully must be subdued. Because of his insecurity, the bully wishes to dominate others, he craves social prestige, and he is insensitive to the feelings of others.[2]

Bullies, like many other types of perpetrators, count on the victim's sub-mission. Using intimidation and threats, they bluff their victims into sub-mission. Of course, some bullies will live up to their threats, but many times, without the cooperation of the victim, the insecure bully could not continue his behavior. It is based on this truth that fathers often tell their children they will be bullied until they stand up for themselves—a very easy adage to share, but a difficult one to practice. One of my teammates when I played ninth-grade football was a bully. He picked on me once or twice, but his attentions were spread among many other students. He wasn't any larger than I was, but I was afraid of him nonetheless. One day he and one of his minions confronted me on the athletic field, out of sight of our coaches. I decided I was going to take a stand. I put up my tiny lit-tle fists and said, "OK, come on." I remember he laughed and made a com-ment to his friend that he feared he would hurt me so he walked away. Many years later I ran into him at a party. We talked about that day I stood up to him, a day he remembered, and he told me that he couldn't believe that I had stood up to him. When I did that, I stole his power and he didn't know what to do.

The bullying behavior of some children is isolated. They pick on a child or a group for a few days or weeks and then either tire of bullying or guilt changes their behavior. Chronic bullies, however, have many victims. They are aggressive toward teachers, parents, siblings, and peers alike, attempting to dominate people in all their environments.[3] Bullies usually dislike school, have poor impulse control, crave social prestige, and are insensitive to feelings of others.[4] Because of their insensitivity, bullies often justify their behavior by saying that their victims asked for the tor-ment that they received.[5] They blame others for their problems and their coping skills are ineffective and dysfunctional. Chronic bullies typically exhibit a host of other problems as well. They may also lie, steal, run away from home, torture animals, vandalize property, smoke, drink, use drugs, engage in sexual behavior, and engage in reckless behavior.[6] Unfortu-nately, bullying behavior doesn't abate with age. One study demonstrated that bullying behaviors remained stable with age.[7] In other words, once a bully, always a bully. Unfortunately, the problem of bullying, both episodic bullying and chronic bullying, is pervasive.

THE SCOPE OF THE PROBLEM

It would be my educated guess that most of the readers of this book have memories of bullies in their respective pasts. Not only was I the vic-tim of bullies, but many other adults have written about their experiences as victims during their childhoods. For example, widely acclaimed writer Frank Peretti, author of *The Oath* and *This Present Darkness*, describes his miserable childhood suffered at the hands of bullies in his book *The*

Wounded Spirit. In this volume, stories are told of rejection and torment and the long-term psychological scars these experiences left on the hearts of men and women.[8] Research on the problem of bullying is consistent. All the data on school bullying demonstrate that a minimum of 10–16 percent of schoolchildren in the United States are bullied each year. Some studies show an even higher percentage.

The problem of bullying is well known to students in our schools. A survey of 823 middle and high school young people indicated that almost 74 percent of kids eight to eleven years old and 86 percent of kids twelve to fifteen years old said bullying occurred at their school and they ranked bullying as a bigger problem than racism, AIDS, or the pressure to try sex, alcohol, or drugs.[9] In the United States and abroad, bullying has been directly linked to a number of school shootings and homicides, and bullying has been linked to many suicides worldwide. Bullying is not tied to socioeconomic status or geography. It occurs equally in rural, suburban, and urban school systems. And it isn't only a U.S. problem. Bullying has been studied in many countries and researchers have found that the percentage of children bullied each year is consistent with the numbers in the United States. In Australia 17 percent are bullied, in England 19 percent, in Japan 15 percent, in Norway 14 percent, and in Spain 17 percent.[10] In France, the problem is significant enough that students are required to buy "bully insurance" at a cost of about $7 per year that covers medical costs for injuries as well as restitution for damaged or stolen textbooks or personal property.

Bullying involves one or more of three types of behaviors—*physical* bullying, *verbal* bullying, and *psychological* bullying. (The U.S. Department of Education includes a fourth category, labeled *sexual* bullying, but I will not address peer sexual bullying in this chapter because it is rare among grade school and middle school children.)[11] Physical bullying involves hitting, beatings, spitting, kicking, pushing, pinching, stealing belongings, cruel tricks (like locking a victim in a closet), knocking food off one's cafeteria tray, and other related behaviors. Verbal bullying involves repeated teasing, name-calling, taunting, and threatening behaviors. Psychological bullying, the type of bullying most often perpetrated by female bullies, involves lying, blackmail, humiliation, social exclusion, passing mean notes, betraying a confidence for the purpose of emotional injury, and malicious gossip.

Name-calling or physical altercations alone do not qualify as bullying. The behavior must be repeated and regular. As one victim described his experience, being teased once is hard, but manageable—being bullied every day "starts to make you crazy."[12] Victims must also perceive themselves to be weaker than the bully, although this can be either a real or perceived imbalance of strength—called an *asymmetric power relationship.*[13] Even though bullying exists across all age groups, the research demonstrates that it is most prevalent between the second and eighth grades. A study by the National Institute of Child Health and Human Development (NICHD) narrows that margin, stating that most bullying occurs between the sixth and eighth grades.[14]

In a fascinating study conducted in Germany and Great Britain over a two-year period, researches interviewed 2,377 children in English primary schools and 1,538 in German primary schools. The results of their study demonstrated that boys were more often perpetrators and that most bullies were also victims—what they called bully/victims.[15] These researchers found no significant differences based on socioeconomic status, that males are victims more often than females, and that girls are more often pure victims as opposed to bully/victims. In this study, about 50 percent of the subjects were either "frequently" or "very frequently" victims of bullies and about 15 percent said they were "frequently" or "very frequently" bullies themselves.

Bullies exist in many places but, by far, most bullying behavior occurs at school, specifically on the playground and in the classroom. Most likely this is due to the fact that most other environments are voluntarily attended by children. If they encounter bullies, they withdraw from that activity or environment, but at school, the child is forced each day to share space with a tormentor.

Peretti describes some bullies as the "cool kid" who thinks that it is cool to push other kids around.[16] Because this type of bully is popular, other children encourage the bullying, teasing, and taunting, especially when the victim is a loner or a friendless child. Even this type of bully, however, is driven by a weak ego—the need to prove something to the victim and/or observers. One child who went to my middle school was unattractive, lonely, and had very bad dental hygiene. Her name was Crystal and most of the time people left her alone, but I recall standing idly by as one of the "jocks," a popular kid in the eighth grade, made fun of her. He teased her about her haircut, her clothes, her awkwardness—it didn't matter. Whenever he felt like teasing her, he would find something to pick on. I never laughed at his jibing, but regretfully I never defended Crystal, either. Not only did I not want to be associated with her because of my own weak ego, I didn't want to risk trading my "popular" friends for Crystal.

Even though I believe that all bullies are driven by similar psychological needs, not all bullies are mean to the core. Because bullies are insensitive to the feelings of others, some just do not consider how deeply they wound their victims. One former bully said, "I didn't really think she [the victim] took the insults to heart because she never really said anything."[17] Other bullies, after their victims have committed suicide, expressed similar remorse for their thoughtlessness and callous behavior.

Victims of bullies experience humiliation, fear, anxiety, and emotional pain. In some cases they endure beatings, bloody noses, and broken bones. At its extreme, bullying behavior leads to death. In 1997, Reena Virk became one such victim when she was beaten twice and then drowned by eight of her peers—all female except one.

REENA VIRK

Reena Virk was a manipulative and emotionally troubled young woman. At fourteen, the ninth-grade student in Saanich, British Columbia, a suburb of just over 100,000 people on the outskirts of Victoria, had spent several months in a foster home. She had accused her father of sexually abusing her, a charge she later recanted, and she fought with her parents over many things, including her desire to smoke cigarettes. The Indo-Canadian teen stood only 5-feet-8-inches tall, but she weighed nearly two hundred pounds. Her weight, her minority race, and her emotional troubles made her the butt of teasing and bullying by her peers.

On Friday, November 14, 1997, the same day she returned home from foster care, Reena received a call inviting her to hang out with some of her classmates and their friends. She called home from a Wal-Mart, a regular teen hangout, saying she would be home by 10:00 P.M. It was the last time her family ever heard her voice. Reena and fifteen acquaintances eventually ended up at the Craigflower Bridge. Two members of group there that night were seventeen-year-old Kelly Ellard and sixteen-year-old Warren Glowatski. The group walked down the stairs from the bridge to a walkway that ran under the bridge. There, the real intentions of the invitation were made clear. Some of the girls accused Reena of spreading rumors about them and another accused her of trying to steal her boyfriend. Then the girls attacked, punching, kicking, and scratching Reena. Some of the girls threw matches at Reena, trying to ignite her hair and another girl stubbed a cigarette out in Reena's forehead. Reena fell down the stairs, but Kelly Ellard pushed her back into the fray. Virk alternately swore at the teens and then begged for them to help, but when no one ventured to help, she pleaded with them to leave her alone. Again, no one offered to help her and when it was clear she was injured, no one used their cell phone to call police or an ambulance. Instead, the group of eighth, ninth, and tenth graders passively watched, cheered on the others, or participated in beating Virk themselves. Finally, Virk fell into the water and it appeared the mob was through with her.

Dazed and bloodied, Virk must have assumed that the beating was over as she staggered up the steps and across the bridge toward a bus stop where she was going to catch a ride home. However, Ellard and Glowatski followed her. Some witnesses said that the pair only followed to make sure she was OK. Others, however, testified that they were only pretending to help her. Their real intentions, they said, were to make sure Virk would not "rat" on them. Apparently, Virk yelled at Ellard and

Glowatski and the two attacked Reena a second time. This time they pummeled her for fifteen minutes. They kicked her in the head, smashed her head into a tree, punched her throat, and attempted to break her arms. As they dragged the severely injured girl toward the river, her pants being dragged down around her ankles, they rolled her into the water and drowned her.

Some accounts say that Glowatski told Ellard to stop and that it was Ellard's decision to drown Virk, while other testimony said it was Glowatski's idea to "finish her off." When the pair pushed Reena into the river, one witness said that Ellard, who only weighed 114 pounds, smoked a cigarette while she held Virk's head under water with her foot for several minutes. "She made it as if it was a joke, like 'Oops, I forgot to take my foot off,'" said a witness.[18]

After Virk was beaten and drowned, the group split up, two of the girls taking Reena's bag. They divvied up her possessions between them and tossed the bag into the river. A sixteen-year-old witness said that he saw Ellard and Glowatski later that night and they told him that they thought they had killed Virk. The next day, Ellard called a friend who later testified that Ellard "Seemed happy...like she was proud of what she did."[19] Ellard and another teen went past the crime scene the next day. Ellard told her what happened and showed her a stick that she had used to hit Virk in the face. Other young people also testified that they heard Ellard bragging about the attack as well, even a week later.

Eight days later on November 22, police divers found Virk's half-nude body just over a half mile from the bridge, after which Saanich police interviewed many of the teens from that night, including Ellard. Initially, Ellard said she knew nothing about the incident, but then as the pressure of the interrogation got to her, she admitted her role. A judge would later disallow the audiotape of Ellard's interview with police because he said she did not understand her rights at the time. As the events of the evening unfolded in the minds of investigators, Ellard and Glowatski were charged with second-degree murder and six other girls were charged with assault with the intent of causing bodily harm.

Glowatski came from a troubled home. His mother was an alcoholic and he had an absentee father, but this brought no sympathy from the court, where he could have been tried as a juvenile. Instead, he was tried as an adult. At his trial, he blamed Ellard, saying he wanted to help Virk, but Ellard had egged him on. In fact, some of the people there that night, including Glowatski, had never even met Virk and had little motive to attack her. He testified that he helped Ellard drag Virk to the river, but he said he "didn't know she was going to die."[20] One must wonder what exactly he had hoped to achieve in brutalizing the defenseless girl. He was convicted of second-degree murder and sentenced to life in prison with a minimum of seven years in prison before parole. Prior to sentencing, the judge asked if he wanted to make a statement to Virk's family. He refused to make any statement or apology. When he had the opportunity to show compassion to the family, he refused.

The six other teens were each also convicted and given prison sentences ranging from sixty days to a year. Finally, more than two years after the murder, Ellard's case came to trial. After her arrest, Ellard spent four months in a youth detention facility before she was released to her mother. She spent the next two years under house arrest until the time of her trial.

At her trial, witnesses testified that Ellard planned all along to lure Virk to the river to beat her up, but when she took the stand in her own defense, she denied having done anything to Virk except for throwing a few punches. Even though he had blamed Ellard in his own trial, Glowatski refused to testify against her at Ellard's trial. "I refuse to testify. Being called here has put my life in jeopardy," he told the court.[21] Glowatski was referring to the treatment that prisoners receive from other inmates when they testify against someone in court. I think it is ironic that Glowatski was apparently afraid he would be bullied. He was later convicted of contempt of court and sentenced to an additional year in prison. Bullies thumb their noses at any authority who attempts to control their behavior. Glowatski's refusal to testify or even be sworn in when he was subpoenaed to testify against Ellard demonstrated his contempt for the legal system and, at the very least, provided evidence that he was unremorseful for his actions.

Powerful testimony at Ellard's trial came from a pathologist who said that Virk's injuries were more consistent with a bad automobile accident than a fight. Her liver, pancreas, and bowel were bruised and torn, she was burned, she had a bruise in the shape of a shoe print on the side of her face, and her brain was swelling prior to her drowning. The pathologist testified that she believed that Virk would have died even if she had not been drowned.

Adrian Brooks, Ellard's attorney, questioned the testimony that placed all the blame on Ellard. He said that all of the teens had reason to lie and that the convoluted, inconsistent, and contradictory testimony that appeared to typify this case was evidence enough to exonerate Ellard. However, the jury was not swayed. After three days of deliberation, on March 31, 2000, the jury returned a guilty verdict. She was given a mandatory life sentence with a minimum of five years in prison before any chance of parole.

As I studied this case, Ellard's character appeared clear to me. She was a bully who showed little remorse for her victim. While being interviewed by police, instead of showing remorse for her heinous actions, she callously told them that she heard that Reena "got her butt kicked" and almost blamed Virk when she said Reena must have been drunk because she "couldn't defend herself very well."[22] Even if she had been totally innocent of any wrongdoing or participation in the crime, one would think that a person would show more respect and compassion than this for a child who had been brutally murdered. Apparently unaware that interrogators were still listening to her when she and her mother were alone in the room, she said, "I swear, I'm going to beat up everyone who said that stuff [about her involvement]. I swear I'm going to kill them."[23] Yet despite this attitude, her mother and her attorney maintained that her daughter wasn't a violent girl.

One psychological report said that it was "difficult to assess Ellard's true attitude toward Virk's death since she admits only to throwing a couple of punches during the first attack."[24] Reality didn't seem to settle on Ellard until the jury returned their verdict. When the verdict was read, her mouth dropped open and she began to cry. In March 2002, Ellard appealed her conviction. In February 2003, a Canadian court overturned her conviction stating that Ellard did not receive a fair trial. She will be retried for the crime. Glowatski also appealed his conviction, but he lost. The Virk family sued Ellard, Glowatski, and a host of others including the Victoria school board. This civil case has yet to go to trial.

VICTIMS AND THEIR RESPONSE

It is estimated that 25 percent of all school children are victimized by a bully at some time during their school career. The victims of bullies are often small, weak, and defenseless individuals compared to their age cohorts. They are usually males, often loners, less confident and less popular, and they may look different from their peers because of race, manner of dress, or some physical handicap. Anything that makes someone stand out from the crowd makes the person a potential target—speech problems, unusual hair, glasses, braces, not wearing the popular brand-name clothing, or living in the "wrong" place. Since some victims are already insecure and vulnerable, they make easy targets. Bullies can pick on them at will with no risk of retaliation.

Some school shooters have blamed bullying for their violent behavior. They were picked on to the point that they decided they wouldn't take it anymore. All victims of bullying experience shame, guilt, remorse, revenge, anger, and hate. By themselves, each of these emotions are very powerful, but when they are experienced together, they create a volatile mix if the individual does not have adequate coping resources. Some victims become bullies themselves, assuming offense as a defense.

Because of the lack of confidence and depression that is common among victims, they often do not know what to do about the treatment they are receiving. Studies show that even though most bullying happens at school, these children rarely, if ever, go to a teacher for help and only about 50 percent of these victims go to a parent for help.[25]

There are few studies on the range of effects of bullying, but there is evidence of physical and psychological effects. Some studies indicate that almost 10 percent of schoolchildren miss one day of class per month because of bullying and just over 40 percent of the schoolchildren studied fear harassment in the bathroom at school. They are subject to injury, depression, low self-esteem, and anxiety. In the long term, the effects of bullying include depression, low self-esteem, and behavior problems.[26]

Bullycide is the word that has been used to describe children who commit suicide because of bullies. In the United Kingdom, suicide because of bullying behavior is a serious problem. It is reported that sixteen children each year in the UK are victims of bullycide.[27] Dawn-Marie Wesley, a victim of bullycide, was a child who decided suicide was the only way she could escape the bullies who threatened her.

DAWN-MARIE WESLEY

Bullies rarely kill their victims. More often, victims choose to take their own lives to escape their tormentors. Dawn-Marie Wesley, a fourteen-year-old middle school girl living in Abbotsford, British Columbia, was one such person. She and a group of her friends had a falling-out and her friends began to torment her. They harassed her with telephone calls and threats telling her they would kill her, and she endured at least one beating at the hands of one of the girls. The girls, two years older than Dawn-Marie, believed that Dawn-Marie had been spreading untrue rumors about them, and they were exacting their revenge by terrorizing her. Dawn-Marie kept her anguish to herself, believing that confiding in an adult would bring no relief. In November 2000, the telephone rang at her home. One last time, the call was for her. "You're f—ing dead," the caller told her as she and two others taunted Wesley over the phone.[28]

After hanging up the phone, Dawn-Marie drafted a letter to her parents. In it, she described the torture she had endured at the hands of these girls, naming the three of them. She couldn't tell her parents, she said in her note, because it wouldn't have made any difference. "There would be no stopping them," she explained.[29] She went on to explain that she believed that death was the only way to escape from the bullies who were tormenting her. "If I ratted to get help," she wrote in her note, "it will get worse and there would be no stopping them."[30] Dawn-Marie went to her bedroom and there she hung herself with a dog leash. Her body was discovered by her younger brother.

Using the suicide note, authorities investigating Dawn-Marie's death arrested the three girls named in the note and charged one of them with criminal harassment and uttering threats; the two others were charged with uttering threats. The trial of the first girl ended with a conviction on both counts. The maximum sentence she could have received was six months in prison and two years on probation. One of the teens charged with uttering threats was acquitted. Cindy Wesley, Dawn-Marie's mother, was pleased with this decision. She told reporters that she believed the other girls were also victims of the first girl's bullying behavior.[31] The trial of the third girl has not yet been completed.

TREATMENT AND PREVENTION

Effective interventions address the bully's behavior, as well as victims and their response to the bullying, and try to prevent bullying to begin with. Suggested interventions with bullies are varied. They run a continuum from "no blame" policies that advocate teamwork projects and reconciliation programs to arresting and incarcerating bullies. One county in Minnesota in 2001, in fact, has jailed a dozen or more bullies since instituting a policy that is tough on bullies ages thirteen and older.[32] Other interventions include community service, counseling, or writing an apology to the victim.[33] The main ingredient in all interventions, however, is adult involvement. When it comes to bullying behaviors, to expect children to monitor themselves and solve their own differences is naïve.

In educational circles, a host of consultants specializing in addressing and preventing bullying behavior have entered the job market. Some of these consultants have their own programs and others take advantage of one of the several hundred antibullying programs available. Most of these programs stress the need for all members of the school organization—teachers, administrators, coaches, bus drivers, and custodians—to learn how to spot bullying behavior and how most effectively to intervene. These programs are pursued voluntarily by the various states and school systems that wish to address the problem of bullying but, in some places, programs like these are mandated by the state. For example, in part because of the Columbine shooting in 2000, the Colorado state legislature mandated that every school in Colorado have a program to reduce bullying by the end of 2001. Kentucky, Florida, Massachusetts, and California have launched antibullying initiatives.[34] Other states, like my home state of Georgia, address bullying through programs emphasizing character development.

Regardless of one's choice of intervention, both victims and bullies need help. Many bullies are unaware of the forces that drive their behavior and they have little notion of the impact their behavior has on others. Victims do not know how to cope with their fear, anxiety, and insecurity. Interventions should include participation from the parents, school, and, possibly, a counselor. Whether victims or bullies, children must take responsibility for coping with and changing their ineffective or dysfunctional behaviors into effective and productive ones.

What Parents Can Do

A parent should be willing to believe his or her child when accusations of bullying are made and the parent should take the threat seriously. Numerous deaths have occurred around the country as a result of bullying. Some of these deaths have been due to bullying behavior, as was the case with Reena Virk. Other deaths have been due to bullycide. Yet some victims also attempt to resolve the bullying problem by killing their tormentors, as was the case for a fifteen-year-old boy in Michigan in 1978. He brought a gun to school to protect himself from two boys who regularly tormented him. That day, as they picked on him in front of his locker, he pulled out the gun and shot both of them, killing one and wounding the other. In extreme cases, these victims target whole groups of students, as has been the case in several school shootings.

If you suspect that your child is being bullied, ask him about it. Check your child's e-mail for evidence of bullying. It is a good idea to monitor a child's e-mail anyway, at least until the child is in middle or high school, and e-mail is an easy avenue for bullies to channel their threats and intimidation. Teach your child to tell an adult if he/she is a victim and report bullying to school authorities. Bullies count on the silence of their victims. "It must have had something to do with the devious power of the old maxim that has protected bullies for generations," writes Frank Peretti. "You don't snitch."[35] Remember, it is likely that your child is not the only victim of the bully and intervention on your child's behalf may also help other victims. Likewise, there is a 50/50 chance that if your child is bullied long enough, he will become a bully himself. Some experts suggest that if the child does not want you, the parent, to contact the school and intervene on his or her behalf, that you should respect that wish. One should balance respect for a child's wishes and need for parental intervention with the perceived level of threat. If it is clear that the child, his or her classmates, or others are at high risk of injury because of the bully, the parent should intervene regardless of the child's wishes, but if the threat is low, respecting the child's wishes for you to stay out of it is acceptable.[36]

Parents should model appropriate behavior for their children. For example, one bully that I dealt with picked on almost every child in his class at one time or another, including the girls. It was later discovered that his mother had been arrested for beating up neighborhood women and his father had been arrested for beating up his workmates. With such a family of origin, it should be no surprise that this young man dealt with his frustrations with his fists.

Parents of victims wonder about calling the bully's parent. At one time this was an effective strategy, but this no longer has much effect. Bullies, as is true with many children these days, are often unsupervised at home because the parent or parents are working. Likewise, if they are abused by their parents already, not an uncommon issue with bullies, calling and reporting the bullying may only increase abuse and, in turn, create an angrier and more vindictive bully. A mediator such as a teacher or a school administrator is usually more effective.[37] Experts remind us that parents view criticism of their kids as criticism of their parenting; therefore, one should choose words carefully, be open-minded, talk about the relationship between the children, and recognize that your child may be contributing to the problem as well.[38]

The adage "Sticks and stones may break my bones, but words will never hurt me" is a myth. Words are harmful and wound deeply. Many people carry emotional scars from careless and hurtful words that are as real as physical scars. Even when these painful words are uttered by people who love us—our spouses, parents, children, or friends—and are quickly followed by apologies, their effects may continue causing pain for years to come. Words intended to sting, delivered by mean people bent on leaving mayhem in their wakes, are potentially even more hurtful and permanent. On the one hand, learning to cope with aggressive individuals, mean words, and hurt feelings is a skill that children need to learn. In fact, many former victims say that being bullied in childhood actually helped them to develop strengths they found advantageous later in life. Research confirms this belief: Several studies have shown that victims, in the long run, fare better than bullies. While many bullies end up in prison, victims learn to cope.[39] However, the parent must effectively distinguish between the normal, day-to-day arguing, "stares," and verbal confrontations that characterize many childhood interactions, and actual bullying. In the case of normal childhood disagreements and arguments, the parent should teach the child how to cope. However, if the child is being bullied, other interventions may be necessary, along with the teaching of coping strategies. For example, telling a child to avoid or "stay out of the way" of a person with whom he/she is having difficulty getting along is a good coping strategy. However, with bullying, saying, "Just stay out of his way" is oversimplifying a difficult situation and doesn't work. Many victims, like me, have discovered that any attempt to stay out of the bully's way just makes the bully more determined to pursue the victim.

Talk to your children about bullying, how to avoid becoming a bully, and how to deal with bullying behavior. In a study conducted by the Kaiser Family Foundation and International Communications Research (ICR), about half of the children surveyed said they wanted and needed more information on bullying. Approximately 80 percent of the 1,249 parents in the survey said they talked to their kids about teasing and bullying, but only about half the kids remembered those conversations.[40] Therefore, parents should not assume that if this topic, or any other topic for that matter, has been addressed once, that it is sufficient.

Be alert for symptoms that your child is being bullied. These symptoms include crying frequently, withdrawing, self-destructive behavior, faking illness in order to avoid going to school, or other excuses to avoid school. Low self-esteem, avoiding certain situations or people, behavior changes, fear when asked about certain situations/people/places, injuries, lowered grades, and unexplained physical symptoms are also signs that bullying is occurring.[41]

Finally, parents should consider the possibility that their child is a bully. In a survey conducted by the Oak Harbor Washington Police Department, 89 percent of local high school students said they had engaged in bullying behavior yet only 18 percent of parents whose children attended the high school thought their children would act as bullies.[42] If your child is a bully, be willing to admit it and seek help for him or her through the school system or a counselor.

What Teachers/School Administrators Can Do

All of us can reduce bullying behavior by treating children with respect. Bullies who don't believe they have been respected are more likely to be aggressive, and children who are outcasts, friendless, and loners, may be more apt to seek help or stand up for themselves if they are respected. Teachers can also teach children to respect one another and they can model respect in how they treat and talk about their students, colleagues, family members, and friends. Teachers and administrators should not challenge a bully in front of others. Humiliation will only antagonize the aggressive child. However, the administrator/teacher should act immediately upon awareness of bullying. This demonstrates to bullies that their behavior will not be tolerated and also demonstrates to victims as well as observers that they will be protected.

Mentoring programs can help both bullies and victims/potential victims. These programs provide modeling of productive behavior, they can teach healthy coping strategies, and they serve as a resource to which victims can turn for help. The Virginia Youth Violence Project is a program designed to address many forms of violence in the school and it has mentoring as a component.[43]

Antibullying programs designed for schools should include training for everyone in school, including janitors, cafeteria workers, teachers, and administrators. They should be trained to recognize bullying and to know what to do when they see it. Open discussions with children about bullying—what it is, how to avoid or cope with bullying—and programs to teach coping skills can help school systems to control bullying behavior. Schools should have a formal policy for dealing with bullies and bullying behaviors. These response plans should include clear, punitive responses to bullying behavior and, at the least, they should teach children to tell an adult if he/she is a victim. Unfortunately, these programs cost money, and funding them at a time when most school systems are cutting their budgets is difficult.

As I mentioned for parents, avoid oversimplifying the situation by telling children to simply avoid the bully. If a child really needs help, a thoughtless remark like this only convinces the child further that he is alone and will not be protected. Also, avoid blaming the victim. Telling a child he must stand up for himself puts the responsibility for the situation back on the child and does not help a child deal with the problem. If it were so simple, there would be very few victims of bullies. In fact, this type of response can easily place the child in a catch-22. If he doesn't stand up for himself, he remains a victim, but if he does, he risks suspension or other punitive consequences because most schools these days have zero-tolerance policies for violent behavior—not to mention his risk of physical injury. Finally, teachers and administrators should refer both bullies and victims to a counselor when bullying situations arise.

Court decisions have demonstrated that the law does not currently hold the school accountable for controlling or preventing bullying behavior. In North Carolina, the state supreme court concluded that the school was not required to protect a boy from harm by classmates.[44] Yet school administrators should not allow decisions like these to excuse their inaction in creating a reasonable environment and protecting defenseless children when they have the power to do so.

What Counselors Can Do

Therapists have a number of treatment tools available that are used to treat bullying behavior. Most therapies involve teaching self-control to bullies. Attention deficit/hyperactivity disorder (ADHD) often occurs in tandem with bullying; therefore, these children will have compounded difficulty with self-control. Bullies do not always realize how their behavior hurts their victims. Treatments that teach these children to understand the perspective of others is also helpful. Group therapy is a treatment that is almost always more effective than individual therapy. However, with bullies, group therapy does not work. The children apparently feed one another's antagonistic behavior and are disruptive.[45] Therapy should be limited to one-on-one sessions.

Role-playing and modeling of appropriate behavior, teaching victims and bullies coping strategies, and teaching bullies self-control are all important interventions. Counselors may also participate in the development of mentoring programs within the school.

Intake evaluations should include a check for generalized anxiety disorders, conduct disorder, dysthymia, and depression in both victims and bullies.[46] Critical in victims is development of efficacy and self-esteem.

Other interventions specifically for bullies include teaching the bully productive use of his strengths, behavior therapy, and loss of privilege when needed.[47]

Educating children about bullying and teaching them to tell an adult if they are victims is important. One author encourages the "walk, talk, and squawk" method. *Walk*, don't run, away from the bully when you can; *talk* to the bully and try to reason and respect him or her; and, finally, *tell* somebody about your situation if you need help.[48]

What Children/Victims Can Do

Teaching children to take responsibility when it is appropriate and possible is an important part of learning how to cope with life's problems. As I have already discussed, children should be taught to respect others. A respectful child is less likely to become a bully. Teach children to include in their activities children who don't fit in—those who are different, less popular, or shy. Being included in a group raises self-esteem and lessens the likelihood that a child will become a victim. Encourage children to talk to their parents about bullying. As research mentioned in this chapter suggests, many children want to talk about bullying with their parents. Encourage them to take the initiative in addressing the subject with their parents. If they need help, children should be told that it is acceptable to seek help. Some psychologists suggest that writing a note to a parent or teacher is easier than talking face-to-face. Finally, students should refuse to participate in teasing, refuse to laugh at cruel jokes or tricks, condemn bullying when they see it happening to others, and defend the victim. There is power in numbers.

CONCLUDING REMARKS

This chapter has provided information on bullying, but the reader should understand that the motives for bullying behavior vary by environment. For example, bullying behavior in gangs or in prison settings is very different than that which is described in this chapter. In those environments, demonstrating that one is tough is a survival technique and is driven by other psychological needs. Likewise, I have not even begun to address bullies in the adult world. Some of you reading this book are currently victims of bullies at work, on the athletic field, or at the community center. There are also adult bullies who are so needy and insecure that they pick on children. I once observed a grown man who was a fellow counselor at a summer camp for children spend much of the week bossing his charges, teasing them, and taking their belongings. Several times I stepped in to protect the children in his "care," but I'm sure for every time I intervened, he successfully pushed around the dozen or so middle school children in his group. This book addresses children in the general population, not those in specific environments like prisons, camps, or detention centers, and I have purposefully omitted discussion of adult bullies. Important as they are, these issues will have to wait for another book.

In this chapter, I've also shared several stories of my own life as a victim. To say that I have recovered from those brutal days would be incorrect. These memories still pain me, and I had no trouble recalling my mental images of those days as I wrote this chapter. But one would be correct in saying that I have overcome those days. I do not have bad dreams or anxiety attacks remembering those bullies and I no longer feel anger toward them. Many of the bullies who picked on me have probably grown up to be fine people, but statistics are against that. One study that tracked highly aggressive boys from age eight until age thirty found that one in every eight had a criminal record by age thirty, while the incidence of criminal records among boys in general is only one in twenty.[49] (Frank Peretti says that bullies either turn their lives around, end up in prison, or end up working for the department of motor vehicles.)[50]

When I was a high school student, I was a volunteer student assistant for a physical education teacher. Each day I spent an hour in his office grading papers, organizing material, or putting away equipment. One day while I was in the gymnasium, two boys confronted me. They accused me of telling on them for using the weight room without supervision. Both of these boys were much bigger than I was, even though they were two years younger. I denied that I knew anything about what they had done, although I would have turned them in if I had known about their actions. For the rest of my senior year, these two boys tormented me. They followed me down the hallways, they threatened me, and, on at least two or three occasions, they struck me. I was able to avoid an all-out fight with either of them, but my last year of high school was miserable. I dreaded going into the building and I feared that these two young men would eventually force me into a physical altercation. One day the boys backed me into a corner in the hallway between classes. Classmates stood around, drooling at the prospect of bloodshed. Because I didn't know what else to do, I asked the ringleader of the two why I was such a threat to him. Neither boy answered and they let me go, but apparently I remained a threat for many months. Two years after I graduated, I was driving down a rural highway near my old high school. One of these two guys was hitchhiking and I passed him by. I recognized him immediately and he apparently recognized me. He shouted obscenities at me and made an obscene gesture that I saw in my rearview mirror. Apparently, in keeping with statistics, he still had not grown beyond his bullying behavior. Thankfully, I had. I'm a doctor and they are both probably still hitchhiking their way through life.

I don't know what became of the bullies in my past, but I wish only good things for them. What I could not see in those days was the fact that the pain they caused me was probably insignificant in comparison to the pain they endured themselves because of neglect or abuse. I fear they grew up to be very lonely people. In fact, the incidence of depression among bullies is almost as high as it is among victims.[51] Hopefully, with greater awareness of the problem of bullying, not only can victims be spared the pain and humiliation of being bullied, but bullying behavior can be seriously addressed, thus saving bullies from the negative outcomes of their own behaviors as well.

NOTES

1. Erica Weir, "The health impact of bullying," *Canadian Medical Association Journal, 165* (October 30, 2001): 1249.

2. Ibid.

3. Ibid.

4. Ibid.

5. "Bullies and their victims," *Harvard Mental Health Letter* (Internet Edition), *18,* November 2001.

6. Ibid.

7. Dieter Wolke, Sarah Woods, Katherine Stanford, and Henrike Schulz, "Bullying and victimization of primary school children in England and Germany: Prevalence and school factors," *British Journal of Psychology* (Internet Edition), *92,* November 2001.

8. Frank Peretti, *The Wounded Spirit* (Nashville, TN: Word Publishing, 2000).

9. "Talking with kids about tough issues: A national survey of parents and kids," Kaiser Family Foundation/Nickelodeon/Children Now (Menlo Park, CA: Kaiser Family Foundation, 2001).

10. Weir, "The health impact of bullying," p. 1249.

11. "Preventing bullying: A manual for schools and communities," U.S. Department of Education, www.cde.ca.gov/spbranch/ssp/bullymanual.htm, November 3, 1998.

12. Denise Rinaldo, "What's a bully?" *Scholastic Choices* (Internet Edition), *17,* October 2001.

13. Wolke et al., "Bullying and victimization."

14. "Study reveals bullying in U.S. schools widespread," *Professional Safety, 46* (July 2001): 41.

15. Wolke et al., "Bullying and victimization."

16. Peretti, *The Wounded Spirit*, p. 5.

17. "A bully apologizes," *Scholastic Choices, 17* (October 2001): 14.

18. Dene Moore, "Accused teen killer acted like death was a joke: Friend," *Canadian Press*, acmi.canoe.ca/CNEWSLaw0003/15_virk11.html, March 15, 2000.

19. Ibid.

20. Dene Moore, "Virk killer in B.C. court to face contempt charges," *Canadian Press*, acmi.canoe.ca/CNEWSLaw0006/19_virk11.html, March 22, 2002.

21. Ibid.

22. Dene Moore, "Teen killer didn't understand her rights: Judge," *Canadian Press*, acmi.canoe.ca/CNEWSLaw0004/04_virk11.html, April 4, 2000.

23. Ibid.

24. Dene Moore, "Ellard sentenced to five years," *Canadian Press,* acmi.canoe .ca/CNEWSLaw0004/20_virk11.html, April 20, 2000.

25. "Bullies and their victims."

26. Brian Pace, "Bullying," *Journal of the American Medical Association, 285* (April 25, 2001): patient page.

27. Neil Marr and Tim Field, *Bullycide: Death at playtime* (London: Success Unlimited, 2000), "Books by Success Unlimited," www.successunlimited.co.uk /books/bullycid.htm, March 25, 2002.

28. Kim Honey, "Everyday war zone," *The Globe and Mail,* www.theglobeandmail .com/servlet/ArticleNews/printarticle/gam/20020330/FCCOVE, March 30, 2002.

29. Ibid.

30. "Bullies," *The National,* cbc.ca/national/news/bully/, March 13, 2001.

31. "B.C. girl convicted in school bullying tragedy," *CBC News,* www.cbc.ca /stories/2002/03/25/wesley020325, March 26, 2002.

32. "New plan to put bullies behind bars," *Christian Science Monitor* (February 26, 2002): 64.

33. Ibid.

34. Marjorie Coeyman, "Schools still working to rein in bullies," *Christian Science Monitor* (December 4, 2001): 14.

35. Peretti, p. 135.

36. For information on risk factors for violent behavior, see Gregory K. Moffatt, *Blind-Sided: Homicide Where It Is Least Expected* (Westport, CT: Praeger, 2000).

37. Jeffrey Zaslow, "Tough kids, tough calls," *Time* (Internet Edition), April 22, 2002.

38. Ibid.

39. "Bullies and their victims."

40. "Talking with kids about tough issues."

41. Pace, patient page.

42. Zaslow.

43. "Virginia youth violence project," Curry School of Education (Charlottesville: University of Virginia, 2002).

44. Coeyman, p. 14.

45. "Bullies and their victims."

46. Weir, p. 1249.

47. "Bullies and their victims."

48. Weir, p. 1249.

49. "Bullies and their victims."

50. Peretti, p. 141.

51. "Bullies and their victims."

CHAPTER 7

The Child Murderer

We don't know the days that will change our lives.
—Stephen King, *Dreamcatcher*

Often when people find out what I do for a living, they tell me how fascinated they are by homicide, why it happens, and especially the investigative aspect of homicide. Nearly every time I speak to any group about homicide, its motives or a related topic, at least one or two people from the audience approach me afterward and express interest in the field of forensic psychology. They want to know what kind of training it takes and how to get into this career field. I answer their questions, but I also explain to them that this field is not for everyone.

"Oh, blood and stuff like that doesn't bother me at all," they say, trying to convince me that they have the stomach for the job.

But they fail to realize that the most painful issues related to homicide are psychological ones, not physical ones. Not many people can handle the gruesome nature of homicide. A dead body, even in a funeral home, is more than some people can handle. To do the work that I do, one has to be able to coexist with the sights, sounds, and smells related to death. The first time I observed an autopsy was at a Veterans' Administration hospital. The patient died of complications related to alcoholism, not homicide, but he was certainly an adequate training tool for our group of fledgling psychologists interested in learning more about the anatomy of the brain. The group of observers of which I was a part numbered about a dozen. The pathologist told us we could either sit in the gallery overlooking the sterile surgical room where the autopsy was to be performed or, he said, we could stand with him at the table. Two others and I stayed on the floor and the rest went to the gallery. The nervous silence of the autopsy room prior to even seeing the body was too much for one student, who left before we ever got started. When the body was brought into the room, the smell of chemicals was powerful. Two others left the gallery for the fresh air outside the building. The sight of bloodless incisions, yellow-fatty material oozing outward from the body, ill-fitting skin pulled back to reveal the inner workings of the man, the sound of the bone-cutting saw, and the crunching of the snips used to clip ribs was enough to finish off most of our group. By the time the physician began moving the circular saw around the cranium to expose the brain, the reason we had come in the first place, only two of us remained. By the end of the autopsy, one classmate and I stood alone with the pathologist as he dissected the brain and made observations about its convolutions, the enlarged ventricles and corpus callosum due to long-term alcohol abuse, and other aspects of brain geography that were pertinent to the examination. Indeed, it takes an especially strong stomach to do this work.

But for me the most difficult part of homicide is pondering what the victims were thinking and experiencing at the time of their deaths. Were they calm or were they so terrified that their hearts nearly exploded in their chests? Were they in pain? Did they beg their attackers for mercy or did they fight back? These are the images that haunt me and these are the thoughts that I hear when I am examining a dead body. My anxiety is increased even more when victims are children. Hard as I try to avoid it, their small, lifeless bodies can't help but make me think of my own three children and how I would do anything to spare them a similar fate. Knowing all that I know about the evil of the world makes me want to clutch my children tightly to my breast and smother them with protection, a foolish response, but nonetheless difficult to resist.

People who want to pursue the field of forensic psychology can never know how these images and voices can prey on one's mind until they experience it for themselves. This work is not a game, a movie, or a novel. The victims will not get up from their morbid poses, ready for another performance. Their unclaimed bodies may lie in storage areas in morgues for weeks until they are identified and claimed. Others will be buried by weeping relatives who blame themselves for the child's death and through their tears they long to trade places with the deceased. They bargain with God to give them one last hug from their babies, to get one last soft kiss from the child's lips, but their wishes are never granted. Their houses are filled with memories of the child, as well as the child's death, now permanently wedded with thoughts of the child. Memories confront them at every turn—a teddy bear, a blanket, and even the silence of the evening, no longer filled with giggling. They would gladly even accept the noise of fighting and complaining just to have the hands of time turned backwards. These are the psychological torments that are harder to deal with than the gruesomeness of flesh and bone.

Equally traumatic is the realization that one's own child is a murderer. Parents, who for one reason or another were unaware of their child's potential, are living their "normal" lives one minute and the next they sit in a visiting room in a jail, talking through Plexiglas to a child who should be running, riding a bike, or playing with friends. Instead of making phone calls confirming attendance at parties or renting prom dresses and tuxedos, they are on the telephone looking for a lawyer. Disrupted routines fill days and weeks to come with trips to the courthouse, the jail, the bail bondsman, or the attorney's office. Savings accounts are drained. Second mortgages are hastily arranged to pay for the child's defense. The telephone never stops ringing. Some callers are friends who want to help, but many callers are reporters hoping for an exclusive interview with the distraught parents of the youthful killer—reporters who will listen empathetically for their two-minute spot on the evening news, but whose true concern is the story, not the people involved in the story. They see the child who kills as "the killer," "the shooter," or "the perpetrator"—not as Timmy, John, Adam, or Steven—children with names, lives, and personal histories. Strangers call as well. They criticize and threaten the parents of the "monster" who killed, unable to see the child-killer as anything but a criminal.

These parents avoid watching the news, listening to the radio, or reading the newspaper. Sensationalists in the media will run the story day and night until something better comes along. Salivating reporters who jump at the chance to spout overused sound bites and phrases will interview people who barely knew the family of the killer, anyone with even a remote self-proclaimed connection, and these subjects will speak with authority, telling vague half-truths that often are nothing more than hindsight or mere speculation. At night the parents lie in bed, staring at the ceiling for hours, wondering what they did wrong and how they could have avoided what happened. Eventually, the case will come to trial and the media circus will start again. Whether convicted or exonerated, the child perpetrator will never be the same and neither will his family ever be the same. Their hopes and dreams for their child to become an astronaut, a doctor, an inventor, or a teacher left their minds the day the county sheriff called them to come to the station—the day that their little boy committed murder. Their hopes now are reduced to the hope for a good night's sleep, the hope for a fair trial, an appeal, peace in prison, or maybe even parole. Nobody wins when children kill. We don't know the days that will change our lives, indeed.

My purpose in the preceding paragraphs is not to depress the reader, although I probably have. Instead, I want it to be perfectly clear that this is not glamorous work. When I'm introduced to someone at a party or an event and the introduction includes a brief biography about what I do, the response sometimes is, "Wow, that sounds really interesting." I can see it in their eyes that their understanding of my work comes from the sanitized, unrealistic version from crime shows on television and suspense novels rather than real life. My work is interesting in many ways, but anyone who really knows this field would never say that. Frankly, they would be more likely to express their condolences.

Children are capable of unbelievably gruesome acts. In Greensburg, Pennsylvania, in 2002, a fourteen-year-old boy bludgeoned his eighteen-year-old brother to death with a hammer. A second youth was also allegedly involved in that murder. Around midnight in December 2001, in suburban Atlanta, a seventeen-year-old boy and an eighteen-year-old boy took turns beating a nineteen-year-old male with a wooden baseball bat in a shopping center parking lot while several others looked on. The fatal beating began over an argument involving stolen stereo speakers. The youths were charged with murder. The murdered male had brought the bat to the parking lot to break up the argument between two groups of young men, but the bat was then used to kill him. The list of cases just like these two could go on and on. As you will see in the following chapter, violence by children is not limited to the United States. It happens in Canada, France, Germany, Japan—this is a problem that occurs worldwide.

Forensic psychologist David Ciampi says that "the ability to appear innocent, harmless and naïve due to one's youthful physical appearance" can make it difficult to identify potentially violent children.[1] He goes on to say that the natural human disinclination to take a human life has been gradually breaking down in our culture.[2] At a time when the overall rate of violent crime is declining, homicides by children are on the rise. This chapter will address murders committed by children and teens. Their victims are siblings, parents, classmates, teachers, and, in some cases, even strangers. Some of them kill deliberately and with clear motive, while the motives that drive others to kill are less clear. In any case, lives are lost and futures, hopes, and dreams are destroyed.

MURDER—A LAST RESORT

In my previous book, *A Violent Heart,* I discussed the development of aggression at great length and in the book before that, *Blind-Sided,* I made the case that by the time people actually commit murder, they usually have left very long and obvious trails of symptoms of their aggressive nature. Therefore, I will provide only a condensed version here regarding the issue. [If readers are interested in more information, I encourage them to pick up a copy of *A Violent Heart: Understanding Aggressive Individuals*[3] and *Blind-Sided: Homicide Where It Is Least Expected.*[4]] As a brief example of how a murderer develops a history of aggression, leaving clues to his potential sometimes years before he commits murder, consider the case of James Ruscitti, whose case I will address in more detail later in this chapter. At age three, he stabbed his stepbrother's puppy to death and later killed a stray cat near his home. He failed the eighth grade, charged his friends interest for loans, smoked marijuana, used cocaine, was expelled from school in the ninth grade for drug possession, and enjoyed tormenting a physically disabled child at his school, purposefully tripping him.[5] He was physically rough with his stepsister's children and was alleged to have suffocated his niece with a pillow, although she did not die.[6] As if these symptoms were not obvious enough, friends expressed concern about the safety of the family and James overtly talked about killing his parents a year before murdering them, asking his siblings, "What would you do if I killed Mom and Dad?" and laughing at their horrified reaction.[7] Far more often than not, the trail of symptoms of one's aggressive potential is clear, as it was in this case.

As I will explain in the chapter on suicide, killing of any kind—either killing oneself or killing another—is the last stop on a deviant path. Adults and children alike will try a number of other options first. They may deal with frustration by arguing, yelling, fighting, fleeing, or crying. However, the major difference between adults and children is that adults are more likely to select their responses from a deliberately ordered hierarchy of options. Children have only a limited number of resources and they pick from their list of options somewhat at random. Therefore, an adult may eventually strike out in anger, but only after trying other choices on one's mental hierarchy of options first—rational discussion, threats, or hateful words. Mentally healthy adults will rarely kill because they have a very long list of effective choices that precede killing. The dysfunctional, mentally unhealthy adult is more like a child. A child has a very short list of choices (i.e., hitting, yelling, telling an adult). In his passion, a mentally unstable child will select the first one that comes to mind.

The reasons that children commit murder are varied. Some kill for revenge against abusive parents, teachers, or peers who have angered them. Narcissistic reasons also motivate some murderers. They may seek fame, like the boys at Columbine, or possessions (i.e., tennis shoes, jewelry, or automobiles). They may also commit murder because of their affiliation with a group or gang. They may kill because of mental illness or because they are under the influence of drugs, and even others kill by accident, not realizing that their actions can lead to serious injury or death, as you will see in the case of Lionel Tate as well as in the murder of Kayla Rowland. Finally, other children kill purposefully, but because of their immaturity, they are incapable of understanding the ramifications of their actions. For example, in early 2002, a twenty-one-year-old college student placed pipe bombs in mailboxes across the Midwest, injuring several people. He said that using the locations of his bombings on the map, he was trying to make a smiley face. He seemed not to have been motivated by any malice toward his victims—only his juvenile desire to make a pretty picture on a map. In the following pages, I will provide cases where children have committed murder because of these various motives.

ANGER/REVENGE

Vengeance can be delivered by the youngest among us—even when one is too young to have any understanding of one's actions. Six-year-old Kayla Rowland was shot to death in her first-grade classroom. The perpetrator was not a family member, a thief, or a child molester. Her killer was a classmate who was only six years old.

On February 29, 2000, at the Buell Elementary School near Flint, Michigan, students were leaving the first-grade classroom on their way to the library. Most of the twenty-two students in the class were lined up in the hallway and their teacher was standing in the doorway supervising their passage. No one was aware that the one of the tots had stuffed a .32-caliber pistol into his pants before he came to school. He and Kayla had scuffled on the playground the previous day and the boy wanted to scare her with the gun that he found at home. As the remaining children prepared to leave for the library, the child pulled the gun and pointed it at a classmate. Then he turned and fired one round at Kayla. The bullet struck her in the neck.

When the shot rang out, one student thought a desk had fallen over but quickly students and teachers realized what had happened. The boy left the classroom and ran to a bathroom where he dropped the gun in a trashcan and then ran to the school office. Teachers pursuing the boy retrieved the gun from the trash as the principal's voice boomed over the PA system, notifying teachers to shut and lock their doors. In spite of their fear, most of the children were calm as the four hundred students, grades K–4, were evacuated to a church across the street.[8] Rescuers worked in vain to save the tiny girl. Sadly, she died at 10:29 A.M.

Police interviewed the boy, but because of his age, there was little they could do and he was released within a few hours. The school could do little as well. They suspended the boy for ninety days. The cry for justice would not be satisfied, however, as numerous charges were brought against his mother and several other men. The national media scrambled for interviews as a picture of the boy's home life began to unfold. His father, Dedric Owens, was in prison for a parole violation on drug and burglary charges. His mother had been evicted from her home because she had fallen behind on her rent, so she had sent her sons to live with her brother—a home she admitted in court was a drug house.[9] The white frame house, a car on blocks in the back and trash strewn about the yard, was occupied by several people and allegedly was a center for drug activity. The boy had been staying in the home for about two weeks before the shooting. While living there, the boy said that Jamelle James, nineteen, would twirl the gun in his hand and pretend to shoot people. James admitted that he would sometimes show off the gun around the house and pretend to shoot people, but said he never did it in front of the boy or his eight-year-old brother—he would just point it at people and play, he said.[10] The gun was kept in an open shoebox in a bedroom where any member of the house, including the children, could easily reach it. It was this gun, a stolen weapon probably seized in exchange for drugs, that was used to kill Kayla.

The boy's mother was charged with neglect and three other men, Jamelle James, Robert Lee Morris III, nineteen, and the boy's uncle Marcus Winfrey, twenty-two, were also charged with a variety of offenses, including contributing to the delinquency of a minor and firearms charges. The boy's grandmother was also charged with running a drug business.[11] After their various pleas, sentences ranging from six to twelve months in prison and fines up to $20,000 were levied.

This child had been aggressive before. He liked violent movies and television shows and he had been suspended for stabbing a girl with a pencil on one occasion, and also for fighting. The sheriff said Dedric Owens told him the boy fought with other children because "he hated them."[12] Several days before the shooting, Kayla's mother had talked with her about the problems she was having with the boy after Kayla told her mother that the boy had been picking on her.[13] Her mother told her to tell a teacher.

At one point the child denied that he shot Kayla, saying that he had given the gun to a friend who did it, but later he changed his story. Even so, it was clear that he did not appreciate the gravity of his actions. According to authorities, while being interviewed he drew pictures and he appeared to "take this as (something) that kind of happens on television."[14] The boy was placed in foster care and may eventually be returned to his parents. One positive result of the shooting was the launching of a mentoring program by Big Brothers/Big Sisters of Flint called Buell Buddies.

Even though many school shootings, like the one at Buell, have revenge or rage as a motive, most shooters are older. Robert Steinhaeuser was nineteen years old when he killed sixteen people at a high school in Erfurt, Germany, on April 2002, almost exactly four years after the shooting at Columbine. Erfurt is an old thirteenth-century cathedral town of about 200,000 people, two hundred miles south of Berlin in former East Germany—a town that was once home to Martin Luther. The Johann Gutenberg High School enrolls 750 students between the ages of ten and nineteen. For the students who were about to graduate, April 26 was not like other days. They had begun a testing process called the "Arbitur" that students are required to pass in order to graduate. Students did not look forward to this series of difficult tests and they sometimes studied for many months in preparation. Around 11:00 A.M., as students pored over the mathematics questions, the first section of the exam, they heard loud noises. Initially, they thought the noise was related to construction in the building until they saw a person dressed head to toe in black, including a black mask and gloves, carrying a shotgun and a pistol. As is often the case, even after seeing the assailant, several students commented that they thought it was a joke until they saw bodies in the hallways and classrooms.

Panic struck the students as they realized this was no joke. Police received their first call at 11:05 from a custodian who said, "Come quick. There is a shooting here."[15] Some students went into the corridor to get out of the building and saw a man with a gun behind them, but many of them fled into the schoolyard. They later told police that there was a second gunman who fled across the schoolyard with them, but police eventually discounted these reports.

Using a 9mm Glock pistol, Steinhaeuser carefully selected his victims, shooting almost all his victims at very close range. Many witnesses said he walked into a classroom, scanned the faces, and then either shot a specific person or walked out, leaving the occupants unharmed. One student made a call on her cellular telephone and said, "He shot a teacher one meter away from me and then just looked into my eyes."[16] In most mass shootings, whether at businesses or schools, perpetrators select a "victim" in advance of the shooting. The victim may be an individual, a group of individuals, or the site itself. If the chosen "victim" is the site, anyone the shooter comes across will be shot. If the targeted victim is an individual or a selected group of individuals, only those people will be shot, unless someone gets in the way or surprises the shooter. Fortunately, Steinhaeuser's victims were a small group—mostly teachers. The two students who were killed died when Steinhaeuser fired through a closed door.

Just minutes after the custodian's call to police, the first officer arrived. Officer Andreas Gorski, age forty-two, who prior to the call was preparing to leave work to attend his daughter's sixteenth birthday party, approached the building. As he did, Steinhaeuser leaned out a window and shot him in the head, killing him instantly. As other officers arrived, they took up positions around the building, just as they did at Columbine. It is my opinion that this was a tactical error. In Erfurt, police arrived just six minutes after the first call, but because they decided to secure the perimeter, Steinhaeuser had almost two hours inside the building before he took his own life. Police officers should never carelessly storm a building with only limited information about the shooter(s), but historically, school shootings have never involved more than two shooters. Some small groups of four or five have conspired to commit school massacres, but these are still very small numbers. When given the opportunity, I encourage SWAT officers to attack quickly. If officers had done so at Columbine, it is possible that police would have been numbered among the dead. However, most of the defenseless students at Columbine were killed in the library at the very end of the attack. A quick rush of the building would have robbed the boys of the time they needed to organize their massacre in the library. I have seen the video footage from the school security cameras that shows the boys leisurely walking through the cafeteria, resting, taking a drink, only to continue their shooting spree. After shooting Gorski, Steinhaeuser continued to freely roam the building for nearly two more hours.

As hundreds of police wearing bulletproof vests surrounded the building, Steinhaeuser strolled the halls, the bathrooms, and the classrooms looking for potential victims. Students hiding in a classroom hurriedly scribbled "HILFE" (HELP) in large letters and taped the sign to the classroom window. Steinhaeuser carried a shotgun, but most of his victims were killed by rounds from the 9mm pistol. During the two hours he terrorized students and teachers, he fired 40 rounds of the 540 rounds he brought with him and had stowed in a school bathroom.

Toward the end of the rampage, a sixty-year-old history teacher named Rainer Heise had been hiding in a closet. When he heard noises on the other side of the door he opened it, expecting to find a student or teacher fleeing the shooter. Instead, he found himself face-to-face with Steinhaeuser and looking down the barrel of the assailant's gun. The boy removed his mask and Heise realized that he knew him. He said, "Robert! Fire! You can shoot me too now ... [but] look into my eyes."[17] The boy replied, "No. That's enough for today, Mr. Heise."[18] Heise convinced Steinhaeuser that they should return to his classroom to talk, but when Steinhaueser entered the classroom, Heise pushed him into the room and away from the door, shut it, and locked it. Minutes later, Steinhaeuser used one last bullet on himself, taking his own life. In the end, Steinhaeuser killed twelve teachers (almost half the faculty at the school), two students, a school secretary, and one policeman. Others were wounded, some because they jumped out of windows or scaled a fence trying to escape.

Germany has a very low murder rate, only one-quarter of the murder rate in the United States, and firearms are strictly controlled. For example, to buy a hunting rifle, one must undergo background and identity checks that can last up to a year, while gun club members are required to obtain a license from the police.[19] Ironically, on the same day the shooting took place, the German parliament was set to approve a new bill tightening gun controls. Guns are estimated to be present in about one-third of all German homes, but there is speculation that the fall of the East has left thousands of illegal weapons in circulation. Police in Germany say that only "0.004 percent of armed crimes are committed with a legally obtained firearm."[20] Despite Germany's restrictive gun control laws, and despite the impression that the United States is the only place with a school-shooting problem, there have been three other killings at schools in Germany since 1999. In 1999, a fifteen-year-old student stabbed a teacher on a dare; in 2000, after being expelled, a sixteen-year-old boy shot and killed his former headmaster; and in 2002, a twenty-two-year-old man murdered the principal of the tech college he was attending.[21]

Steinhaeuser owned his guns legally. He was a member of two different gun clubs and it appears that he may have been planning the attack for up to a year.[22] In Germany, purchase of ammunition is tightly regulated and it would have taken him nearly a year to amass the 1,000-plus rounds of ammunition he had, 500 at home and the 540 rounds he carried with him to the school.

Steinhaeuser, who lived with his mother who was separated from his father, was not the typical social outcast that one has grown to expect in school shootings. "Everybody liked him," said a classmate.[23] He was popular, played handball, and a teacher said he was a "very calm, reasonable guy."[24] He appeared to be at least somewhat concerned about his academic life. In August 2001, he quit the handball team to prepare for Arbitur.[25] Yet not all accounts of his behavior were positive. Even though students said he was well liked, he had few friends. He was said to have been a poor student, who often missed classes. He had already failed the exam once and he had tried to cover his absences by forging a doctor's note, but administrators caught him and he was expelled. Even though he was liked and known to joke around, a number of his peers had seen him point his index finger at teachers and pretend to pull an imaginary trigger.[26] He was described as an insubordinate at school, one who enjoyed attracting attention, and he told a friend he "wanted to be famous."[27] I suppose he got his wish.

His motive appears to be linked to his anger at being expelled. A search of his home and possessions revealed violent comic books and video games, as is common among school shooters. His parents were unaware of his expulsion and even up to the day of the shooting, they believed he was still attending classes. He apparently was under great pressure to pass the exam, a test he was not able to take because of his expulsion, and he was seeking revenge against the teachers at the Erfurt school. He may have begun his plans the previous May when he failed the exam the first time. It was only a few weeks after failing that test that he applied for a gun license. After being suspended from the Johann Gutenberg High School in October, he briefly attended another high school, but quit attending after just a few weeks of class.[28] In workplace violence, when a person is fired from his job, even if he gets a better job, the anger at being fired smolders for weeks and even years. These people sometimes return to their former workplace two or three years later to seek revenge. I believe the same thing occurred with Robert Steinhaeuser.

Derek and Alex King

Some children seemingly don't have a chance from their earliest days. Derek, age thirteen, and Alex King, age twelve, were born to Janet French, a nightclub dancer who never married Terry King, the boys' father. French lived with King, then with her mother, and later with other men, some of whom she married and some of whom she did not. During the periods when the boys lived in French's care, instead of altering her lifestyle to meet their needs, she altered their lifestyle to match hers. As infants, they spent much of their day in a playpen, out of French's way. She enjoyed staying up into the early hours of the morning and then sleeping during the day; therefore, she kept the boys up late so they, too, would sleep all day. Because of their unusual sleep schedules, on the occasions when they attended school, they were almost always late. When Terry King took responsibility for his boys, he was not much better. Instead of sending the boys to school on a regular basis, he sometimes chose to take his sons to the print shop where he worked. They would nap, read, or study while he worked.

During their childhood, Derek and Alex sometimes lived with their mother, sometimes with their father or grandmother, at least once with their grandmother's ex-husband, sometimes together, and sometimes separated. Both boys spent time in an orphanage and in different foster homes, but they both eventually returned to the custody of their father. In the fall of 2001, Derek was returned to his father for the last time. He and his brother, who was living with King at the time, had been separated for four years and they had not seen their mother in six years. Terry King had become friends with Ricky Chavis, a forty-year-old man who helped King work on cars. It is unclear whether or not King was aware of Chavis' history as a convicted child molester. Chavis took an interest in the boys and over time, his friendship with King waned in comparison with his relationship with Derek and Alex. It is alleged that Chavis repeatedly tried to convince the boys that their father was mentally abusing them. Alex was especially influenced by Chavis. In a note, he said his life had been "cloudy" before he met Chavis, "but now his goal was to share his life with someone. Before I was straight, now I am gay."[29]

Despite comments from Chavis, there is no evidence that King was mentally or physically abusive to the boys. Although he had a criminal record, the charges were for DUI, passing bad checks, and driving with a suspended license. In fact, just before his death, King wrote in a diary that he wanted custody of all four boys—Derek and Alex as well as twin boys French had given birth to by another man who were in the permanent care of another couple—and he wanted to establish a good home for them.[30] Perspective is everything, however. Fueled by Chavis's influence, the boys apparently believed that they were being abused. A child's perspective is easily skewed. Undoubtedly, many readers of this book can remember a time in childhood when they believed their parents were abusing them because they were punished or were forced to do household chores. The repeated message that their father was mentally abusing them, delivered by an influential person in the boy's lives, had a potent impact. In their short lives, the boys had only sporadically had a stable home life, their mother was completely disengaged from their lives, and they feared their father. Their father's criminal record, while not abusive, certainly implies personal life problems and one might assume that those difficulties had some effect on the children. Alcohol and financial problems almost always have negative effects on children. Finally, the most accessible and influential person in their lives was a pedophile almost three times their ages.

In part because of their increasingly dependent relationship with Chavis and their belief that their father was abusing them, on November 16, the boys ran away from home and went to live with Chavis. They stayed with Chavis for approximately a week before returning home to their father. The boys allege that they were afraid their father would punish them for running away. Their anger over their alleged abuse grew. "We wished him dead," said Alex.[31] On November 26, as their forty-year-old father was sleeping in a chair, Derek and Alex came into the room with a baseball bat. Derek struck him ten times with the bat, killing him. The boys then set fire to the house and fled. They later contacted an acquaintance who, after persuading them to turn themselves in, drove them to sheriff's office. Derek, thirteen years old, and Alex, only twelve, were charged in adult court with first-degree murder.

During their trial, a tape-recorded confession was played in which Derek admitted waiting for his father to go to sleep and then bludgeoning him to death with a baseball bat. Their defense counsel argued that the boys had recanted their confession and they accused Chavis of the murder. The boys said they weren't present for the murder and that Chavis killed their father during a fight, set fire to the home, and left. They said that Chavis told them that if they took responsibility for the murder they would be acquitted on grounds of self-defense because they were juveniles.

In an unusual legal twist, Chavis was actually being tried for the murder in another court at the same time. Unknown to the jury in the trial of the King boys, Chavis was acquitted of the murder at his trial. On September 6 in their own trial, Alex and Derek were found guilty of arson and second-degree murder (rather than first-degree murder) in part because the jury believed the boys had allowed Chavis to enter the home and commit the murder. Following their decision, jurors in the Kings' trial were stunned to learn that Chavis had been acquitted.

But the story doesn't end there. At their sentencing one month later, a judge threw out their convictions stating that he did not believe the boys had received a fair trial. He ordered a new trial if mediation between the defense and prosecution could not prevent going forward with a new trial. Mediation prevailed and the boys pled guilty to arson and third-degree murder. Derek was sentenced to eight years in state prison and Alex was sentenced to seven years in state prison instead of the potential life sentence they each could have received for the second-degree murder conviction. The boys could be released early, but both are required to serve 85% of their sentences. Even though he was acquitted of the murder, Chavis was charged in December 2002 with ten lewd and lascivious charges, kidnapping, accessory after the fact, and evidence tampering. His trial is pending. If convicted, he faces 170 years in prison.

In her comments about her sons' behavior, French said the boys had attention deficit/hyperactivity disorder (ADHD), but ADHD does not cause children to kill their parents. In fact, ADHD is such a common diagnosis that more than half the children I've seen in my practice over the years would be a risk to their parents if ADHD were a cause of homicidal behavior. More likely, the multiple homes, dysfunctional role models, and unstable upbringing these boys were forced to endure created the framework for how these boys would deal with their anger and revenge.

Parricide

Revenge is always taken against a person or an object that has personal meaning and family members are often the target of a child's anger or revenge. Children, sometimes in their adult years, kill their mothers (matricide) or their fathers (patricide). *Parricide* is the generic term for killing one's parent or parents. In the United States, about a hundred children kill their parents each year.[32] History is laden with stories of parricide. Although she was exonerated at trial, Lizzy Borden was accused of murdering her mother and father with an ax in 1892. Greek mythology provides us with the story of King Oedipus, who killed his father, although unknowingly, and married his mother. It is the story of Oedipus that Sigmund Freud used to demonstrate his theory that boys wish their same-sexed parents dead because of their love for their mothers—a phenomenon he termed the *Oedipus complex*. Even though Freud may have taken the idea of one's love for the opposite-sexed parent to an extreme, it is through the child-parent dyad that children first develop love and attraction to members of the opposite sex. "Ideally, the child should have two parents: a parent of the same sex with whom he or she identifies and who forms a role model to follow in adulthood, and a parent of the opposite sex who becomes a basic human love object and whose affection provides the child with a sense of worth," writes psychologist José Silberstein.[33] In general, a girl's first love is her father and a boy's first love is his mother. When these dyads are healthy, respectful, nurturing, and balanced, children develop confidence, self-esteem, and efficacy, and they learn how to give and to receive love and affection. However, when these relationships are cold, distant, unfeeling, hurtful, or abusive, children fail to learn to trust and to give of themselves in a healthy, balanced way. Silberstein notes that, "When the primary parent is physically and emotionally sadistic, the child will usually establish a sadomasochistic primary attachment."[34] Therefore, when this attachment is dysfunctional, children perceive their mothers (or fathers) as threats, what Silberstein calls a "maddening object."[35]

Most researchers divide parricide perpetrators into three categories. The first category includes those who commit murder because of abuse. The murder relieves them of their real or perceived abusive situation. The second category includes those who murder for selfish reasons. It is alleged, for example, that Lyle and Erik Menendez, who were convicted of the 1989 murder of their parents, did so for financial gain. The final category includes those children who murder their parents because of severe mental illness. Kip Kinkel, the school shooter from Springfield, Oregon, who in May 1998 shot his parents to death, would fit into this category.

Parricide offenders are more likely to be adults themselves, rather than children. The typical perpetrator of parricide is Caucasian and those who kill their fathers tend to be younger than those who kill their mothers.[36] Although parricide occurs in both blended and intact families, stepparents are especially at risk from younger perpetrators. About one-third of murdered stepmothers and stepfathers are killed by children under eighteen.[37] Finally, matricide is most common in a family where there is a dominating, abusive mother and a passive, uninvolved father.[38]

Emotional attachments to family members are very strong. Those passions may be anger, hate, or jealousy, as easily as they may include love and affection. Even in adults, the power of those negative emotions can drive one to say hurtful things or behave in ways that are damaging to oneself or the relationship, and they can also drive one to kill. Children who are less mature and who have fewer resources for coping with their stress and emotions are even more likely to behave unproductively. Consider the case of James Ruscitti whom I mentioned earlier in the chapter.

James Ruscitti was adopted by an Italian immigrant and his family who lived in Canada. Despite the nurturing home where he was raised, James held grudges against anyone who threatened him or, in his view, wronged him. On June 22, 1996, James and a friend who had spent the night with him shot and killed his fifty-four-year-old father, his forty-nine-year-old mother, his brother's seventeen-year-old common-law wife, and a forty-six-year-old male who was boarding at the Ruscitti home. James, carrying a .30-.30 Winchester and a .22-caliber rifle, first shot the boarder in the chest and head as he slept. James and his friend then met his father in the hall as he came to investigate the sound of gunfire. There, they shot him in the chest and head. Next, they entered his mother's bedroom where she apparently tried to defend herself. She raised her arm, but was shot through the arm, chest, and head. Finally, the boys went to the seventeen-year-old woman's room. She was sitting upright in bed, undoubtedly terrified as she listened, one-by-one, as her loved ones were murdered. The boys entered the room and shot her in the leg and the head. Before leaving the house, they dragged his father's body to the bedroom, locked the door, and then returned to the boarder's room where they shot him once again in the head.[39]

A two-month-old baby belonging to his brother's common-law wife was found lying beside her mother's body. The baby was dehydrated, but otherwise unharmed—the only person to survive. James was fifteen years old and his accomplice, Chad Bucknell, was only fourteen. James didn't like being told what to do by anyone, including his parents, and records indicate that he believed he had been wronged at one time or another by each of the victims. After the killings, the boys stole a family car, spent the day at a video arcade, and then went to stay with a friend, to whom they bragged about the murders. Ruscitti's uncle found the gruesome crime scene the next day and alerted authorities. The boys were arrested by the Royal Canadian Mounted Police on June 26 and James pled guilty to all four counts of murder and was sentenced to four life sentences of twenty-five years each.

NARCISSISM

Among the oldest motives for murder are greed and narcissism. The word *narcissism* comes from the ancient Greek myth of Narcissus who, because of his cruel response to the nymph Echo who was in love with him, was cursed by the gods to spend his life gazing at his reflection in a pool of water—experiencing love of self, but not receiving love in return. He could not bear to take his eyes off of himself and he gazed at his reflection until he wasted away and died. The term "self-centered" is a synonym that approaches the meaning of narcissism. I could easily fill this book with stories about narcissistic adolescents who were so wrapped up in their own immediate desires that they committed murder for things so trivial as money, professional athletic team Starter jackets, jewelry, or stereos. Carjackings sometimes end in death when an equally narcissistic victim is willing to sacrifice his life to protect his car. In recent years, a number of cases have arisen where children have committed violent crimes not for money, but for fame. The boys from Columbine wanted to become famous and, in a way, they achieved their goal. They are well known, but not in the way they wanted. Instead, they are better known for their stupidity and incompetence and I refuse to use their names in any lecture, book, or presentation unless it is absolutely necessary. Sadly, their perverted narcissism is not isolated. In 2001, a group of five classmates at a high school in New Bedford, Massachusetts, planned to repeat the Columbine tragedy.

"Bigger than Columbine"

These five young people were not much different than the Columbine criminals. They thought they could do it better than other people who had planned and executed school shootings and they thought they were more original. In reality, just like the boys at Columbine, they were merely copy-cats. They took on the name "Trench Coat Mafia" used by the Columbine boys and they planned to detonate bombs inside the building, waiting outside to shoot the innocent victims as they left the building—just like the original plan at Columbine. Fortunately, even though they planned an attack that was "bigger than Columbine," they were equally incompetent and were never able to execute their plans.

Their plot was totally narcissistic. They weren't angry with teachers. They were not angry with classmates. They simply wanted to see the reaction of the community and to make a name for themselves. In his tape-recorded interview with police after his arrest, one of the perpetrators, seventeen-year-old Eric McKeehan said, "I wanted to do it ... Just to see what the shock would be in New Bedford."[40] He just wanted to "see the publicity. See how big it would get," he said.[41]

New Bedford, a town fifty miles south of Boston, was launched into the news after the filming of the movie *The Accused*, based on a gang rape at Big Dan's tavern in March 1983. The five students, Eric McKeehan, his fifteen-year-old brother Michael, seventeen-year-old Amylee Bowman, and Steven Jones and Neil Mellow, both sixteen, plotted to set off explosive devices and then shoot students, teachers, administrators, and police as they fled the building. This plan was very similar to the original plan at Columbine as well as the shooting in Arkansas where two boys set off a fire alarm in the school building and then shot students and teachers as they exited.

In November 2001, a janitor found a letter in a trash can at the New Bedford High School, a school of about 3,250 students and the second biggest in Massachusetts, which described a plan to massacre students that would take place on "Monday," but did not specify which Monday. Police moved in and arrested the teens. As the details of the plot unfolded, it was alleged that the students were planning to kill themselves after the massacre, again copying the Columbine duo. A search of the homes of the teens turned up directions for making bombs, as well as shotgun shells and knives, and photographs of people posing with weapons. There had been an investigation under way since October 17 when Amylee Bowman told a counselor about the planned attack. However, investigators did not have enough evidence to arrest anyone. When the note was found a month later, police had the evidence they needed to make arrests.

Although students said he was only joking, McKeehan had commented about "how cool it would be to pretend to blow up the school."[42] In light of the Columbine attack two and a half years earlier, as well as other school shootings in recent history, I can't imagine who would think this was funny.

In the McKeehan boys' home, investigators found gas masks, satanic writings, a voodoo doll, a Confederate flag, and pictures of Adolf Hitler. Also recovered were a black-handled knife, a brass-knuckle dagger, a hatchet, a meat cleaver, live ammunition, and a doll hanging from a noose.[43] The boys had painted the walls, doors, and windowsills of their room with symbols and initials, song lyrics, and phrases like, "Kill everyone" and "I hate the world," in large black letters.[44] Either McKeehan's mother, Carol McKeehan, who is divorced from their father, allowed the extreme attitude as depicted by these paintings and objects in their rooms, or, like the parents of the Columbine shooters, she was so disengaged from her son's activities that she wasn't even aware of what they were doing. Regardless, their mother downplayed the incident saying Eric's only problem was "talking with the wrong people, getting in the wrong conversations," and she accused prosecutors of being overzealous in their handling of the case.[45]

How she could make such a comment is beyond my imagination. "I wanted to see how New Bedford would be if they were on top, because it's such a little P-town ... Just imagine another Columbine but at New Bedford High, you know what I mean," Eric said.[46] "I didn't give a shit if it was a teacher, cop, mother, whoever. You're in my way, you're getting a bullet.... Whoever's going with me is going with me."[47] After hearing these outrageous statements made by her son in the twenty-nine-minute taped police interview, one has to wonder how she could make such comments excusing her son's behavior. If these were my sons, I would be horrified that they would utter such threats, yet this woman unbelievably saw little wrong with it, casting blame on others rather than addressing her sons' behavior. Downplaying the responsibility of one's child in a case like this is very common and reflects an attitude that undoubtedly contributed to the child's behavior.

McKeehan's mother wasn't the only one to suggest that police and the prosecutor overreacted. McKeehan's attorney downplayed the plot as well. In court, the prosecutor presented a notebook belonging to Michael McKeehan that included excerpts from *The Anarchist Cookbook* that outlined how to build a tennis-ball bomb ("Throw it at a geek—he will have a blast") and other explosive devices.[48] "Not exactly Osama bin Laden stuff," he said.[49] I'm not sure what it would take to convince this attorney that something *was* a problem. A police officer on the stand noted that the initials FTW (fuck the world) and TCM (Trench Coat Mafia) were found in Stephen's room on a piece of paper. The defense countered that TCM may have stood for Turner Classic Movies—a comment that was so ridiculous that some in the courtroom laughed out loud.[50] He went on to say that the alleged plot was nothing more than brainstorming ideas, never seriously considered.[51] Brainstorming? I wonder if this attorney would have a similar attitude if a former client, whose case he lost, "brainstormed" about killing him and his family. I would guess he might take such threats more seriously. Even if police and prosecutors were "overzealous," if they had not intervened and an attack had taken place, as it did at Columbine, they would have been sued for not taking the threats seriously and failing to act soon enough.

A neighbor said that "Eric seemed very quiet."[52] Yet again, this was very similar to comments made about the boys from Columbine. Another parent claimed that the ammunition found on her son was only a souvenir from a hunting trip.[53] After the tape of McKeehan's interview was played in court, a friend of the accused told reporters, "They wouldn't have gone through with it. Nothing major was going on. Things look real bad. You'd have to know them to understand."[54] What an understatement. Frankly, without actually committing the act, I don't see how it could have been much worse.

Police said that Bowman had agreed to smuggle guns into the school building and was to take part in the shooting, but her conscience drove her to divulge the plan. Some accounts say she was concerned about her favorite teacher, English teacher Rachel Jupin, but Bowman said she was concerned about everyone and didn't want anyone to die. "I didn't want the lives of 4,500 people (students, faculty, administrators) resting in my hands," she said.[55]

Bowman, charged with conspiracy to commit assault with a dangerous weapon, and Eric McKeehan were both charged as adults. The other three boys were charged as juveniles. Bowman was freed on bond pending her trial. The judge in the case created a firestorm of protest in the community when he released Eric McKeehan as well. Even though the judge considered him a danger, he released him on bail, placing him under house arrest where he was required to wear an electronic ankle bracelet. After this decision, nearly one hundred students were suspended from New Bedford High School when they staged a mass walkout, protesting the decision. But Eric didn't remain free for long. He was instructed as a condition of bail that he should not contact any of the charged individuals, any witness, or any student from the high school. Yet while at home, he telephoned a student from the high school and when the court was notified, his bail was revoked.

McKeehan, who said he wanted to shock the city, pled innocent to the charges and the case is yet to be tried. Based on pictures of the youth with guns, police searched for the weapons, but did not find any in searches of the homes of the accused. Bowman felt betrayed by the charges. Saying she was trying to do the right thing by divulging the plan, she now believes her life has been ruined.[56] She was suspended from high school just short of graduation, expelled from her Junior Reserve Officer Training Corps (JROTC) program, and her plans to enter the Army as a military policewoman and her desire to eventually become a state police officer are in jeopardy.[57] Her military service would have included a guarantee of $40,000 in education scholarships.[58] Even though this was a high price for her to pay, all these losses seem to be a reasonable trade for the lives of several hundred students and faculty members.

MENTAL ILLNESS

In most of my books, seminars, and lectures, I suggest that anyone who commits murder is mentally ill at some level, although the illness is sometimes undiagnosed. It is abnormal for one person to kill another and it is especially abnormal for children to deliberately murder playmates. There are a number of diagnoses that could apply—psychosis, reactive attachment disorder, schizophrenia, and delusion—but regardless of the diagnosis, in some cases mental disruption is clear. This was clearly the case when on April 15, 2002, six-year-old Jackson Carr was cruelly murdered by his ten-year-old brother and fifteen-year-old sister. In the town of Lewisville, twenty miles from Dallas, Texas, a neighbor saw Jackson riding his bicycle alone in front of his house in the late afternoon. Just thirty minutes later, when his mother, forty-two-year-old Rita Carr, returned home from work, the boy could not be found. Her ten-year-old son said that he and Jackson had been playing hide-and-seek. He said that he told Jackson to go and hide and that he would count to fifty, but after counting he couldn't find Jackson.[59]

Around 5:00 P.M., police were notified and the boy was reported missing. A massive search for the first grader was conducted and volunteers from the neighborhood joined the police officers, firefighters, rescue workers, search dogs, and helicopters with thermal-imaging devices already engaged in the hunt. "When everybody was searching, we weren't looking for a grave. We were looking for a lost little boy," said a neighbor.[60] In an act that is common in cases like this, the murderer joined the search when Jackson's fifteen-year-old sister volunteered to help look for him. Police, who had been given permission by the Carrs to search the house, found evidence that suggested the siblings knew something about the disappearance of their brother. After thirty minutes of questioning the girl, the six-hour search came to an end. At 12:45 A.M. she said, "I know where my brother is, and I'll take you to him."[61] She led authorities to the body, buried one hundred yards behind the house under two feet of mud, just beyond a tent where the children regularly played. According to her statement, her brother had held Jackson down while she choked him, holding him face down in the mud and water, and stabbed him in the neck. Jackson died of blood loss when the stab wound punctured his jugular vein. The ten-year-old admitted to authorities that he held Jackson down and then helped to bury him.

Both children had a history of troubles. The fifteen-year-old was a seventh grader, two grades behind most children her age, and she had a history of discipline problems in school.[62] In 1998, she set fire to the Shorehaven Elementary School building and just a few weeks before the murder of her brother, she vandalized her middle school. Noting the way she dressed, a friend said she even looked like she was troubled. According to those who knew her, she was emotionally disturbed and fought with her brothers.[63] On one occasion, when a classmate called her a name, she cut him in the face with a pair of scissors. This child was clearly disturbed. There are three symptoms, called the *terrible triad*, that are always troubling signs with children and are usually the by-products of physical abuse. They include cruelty to animals or people, bed-wetting, and arson. This child exhibited at least two of these symptoms.

The ten-year-old allegedly had been diagnosed with a learning disability and Tourette's syndrome.[64] He reportedly also participated with his sister in the arson and vandalism attacks on the two school buildings. Neighbors reportedly were concerned about all the Carr children because all three "seemed to have developmental or behavioral problems."[65] One neighbor said that she began locking her gates and doors because she feared Jackson would wander into her home and fall in the swimming pool.[66]

There were other reports of difficulties in the home. Rita and her husband, Michael, divorced in 1997, but later reconciled, and had been living in the house in Lewisville for only about four months. Child Protective Services had investigated the family three times over allegations of emotional and physical abuse of the two older children, but no proof of abuse was found.[67]

The siblings were charged, the younger as a juvenile and the elder as an adult. If convicted as an adult, the girl could receive as much as forty years in prison. Even charged as a juvenile, the younger boy could potentially be held even longer than his eighteenth birthday. The prosecutor noted the complex issues involved in charging children in a crime like this. It is a difficult balance between seeking rehabilitation and protecting the community. "Some kids you can fix and some you can't," he said.[68] Rita and Michael Carr refused to participate in the girl's psychiatric evaluation and even though they asked for the boy to be released, they did not want their daughter released on bail. As of the publication of this book, the case has not yet been tried.

IMMATURITY

Because of developmental limitations, children cannot fully understand the ramifications of their actions. We have to teach children not to play in the street so they will not be run over by a vehicle and we have to keep medicines and poison out of reach so they will not eat them. Even though they may know not to play in the street or not to eat poison, until they reach full cognitive development, they cannot fully know *why* they shouldn't do those things and all the possible results of those behaviors. In January 2000, a fifteen-year-old boy in Utah spent the night with his fourteen-year-old friend in the small trailer he shared with his mother, sister, and two dogs. The boys spent the late evening playing violent video games while the others were sleeping. Prosecutors claim that the older boy attacked and killed the younger while he slept on the couch, stabbing him thirty-nine times with a kitchen knife, but the boy's account of the events varied. He said at first that his friend fell on the knife, then that he acted in self-defense, and even that the mother had participated in the murder. He also said that the two had wrestled for a half hour before the killing, but prosecutors noted the unlikelihood of that story because such behavior surely would have awakened the mother or sister or aroused the family dogs, but that did not happen. The boy was convicted of first-degree murder and tampering with evidence and he was sentenced to life in prison. The boy's attorney appealed for a new trial in 2002, stating that the trial judge improperly instructed jurors. I find it less than believable that someone could stab someone else thirty-nine times in "self-defense" and it is clear to me that this was a very angry child. No doubt, he understood that stabbing his friend would cause his death, but at his age I think that it is unlikely that he fully understood all the ramifications of committing murder.

An even more complex case of development and murder happened in Florida in 1999. A twelve-year-old boy named Lionel Tate killed his six-year-old playmate while he imitated wrestling moves he had seen on television. Lionel lived with his mother, Kathleen Gossett-Tate, a Florida Highway Patrol officer. She had divorced Lionel's father in 1987. On July 28, 1999, Lionel's mother agreed to babysit for a longtime friend's daughter, Tiffany Eunick. Eunick was only four feet tall and was dwarfed by Lionel who was large for his age at 166 pounds. After spending time at the library, and then eating lunch at home, Lionel's mother left the two children in front of the television for the afternoon while she slept in her bedroom. She arose around 7:00 P.M. and, after fixing them dinner, she returned to bed. At 10:00 P.M. she heard noise and told the children to be quiet.[69] About forty minutes later she was awakened when Lionel entered her room and said that Tiffany wasn't breathing. She raced downstairs and administered CPR until rescue workers arrived, but Tiffany died despite all efforts to revive her.

Initially, Lionel said that they had been playing and that Tiffany fell and hit her head on a table, but he later said they punched each other and he swung her into the stairs and she hit her head on the railing.[70] He also said he put Tiffany in a headlock, and there was indication that he slammed her into the floor. Her injuries were massive, thirty-five in total. She suffered a lacerated liver, hemorrhaging around her kidneys, a skull fracture, broken ribs, cuts, and bruises. Testimony at the trial indicated that the severity of her injuries was consistent with a fall from a three-story building.

The prosecutor tried to avoid a trial by offering Lionel's attorney a plea bargain. In exchange for a guilty plea, Lionel would have served three years in prison, ten years' probation, counseling, and community service. However, Lionel's mother rejected the offer. Instead, Lionel pled innocent. His attorney tried to cast blame on the World Wrestling Federation (WWF), saying the televised wrestling bouts negatively influenced children like Lionel who did not understand that it was make-believe and the WWF thereby caused aggressive behavior. The WWF countered this attack by suing the attorney for libel. There is no question that television and movies do have an influence on children's behavior. In fact, in 1999 alone, there were three separate deaths where children were imitating wrestling moves. A twelve-year-old boy was convicted of second-degree murder in Washington State after killing a nineteen-month-old cousin by slamming his head into the ground; a seven-year-old Dallas boy clothes-lined (striking an opponent with an extended arm across the neck, as if running into a clothesline) his three-year-old brother, who died when he fell and hit his head against a table (no charges were filed); and in Georgia, a four-year-old left home alone with his fifteen-month-old sister by a babysitter stomped the baby to death (the sitter was charged with involuntary manslaughter).[71]

Lionel had admitted that he knew television wrestling was not real, but even so, that does not mean he understood that his behavior would kill Tiffany. In the eyes of the jury, I suspect his size worked against him. They saw an adult-sized boy in front of them and the victim was a tiny first grader. However, just because he was large for his age does not mean his cognitive development was comparably advanced. Cognitively, he was still only twelve.

The prosecutor said that Tiffany's injuries were so severe that they had to be deliberately inflicted. In Florida, a charge of first-degree murder does not require "proof that Tate actually intended to kill the girl, but only that he intended to commit the acts that led to her death."[72] This is an inappropriate law when applied to a child of Lionel's age. An act could be intentional and yet still be an accident. Lionel may have intentionally "wrestled" the child, but because of cognitive limitations, not understood that his actions would lead to injury—hence, injuring her unintentionally.

After deliberating for three hours, the jury returned its verdict of guilty and, in turn, the judge was required by law to sentence him to life without parole. Tears streamed down Lionel's face as the sentence was read. He was totally unaware that he might receive such a sentence. His mother had not discussed the possible sentence with him because, she said, she did not believe the case would make it that far.[73] It could have been even worse. If he had been sixteen years of age, he could have received the death penalty.

After the guilty verdict at his trial, Lionel's attorney petitioned the judge to reduce his sentence because he said that neither he nor Lionel's mother had understood the ramifications of rejecting the plea offer from the prosecutor and going ahead with the trial.[74] The judge rejected the petition. Lionel was led away from the courtroom in shackles and was sent to a juvenile facility where he will live until he is eighteen years old. He will then be transferred to an adult prison.

Lionel's attorney petitioned Governor Jeb Bush for clemency, as did a group of Episcopal priests in Florida. Several jurors who convicted Lionel have also come forward to support a lighter sentence.[75] Even the prosecutor has supported clemency from the governor, although one has to wonder if his support has more to do with the public support for clemency and its impact on his own political future than his belief that Lionel's sentence should be reduced. If he had been concerned about such a sentence, it seems reasonable to suppose that he would have charged Lionel with a lesser crime, but chose instead to pursue the murder charge.

Even though a psychologist who interviewed Lionel said he was a "kid with a history of problems,"[76] that does not mean he had a cognitive understanding of his actions. Unfortunately, Florida is not the only state that tries children like Lionel as adults. Between 1992 and 1997, all but six states made it easier to try children as adults.[77] In some cases, children should be tried as adults, but the public, the media, and prosecutors let the heinous nature of the act determine the charge rather than the development and intent of the offender. Clearly, all states in the United States recognize an age of accountability. For example, in the case of Kayla Rowland mentioned earlier, no charges were filed against her perpetrator because of his age. If the law had allowed six-year-olds to be tried either as juveniles or adults, I wonder if the prosecutor in that case would have filed charges. One can only speculate. When the child borders on adolescence, like Lionel, it appears the question of developmental culpability is not even considered.

CONCLUDING REMARKS

We don't like to believe it, but children are capable of cold-blooded murder. Their actions are often hard to fathom. In an eerie premonition of the September 11 terrorist attacks, one of the two boys involved in the Columbine massacre fantasized about hijacking an airplane after shooting his classmates and then flying it into the World Trade Center. Fortunately, the incompetence of these two thugs prevented them from fully realizing their plans.

Like adults, children do not act out of the blue. Symptoms of the potential they have for aggressive behavior can be seen for weeks, months, or even years before a violent act is committed. Kip Kinkel demonstrated his aggressive tendencies for years prior to his shooting spree. Jackson Carr's sister vandalized a school building, slashed a classmate in the face with scissors, and committed arson prior to killing her brother. I am confident that even accidental deaths committed by children like Lionel Tate can be prevented. The day Lionel killed his six-year-old playmate was surely not the first time he had acted boisterously, mimicking wrestling moves. One has to wonder how many times a day his mother had to tell him to "settle down." For Lionel, adequate supervision may have been the only prevention needed to save Tiffany's life.

Prevention of such acts of violence involves not only awareness of the signs of aggressive potential, an issue that I will address in Chapter 11, but also parental supervision and involvement. Even though there are cases like Kip Kinkel's where the parents did everything they could to provide a nurturing home and to intervene when his aggressive tendencies became evident, more often violent children are created by abusive, neglectful parents. Prevention, therefore, begins with healthy parenting. In Savannah, Georgia, in March 2001, a sixteen-year-old girl received a ten-year prison sentence after pleading guilty to conspiring to kill her mother. She said that for two months her father and her twenty-year-old boyfriend together had plotted the murder. Her mother was stabbed to death and her body was left in her van outside a business. The girl's guilty plea was accepted in exchange for testimony against her father. Her father had been arrested on domestic violence charges prior to planning this murder. He certainly wasn't much of a role model. Teaching parents to properly nurture their children, avoid abuse, and how to build self-esteem is part of the parent's job in prevention of aggression. Social services needs to take an active role in removing children from abusive and neglectful homes until the parents' behavior can be corrected or until the children can be placed in a foster home where their needs will be met.

We currently have a generation of aggressive children that surpasses the violent behavior of past generations. Our culture fosters aggression in television, advertising, movies, music, comedy, and even in athletics. Only with concerted effort will parents be able to counter the aggressive cultural influences on their children. Parents must be actively involved in their children's lives, monitoring what they read, with whom they associate, and how they spend their free time. Parents must be willing to say,

"No. That behavior is not acceptable." I once read a column by Erma Bombeck where she addressed her daughter's accusation that she didn't love her. "How much do I love you?" she wrote. "I loved you enough to say 'no,' even when you hated me for it. And that was the hardest thing of all." Courageous parenting will help us make great strides in stemming the tide of violence in our culture.

NOTES

1. David Ciampi, "Perpetrators of violence: Adolescents in America," *The Forensic Examiner* (September/October 2001): 33.

2. Ciampi, p. 32.

3. Gregory K. Moffatt, *A violent heart: Understanding Aggressive Individuals* (Westport, CT: Praeger, 2000).

4. Gregory K. Moffatt, *Blind-sided: Homicide where it is least expected* (Westport, CT: Praeger, 2000).

5. Richard Skelly, "Massacre at Buffalo Creek," *Alberta Report/Newsmagazine* (February 24, 1997): p. 20.

6. Ibid.

7. Ibid.

8. "Michigan first-grader fatally shot by classmate," *CNN On-Line*, www.cnn.com/2000/US/02/29/school.shooting.04/index.html, February 29, 2000.

9. "Mother of boy accused of first-grade shooting admits neglect," *CNN On-Line*, www.cnn.com/2000/US/05/03/schoolshooting.custody.ap/index.html, May 3, 2000.

10. "6-year-old boy testifies he didn't shoot first grade classmate," *CNN On-Line*, www.cnn.com/2000/US/03/31/school.shooting.ap/index.html, March 31, 2000.

11. "Kayla's death spurred outrage, not change," *Detroit News*, detnews.com/2000/metro/0012/11/a01-160171.html, December 10, 2000.

12. "Boy shooter, siblings in aunt's custody," *Atlanta Journal/Constitution* (March 2, 2000): A6.

13. Rani Goldberg, "Mom urged Kayla to tell her teachers about bully," *Atlanta Journal/Constitution* (March 7, 2000): A1.

14. "Authorities say 19-year-old may be charged in relation to Michigan school shooting," *CNN On-Line*, www.cnn.com/2000/US/03/01/school.shooting.03/index.html, March 1, 2000.

15. Charles P. Wallace, "Massacre in Erfurt," *Time Atlantic* (Internet Edition), May 6, 2002.

16. Ibid.

17. David Holley, "Teenager legally owned weapons," *Atlanta Journal/Constitution* (April 28, 2002): A15.

18. Ibid.

19. "Mourning for victims of German school rampage," *CNN On-Line*, www.cnn.com/2002/WORLD/europe/04/26/germany.shooting/index.html, April 26, 2002.

20. "German gun controls to be tightened," *CNN On-Line*, www.cnn.com/2002/WORLD/europe/04/26/germany.guns/index.html, April 26, 2002.

21. Wallace, "Massacre in Erfurt."

22. "German horror 'planned for a year,'" *CNN On-Line,* europe.cnn.com /2002/WORLD/europe/04/30/erfurt.plan/index.html, April 30, 2002.

23. Michael D. Lemonick and Charles P. Wallace, "Germany's Columbine," *Time* (May 6, 2002): 36.

24. Wallace.

25. Ibid.

26. "German horror 'planned for a year.'"

27. Wallace.

28. "German horror 'planned for a year.'"

29. Ginny Graybiel, "When children kill parents," *Pensacola News Journal,* www.pensacolanewsjournal.com/news/011302/Local/ST001.shtml, January 13, 2002.

30. Ibid.

31. Ibid.

32. Ibid.

33. José Alejandro Silberstein, "Matricide: A paradigmatic case in family violence," *International Journal of Offender Therapy and Comparative Criminology,* 42 (1998): 213.

34. Ibid., p. 216.

35. Ibid., p. 217.

36. "Parricide mostly committed by adult offspring," *Brown University Child and Adolescent Behavior Letter, 10* (February 1994): 4.

37. Ibid.

38. Silberstein, "Matricide," p. 218.

39. Skelly "Massacre at Buffalo Creek," p. 20.

40. "Court hears of school shooting plot," *CNN On-Line,* www.cnn.com /2001/LAW/12/03/crime.school.reut/index.html, December 3, 2001.

41. Neil Miller, "New Bedford confidential," *Boston Phoenix,* www.boston phoenix.com/boston/news_features/top/features/documents/02063814.htm, June 5, 2002.

42. "Mass. police say they spoiled school massacre," *CNN On-Line,* www.cnn .com/2001/LAW/11/25/school.plot.ap/index.html, November 25, 2001.

43. Miller, "New Bedford confidential."

44. Megan Tench and Scott S. Greenberger, "Jokers or killers?," *The Boston Globe,* nl1.newsbank.com/nl-search/we/archives, December 2, 2001.

45. "Teen accused in plot confined to home," *Cape Cod Times,* www.capecodonline .com/cctimes/archives/2001/dec/5/teenaccused5.htm, December 5, 2001.

46. Miller, "New Bedford confidential."

47. Ibid.

48. Ibid.

49. Ibid.

50. Ibid.

51. "Teen accused in plot confined to home."

52. "Columbine-style massacre stopped," *Safer Schools News,* keystosafer schools.com/NewBedford112601.htm, November 26, 2001.

53. "Teen-age girl arraigned in Massachusetts school bomb plot," *CNN On-Line,* www.cnn.com/2001/LAW/11/27/school.plot.arraignment/index.html, November 27, 2001.

54. Miller, "New Bedford confidential."

55. Bill Alexander, "Whistleblower: 'My life ruined'," *Youth Today*, www .psrn.org/News%20articles/school%20climate%202-10-02.html, February 10, 2002.

56. Ibid.

57. Ibid.

58. Ibid.

59. "Siblings suspected in killing of brother, 6," *CNN On-Line*, www.cnn.com/2002/US/04/16/sibling.suspects/index.html, April 16, 2002.

60. "Texas police say siblings confessed to murder of boy," *USA Today*, www.usatoday.com/news/nation/2002/04/16/texas-killing.htm, April 17, 2002.

61. Doug Fox, "Lewisville case latest in rising number of juvenile killings," *WFAA.com*, www.wfaa.com/dfox/stories/wfaa020416_am_lewisvillefolo.80d45e 6a.html, April 17, 2002.

62. Paul Duggan, "Texas police charge siblings in death of 6-year-old boy," *Washington Post*, www.washingtonpost.com/ac2/wp-dyn?pagename=article& node=&contentId=A63051-2002Apr16, April 17, 2002.

63. Susan Parrott, "Texas kids accused of fratricide," *The Nando Times*, www .nandotimes.com/nation/story/379566p-3032518c.html, April 25, 2002.

64. Ibid.

65. Domingo Ramirez and Mike Lee, "Texas siblings suspected in death of brother, 6," *The Salt Lake Tribune*, www.sltrib.com/2002/apr/04172002/nation_w /729105.htm, April 17, 2002.

66. Ibid.

67. Parrott, "Texas kids accused of fratricide."

68. Rachel Horton, "Lewisville siblings to be held until May 15," *Dallas News*, www.dallasnews.com/latestnews/stories/050102dmnlewsiville.ca0a2.html, May 2, 2002.

69. Nick Charles, Siobhan Morrissey, Linda Trischitta, and Deweese Eunick, "Judging Lionel," *People* (Internet Edition), February 12, 2001.

70. Ibid.

71. Terry Springer, "Boy who killed blames wresting," *Atlanta Journal/Constitution* (January 14, 2001): A10.

72. "Stiff sentence," *ABC News*, www.abcnews.go.com/sections/us/Daily News/tate_sentence010309.html, March 9, 2001.

73. Ibid.

74. "Sentencing proceeds for boy facing life term," *CNN On-Line*, www.cnn.com/2001/LAW/03/09/wrestling.sentence.02/index.html, March 9, 2001.

75. Ibid.

76. Charles et al., "Judging Lionel."

77. Amanda Ripley and David S. Jackson, "Throwing the book at kids," *Time* (March 19, 2001): 34.

CHAPTER 8

Violence against Self

> I am afraid I am becoming out of control. I am afraid that I am becoming less afraid of immoral behavior. I am most afraid that my life will end up being mere existence and I will never be able to appreciate the colors of life ever again.... I usually do whatever I intend to do, both good and bad, motivated by pure desire to act.
>
> —Note from a suicidal teenager

"I think sometimes about being in a car crash," the twelve-year-old girl told me as she massaged a lump of Play Dough in my office. "A car crash happens really fast and if I died, my heart wouldn't hurt anymore. Nobody could hurt me or make fun of me anymore and I wouldn't be alone. I would be with my dad in heaven."

The child who made these statements to me was suffering from depression. Her father had died suddenly and her mother was having a very difficult time coping with his death. The child had no siblings and even before her father's death, she was an isolated, peculiar girl who had very few friends. Her suicidal thinking was overt. Self-destructive behaviors are similar behaviors to vandalism, bullying, and homicide. The major difference between them is that suicide, eating disorders, and self-mutilation are aggressive behaviors turned inward, while the others are externalized aggressive behaviors. When a child does not know what to do with his rage, frustration, and pent-up aggression, it is easily focused upon himself. For example, an eight-year-old client of mine had a habit of hitting himself in the head with his fists when he became frustrated. He never did any damage or left any bruises, but this behavior clearly was internalized aggression. He hit himself because he could not hit his mother, the real cause of his anger, and he did not know how to express his anger in any other way.

Over the years I have worked with many clients, both children and adults, who were self-destructive, had eating disorders, or were suicidal. To date, none of my clients have ever died, but it may be inevitable that I lose a client eventually. There are many factors that drive these behaviors (attention, body-image problems, esteem problems, etc.), and these clients not only have the presenting issue to deal with, but they usually have other diagnoses as well. Depression, borderline personality disorder, and other similar disorders must be treated concurrently with the eating dis-order or the self-destructive/suicidal behaviors. Many of these self-destructive people deeply want to find a better way to deal with life's problems, but they do not know how to do it. Guidance from a caring indi-vidual and someone who can provide a sense of hope for a better future can at least temporarily help abate the self-destructive symptoms; how-ever, the behaviors described in this chapter are almost always driven by deep psychological issues and recovery requires trained, professional intervention, and full recovery may take a very long time.

As I discussed in Chapter 6, it is a balance of the three elements of our personality—the id, the ego, and the superego—that keeps us healthy. When the superego, the conscience, takes the lead, one feels guilt. Freud tended to view guilt as a bad thing, but I disagree. Guilt can be very pro-ductive. Guilt allows us to recognize that we have wronged someone else; thus, in seeking to resolve our guilt, we are motivated to make resti-tution. If I have said something unkind to my spouse, either deliberately or accidentally, it is the recognition that I have done something hurtful that goads me to repair the damage that I caused. The drive to resolve my guilt and to know I have set the world right again prompts me to demon-strate the value of another. Without guilt, people would say and do cruel things with no remorse and no drive to repair the damage that they have caused. The real problem is not guilt, but rather inappropriate guilt. Once I have done my best to repair the damage that I have done, I must let it go. I have no control over the response from the other person. Again, sup-pose I have said something hurtful to my spouse. Once my guilt helps me to recognize my thoughtlessness, I apologize, and I resolve to try to avoid similar comments in the future, my responsibility is complete. My wife, however, may choose to accept or reject my apology. She may forgive me (as she always does!), and all will be right with the world, or she may choose to hold a grudge or remain angry. Regardless of her response, if I continue to feel guilty, even though I've done all I could to correct the sit-uation, I am then experiencing inappropriate guilt.

Inappropriate guilt can also be caused by unrealistic beliefs we create about who we should be and how we should act. Some theorists call these things the self-created "musts" of our lives. We "must" be perfect. We "must" look a certain way. We "must" reach certain goals. This set of ideas about how we ought to be is called the *ideal self* or what Freud called the *ego ideal*. Nobody fully achieves the ego ideal and, for most of us, we recognize some of our goals and aspirations as unrealistic. However, when one sets unrealistic goals, one feels bad for consistently failing to achieve that which was unreachable in the first place. For example, I may have an ego ideal that drives me to be a best-selling author. I would like all my books to be best-sellers. However, I understand that of the thousands of books published each year, only a few will make it to that level of success. I still want to achieve best-selling status, but I am not too disappointed or surprised if I don't. Therefore, my ego ideal drives me to do my best, but I do not allow my superego to make me feel inadequate when I do not achieve that ideal goal. Dysfunctional or immature individuals set goals that are unrealistic and then they are devastated when they do not achieve those goals. For example, a woman may have an ego ideal that says she should weigh less than one hundred pounds. With the exception of disease or starvation, it may be impossible for her, given her height and heredity, to weigh so little. Each time she steps on the scale, regardless of how thin she becomes, she feels guilty because she isn't "thin enough" and she "must" lose more weight. In this way, the ego ideal inappropriately prompts the superego to generate guilty feelings.

Inappropriate guilt does not always lead people toward dangerous behaviors. Sometimes inappropriate guilt even causes people to *sublimate*—to channel their inappropriate desires into productive ones. For example, I once had an adult client who felt guilty because she was wealthy. She spent much of her time and money on benevolent activities with homeless people at shelters in downtown Atlanta. There is nothing wrong with her benevolence, but the thing that drove it was dysfunctional. There was nothing wrong with being wealthy. If she had earned her wealth by stealing, defrauding, or some other dishonest means, then guilt would have been appropriate. As it was, she had a successful business and she had earned her money honestly. Therefore, she had nothing about which she should have felt guilty. A more appropriate response to her wealth would have been a desire to share her money and time because she was grateful for what she had, rather than because of guilt.

Inappropriate guilt is more often destructive, though, and it leads people to overindulge in food, shopping, drugs, or alcohol. Inappropriate guilt can drive people to cut themselves, bang their heads against walls, mutilate their genitalia, or take their own lives. One of my clients was a childhood victim of sexual abuse and she believed that she was responsible for her sexual victimization in childhood. In order to deal with the inappropriate guilt she felt over having been sexually abused, she ate compulsively for several days at a time. She would buy boxes of cookies, ice cream, doughnuts, and other junk food and consume them while sitting in front of the television. Then, not only did she have inappropriate guilt because of her abuse, she would also feel guilty about bingeing. Therefore, she would spend the next several days starving herself. She had a distorted perception of herself, believing that she was never thin enough, never pretty enough, and never smart enough, and that she was responsible for the hideous behavior of her abuser.

Guilt is only one of many causes of the destructive behaviors—self-mutilation, eating disorders, and suicide—addressed in this chapter. In the following pages, I will present other causes of these disorders, spotlight symptoms that aid in diagnosing and recognizing them, and provide some suggestions for intervention.

SELF-MUTILATION

The most overt self-mutilating client I have ever seen was the one I mentioned in Chapter 5 who used a knife to carve the word "HELP" into her calf. Many of my clients have used knives, razor blades, fingernails and other sharp objects to scratch or cut their arms, breasts, abdomens, legs, or neck. Others have beaten themselves with boards or books, or thrown themselves repeatedly against walls. Self-abusive individuals may pinch, cut, or burn their genitals. Other self-abusive patients have been known to use a syringe to withdraw blood from major veins or arteries. These behaviors are quite bizarre, but you would be surprised at how many seemingly "normal" people do such extreme things to themselves. Princess Diana, one of the most famous and "glamorous" women in the world in the 1980s, was a self-mutilator. She publicly admitted throwing herself down stairs and cutting herself with razors, penknives, and other kitchen tools because of her torment over her marriage relationship. B. F. Skinner, a pioneer in psychological behaviorism, also admitted cutting himself at one point in his life because of his pain over a failed relationship. It is estimated that between 2 million and 3 million Americans cut or burn themselves, break bones, or otherwise mutilate themselves each year.

Self-mutilation has been linked to guilt, perfectionism, self-demanding personalities, and controlling behavior. Other evidence links this disorder to mental illnesses such as autism, borderline personality disorder, depression, dissociative identity disorder, and obsessive-compulsive disorder, to name just a few. Some individuals who self-mutilate do so because they feel guilty and believe they deserve punishment, while others do so because of a desire to control other people or to control their sexual selves. Others cut themselves as a result of dysfunctional thinking brought about by mental disorder. Still others do so because they are dealing with some unresolved trauma. In Chapter 5, I described abreaction and how children will relive their trauma. It is suggested that some self-mutilators use their bodies as a "theater to reenact the trauma of abuse."[1]

Each case has its own cause, and understanding the cause for a given client's self-mutilation is an important starting point for treatment.

Self-mutilators are not masochists, as some people mistakenly suppose. Masochists derive pleasure from receiving pain and they either abuse themselves or allow others to do it for them for the explicit purpose of receiving the pleasurable sensations pain produces for them. Self-mutilators, on the other hand, do not find pleasure in pain, per se. In fact, because of the dissociative nature of this activity, some mutilators have very little sensation or feel no pain at all when they cut or burn themselves. It is not unusual for a person to be unaware of what he or she is doing during the act of cutting. Rather than seeking pleasure from pain as masochists do, self-harmers seek relief from a painful emotional condition and self-injury is the medium through which they gain that relief.

Self-mutilators are not trying to commit suicide, either. Instead, their goal is to inflict injury, always stopping short of terminal behaviors. In essence, they are exhibiting a suicidal impulse on part of the body instead of the whole body.[2] One researcher even called self-mutilation "anti-suicide" in that the behavior replaces suicidal urges.[3] This does not mean that self-mutilators are not at risk for suicide. With some specific populations, such as borderline personality–disordered (BPD) clients who self-mutilate, their risk of suicide is double that of BPD clients who do not self-mutilate, and research indicates that these patients can easily escalate to suicidal behaviors.[4] In fact, suicide is sometimes thought of as the ultimate form of self-injury.

There is variability among the different types of self-mutilators. For example, some self-mutilators focus their attention exclusively on their genitalia. Almost all self-mutilators who focus their mutilations exclusively on their own genitalia are psychotic (87%).[5] Those who focus their mutilations on other body parts, excluding their genitalia, are often also diagnosed with borderline personality disorder. Most of my own clients who were mutilators were BPD. The common theme among all self-mutilators is that they are expressing aggression inwardly because they are unable to effectively express their anger, hostility, or frustration with words or other appropriate means.

The average age of onset for mutilation behaviors is the early to mid-teens, but self-mutilators may be ten years of age or forty. There is no rule or limit. The relationship between childhood sexual or physical abuse and self-mutilation is almost unquestioned. Theoretically, it makes great sense that the two would be linked. Abusive and painful acts related to the body are experienced and at the same time, the individual does not know how to productively express the anger and hostility that accompanies that abuse. Anger becomes internalized, turning to guilt, and, in response, the individual punishes the self. Researcher Shanti Shapiro notes that victims blame themselves for abuse, their self-blame becomes guilt, guilt becomes shame, which leads to a negative self-image and eventually to self-hate.[6]

Some studies indicate that upwards of 80 percent of all self-mutilators have some history of sexual or physical abuse in their pasts. Other studies have demonstrated a weaker relationship of only 60 percent between the two. Either way, incidence of sexual and physical abuse is present in mutilators in a far greater frequency than in the general population.

Most self-mutilators are female, adolescent, single, intelligent, and live in middle- to upper-middle-class families.[7] Cutting of one's wrist is the most common form of self-mutilation. However, girls are most likely to cut themselves on their wrists or the backs of their legs, while boys are more likely to bruise their arms or legs, or to burn their arms with cigarettes.[8] Self-injury is usually not isolated to one or two episodes. One study demonstrated that those who mutilate had an average of 93 scars.[9]

Many self-mutilators engage in sexual activity with older people.[10] It appears that sexual engagement with an older parental figure provides a sense of acceptance and security. About half of all victims of self-mutilation live in disrupted families (abuse, domestic violence, family dysfunction) and victims also lack an effective social support network, sometimes pairing together with other suicidal or self-mutilating individuals. This association only perpetuates their dysfunction. These individuals find it difficult to accept comfort from others.[11] This inhibits their ability to trust, which may explain why they associate with other mutilators—they assume if the person mutilates, then she can be trusted. This lack of trust, even of one's counselors, makes therapy difficult.

Well over half of all self-mutilators also have an eating disorder. Just as patients use eating disorders to control their parents or other authority figures (including unskilled therapists) and to deal with their frustrations, self-mutilation can be used as a form of manipulation and control as well. It is not just an attempt to gain attention, although attention is an issue. Clients who use self-harm as a means of control want the authority figure to recognize that he or she cannot stop the self-mutilation from occurring; this gives the patient a sense of power—knowing she has found a way to calm herself and control her negative feelings.

Some studies have noted sexual confusion among nearly all subjects who self-mutilate.[12] Because of sexual urges, homosexuality, or guilt related to sexual thoughts, impulses, or behaviors, some individuals punish themselves by damaging their bodies. Lesbians and gays have resorted to self-mutilation in an attempt to cope with the conflict between their sexual orientation and the social taboos against such behaviors. Coping with sexual maturation, alone, has been related to self-mutilation.[13] The many emotions and social issues involved in pubescence, combined with dysfunctional thinking or mental illness, may lead to self-mutilation. When one is painfully uncomfortable with one's gender or sexual identity, genital mutilation is not unlikely. Genital mutilation has been described as a substitute for self-castration.[14] Religious issues, while not always related to sexual issues, are sometimes the source of self-harm. Religious teachings regarding sexuality contribute to the development of the superego, sometimes creating overwhelming guilt that cannot be appeased. The ego ideal may involve aspirations that one should never lust or engage in certain types of sexual behaviors—homosexuality, masturbation, or premarital sexual intercourse. Yet the drive to engage in those behaviors may be overpowering and to suppose that one would never have sexual desires is unrealistic. It is important to note that religion, by itself, does not cause self-mutilation. Individuals who self-harm have many issues in their lives, apart from self-mutilation. For instance, their lack of coping strategies, immaturity, narcissistic needs, mental disorders, and other related issues contribute to cutting. Therefore, it would be oversimplistic and inappropriate to conclude that religious taboos regarding sexual behavior cause self-mutilation behaviors, but oppressive religions that condemn behavior without providing resolution are apt to create this type of powerful guilt.

Typical of clients with borderline personality disorder, self-mutilators divide the world into two distinct groups, black and white, good and bad. There is no gray area whatsoever. Not only do they see their friends, family and therapists as either all good or all bad, they see themselves this way, as well. When they fail to live up to their own unrealistic expectations, they see themselves as totally bad, unworthy, and deserving of punishment. These negative feelings lead them to punish and destroy themselves.

THERAPY

Therapeutic models for self-mutilators include psychodynamic therapy, behavioral and cognitive methods, group therapy, as well as pharmacological interventions. If the client is a clear danger to self, hospitalization may be necessary. Art therapy can be very effective with this population. Advocates for this form of therapy argue that it provides an alternative language (paint, sculpting, etc.) for communicating one's thoughts and that it also provides an outlet for hostility when one cannot effectively express anger verbally.[15] In short, one can paint, sculpt, or draw one's rage more easily than one can talk about it. The primary goal in counseling is to help the client manage his or her affect and channel emotions into productive outlets. Rochman writes that therapists must understand that self-mutilators do not see their behavior as a problem. Instead, they perceive this behavior as "something positive and helpful because it has enabled them to function in life."[16] This perspective must be altered.

In summary, self-mutilation is a dysfunctional coping strategy that provides catharsis for one's guilt, shame, or self-hate. It may be used to manipulate and control others and it may also be an expression of one's degree of pain. These patients often suffer from many dysfunctions, including family problems, coping difficulties, mental disorders, and eating disorders that must be addressed in conjunction with self-mutilation. Self-mutilators need professional intervention, especially borderline personality–disordered clients, because of the high risk of escalation to suicide.

EATING DISORDERS

In effect, people with eating disorders are mutilating themselves. Not only does the disorder often result in visible bodily changes, but it can also be fatal. In a sense, I suppose that makes it a form of unintentional suicide as well. Most individuals with an eating disorder have a distorted view of self. No matter how thin they become, even when their bones show through their clothing, they still perceive themselves as overweight. A lovely young lady, only seventeen years of age, sat across from me in my office one day. It was our third session. She was suicidal and also had anorexia nervosa, an eating disorder that led her to starve herself. "What do you see when you look in the mirror?" I asked her.

"I'm fat and ugly," she said very matter-of-factly and I know she believed that about herself, even though she was quite beautiful and weighed less than one hundred pounds. When she looked in a mirror, it was as if she were looking into a warped fun-house mirror. Her perception of herself was so distorted that it was impossible for her to see what I was seeing as I looked at her. Her distorted perception was brought about by a combination of depression, family problems, esteem problems, and immaturity. Treating this woman took a very long time and, at one point, I nearly lost her when she attempted suicide.

This distortion, as is so common among eating-disordered clients, sometimes has its roots in sexual abuse. Maria, who suffered from bulimia nervosa, had been sexually violated repeatedly by her father. Maria's father, who had a host of psychological problems himself, consistently made it clear to his daughter that she was disgusting to him, calling her "little fat girl" and other unkind names. Yet sometimes, just minutes after verbally berating her, he would molest her. Over time she began to associate the pain of molestation with his hurtful words about her appearance. This association was converted into an irrational belief that if she were skinnier, the sexual abuse would stop, and yet, another part of her psyche told her that if she were prettier (if she looked "right" given her perception of what she was supposed to look like), the molestations would only become more frequent. Therefore, as Maria battled between these conflicting thoughts, she would alternate between starving herself to get "thin enough" and gorging herself on boxes of cookies, ice cream, and potato chips so she would be "too fat and undesirable" for him to molest.

There are two types of eating disorders identified by the *Diagnostic and Statistical Manual of Mental Disorders, Fourth Edition, Text Revision (DSM IV-*

TR). Anorexia nervosa involves an intense fear of weight gain that results in self-starvation. Individuals who are suffering from anorexia nervosa are often very thin. They dress in baggy clothing to disguise their skeletal forms, but they cannot hide their gaunt faces, bony fingers and wrists, and emaciated necks. Anorexic individuals either binge briefly, followed by purging (self-induced vomiting, laxatives, etc.) or they are "restrictive," meaning they do not binge/purge at all. Anorexia is a very serious disorder that can even be fatal. Musician Karen Carpenter died of heart failure at just thirty-two years of age. She had struggled with anorexia for years and the resultant heart damage directly contributed to her death.

Bulimia nervosa is a disorder in which one alternates between self-starvation and bingeing, just as Maria did. Many bulimics are either normal in weight for their for age and height, or they are slightly overweight. Maria weighed about fifteen pounds above normal for her age and height. There are two forms of bulimia—the purging and nonpurging forms. After bulimics binge out of control, sometimes on 20,000 calories per day, they are driven to rid themselves of the food they have eaten. In the purging form, they rid themselves of food through the use of laxatives or self-induced vomiting. In the nonpurging form, they rid themselves of the food through excessive exercise or the use of diet pills. A bulimic's weight may frequently fluctuate by ten or more pounds as she cycles between bingeing and purging. Bulimia is often accompanied by other compulsive behaviors like sexual promiscuity, shoplifting, and drug abuse.

Other eating disorders that are not official diagnoses in the *DSM IV-TR* include anorexia athletica (compulsive exercising), orthorexia nervosa (eating only "superior" food), and pica (the eating of nonfoods such as chalk or paper). These disorders would be classified as "Eating Disorders Not Otherwise Specified" by the *DSM IV-TR*. All eating disorders are expressions of underlying psychosocial problems.

Frequency and Origins

More than 7 million females as well as approximately 1 million males in the United States have an eating disorder and it is estimated that 6 percent of these 8 million people die annually as a result of their eating disorders. Bulimics outnumber anorexics by 4:1. Even though 90 percent of the people with eating disorders are female, males are growing in number, especially among jockeys, runners, wrestlers, models, and others whose careers or hobbies depend on body image. Almost 90 percent of those with eating disorders began prior to age twenty and the number of children as young as eight or nine years of age with eating disorders is on the rise. This is not a small problem. One study of senior high school students in twenty different high schools and eighteen different states, conducted in 1990, found that 11 percent of all students suffered from anorexia or bulimia.[17] The perception that one does not look right is perpetuated by a Western culture that idolizes thinness to the point that is not only unrealistic, but sometimes downright unhealthy. One research study noted that 32 percent of female TV network characters are underweight while only 3 percent of female TV network characters are overweight—in the general population, by contrast, 5 percent of all females are underweight while 25 percent of all females are overweight.[18] Study after study indicates that our culture creates an impression of a "normal" body, especially for females, that is unrealistic. More than half of all teenaged girls diet or think they should be on a diet. An interesting study done in 1995 in the Pacific paradise island of Fiji found that before they had television, the people of Fiji thought the ideal body was "round, plump and soft." "Then, after 38 months of *Melrose Place* and *Beverly Hills, 90210*, and similar Western shows, Fijian teenage girls showed serious signs of eating disorders."[19]

Many of the same issues that lead to self-mutilation are also variables related to eating disorders. A dysfunctional home life, poor communication at home, guilt, shame, and the inability to verbalize one's feelings and thoughts in a healthy way are all causes of these disorders. Families of bulimics have higher rates of affective disorders and obesity, while anorexics often have difficulties related to autonomy and expressiveness (including the direct expression of anger).[20] Anorexia has been described as a "symbolic language used by people who don't know how to, or are afraid to, express powerful emotions directly with words."[21] Instead of telling a parent, for example, "I do not want you to control my life," an anorexic communicates that the parent cannot control her by refusing to eat.

Mental illness—specifically, depression, borderline personality disorder, and obsessive-compulsive disorder—is also closely linked to eating disorders. For example, as I described earlier, a symptom of borderline personality disorder is the tendency to divide the world into two distinct parts—good or bad. In a similar way, these patients divide other things into discrete halves as well. They approach tasks with an all-or-nothing attitude, so they either don't engage in an activity at all, or they are obsessed with the activity. If BPD patients also have an eating disorder, they will diet to the extreme (anorexia) or eat to the extreme and then purge to the extreme (bulimia). Their perfectionistic approach to life makes it very difficult for them to do anything in moderation and they have unrealistic expectations of themselves and others that lead to continual disappointments; hence, more guilt, shame, and depression.

The relationship between sexual abuse and eating disorders is unclear. Some research indicates no more frequent incidence of sexual abuse among eating-disordered clients than in the normal population, while other studies show a high degree of correlation between the two. The contradictory data may be due to the fact that it is often difficult to distinguish truth from fiction with these clients. Some clients with eating disorders choose to deceive even their therapists because they don't trust them, or because they believe they will gain pity or attention by their fabrications. In Chapter 3 I described my client who denied sexual abuse when I was certain it had occurred. Likewise, I have had clients who have claimed to have been sexually or physically abused, but there is neither physical evidence of abuse nor is there any evidence of abuse in their psychological workup. These clients fabricate rape, molestation, physical abuse, and other issues as a symptom of their psychological dysfunction, making therapy very challenging. These are very frail people who would not take it very well if you called them liars, yet it is not productive to perpetuate their fabrications. Their treatment requires a delicate touch.

People with eating disorders are more likely to be raised by parents who overvalue physical appearance. Their mothers tend to be emotionally "cool"; their fathers emotionally distant or absent; and the family structure overprotective and lacking in effectual conflict resolving skills.[22] There is even evidence that brain physiology is related to eating disorders. Eating stimulates areas of the brain, activating chemicals that create peaceful or pleasurable feelings. Finally, even though bulimics may be promiscuous, some anorexic patients use their eating disorder to avoid sexual intimacy, perhaps because of sexual issues in the past. Several things can trigger eating disorders or cause them to recur, including trauma, loss, relationship problems, stress, loneliness, and guilt, as can the affiliation with "appearance-obsessed" friends (i.e., sorority sisters, members of a theater troupe, models, dancers).[23]

Physical Results of Eating Disorders

Anorexia and bulimia have differing physical ramifications. For anorexic patients, physical weakness, heart damage, cognitive impairment, apathy, dizziness, and loss of sexual interest are all likely. Some of my clients with eating disorders have not menstruated in over a year, another side effect of anorexia. Bulimia can result in tooth decay due to the exposure of the teeth to gastric fluid because of excessive vomiting. Like anorexic patients, bulimics may experience chest pains, heart palpitations, weakness, and lethargy. Both anorexics and bulimics may suffer from dehydration and kidney damage. Emotional problems, such as depression, shame, guilt, low self-esteem, and mood swings are not unusual.

Warning Signs

Tables 8.1 and 8.2 outline the warning signs for anorexia and bulimia. Especially at risk are children who are eager to please, who have problems with impulse control and who have been diagnosed with depression.[24]

Table 8.1
Warning Signs for Anorexia Nervosa

- ❑ Self-starvation
- ❑ Fear of weight gain
- ❑ Noticeable weight loss
- ❑ Skeletal appearance
- ❑ Obsession with clothing size
- ❑ Constantly drinking diet sodas
- ❑ Spits out food
- ❑ Won't eat in front of others
- ❑ Lies about eating habits
- ❑ Skips meals
- ❑ Refusal to eat
- ❑ Shows disgust around formerly favorite foods
- ❑ Compulsive exercise
- ❑ Wears baggy, loose clothing that covers all body parts, even when inappropriate for the weather
- ❑ Unrealistic body image
- ❑ Loathing of one or more body parts
- ❑ Absent menstruation

Also at risk are those who have difficulty talking about their feelings, those who have superficial relationships, and those with a very poor self-image.

Treatment

Treating eating disorders requires experience and training. These disorders ordinarily do not go away by themselves and, as I mentioned earlier,

Table 8.2
Warning Signs for Bulimia Nervosa

- ❑ Preoccupation with food
- ❑ Binge eating in secret
- ❑ Noticeable weight fluctuation
- ❑ Constantly drinking diet drinks
- ❑ Lies about eating habits
- ❑ Vomiting
- ❑ Diet pills
- ❑ Laxatives
- ❑ Unrealistic body image
- ❑ Obsession with clothing size
- ❑ Denial of hunger
- ❑ Compulsive exercise
- ❑ Shoplifting
- ❑ Sexual promiscuity

can lead to serious health problems and even death. Treatment must involve addressing one's unrealistic self-image and these distortions need to be modified. These clients, like chemically dependent clients, are very unreliable and cannot be trusted. They will hide their destructive behaviors from their therapists and continue in their dysfunctional habits if they are not held accountable and if therapists do not follow up on them.

A team approach to treating these disorders may be helpful. Nutritional counseling, rehabilitation counseling, and psychotherapy to address the underlying causes of the eating disorder are all important. Some change in behavior should be seen in a short period of time, but complete treatment of eating disorders is normally long term, taking two or more years. Even with professional intervention, about half of all patients who seek treatment will revert to their destructive habits. One study tracked adolescent patients with anorexia who had been hospitalized. A fifteen-year follow-up study showed that about three-quarters of all patients recovered fully, but the time for full recovery ranged between fifty-seven and seventy-nine months.[25] Treatment is expensive, especially if it involves hospitalization, and may cost thousands of dollars per month. Health insurance sometimes covers the majority of these costs, but HMOs and PPOs vary widely in the treatments they will cover. It is an unfortunate truth that many people with eating disorders go untreated simply because they do not have the financial resources to overcome the problem.

SUICIDE

While doing my research for this chapter, I came across a number of theorists who talked about "serious suicide attempts" as predictors of suicide. I know what they mean when they use the term "serious." They are actually referring to how potentially lethal the method was, but this language perpetuates the belief that some attempts are not serious. Even though some attempts are clearly more lethal than others, all attempts are serious. Once a client told me he tried to kill himself by holding his breath. Another child told me he tried to kill himself by dreaming that he fell off a cliff. It is impossible to kill yourself by holding your breath or through your dreams. Therefore, one might suppose these attempts were "not very serious." However, there are at least three mistaken notions about this assumption. First of all, these two children did not know it was impossible to commit suicide in the way they were contemplating. In their minds, holding one's breath or dreaming one's death was the same as putting a gun to their heads. Second, the most important issue is that these boys both were serious in their consideration of suicide, even if their attempts were feeble. To assert that only lethal methods of suicide are serious supposes that the attempts are less of a cry for help than nonlethal methods. Third, most people who attempt suicide do not want to die. If so, nobody would ever call a suicide hot line. Instead, they are looking for a reason to live; only in the absence of any credible evidence as why one should go on living will they commit suicide. They tell others of their plans, either directly or in a coded manner, in hopes that someone will hear them calling for help. Many times, when referring to a suicide attempt, someone says, "He was only trying to get attention." Of course he was. The motive for that attention varies, but most suicidal people want to be noticed, they want to be considered important, they desperately want some meaning in their lives, and they want relief from the pain (psychological and/or physical) that they are experiencing.

In January 2002, fifteen-year-old Charles Bishop left an airport near Tampa, Florida, on a solo training flight. Less than fifteen minutes later, he flew the single-engine Cessna into the forty-two-story Bank of America Plaza building in Tampa, killing himself, but injuring no one else. Just four months after the September 11 terrorist attacks, authorities feared a connection with terrorism. In fact, they found a note in the boy's pocket expressing support for Osama bin Laden and the September 11 attacks. However, upon further investigation, it was determined that Bishop was no terrorist. Instead, he was a high school freshman, described by authorities as a troubled boy with few friends. Teachers and relatives claimed he was well liked and sociable and they denied they saw any signs of his suicidal intent prior to the crash, but he was in the midst of his freshman year, having transitioned from a small school of only 275 students to a high school of 2,200 students in Dunedin, Florida, and he fit many of the predictors for suicide. He was lonely and had made few friends at his new school. He had just experienced a significant life transition and he was in the midst of his pubescence.

His mother argued that her son's behavior was due to the acne medication Accutane that he had been taking, and she filed a $70 million wrongful death and negligence lawsuit against the manufacturer of the medication. As with many suicides, the real motives behind his decision may never be known, but it is reasonable to suppose that he wanted to be recognized as someone important. It would be easy to get lost in the large high school he was attending and his comments supporting bin Laden do not match the history of the boy who apparently wanted to join the military to help fight the war on terrorism. As with all public suicides, his death made a statement. It appears to me that the statement he wanted to make was "Notice me."

Suicide is relatively rare compared with other causes of death. Only about 2 percent of all deaths are suicides.[26] But suicide is often more difficult to deal with than other forms of death because we like to think that people will always have hope and something to live for. Even though most of us at one time or another have considered suicide as a way to deal with our problems, we have quickly realized that we have other coping skills that we believe to be more effective. For those who attempt or commit suicide, they have chosen it when all other coping mechanisms have failed. People who are seriously considering suicide are faced with hopelessness, isolation, and a desire to be loved and needed, and they are overwhelmed by life's challenges, embarrassed that they cannot cope. They often feel totally alone, as if they were the only ones who have ever felt this way. The more they believe their condition will never improve, the more energy they invest into a plan for self-termination. In despair and frustration, they dread the everyday business of life. By far, most people who think about suicide don't want to die and they would welcome some other option—they just can't figure out what that option might be.

There are varying degrees of risk for suicide. A fleeting thought does not pose as serious a risk as when one actually makes a plan to commit the act. The next step toward high risk is to make an attempt, and various attempts have differing levels of risk as well. Once I had a client who tried to commit suicide by consuming a handful of antacid tablets—not a very lethal method. It is this kind of attempt that leads some to say it was not a "serious" attempt, but the fact remains that she did make an attempt. Sometimes even a lethal attempt is not a "serious" attempt. It is not unheard of for people to attempt suicide, hoping to be found and saved. For example, a woman may overdose on medication, but she chooses to do it just minutes before her roommate or spouse is due to return home. She hopes she will be found and the spouse or roommate will call an ambulance; thus, she will be saved and people will realize how "serious" she is. However, when her roommate or spouse is caught in traffic or delayed at work, she accidentally succeeds. Therefore, all attempts are serious statements. They all communicate the same message: "I need help."

On the whole, people who commit suicide do not want to die as much as they want relief from their loneliness, sorrow, and pain. By the time they make an attempt, they have expended all their resources. Once when I was working with a highly suicidal client, she asked me, "What do I have to live for?" It was a hard question to answer. Honestly, many times during our therapeutic relationship I had thought about how glad I was that I was not her. She was seventeen years old and had, for all practical purposes, been abandoned by her parents. She was an obnoxious, unlikable person, who was angry or depressed almost all the time. She snipped at everyone and when she was in a bad mood, which was most of the time, she was downright mean. She was very lonely and the fact that she had almost no social skills only made her loneliness worse. Part of her psychological dysfunction caused her to refuse to allow anyone to get close to her or show her affection. Whenever people tried to reach out to her, her ungratefulness and foul temper, driven by this dysfunction, eventually turned them away. This only confirmed to her that she was unworthy of love and made her more bitter. She was intelligent, but she did not see that in herself and, because of her laziness and preoccupation with her childish passions (television, video games, and other such things), she earned very poor grades. Therefore, she had very little immediate prospect for "happiness" as the term is usually applied. What could I say? Times will get better? Her experience had told her that times only got worse and, unless something changed, she was in for more of the same. To talk about the future, relatives and people who would miss her, and hope for a better life would have had no impact. It was a very hard question, indeed.

Statistics

Suicide is a problem across the life span. Even though elderly people are statistically at the highest risk for suicide, young people come in second. Children and young adults between the ages of fifteen and twenty-four are at the highest risk among the young. In 1999, suicide was the third leading cause of death among this age group.[27] Even more startling is the fact that two hundred or more children younger than age fourteen commit suicide each year and the number is increasing. Between 1980 and 1997, the suicide rate for children ages ten to fourteen increased by 109 percent. Suicide is the sixth leading cause of death for children ages five to fourteen.[28] The number of actual suicides may be even higher because many deaths that are ruled as accidents may in fact be suicides. A child will commit suicide by the only means he or she knows—jumping off a high place, running into traffic, consuming poisons or medications, or stepping in front of a train. Because of the age of these young victims, suicide is rarely considered a possible cause of death. Homicides and suicides account for three-quarters of adolescent deaths.[29] The surgeon general notes that somewhere in the United States a child commits suicide every two hours.[30]

Females are far more likely to attempt suicide, but males are at least four times more likely to succeed. Males succeed at suicide more often than females because males are more likely to choose violent methods. For example, males are more likely than females to use a firearm. Females, however, are more likely to take pills. If caught in time, the chance of recovery from an overdose of medication is much better than the chance of recovery from a gunshot wound to the head (although I have had clients who survived self-inflicted gunshot wounds to the head). Drug overdose, hanging, poison, jumping from a high place, and use of a firearm are all common means of suicide by children. Whether attempts or completions, the thought that a child or adolescent—one who has so many possibilities lying ahead in his future—believed his life was so hopeless that he wanted to end it is sobering.

Risk for Suicide

Only about half the time do those who commit suicide leave a note explaining their reasons. In cases where no note is left, survivors can only speculate about the cause. People vary in their psychosocial situations, but suicide has been very well researched for many years, allowing us to draw some general conclusions. For example, children in families where a suicide has occurred are nine times more likely to attempt suicide than children who have no exposure to suicide.[31] Exposure to suicide through the media also increases risk. Known as *suicide clusters*, children are more likely to commit suicide when stories about suicide are present in the news or in other areas of their daily lives. Children imitate what they see. According to the surgeon general, almost all children and adolescents who commit suicide (90%) have a mental disorder before their death.[32] Even though not all people with diagnosed mental disorders are suicidal, it is a very common symptom among both adults and children. Some diagnoses are more directly related to suicidal attempts and completions than others. The most common disorders of suicidal patients are mood disorders, anxiety disorders, substance abuse disorders, and borderline personality disorders. Depression, a specific mood disorder, is highly correlated with suicide. Children are twelve times more likely to commit suicide if they are diagnosed with depression than if they are not.[33]

Pubescent children are more likely to commit suicide than younger children. Young children, even though they think about suicide, don't have the cognitive skills to formulate and execute a suicidal plan, nor do they have the freedom or means to do so until they reach adolescence. By the time they reach adolescence, they have means, cognitive ability to develop a plan, and freedom to go out and do it, not to mention the peer influence and stress of adolescence. Puberty also brings with it a host of sexual issues, including homosexuality, breakup of romances, and pregnancy, increasing the risk for suicide. One's developing sexuality and confusion that accompanies that development play an important role in suicidal ideation. Peer influence during puberty, a time of "vibrant sexual consciousness," is directly related to attachment issues with the parent and the anxiety related to the severing of those attachments as one approaches adulthood.[34] In brief, one's sexuality plays a significant role in suicidal thinking and behavior.

Children who experience rejection from their family or friends are at greater risk for suicide, as are children who experience excessive pressure to conform, to achieve athletically and academically, and children whose family lives are in disarray as a result of divorce, separation, or remarriage. Families who do not communicate effectively with their children are also at risk because children rely on guidance from their parents to teach them how to cope with life's problems. For example, my nine-year-old daughter came into my office at home one day. In one hand she held the case for my one-hundred-foot tape measure and in her other hand was a tangled mass of about fifty feet of tape. She was crying because she had gotten the tape out to "measure her head," but then she couldn't get it back in the case. She didn't know there was a fold-up handle on the side that was used to rewind the tape. Even though this was a very small issue for me, it was an insurmountable problem for her. She felt better when she realized the problem could be fixed and the world was not going to end as a result of her actions. Adults easily forget how overwhelming seemingly little things can be to children who have far fewer resources for problem solving. Children need their parents to help them cope with academic stress, loss, rejection, disappointment, mistakes, and other daily issues in life. When parents are not accessible to their children, or when their communication is dysfunctional, children are left to come up with their own problem-solving ideas and coping strategies.

There is even some evidence that those who commit suicide by violent means have measurable brain chemistry changes. There have been some studies that have correlated suicide by violent means with low levels of a chemical in cerebrospinal fluid called 5-hydroxyindoleacetic acid (5-HIAA).[35] It is helpful to note the possible physiological connection to suicide, but the more likely contributors are psychological and sociological.

It is important to recognize symptoms in individuals that are indicative of suicidal ideation. Perhaps the most obvious warning sign of one's suicidal potential is a prior attempt. It is estimated that people attempt suicide between eight and twenty-four times before they actually succeed.[36] This is especially significant for males who have made suicide attempts. Females who have made previous attempts at suicide are three times more likely to kill themselves and males with previous attempts are thirty times more likely to commit suicide.[37] Ironically, when someone attempts suicide several times, friends and family members become desensitized and take the attempts less seriously. Therefore, the more often a person attempts suicide, the *less* serious people think he is, when just the opposite is true.

Table 8.3 outlines a list of variables that are correlated with increased risk of suicide. These items are not in any formal order. However, the items toward the top tend to be universally agreed-upon warning signs among researchers and suicide experts, while the items toward the bottom are mentioned in some studies, but not others. The list is mostly self-explanatory, but I will elaborate on a few issues.

The availability of firearms, especially handguns, greatly increases the likelihood of suicide because firearms are used in three-fifths of all suicides. Researchers and gun-control advocates note that because handguns are used for home protection, they are thirteen times more likely to be kept both loaded and unlocked than rifles.[38] For this reason, many have called for restrictions and even a ban on handguns. There is no question that firearms increase risk of injury, suicide, and death. Guns in the home are not only a risk to the children in that home, but also to any child who visits that home. Therefore, parents may have no weapons in their own homes, but their children could still commit suicide using a firearm discovered at a friend's home or one provided by a friend. However, these

Table 8.3
Warning Signs for Suicidal Behavior

- ❑ Suicidal attempts
- ❑ Direct threats and/or an overt suicide plan
- ❑ Letters/notes that imply closure (i.e., writing a will)/statements of finality
- ❑ Neglect of personal hygiene
- ❑ Drug or alcohol use
- ❑ History of psychiatric hospitalization
- ❑ Diagnosed psychiatric disorder (especially depression, anxiety, borderline personality disorder)
- ❑ Feelings of hopelessness/powerlessness/worthlessness/guilt/shame
- ❑ Giving away of important possessions
- ❑ Behavioral changes
- ❑ Preoccupation or fascination with death
- ❑ Risk-taking behaviors
- ❑ Social isolation
- ❑ Self-mutilation, head banging, breath holding, and hair pulling
- ❑ Sleep disturbances
- ❑ Change in appetite/eating habits
- ❑ Decreased pleasure in activities that were once pleasurable
- ❑ Withdrawal
- ❑ Impulsivity
- ❑ Racing thoughts/distractibility/inability to concentrate
- ❑ Running away
- ❑ Promiscuity
- ❑ Home-life problems
- ❑ Availability of a firearm
- ❑ Recent loss
- ❑ Failure to attend school or work
- ❑ Declining school performance
- ❑ Arrest record
- ❑ Externalized violence in the past (bullying, behavioral problems)

statistics may be somewhat deceiving. It is obvious that people are more likely to be injured or killed by guns when they have access to guns than when they do not. We don't need research studies to tell us that. Calling for a ban on handguns based on this statistic is overreactive and misleading. No one wants children to be harmed and we all want a safe environment, but using this logic, we might also call for a ban on boats, personal watercraft, automobiles, and other items that contribute to the deaths of children. After all, one cannot be killed in a boating or automobile accident if no boats or cars are available. Even though I agree that firearms pose a significant risk, the responsible storage and use of handguns is equally as important an issue as the presence or absence of a weapon. If gun owners properly secured their weapons and found other means for protecting their homes, the number of deaths by firearm would decline.

The item described in Table 8.3 as "recent loss" could include a number of things. The loss of a girlfriend or boyfriend, the death of close friend or relative, or the suicide of a friend or family member are all forms of loss. Loss of freedom because of an arrest or perceived loss of one's future because of bad grades, low standardized test scores, or rejected college admissions applications are also related to this item. Finally, the loss of one's health due to disease or an accident should also be considered.

Home-life problems would include divorce, separation, or remarriage of a parent, and certain times of the year can trigger suicidal ideation. Events, days, or traditions that have symbolic meaning to a person, such as anniversaries, holidays, and birthdays, are times that a therapist or parent should recognize as times of high risk.

Not only is it helpful to know the risk factors and warning signs for those who have an *increased* risk of suicide, it is also helpful to know the variables that *decrease* risk of suicide. Among the variables that help decrease risk are high levels of sociability in the mother and father, an accepting nature in the mother and father, religiosity, a large social support network, high ego strength, high self-esteem, calm mood, replacement as coping style, and overcoming as coping style.[39] Fostering these variables can help decrease suicide risk.

Suicide Pacts

For survivors, suicide is painful enough when it involves only one child. When a group commits suicide together, it is even more devastating. Many times over the past twenty years, groups of two, three, five, or ten young people have taken their lives at one time. For example, in Seoul, South Korea, two teens and an adult jumped from the twenty-eighth floor of an apartment building after making a suicide pact on an Internet site. A fourth man had also agreed to jump with them, but he changed his mind. In Australia, fifteen Middle Eastern teens being detained by immigration threatened a mass suicide to protest the conditions of their detention. Adults commit suicide in pairs, but they are usually elderly couples, one or both of whom are suffering from a terminal disease, who decide they have lived long enough and that they can neither bear the suffering of the other, nor the thought of living alone. Children, on the other hand, commit suicide in groups for far different reasons. Author Michael Conner provides several reasons why children commit suicide in groups. Teens look to each other for support, especially when they have little support at home. When they are in the midst of severely painful emotions, they look to their peers for help, rather than to their parents. When troubled children find each other and as they commiserate about their problems, the idea of suicide becomes more appealing and less frightening. Finally, if their mental state does not improve, they lose hope. Conner suggests that nobody wants to die alone and a group suicide gives their lives, and deaths, some meaning.[40]

Also contributing both to the suicide rate among teens overall as well as suicide pacts, young people have a tendency to romanticize suicide. In one study, the majority of students surveyed considered suicide a reasonable problem-solving strategy.[41] Rather than seeing suicide as a desperate and dysfunctional means of dealing with life's problems, many adolescents hold an almost Shakespearean "Romeo and Juliet" romanticization of lovers who commit suicide. Likewise, the ease of communication via the Internet has contributed to the problem. Internet pacts like the one mentioned above have been associated with a number of deaths. Through Internet chat rooms, troubled teens (people of any age, actually) can congregate, feed one another's depression, and make plans for their own demise. Using the Internet, they can also look up methods for killing themselves on suicide Web sites and even order poisons over the Internet from sites that specialize in suicide. The Internet is a wonderful tool. Much of my research is done via the Internet and there are far more suicide prevention sites than sites for helping people commit suicide. However, parents need to understand that when its use is unsupervised, the Internet can be extremely dangerous.

The Media

Regardless of their claims to the contrary, the media play a significant role in suicidal behaviors among teens. There is no doubt that radio, television, music, films, magazines, and newspapers have an influence on our lives. That is why a business will pay millions of dollars for a single, strategically placed advertisement. How members of the media can then argue that movies, music, and television shows with violent themes have no effect on our children is a mystery to me. "Then shall we simply allow our children to listen to any stories that anyone happens to make up, and so receive into their minds ideas often the very opposite of those we shall think they ought to have when they grow up?" This statement was not made by some 1990s conservative religious leader about television and movies. It was a question posed by Socrates to his student Plato in Plato's magnificent work *The Republic*.[42] Thirty years ago in 1972, the surgeon general announced his concern about the relationship between television and aggression. He said, "Televised violence, indeed, does have an adverse effect on certain members of our society."[43] A joint statement released by the American Medical Association, the American Academy of Pediatrics, the American Psychological Association, the American Psychiatric Association, the American Academy of Family Physicians, and the American Academy of Child and Adolescent Psychiatry proposed that viewing violence leads to desensitization, to perceiving violence as an effective way to solve problems, and perhaps to real-life violence.[44] Yet we still produce hours of filthy television programming, music, movies, and print media every week—all under the ridiculous notion that it has no effect on children, the most vulnerable members of our community.

The courts and public opinion alike seem to discredit the influence musicians and actors have on impressionable teens. In 1991, a judge threw out a lawsuit brought against singer Ozzy Osbourne. The parents of a sixteen-year-old boy claimed that Osbourne's song "Suicide Solution" contributed to the death of their son who listened to it repeatedly. The song lyrics instructed the listener that suicide was the only option, advice this young man decided to follow. Granted, this boy was very troubled, but healthy young people are at less risk for suicide anyway. Likewise, it should come as no surprise that a troubled teen with poor coping skills might select a coping strategy presented by a music idol rather than seeking help from a more responsible source. Many artists, however, criticize the suggestion that the music had anything to do with this suicide. Here are the words of one musician responding to this case: "The guy killed himself with his father's gun, which should have been put away. Besides, he'd drunk eight beers. And yet they were claiming that the suicide was a result of hearing a rock 'n' roll record. I mean, it's all pretty thin."[45] The victim had many problems, but the influence of alcohol was not the only factor contributing to his suicide, any more than the music was the only contributing factor.

In a similar case, a twenty-year-old man named James Vance and his eighteen-year-old friend shot themselves in the head with a shotgun on a church playground. They had consumed drugs and alcohol prior to the shooting and they had destroyed everything in Vance's room—everything except his albums and his stereo. Vance's friend died in the shooting, but Vance, despite a shotgun blast to the head, lived three more years. Vance had a very troubled past. He ran away from home more than a dozen times, he admitted using a variety of drugs and alcohol, and he had an unstable home life. Yet also contributing to his frame of mind was his music. A favorite was a British rock band called Judas Priest whose music contained violent themes. His mother said that James would "quote lyrics just as if they were scriptures." Yet when the Vances brought a lawsuit against the rock band, it was thrown out of court.

I am not suggesting that either of these music groups were solely liable for the suicides of these young men, but I am suggesting that it is absurd to assume that their music had *no* influence on them. Media icons have a greater ability to affect behavior than nonfamous people do. That is why companies pay millions of dollars to superstars to have them pitch products. Do you think that Jamie Lee Curtis pitching a cellular telephone company is more effective than if I did it? Of course! Therefore, a musician, actor, or athlete who is well known and idolized will have more influence on the viewer's behavior than one who is not famous. The influence these idols have can be either positive or negative, but it is unquestioned that they do have an influence.

Suicide Summary

Suicide is almost always preceded by attempts to deal with pain, loneliness, and despair in some other way. When people have expended their resources, they are at high risk for suicide, especially if they suffer from mental illness and if one or more of the many variables correlated with suicide apply to them. Drugs, alcohol, sexual issues, and a host of other factors contribute to suicidal ideation and attempts. Likewise, the media, the availability of lethal means, and a dysfunctional home and/or peer group all contribute to the suicide rate. In Chapter 11, I will provide ways that suicidal behavior can be addressed both by clinicians and by the layperson. Intervention often boils down to a concerned listener who is willing to invest time and energy in another human being and who can provide a sense of hope for tired and desperate people.

CONCLUDING REMARKS

Self-destruction takes many forms. It exhibits itself in risk-taking behaviors—reckless driving, smoking, drug use—and as it grows more serious it can cause the individual to attempt to destroy one's body through cutting, burning, bruising, self-starvation, and eventually self-termination. All these behaviors have psychodynamic causes and the propensity for such behaviors can be seen before they fully emerge if one knows what to look for. No suicidal individual, for example, goes from being a happy, healthy individual one day, only to attempt suicide the next. Many warning signs precede the individual's self-destructive behavior. Psychotherapeutic intervention can prevent death and greatly reduce the risk of long-term damage from self-destructive behaviors if it is done properly and quickly enough.

Returning to the story earlier in the chapter of my client who felt life was hopeless and who asked me what she had to live for, there was little I could tell her. As much as I wish that I could have, I could not promise her a rosy future. Frankly, I knew she would probably always have significant difficulties in her life, but I have never lost a suicidal client and I didn't intend to start with her.

"What do you want in life?" I asked her.

She paused, started to speak, and then closed her mouth. As she furrowed her brow, I realized she didn't really know what she wanted.

"Something other than this," she finally answered.

"Maybe," I began, "instead of looking at what you *have* to live for, we might be better served if we look for what it is that you want to *achieve* that you don't have right now."

She thought for a few minutes. "I want to feel like I have some purpose," she said. "I want friends and I want a job."

The conversation continued and by the end of that session, she was no longer focusing only on what she didn't have. Instead we began working on how she could get what she wanted in life. In the coming sessions, she began to see a future for herself and she was working on ways to achieve her goals. We worked together for several months and then off and on for eight years. Even today we still have occasional contact. Her life is still difficult, as I predicted. She has had one or two very difficult dating relationships and she remains unmarried, but she has learned to cope with her disappointments in much healthier ways. She set career goals for herself that she has attained and she has dramatically improved her social skills. As a consequence, she has several friends and a life that is not nearly as lonely. She hasn't talked about suicide in years. I have high hopes for her.

As a final note, the quote at the beginning of the chapter was written many years ago by a client of mine. She was in serious distress at the time and suicide was an ever-present risk for her. After extensive therapy, her condition greatly improved. She went on to college, later married and earned a master's degree, and now is a therapist in practice. I believe her personal experience with depression and suicidal ideation will prove to be useful tools as she works with her own clients in the years to come.

NOTES

1. Diana Milia, "Art therapy with a self-mutilating adolescent girl," *American Journal of Art Therapy* (Internet Edition), *34*, May 1996.

2. Laurie MacAniff Zila and Mark S. Kiselica, "Understanding and counseling self-mutilation in female adolescents and young adults," *Journal of Counseling and Development, 79* (Winter 2001): 47.

3. Elizabeth Faulconer and Matt House, "Arterial blood gas: A rare form of self-mutilation and a review of its psychological functions," *American Journal of Psychotherapy, 55* (2001): 411.

4. J. Christopher Fowler, Mark J. Hilsenroth, and Eric Nolan, "Exploring the inner world of self-mutilating borderline patients: A Rorschach investigation," *Bulletin of the Menninger Clinic, 64* (Summer 2000): 366.

5. N. Eke, "Genital self-mutilation: There is no method in this madness," *BJU International, 85* (2000): 295.

6. Shanti Shapiro, "Self-mutilation and self-blame in incest victims," *American Journal of Psychotherapy, 16* (January 1987): 47.

7. Zila and Kiselica, "Understanding and counseling self-mutilation," p. 46.

8. Sue Rochman, "The cutting edge," *Advocate* (Internet Edition), May 23, 2000.

9. Zila and Kiselica, "Understanding and counseling self-mutilation," p. 48.

10. Shapiro, "Self-mutilation and self-blame," p. 52.

11. Zila and Kiselica, "Understanding and counseling self-mutilation," p. 49.

12. Ibid., p. 48.

13. Faulconer and House, "Arerial blood gas," p. 411.

14. Milia, "art therapy with a self-mutilating adolescent girl."

15. Ibid.

16. Rochman, "The cutting edge."

17. "High school study on eating disorders," National Association of Anorexia Nervosa and Associated Disorders, www.anad.org/hsstudy.htm, June 11, 2002.

18. "What causes eating disorders?" National Association of Anorexia Nervosa and Associated Disorders, www.anad.org/causes.htm, June 11, 2002.

19. Ibid.

20. "Disease definition, epidemiology, and natural history," American Psychiatric Association, www.psych.org/clin_res/guidebk-4.cfm, June 11, 2002.

21. "Who is at risk for developing an eating disorder?" National Association of Anorexia Nervosa and Associated Disorders, www.anad.org/who.htm, June 11, 2002.

22. "What causes eating disorders?"

23. Ibid.

24. "Who is at risk for developing an eating disorder?"

25. "Disease definition, epidemiology, and natural history."

26. "What can I do to help someone who may be suicidal?" metonia.org, www.metanoia.org/suicide/whattodo.htm, June 11, 2002.

27. "Suicide facts," National Institute of Mental Health, www.nimh.nih.gov/research/suifact.htm, March 25, 2002.

28. "Teen suicide," American Academy of Child and Adolescent Psychiatry, www.aacap.org/publications/factsfam/suicide.htm, 1997.

29. Edward F. Zigler and Matia Finn Stevenson, *Children in a changing world: Development and social issues,* 2nd ed. (New York: Brooks/Cole Publishing Company, 1993), p. 515.

30. Carol Watkins, "Suicide and the school: Recognition and intervention for suicidal students in the school setting," Northern County Psychiatric Associates, www.baltimorepsych.com/Suicide.htm, June 11, 2002.

31. Charles Thompson and Linda B. Rudolph, *Counseling with children,* 4th ed. (New York: Brooks/Cole Publishing Company, 1996), p. 446.

32. "Depression and suicide in children and adolescents," Surgeon General, www.surgeongeneral.gov/library/mentalhealth/chapter3/sec5.html, June 6, 2002.

33. Ibid.

34. Katharine Davis Fishman, *Behind the one-way mirror: Psychotherapy with children* (New York: Bantam, 1995), p. 166.

35. Robert Blutchic and Herman M. Van Praag, "Suicide, impulsivity, and antisocial behavior," in David M. Stroff, James Breiling, and Jack D. Maser, eds., *The handbook of antisocial behavior,* pp. 101–108 (New York: Wiley & Sons, Inc., 1997), p. 102.

36. "Suicide facts."

37. "Depression and suicide in children and adolescents."

38. Katherine Kaufer Christoffel, "Firearm injuries affecting U.S. children and adolescents," in Joy D. Osofsky, ed., *Children in a violent society,* pp. 42–71 (New York: Guilford Press, 1997), p. 55.

39. Blutchic and Van Praag, "Suicide, impulsivity, and antisocial behavior," p. 105.

40. Michael G. Conner, "Understanding and dealing with violence and suicide pacts," Mentor Research Institute, http://www.oregoncounseling.org /ArticlesPapers/Documents/SchoolViolence/SuicidePact.htm, June 6, 2002.

41. Fishman, "Behind the one way mirror," p. 11.

42. Madeline Levine, *Viewing violence: How media violence affects your child's and your adolescent's development* (New York: Doubleday, 1996), p. 14.

43. Craig A. Anderson and Brad J. Bushman, "The effects of media violence on society," *Science, 295* (March 29, 2002): 2377.

44. "Joint statement on the impact of entertainment violence on children congressional public hearing summit," *Lion and Lamb*, www.lionlamb.org/jointstate ment.htm, July 26, 2000.

45. David M. Given, "Interview with Frank Zappa," *The Entertainment and Sports Lawyer, 9* (Summer 1991): 32.

CHAPTER 9

Sexual Assault by Children

We do not know how he may soften at the sight of the child:
The silence often of pure innocence persuades when speaking fails.
—William Shakespeare, *The Winter's Tale*

Dominic McKilligan was born in Bournemouth, England. By the time he reached his teen years, he was already known to police in town. At age thirteen, he began molesting children and in 1994, at fourteen years of age, he was convicted of "gross indecency against four boys aged seven to eleven whom he lured into playing games which turned to torture."[1] McKilligan was sentenced to three years' detention at Aycliffe Young People's Centre, a sentence that was supposed to provide assessment and treatment for seriously disordered children like McKilligan. During his three years at Aycliffe, McKilligan saw dozens of counselors and received numerous evaluations, including two evaluations just weeks apart—one that said he was a danger to others and another just prior to his release that said he was not. Records show that while at Aycliffe he engaged in "15 very serious incidents ... , 13 of which were of a clearly sexual nature."[2] Yet despite these incidents, he was released from Aycliffe in August 1997.

McKilligan, now eighteen years old, did not return to his hometown, but instead moved to Newcastle, England, where he enrolled in college to study music. If he had been held one day longer at Aycliffe, he would have been required by a new law to register as a sex offender, but the law was not in effect at the time of his release; therefore, authorities, classmates, school personnel, and neighbors were unaware of McKilligan's dangerous past. In a short time, he met eleven-year-old Wesley Neailey on the street in Newcastle and befriended him. Wesley began visiting McKilligan at McKilligan's house as he worked on cars. Wesley had no reason to distrust him.

On Friday, June 5, 1998, just a few months after McKilligan was released from Aycliffe, Wesley's mother picked him up from school and brought him home. Shortly thereafter, Wesley set out on his bike for McKilligan's house. An hour later, he would be dead. While at McKilligan's home, prosecutors claim that McKilligan sexually assaulted the boy and then, fearing that Wesley would talk, he put a bag over his head, strangled him, and beat him in the head with a wrench. Next, he wrapped the body in trash bags, loaded him in his car, and drove a few miles away, where he dumped the body along a quiet deserted road. His bicycle was later found in an alley near McKilligan's home. McKilligan tried to get out of going to work as a pizza delivery man that night, but apparently was unsuccessful. Coworkers and others who saw him that evening did not notice anything unusual.

For the next four weeks, investigators searched for Wesley, hoping he was still alive. During that time they had no reason to suspect McKilligan who, in an unbelievably bold move, came to detectives as an "ordinary citizen" and said he had seen Wesley.[3] Three weeks after Wesley's disappearance, a social worker aware of McKilligan's history came forward to police and told them about McKilligan's past. At that point, the investigation focused on him. Upon searching his home, police found a torn-up check for £150 (approximately U.S. $230) made out to Wesley in a wastebasket and later they also found traces of Wesley's blood in McKilligan's car. McKilligan told police that he had lost his checkbook, but later changed his story, saying he had given the check to Wesley because Wesley had promised to work on the brakes of his car.[4] As his story fell apart, McKilligan eventually told police that Wesley had fallen from a car in his garage and hit his head on a wrench. In a panic, he said, he dumped the boy's body. However, in one police interview described later in court, McKilligan admitted to a police officer that he had choked Wesley. When the officer asked him if he had done that to stop him from breathing, McKilligan said, "to stop him breathing."[5] Four weeks after the murder, McKilligan led police to Wesley's body.

In 1999, McKilligan was tried for rape and murder, charges on which he was convicted, but the rape conviction was later overturned. After his conviction, McKilligan was sentenced to life in prison. If the sexual predator law had been in effect one day earlier, perhaps Wesley would still be alive. Almost certainly, if the police had known of McKilligan's past, they would have recognized McKilligan as a suspect almost immediately, serving if nothing else to close the case earlier and ease the pain of Wesley's grieving parents.

After nearly two decades of research and clinical practice, very little surprises me anymore. Stories people tell that once made my jaw drop no longer elicit a reaction from me. Even though I am often saddened by these narratives, I am almost never surprised. One exception, however, is when children sexually assault other children or adults. Even though I've seen it many times, I still find it hard to picture innocent seven- and eight-year-old children deliberately molesting, sodomizing, and raping toddlers, infants, and in some cases adults. Movies and books many times have played the theme of "evil" children. These movies are eerily disconcerting because it is so hard for all of us to juxtapose our inclination to always see children as victims with the fact that sometimes they are not victims, but perpetrators.

Children who perpetrate sexual crimes can be just as cruel and frightening as adults. Adolescent perpetrators have been known to attack grown women, forcing them with a knife or a gun into engaging in sexual behaviors, but sexual crimes are perpetrated by children even younger. Six- and seven-year-old children have been known to stick pins in an infant's scrotum or penis, insert objects into a child's anus or vagina, or pinch a child's penis or vagina with the intent of causing pain. They may force a child to engage in oral sex or they may even engage in full sexual intercourse with a younger or defenseless child, sometimes with the help of playmates. Writers Terry and Kunz chronicle the behavior of an eight-year-old boy named Henry. Henry, with the help of other boys on a playground, tried to forcibly engage in intercourse with a female playmate.[6] Within two years of this incident, he molested two other children and eventually even frightened an adult female counselor to the point that she refused to work with him. He was described as charming but manipulative, and when his counselor asked him what he was thinking when he frightened the female counselor, he said he was "visualizing that he had a baseball bat in his hands and was slamming the bat back and forth at her head. He imagined her brains came out, then her head rolled off, and he was slamming it, and the mouth was open and yelling for help."[7] Children who sexually abuse other children are not always males. Tales of sexual abuse by female children include a five-year-old female offender who sexually violated a boy and a girl, both under one year old, and six-year-old twin girls who, after having been forced to perform oral sex on their uncle two years earlier, nearly bit off of their eighteen-month-old brother's penis.[8]

Unhealthy or dysfunctional sexual urges and behaviors are called *paraphilias*. According to the *DSM IV-TR*, paraphilias involve behaviors that include intense, sexually arousing urges, fantasies, or behaviors. Paraphilias may involve exhibitionism, fetishism, frotteurism, pedophilia, sexual masochism, sexual sadism, and voyeurism. These behaviors not only interrupt one's ability to function normally within society, but they can also be harmful to others. Even though we most often think of adult males when we use words like sexual abuse, rape, and so forth, as you will see in this chapter, children under the age of eighteen are statistically equally likely to perpetrate these offenses.

PREVALENCE

Approximately 30 percent of all rapes and half of all child molestations are committed by people under the age of eighteen.[9] Children under the age of eighteen are also responsible for 30 percent of all sexual assaults on adults.[10] Between 1980 and 1995, arrests of children under the age of twelve years old increased 125 percent for sex offenses (excluding rape) and 190 percent for forcible rape.[11] It appears that sexual crimes by children under age fourteen are on the rise. In 1992, the state of Washington's Department of Social and Health Services reported 691 sexually aggressive youth in state custody, 33 percent of whom were under twelve.[12] In a Utah survey 18 percent of sexual perpetrators were under thirteen.[13] Sexual aggression by children may be even more widespread than these numbers indicate because, like almost all sexual crimes, many cases go unreported. Parents who learn that their child has been molested by another child may minimize the significance of the molestation, supposing it to be normal childhood play. Other times, they know the assault is not normal, but they still deny that anything abnormal occurred because it is easier to deny it than it is to deal with the legal, social, and emotional issues related to the assault.

The vast majority of all sexual offenders are male (98 percent), although females do perpetrate sex crimes. Not only are we less suspicious of females than males, as I discussed in Chapter 3, but because females are more likely to bathe, change, and care for children, their inappropriate fondling of a child could easily be disguised by one of these behaviors; therefore, they do not get caught or even fall under suspicion.

America is not alone in grappling with this problem. In Great Britain, for example, more than 450 children are convicted of sexual offenses against other children each year.[14] These are just the convictions; these numbers do not include all the abuse cases that do not end in conviction, abuse cases that never make it to the court system, and abuse cases that are never even identified.

All the data above translate into thousands of juveniles who commit sexual crimes every year.[15] These juvenile sexual predators commit multiple offenses, they usually have more than one victim, and they may not limit their offenses to one type of victim. In the end, these numbers represent thousands of victims every year.

A PROFILE OF JUVENILE SEXUAL OFFENDERS

Very little is consistent in the research on juvenile offenders, but one thing that most researchers agree on is that there is no single profile that fits all juvenile offenders. This is a heterogeneous population with no consistent findings with regard to age, race, motive, or socioeconomic class.

Some research has found that juvenile sexual offenders are very bright and socially competent, while other studies show them to be below normal in IQ and socially inept. About half of all juvenile sexual offenders live in homes with both parents, while others live in unstable homes or with only one parent. About half of all juvenile sexual offenders have a history of sexual abuse, physical abuse, or neglect in their history, but the other half does not.

The Federal Bureau of Investigation pioneered the process of profiling criminal offenders. FBI special agents like Roy Hazelwood, Robert Ressler, and John Douglas interviewed serial killers, and through their research, the FBI opened the door to what we know of as psychological profiling. Profiling research is now common in research among many types of offenders. In fact, the profiling work of the FBI served as a model for my own research in the development of a profile of workplace killers that I presented in my book *Blind-Sided: Homicide Where It Is Least Expected;* this is the subject that I lecture on at the FBI Academy. I have also provided general profiles of other types of perpetrators in previous chapters in this book. For all of this, we can thank the FBI. However, it is fortunate that the researchers with the FBI started their work with serial killers instead of some other population of criminals because serial killers are more similar than they are different. Their homogeneity makes this group a perfect population for profiling—perhaps more so than any other single group of criminals. I suspect that if they had begun their research with juvenile sexual offenders, their funding would quickly have evaporated. No tidy picture of these offenders has yet come to light. The information in this section is controversial. Among one hundred experts on juvenile sexual crime, ninety-nine of them would probably disagree with at least some of the information that I present here. My attempt is not to provide a conclusive profile. Rather, I have examined the research that exists on these offenders and have presented the issues that appear to be most closely related to sexual offending in childhood.

With rare exception, as is true with almost all forms of aggression, sexual abuse does not "suddenly manifest itself."[16] There are symptoms that problems exist before a child ever attacks another child. The symptoms, behaviors, and social circumstances that precede or accompany juvenile sexual offenders are the warning signs from which we can derive a profile. These symptoms and related issues are outlined in Table 9.1.

Family Problems

Family problems are not uncommon. One study of two thousand juvenile offenders showed that only 28 percent were living with both parents.[17] This leaves more than 70 percent of all juvenile offenders who live

Table 9.1
Related Issues with Juvenile Sexual Offenders

- ❏ Dysfunctional family environment
- ❏ One or more parents who were victims of sexual crime/abuse
- ❏ History of physical abuse, sexual abuse, or neglect
- ❏ Exposure to age-inappropriate sexual content (pornography, sexual abuse of a sibling, etc.)
- ❏ School problems
- ❏ Underachiever
- ❏ Nonsexual delinquent behavior
- ❏ Preference for playing with younger children
- ❏ Unsupervised access to children
- ❏ Obsessively self-absorbed
- ❏ Male
- ❏ Low self-esteem
- ❏ Atypical sexual fantasies
- ❏ Poor impulse control
- ❏ Poor social skills
- ❏ Neurological and/or cognitive deficits
- ❏ Mental disorder (especially conduct disorder, attachment disorder, or depression)
- ❏ Manipulative
- ❏ Antisocial behavior
- ❏ Lack of social skills
- ❏ Social isolation
- ❏ Poor peer relationships

in homes with only one parent or guardian or are in the care of group homes—public or private. Instability at home is related to many forms of delinquency, sexual abuse being no exception. Other experts have demonstrated that "poor family relationships," even in intact families, correlate with juvenile offending.[18] Also, a parent's troubled past can have an effect on his or her own children. Researchers have found that many parents of juvenile sexual offenders have been victims of abuse themselves.[19] Whether this connection is coincidental, genetic, or social is unknown, but I doubt that this is merely coincidental and there is minimal evidence for a genetic connection. This means that, in some way, parents may either intentionally or unintentionally, overtly or subtly, behave in a way that makes sexual abuse by their children more likely. Almost no research exists with regard to this cause-effect relationship and much needs to be done before any conclusive assessment can be made.

Abuse

There is little doubt that child abuse plays a role in children who sexually abuse other children. In one study of 1,616 sexually abusive children, 41 percent had been physically abused and 39 percent had been sexually abused.[20] Similar numbers appear consistently across research studies, with some demonstrating a history of victimization as high as 80 percent. For example, one U.S. study showed that 60 percent of adolescent sexual offenders had been physically abused, almost half had been sexually abused, and 70 percent had been victims of neglect.[21] Even though males are by far more likely perpetrators than females, sexual abuse appears to be a much more significant factor in causing sexual abuse by females than by males. In a review of three different studies, researchers found that 100 percent of the female offenders were molested as children.[22]

One's age when sexual abuse occurs also appears to be significant. In a study of children who started molesting at age six or younger, 72 percent had been sexually abused, but for those who started molesting between the ages of seven and eleven, only 42 percent reported abuse.[23] Finally, of those who started molesting other children after age eleven, only 35 percent reported abuse in their past.[24]

Researchers must carefully validate claims of abuse by sexual offenders. An interesting study was done with sexual offenders who claimed sexual abuse in their history. Initially, 67 percent of these offenders reported child abuse in their respective pasts, but when these offenders were administered a polygraph while being interviewed, the number reporting abuse as a child fell to 29 percent [25] Whether abuse is present 80 percent of the time or 29 percent, the role of abuse in the histories of juvenile sexual offenders is apparent, but it is certainly not the only issue. It must be considered as an issue "intertwined in complex patterns in the developmental histories" of these sexually aggressive juveniles.[26]

Types of Offenses

Sexual aggression by children involves many different activities. In one study of fifty-seven children between the ages of six and twelve who had engaged in sexual behavior with other children, 67 percent engaged in touching, 63 percent fondled another child's genitals, 48 percent made inappropriate sexual comments to a child, 35 percent exposed themselves, 26 percent masturbated in public, 23 percent engaged in oral sex, 14 percent engaged in penetration, and 4 percent forced sex by means of a threat or use of a weapon.[27] The range of sexual offenses includes "hands-off" crimes—exhibitionism, sexual talk, and voyeurism—as well as "hands-on" sexual contact that includes mutual play where no force is used as well as forced sexual interaction. Hands-on sexual contact may include fondling, oral-genital contact, or penetration. Older perpetrators are more likely to use force than younger perpetrators and adolescent rapists are more likely to attack strangers than their younger counterparts, who are more likely to prey on people that they know. Also, juveniles who threaten their victims or use physical force will do so most often when their victims are older.[28]

Victims

Most offenders (90 percent) know their victims.[29] They prey on neighbors, younger siblings and other relatives, friends, and even the children in their care as babysitters. One study showed that 38.8 percent of victims were blood relatives and 46 percent were other family members.[30] Victims of juvenile sexual perpetrators range in age from infancy through adulthood, but most victims are young females. Studies show that most victims are under twelve (62 percent) and a large number are under the age of six (44 percent), with six being the average victim age.[31]

Juvenile sexual offenders prey on females three times as often as males and they will repeat their abuse. Sixty-one percent of adolescent sex offenders abuse more than one victim, abusing seven different victims on average, not to mention the fact that many perpetrators abuse the same victim more than once.[32] Unlike adult rapists, juvenile sexual offenders do not necessarily limit their aggression to victims of a certain type (i.e., race, age, hair color).

Behavioral Problems

Sexual offenders are three times more likely than nonoffenders to have been convicted of nonsexual crimes, as well.[33] One study showed that sexual offenders had two or more convictions on average.[34] These offenders are more likely to have behavioral problems, including antisocial behaviors and school behavioral difficulties than nonoffenders.

Cognitive Deficits and Mental Illness

Neurological and cognitive problems are not uncommon, although the correlation between these problems and sexual aggression remains unresolved. Even though a few studies have shown that sexual offenders achieve "average" grades, more often research has demonstrated that sexual delinquents tend to have lower IQs than nonsexual delinquents. Consequently, they have more academic problems. One study showed that only 57 percent of all adolescent sexual offenders had "attained their appropriate or superior grade placement" and over 80 percent had learning and/or behavioral problems.[35] Another study of 286 male adolescent sex offenders showed that over half (53 percent) had school problems.[36] The variability in research results may be due to the complex interaction of variables found within the adolescent sexual offender population, especially age, history of abuse, level of social skills, and peer relations. More research is needed to clarify the effect of these individual variables and their effects in combination.

Mental illness may be an important factor. In a study of 852 subjects, sex offenders who had been sexually abused in the past had a higher depression rate than non-abusive adolescents.[37] What is unclear in this study, however, is whether depressive symptoms appeared after the child sexually abused or whether they were present prior to the abuse. In order for mental illness to be considered a cause rather than a symptom, it would have to have preceded the behavior. Other forms of mental illness associated with juvenile sexual offending include conduct disorder, a very common diagnosis, as well as substance abuse disorder and attachment problems. In summary, adolescent and child perpetrators of sexual crimes exhibit a "wide range of mental and emotional problems which do not fit a standardized mold" including "feelings of male inadequacy, low self-esteem, fear of rejection and anger toward women, atypical erotic fantasies, poor social skills, sexual abuse in the past, and exposure to adult models of aggression, dominance, and intimidation."[38]

SEXUAL DEVELOPMENT IN CHILDREN

One of the questions that I am asked most frequently by parents has to do with the normalcy of their children's behavior. "My child masturbates. Is that normal?" "I found pornographic pictures on my son's computer. Is that normal?" "I caught my daughter and her cousin in the bathroom playing naked. Is that normal?" "Normal" is based on a number of things. I have to consider the child's age, his environment, and the behavior itself. What may be normal for a five-year-old may be highly abnormal for a ten-year-old. What may be normal in one context may be highly abnormal in another. Some behaviors are exhibited by almost all children at one time or another and others are almost never exhibited unless there is a serious problem. In order to have an understanding of the origins of sexual crime—what is normal and what is abnormal—one must first have an understanding of how we develop as sexual beings.

We first begin to recognize our sexuality in infancy. Baby boys will pull on and fondle their own penises in the same way they play with their toes. At this point in life, the penis is not a sexual organ. It is just another body part. Around age two, children believe that all people have the same body parts, eyes, ears, nose, arms, and legs. If a toddler sees someone with an amputated leg, the child will stare because he realizes that having only one leg is not normal. By age three, children learn that there are body parts that we normally keep covered. These parts are "mysterious"—the penis, the breasts in women, the buttocks, and the vagina. They don't understand why we cover them, but they know there is something different about these parts. By this age, if a child sees someone undressed, he will giggle or express surprise because these parts are not often seen. It is around this time that boys and girls begin to recognize that there is something physical that distinguishes maleness from femaleness. Prior to this realization, "gender" in their minds is based on clothing, hairstyle, and one's name.

Even in these very early years, children are learning gender roles—those behaviors and attributes that a given culture identifies with one gender or the other. Gender roles and stereotypes lead children to believe such things as "Boys are better than girls" or "Girls are smarter than boys." Stereotypes cause them to limit their play to certain toys and limit their dress to certain types of clothing. What a person can and can't do or should and shouldn't do is based on gender stereotyping that has its genesis in these early years.

By grade school years, children are well aware that boys and girls have different sexual parts, and as they approach grades 4 or 5, they begin to create ideas in their own minds about where babies come from. In early childhood, children may think babies come from the stork, swallowing a watermelon seed, kissing, or getting married. They attribute no connection between babies and genital contact. Ordinarily, it is not until preadolescence that children understand a connection between the sexual organs of males and females and reproduction, but even then, their knowledge of intercourse and conception is still based more on myth than fact.

Physical sexual maturation occurs as early as age nine in some girls and ten or eleven in some boys. Puberty may take four to six years for girls to complete and two to four years for boys to complete, and it involves the development of pubic hair, change in skeletal form, development of muscle tone, enlarging and changing of the sexual organs, the onset of menstruation in girls, and the deepening of the voice and the appearance of facial hair in males. All these changes are almost exclusively the result of hormones that flood the child's system. Accompanying the physical changes that occur during puberty is a dramatically increased interest in sex. Even though all children are different, nearly every pubescent child has some interest in sex. Compounded with the shifting influence from parents to peers, sex is a common topic of discussion, jest, and inquiry.

Sex continues to be an important part of our lives even into old age. Notice how many comedians, television situation comedies, and movies rely on sexual innuendo or sexual jokes to make people laugh. Sex can be funny, in part because sexual issues make us nervous, but also because we can never escape our sexual selves and almost all of us can easily relate to these situations. Not only do most adults find sex play an enjoyable recreational activity, it is perceived to be an integral part of a marriage relationship. In fact, consummating the marriage is still considered a part of the legal definition of marriage in some states. If a couple never has sexual intercourse, the marriage can easily be annulled. We are influenced by our sexuality more than anything else—more than our age, race, religion, family, career, or citizenship.

In order to develop a healthy attitude about sex, one must recognize that sexual interaction with other people involves a relationship, not exclusively the pursuit of one's personal interests or desires. Most religions require a covenant of some form in order to engage in a sexual relationship, but the recognition that sex is always a part of a relationship goes beyond religion. In order for it to be a satisfying experience for both parties, even nonreligious people who are interested in sexual experimentation or sexual activity with each other must negotiate the sexual relationship, deciding at the very least on what behaviors they will engage in. Rape and other forms of sexual exploitation bypass the relationship aspect of sex, substituting physical force or psychological coercion for a healthy, mutually satisfying sexual interaction. Therefore, the offender may find the experience satisfying, but it comes at the expense of the victim. Children begin learning the relationship aspect of sex in their very early years. By watching their mothers and fathers, they learn how people in a relationship should talk to each other, negotiate problems and arguments, and express love and affection. During childhood, children must learn the nature of relationships, how to behave in their varied relationships, and what the boundaries of those relationships are. For example, mothers are often the first love objects for their sons. These boys talk and fantasize about marrying their mothers. They are not yet old enough to understand the boundaries of love relationships between family members, nor can they distinguish the powerful emotion of love for one's mother from love for a mate—love that has the capacity for erotic attraction. Note how complex all of this is even in normal childhood. A child who is sexually active with a sibling, father, mother, or other relative during these years begins to equate sex with the normal development of a relationship. It should then come as no surprise that when these children reach adolescence many of them become promiscuous.

Even though parents are the primary role models for children as they learn the nature of relationships, there is no question that movies, books, and television shows also contribute to this understanding. There is a vast body of research that has demonstrated that aggressive images, including those that degrade women, desensitize males in their view of women. To my knowledge, there is little data to support this same conclusion among children who view nonaggressive programs with sexual content, but it certainly stands to reason that such programs would have some effect. Movies and television situation comedies, which consistently portray relationships as fleeting sexual liaisons, devoid of the commitment and work required to sustain meaningful and lasting relationships, surely do not help in the development of reasonable attitudes toward and expectations for those relationships.

During childhood, a person must learn socially appropriate sexual expression. One Sunday morning many years ago as I was waiting to greet a minister before leaving church, his three-year-old daughter who was standing beside him was uncomfortable so she decided to remove her dress. Before he realized what was happening, she dropped her dress and underwear to the floor and, to his horror, sprinted up the center aisle of the sanctuary wearing nothing but her patent leather shoes. This was cute for a three-year-old (to everyone except her parents, of course) because no one expects a three-year-old child to know the social rules for dress. However, it wouldn't have been cute if the child was ten or twelve years of age.

Social expression of sexual behavior also involves learning what words to use and when to use them in varied contexts. For example, parents wrestle with whether or not to teach their children the proper names for sexual body parts or to use some euphemism. My suggestion has always been if you don't mind a child yelling across the grocery store, "My penis itches!" then you can use anatomically correct names. If you do mind, then use pet names. It takes time for children to learn the social constructs that guide when and how we use words and phrases related to our own sexuality and the sexuality of others. As children approach puberty and begin to experience erotic attraction, they must learn socially acceptable ways to express their feelings and how to negotiate their erotic attraction to another person.

Psychologists and authors Bukowski, Sippola, and Brender summarize the complexity of our learning and developing as healthy sexual creatures. According to these authors, one must learn how to be intimate, to develop personal relationships, to adjust to physical changes especially in adolescence, to integrate erotic feelings and experiences into one's life, to learn societal standards regarding sexual expression, and to understand reproduction.[39] Complications in any of these areas because of physical problems, social limitations, or dysfunctional models make this challenge even more difficult.

The Development of Sexual Interest

It would not be inaccurate to say that even infants have sexual interest, but not in the same way that older children and adults have sexual interest. Babies are interested in their bodies. As I mentioned earlier, upon the discovery of their penises, boys are interested in this body part just as they are when they discover their toes. This doesn't mean they are obsessed with it, although it may seem like it. The penis is within easy reach of an infant, even more so than toes. It should not be surprising that baby boys play with it once they have discovered it. As children discover erotic sensations, they pursue those erotic feelings without consideration of any social rules or relationship. This egocentrism develops into a mutually shared interest in sexuality with a partner as one becomes an adult. Between infancy and adulthood, the child must learn when, where, and how it is appropriate to touch himself or others. Both parents and one's culture participate in this acculturation regarding proper and improper touching. Nothing in our genetics teaches us culturally appropriate sexual contact. In fact, the only thing in genetics that addresses sexuality is the drive to reproduce.

The drive to reproduce is one of the five basic human needs, along with food, water, shelter, and sleep. Prior to age five, children will touch an adult in many ways that would be inappropriate for an older child for two reasons. First, the younger child does not know any better. When he climbs into his mother's lap, he does not consider touching one body part any different from touching any other body part. Therefore, he may touch her breasts to hold on just as he might touch her arm or leg. Second, there is no sexual intent. This child is not touching his mother's breast in an erotic way. Again, he is touching it as he would any other body part. An older child, on the other hand, should know the difference between erogenous zones and nonerogenous zones. Likewise, after age five, a child will begin to experience erotic desire and he is more likely to touch a sexual body part with an erotic purpose.

By age three, as children learn that boys and girls are physically different, there is an increased interest in the opposite sex and a fascination with the differences between the two. At this age, anything sexual, including bowel movements, gas, and urination, is interesting to children. This childlike interest lasts until puberty. Prior to age nine or so, "sex" from a child's perspective involves things that he or she has seen. Since most children are not exposed to sexual intercourse, their idea of sex involves hugging, kissing, or hand-holding. For this reason, it is unusual for a child under the age of eight or nine to talk about or express interest in intercourse and it is abnormal to have this interest prior to this age.

Prior to age nine or ten, there is little understanding of love other than personal desire and that desire is wrapped up in getting what one wants. Therefore, a child will "love" his mother when he gets a present, but not "love" her when he is being punished. During this stage, what Freud called *latency* or the stage where sexual interest is "sleeping," boys and girls tend to engage in same-sexed friendships. However, I do not totally agree with Freud's assessment of the latency stage. Children at this stage clearly have interests in the opposite sex, but they just do not act upon it nearly as much as they do at puberty. This reservation to act is fostered by naïveté, lack of experience, and lack of hormones that drive sexual interest.

As children approach puberty and their bodies begin to generate hormones that precede sexual maturation, their interest in sex changes. They begin to think about sex (given their limited understanding of it) and obtaining a boyfriend or girlfriend grows in importance. Not only is having a pseudo-partner a part of their sexual development, but they gain prestige from peers and having a "mate" mimics adult behaviors. During pubescence, many boys and some girls will experiment with pornography. This interest is driven by hormones and curiosity as well as a sexual awakening that, when fully developed, will allow for a normal marital relationship in the future. Hollywood panders to this drive by producing trashy films with cheap gags that rely heavily on sexual innuendo, flatulence, and women removing their shirts. These gratuitous scenes serve no other purpose than to draw a crowd made up of hormonally driven adolescent boys.

Early maturation tends to be psychologically and socially beneficial to boys, but unproductive for girls. Western culture values athleticism in males. If a boy reaches sexual maturity earlier than his peers, his muscles will be more developed than those of his peers and he will perform better in athletic events. Excelling in athletics produces accolades from peers and adults alike, generating positive self-esteem in the child. However, there is little benefit for girls who mature early because Western culture has a different set of values for females. Girls tend to be self-conscious about their bodies when they mature earlier than their peers and this leads to a diminished self-concept. Physical strength is not as important among girls and a female who matures early is more likely to be treated as if she were the age she appears to be rather than the age that she is. Therefore, a fourteen-year-old female who looks eighteen years old will more likely be treated as if she were eighteen. Even adult men will pursue a sexual relationship with these little girls, responding to their appearance rather than realizing that even though she may appear to be an adult physically, in the rest of her development—cognitive, emotional, and social—she is still a child.

By the mid-teens, young people begin sexual experimentation. By this time, when their hormones are in full swing, they should have some awareness of the biology of sexual relationships, but, even then, much of their understanding of sexual behavior is based on minimal sex education from parents or teachers. More likely, the bulk of their knowledge about sexual issues comes from movies, myths communicated by their friends, and their own limited experience. All this drives an interest in sexual intercourse. Whether or not children act on this drive is a whole other discussion and is based on peers, parents, culture, religion, history, and a host of other variables. For our purposes here, sexual development is complete by the late teens and, assuming a healthy sexual education, a healthy parental relationship as a model, and normal psychosocial development, the young adult is now prepared to enter an enduring, mutually rewarding relationship.

Normal Sex Play in Childhood

So what is normal? Toddlers may be interested in a woman's breasts because they have seen her or another woman breast-feeding, or because they recall their own experiences breast-feeding. There may be an interest in seeing an opposite-sexed parent nude, not for erotic pleasure as much as curiosity. Many children touch themselves, show their genitals to each other, and "play" sexually, perhaps touching one another.[40]

Sexual experimentation, especially masturbation, is common among children and a normal activity throughout late adolescence and adulthood. In fact, by age eighteen virtually all males and about 75 percent of all females have masturbated at least once, and by late puberty, about three-quarters of all boys and nearly as many females masturbate one to four times each week. Many children masturbate, even in infancy, if they discover that rubbing their genitals on a blanket or stuffed animal produces a pleasurable feeling. Even though there is no clear conclusion on the frequency of masturbation, it appears that females masturbate in higher numbers than males until puberty, at which time males take the lead in frequency, and frequency for both genders increases dramatically around puberty and wanes slightly in the late teens. However, masturbation is a behavior that is often attached to guilt, religious taboos, and myth. A parent's nervousness about such issues only makes learning about one's sexuality confusing and adds to the mystery of the sexual self. Autoerotic behavior troubles parents, especially if they have religious beliefs that prohibit such behaviors. When I work with children who masturbate, I usually suggest to parents that they teach privacy rather than condemning the behavior. Children who masturbate on a regular basis will do it even if their parents tell them not to. The child has discovered something that feels very good and he/she has ready access to it. Imagine a child who has free rein in a candy store. A parent's instruction "Don't eat the candy" would do little to inhibit the child from sneaking candy when no one was looking. To condemn children for masturbating will only create guilt and shame, potentially complicating their sexual lives in the future.

As boys reach puberty, nocturnal emissions, also called "wet dreams," are not uncommon. Fantasies about sex, love, and marriage are common for both genders. Same-sexed sexual play is not uncommon either and does not necessarily indicate that one is homosexual. In early adolescence, sexual drives are somewhat like a boat with no rudder. These drives exhibit themselves in a variety of ways, including pornography, autoeroticism, and same-sex sexual play. Counselors, especially homosexual advocates, may easily confuse normal sexual experimentation with the emergence of a homosexual self. To suppose that a child is homosexual just because of homosexual play is an inappropriate interpretation.

Normal sexual play between children always happens in an interpersonal context.[41] These playmates may be friends, relatives, or neighbors, and they are usually the same age or very close to the same age. Therefore, sexual play between two children who do not know each other, between two children who are more than three or four years apart in age, or sex play that is forced is abnormal. Determining normal age-appropriate sexual exploration/experimentation must take into account the behavior, the child's age, and the child's playmate, if any.

ORIGINS OF SEXUAL AGGRESSION IN ADOLESCENCE

There have been a number of theories proposed as to why children molest other children, but the debate as to the etiology of sexual aggression in children is heated and there is little consensus. The fact is there are a number of reasons why children sexually abuse other children and each motive has a different set of related issues, precursors, and symptoms. There have been a number of attempts to classify sexual offenders, but I have chosen to categorize them into five types. Type I offenders include those who sexually abuse, but who have no intent to cause harm. They are curious and are experimenting with their bodies and are what Cashwell and Caruso call *normal explorative* children.[42] These children do not have "sexual" intent, per se, and their behaviors fall within the range of normal child sexual play. Their victims are most likely friends, siblings, or neighbors, and are close in age to the offender.

Type II offenders include children who are themselves victims of abuse. They are children who have been physically abused, sexually abused, or neglected, and they are acting out their abuse. These sexual offenders are repeating the behaviors they have experienced as victims and the characteristics of their victims are more likely to be reflective of their own experience.[43] Reenacting their abuse is their attempt to resolve and "gain mastery" over their abusive pasts.[44]

Type III sexual offenders include those with mental and/or cognitive deficits. Conduct disorder, attachment disorder, impulse-control, depression, and antisocial personality issues may contribute by compromising one's ability to make decisions, interpret social cues, and empathize, and these issues also may interfere with normal peer relationships—a vital governor of one's behavior.

There is little research on the role of mental retardation and sexually aggressive behavior, but even though most mentally disabled individuals are not a high risk for sexual offenses, approximately 23 percent of developmentally disabled adolescents in treatment have been found to have engaged in sexually abusive behavior.[45] These offenders are more likely to engage in socially inappropriate, nonassaultive "nuisance" behaviors, such as public masturbation, exhibitionism, and voyeurism, than in hands-on assaults.[46] This may most likely be attributed to poor impulse control and social skills deficits rather than any intent to cause harm.

There are some theorists who attribute these deficits and the subsequent aggressive sexual behavior to hormonal levels within the endocrine system that go awry in response to stress. This area of study, called *psychoneuroen-docrinology*, supposes that sexual aggression may be, at least in part, a mal-adaptive response to stress. "The stress response system is composed of psychological elements (the interpretation and labeling of threats), the neu-ral system, that subserves this interpretation, and finally the endocrine sys-tem permitting the organism to treat threats with a physical response such as flight or fight, and as such is vital for self-protection."[47] While most the-orists would discount psychoneuroendocrinology as a primary cause of abuse, it is certainly a possible contributor.

Type IV juvenile sexual offenders are most often adolescents who are deliberate perpetrators. They do not come by their victims by chance or opportunity. They plan their assaults, sometimes using threats or weapons. These are the most difficult children to treat. They have repeatedly abused many victims and their sexually aggressive behavior has become a part of their lives. For these children, their sense of self has become enmeshed with their sexuality and the two are inseparable. Instead of their sexual nature being one contributing component of their lives, it is the primary driving force for their behavior. Even though this group of offenders may have a diagnosable mental disorder, as with Type III offenders, and they may be victims of abuse, like Type II offenders, they are much more aggressive and their mental illness or abuse is closely wedded to their histories as well as their decisions to sexually abuse. In other words, their abuse is more than abreaction, as with Type II offenders, and their mental illness is more than just a correlate. These offenders are primed to become violent, angry, and dangerous adult sexual offenders.

Type V sexual offenders, the final group, would include those who are influenced by a social group to engage in sexual assault. Their social behavior may be gang related or, as was the case for Henry's friends whom I described at the beginning of this chapter, they may have little interest in sexual assault, but are following the direction of a charismatic leader or mentor. Their participation in sexual assault serves them in their desire to affiliate rather than serving them sexually.

Among these five types of sexual offenders, variables such as one's physiology, family of origin, sexual history, history of abuse and neglect, and social experiences contribute to either a healthy or unhealthy approach to one's sexual self.

EVALUATION AND TREATMENT OF ADOLESCENT SEXUAL OFFENDERS

If there is any good news in all this, it is that the recidivism rates for ado-lescent and child sex offenders is significantly lower than that of the adult population. It appears that developmental issues and/or treatment have an effect on their behavior as they move into adulthood. However, many adult sex offenders began their sexually abusive careers in adolescence. One study of eighty-four adult sexual offenders showed that 45 percent had engaged in voyeuristic behavior as an adolescent and 37 percent had a history of exhibitionism.[48] Across research studies, the data consistently show that about half of all adult offenders began sexual offending prior to age eighteen. Without assessment and treatment, recidivism is certainly a risk. Likewise, without treatment the offender is an ever-present risk to his or her community. A sex offender "perpetrates an average of 581 acts against an average of 380 victims over the course of the perpetrator's life."[49]

In general, psychotherapeutic treatment has not been very well researched for any disorder, including sexual offending. There are only a very few therapeutic models that have been empirically validated to have long-term effects and those models (i.e., alcohol and drug treatment) have only been thoroughly studied for specific populations. What research does exist for juvenile sex offender therapy looks promising. A Canadian study, for example, found that with at least twelve months' intensive treatment, recidivism rates were reduced to 5 percent for sexual offenses, 18 percent for violent offenses, and 20 percent for nonviolent offenses, compared to 17 percent, 32 percent, and 50 percent, respectively, for those who do not receive treatment.[50] Even though therapy is easier and more productive when the client is a willing participant, these success rates demonstrate that the offender's willingness to participate in therapy is not essential. Several writers have observed that it would be rare for a sexual offender to voluntarily come forward for therapy. Instead, court action is usually the precipitating event for sexual offenders who seek therapy. Therefore, almost all sexual offenders will be "unwilling" clients. Compounding this difficulty, child abusers, in general, are manipulative and deceptive. These offenders can be very convincing liars and the unskilled therapist may easily be misled and manipulated. Treating these offenders requires training beyond normal psychotherapeutic skills.

Unfortunately, treatment for juvenile sexual offenders, even children at five or six years of age, has traditionally involved the application of adult models. Recent advancements in therapy have provided new approaches that are multifaceted, involving some traditional therapies as well as some new models, and take into account learning styles, development, family dynamics, and a number of other issues that have been neglected in the past.

Assessment

Treatment begins with assessing the type of offender one is working with. Assessment must include the details of the offense(s), whether it was opportunistic or planned, how long the perpetrator has been offending, the number of offenses, the degree of force, the perpetrator's honesty and motivation for help, his/her level of antisocial behavior, sexual fantasies, and any history of sexual abuse.[51] Also of importance would be information regarding the child's support system, cognitive abilities, communication skills, developmental adjustment, an assessment of family relationships and family stress, social competence/skills, medical history, and prior involvement in therapy. Assessment protocols that omit any of these areas would provide an incomplete picture of the offender and inhibit the construction of a properly tailored therapeutic plan for the offender.

Recognition of Responsibility and Development of Empathy

Once assessed, the second step is to address the crime and evaluate the perpetrator's willingness to admit that he has done something wrong. Juvenile sexual offenders almost always deny, minimize, or blame their victims when they are confronted or caught. One study of over 1,600 juvenile sexual offenders demonstrated that 62 percent showed no sympathy for their victims, 51 percent showed no remorse, and 33 percent blamed their victims for the assault.[52] Another study of forty-five adolescent male sexual offenders showed they were lower in empathy than nonoffenders.[53] In 1993, Barbaree and Cortoni conducted an interesting study on denial and failure to accept responsibility. These researchers interviewed 114 incarcerated sex offenders. Of these offenders, 41 percent admitted their offenses while 59 percent denied their offenses, but both groups of offenders justified their behavior at some level and minimized their responsibility.[54] They also found that 31 percent of deniers said they had been provoked by their victims, 34 percent of deniers and 24 percent of admitters said their victims meant "yes" even though they said "no," 69 percent of the deniers said the victim eventually relaxed and enjoyed the rape, and 69 percent of deniers and 22 percent of admitters alluded to the victim's "unsavory sexual reputation" as an excuse for rape.[55] Barbaree and Cortoni isolated three different forms of denial: total denial; saying the victim consented because she did not resist; and arguing that the sexual interaction was nonsexual (i.e., "I was just putting suntan lotion on her skin.").[56] They also present three forms of minimizing responsibility that include blaming the victim, attributing the responsibility for their behavior to some external issue (i.e., troubled childhood, alcohol, family problems), or making irresponsible internal attributions.[57] Unfortunately, these researchers also found that family members and friends often support the offender in his denial, often against the allegations of another family member, and this leads the offender to behave as if he were the victim rather than the perpetrator.[58]

Learning to empathize includes making the offender aware of the impact of his actions on victims. Not only are sexual offenders sometimes unaware that they are hurting their victims emotionally and physically when they abuse them, but they often have no insight into the long-term emotional, social, and sometimes physical pain their abuse causes their victims. Even though there are dozens of approaches to therapy with sexual offenders, researcher David M. Burke notes that victim empathy is used almost universally, showing up 96 percent of the time.[59]

Altering the System

Intervention with sexual offenders must address the many systems that interact to allow, or even perpetuate, their offending behavior. Family therapy, individual and group cognitive therapy, and behavior modification, social skills training, and anger management alone are all potentially effective treatments, but the most effective treatment includes all of these approaches. It is a consensus among researchers that no one therapy model is an effective template in all cases and treatment must be personally tailored to the client's circumstances based on a thorough assessment at intake.

Family therapy can help the offender understand the origins of his offending behaviors (i.e., abuse) and it can also help family members recognize how they may be contributing to the offender's behavior, but parents are not always willing participants in the offender's therapy. Unlike offenders who may be mandated by the court to attend therapy, the family of the offender may be under no such order. Therefore, if they refuse to participate or if they interrupt therapy, this component of therapy may need to be abandoned.

Individual and group therapy, both cognitive and behavioral, can address self-awareness, effective coping strategies, and anger management. Many sexual crimes are driven by rage. Controlling that anger is a part of social skills training. Burke notes that anger management is a common component of treatment for sexual offenders, appearing as a part of treatment 94 percent of the time.[60] Behavioral therapy often includes arousal conditioning in which the offender is trained to adjust his sexual response to conditions that have contributed to his offending behavior.

Social skills training addresses, among other things, reading social cues. Many sexual offenders mistakenly believe that their victims wanted and enjoyed the assault, completely overlooking the victim's verbal messages as she screamed for him to stop. Also a part of social skills training is addressing peer relationships. Many juvenile sexual offenders are socially isolated due to their social awkwardness and ineptitude. The ability to form peer relationships is imperative, especially in the case of disrupted bonding.[61] Just as a social group can be a contributor to delinquent behavior, as with Type V offenders, social groups can also inhibit delinquent behavior and encourage prosocial behaviors. Removing the child from a social setting where he was influenced by a delinquent social group and teaching the offender to form nondelinquent friendships is a part of this training.

Finally, the offender must be taught to understand the cues and precursors to his deviant behavior.[62] In the words of researcher Joyce F. Lakey, the "offender must understand the connection between events, his thoughts, and his feelings, all of which triggered his offending behavior."[63] Recognizing events, conditions, and situations that can lead one to offend can help the sexual offender reduce or even eliminate the drive to take sexual advantage of victims.

Other therapies, specifically art therapy, music therapy, and drama therapy, are also used with this population. Not only do these expressive forms of therapy tap the right hemisphere of the brain, bypassing the inhibitions of the left hemisphere, but participants who may be reluctant to express themselves in words can more easily express their thoughts and feelings through artistic expression.

Altering One's View of Sex and Sexual Conduct

Effective treatment must address the way the offender perceives his or her sexuality and the sexuality of others. In some cases, sex education by itself, especially among Type I offenders, may be the primary treatment. For those offenders who abuse because of ignorance, lack of information, or curiosity, education about one's sexuality may be the most efficient treatment, even though sex education should be a part of all treatment programs. Burke reports that 93 percent of all therapy programs for sexual offenders included a sex education component.[64] Sex education includes the biology of gender, development, reproduction, sexually transmitted disease, and masturbation as well as information on mutually rewarding sexual foreplay and intercourse.

Sexual offenders must learn to control their sexual fantasies, replacing deviant fantasies with appropriate ones. The offender must learn to gain control over his deviant sexual urges and behavior and recognize his distorted thinking.[65] Learning to fantasize about age-appropriate partners and slowing his reaction time are a part of self-control that leads to overcoming sexual offending.[66]

Psychopharmaceutical Treatment

Medical interventions for sexual offenders are controversial. Adult offenders have been treated with drugs like Depo-Provera, a form of chemical castration, but the effectiveness of these drugs is questionable. Psychotropics like Prozac and Anafranil have been prescribed to treat disorders related to sexual offending (i.e., depression), but these drugs do not directly address sexual behaviors, although a physician may prescribe an antidepressant medication like Paxil that reduces sex drive as a side effect. At this time, there is no clear evidence that juvenile sexual offenders can be effectively treated with medications alone, but in conjunction with other interventions, psychotropic medications can be helpful.

Relapse Prevention

Reducing the rate of recidivism among sexual offenders is a primary goal of researchers and therapists alike. This requires that offenders complete their therapy and that some follow-up regimen be established. Barbaree and Cortoni note that while the offender is in therapy, the therapist has an ethical obligation to notify social and/or criminal authorities if the offender fails to adequately participate in therapy or if he stops attending treatment altogether.[67] As with any program that addresses dangerous behavior, some form of follow-up must be included in the treatment plan. At the very least, there should be some level of accountability for one's behavior both during therapy and in the months following the completion of therapy through periodic visits with one's therapist.

Protecting Potential Victims

The responsibility for protecting children from sexual predators falls to teachers, clinicians, social workers, and others who have responsibility for and oversight of children, but parents by far have the greatest responsibility. Parents should never expose their children to their own marital sexual behavior and children should be shielded from sexual images on television, in movies, and in pornographic materials. Children should be taught rules of privacy, appropriate and inappropriate touch, and modesty when it comes to bathroom use and changing of clothes. Parents should be cautious about allowing their children to play with other children, especially males, who are older than their children by three years or more. Most parents are cautious about which adults they leave their children with, but rarely do they give much thought to their children's playmates. Because young people have access to other children, they also have easy opportunity to molest them if they choose. Therefore, equal care should be taken in deciding which children will spend the night or travel together with one's children— circumstances that increase the probability of sexual play or abuse. Perhaps most important of all, parents should supervise their children. Sexual offenders never sexually violate children in the presence of some authority; therefore, supervision may be the most effective form of prevention.

CONCLUDING REMARKS

"Sexuality is more than just behavior."[68] It involves our psychological and social selves, as well as our behavior. There is no sexual behavior without these two components. What is considered "sexual" is driven by social definition, history, religion, and personal intention. Development plays an important role in learning about one's sexual self and in understanding how to appropriately express sexual feelings and thoughts. Dysfunction, almost by definition, occurs when some part of this process goes awry.

Identifying and treating these offenders begins with believing that they are capable of committing these crimes. Hard as it is for us to admit, seemingly innocent children can be cruel sexual predators, just like adult pedophiles. Perhaps even more important than treatment is prevention. The divorce rate, as well as the haphazard approach to relationships that is becoming ever more common in our culture, diminishes the sanctity and value of long-term commitments. This results, at the very least, in poor modeling and perhaps even perpetuates shallow, egocentric relationships in children who observe these relationships. They learn by watching us.

It is a waste of time to call on the media to broadcast responsible programming. They will generate trash and smut as long as it sells. Our energies would be more productively focused on calling on parents to monitor the music, books, movies, and television shows that their children consume. Protecting children from perpetrators can also assist in breaking the cycle of violence. When a child is assaulted, intervention for both the perpetrator and the victim is imperative. The earlier intervention occurs, the higher the probability of success. The stakes are high. Today's child sex offenders are the predatory adults of tomorrow.

NOTES

1. Martin Wainwright, "Care muddle let teenage sex abuser slip through net to kill boy," *The Guardian,* www.guardian.co.uk/child/story/0,7369,593590,00.html, November 15, 2001.

2. "Young offenders units," *House of Commons Hansard Debates,* www.parliament.the-stationery-office.co.uk/pa/cm200102/cmhansrd/vo)11121/debtext/11121-35.htm, November 21, 2001.

3. "'Callous paedophile' jailed for murder,'" *BBC News,* news.bbc.co.uk/hi/english/uk/nesid_402000/402059.stm, July 23, 1999.

4. "Schoolboy's head 'smashed with wrench'," *BBC News,* news.bbc.co.uk/hi/english/uk/newsid_387000/387461.stm, July 6, 1999.

5. "Schoolboy's 'killer' acted normally, court told," *BBC News,* news.bbc.co.uk/hi/english/uk/newsid_388000/3885030.stm, July 7, 1999.

6. S. Terry and A. Kunz, "Sins of the innocent," *Rolling Stone* (Internet Edition), October 31, 1991.

7. Ibid.

8. Ibid.

9. "Adolescent sex offenders," *Sexual Deviancy,* www.sexualdeviancy.com/New_Folder/adolescent_sex_offenders.htm, June 2002.

10. "Sexual offenders," Illinois Coalition Against Sexual Assault, www.icasa.org/uploads/sexual_offenders.pdf, 2001, p. 92.

11. Ibid., p. 91.

12. Ibid.

13. Ibid., p. 92.

14. Natalie Valios, "Damaged beyond repair?" *Community Care* (Internet Edition), January 17, 2002.

15. "Adolescent sex offenders."

16. "Adolescent sexual offenders," The National Clearinghouse on Family Violence (Ottawa, Ontario: Family Violence Prevention Division, January 1990), p. 3.

17. "Adolescent sex offenders."

18. Ian W. Shields, "Young sex offenders: A comparison with a control group of non-sex offenders," International Child and Youth Network, www.cyc-net.org /ft-shields.html, June, 2002.

19. "Sexual offenders," p. 93.

20. Ibid., p. 94.

21. "Adolescent sexual offenders," p. 3.

22. "Children who act out sexually," *Sexual Deviancy*, www.sexualdeviancy.com /New_Folder/sexualized_children.htm, June 2002.

23. "Adolescent sex offenders."

24. Ibid.

25. David M. Burke, "Empathy in sexually offending and nonoffending adolescent males," *Journal of Interpersonal Violence, 16* (Internet Edition), March 2001.

26. Raymond A. Knight and Robert A. Prentky, "Exploring characteristics for classifying juvenile sexual offenders," in Howard E. Barbaree, William L. Marshall, and Stephen M. Hudson, eds., *The Juvenile Sex Offender*, pp. 45–83 (New York: Guilford Press, 1993), p. 77.

27. "Adolescent sex offenders."

28. "Adolescent sexual offenders," p. 3.

29. "Adolescent sex offenders."

30. Carol Veneziano, Louis Veneziano, and Scott LeGrand, "The relationship between adolescent sex offender behaviors and victim characteristics with prior victimization," *Journal of Interpersonal Violence, 15* (April 2000): 365.

31. Ibid.

32. "Sexual offenders," p. 92.

33. Ibid.

34. Shields, "Young sex offenders."

35. Knight and Prentky, "Exploring characteristics for classifying juvenile sexual offenders," p. 77.

36. Joyce F. Lakey, "The profile and treatment of male adolescent sexual offenders," *Adolescence, 29* (Internet Edition), Winter 1994.

37. Shields, "Young sex offenders."

38. Lakey, "The profile and treatment of male adolescent sexual offenders."

39. William M. Bukowski, Lorrie Sippola, and William Brender, "Where does sexuality come from?: Normative sexuality from a developmental perspective." In Howard E. Barbaree, William L. Marshall, and Stephen M. Hudson, eds., *The Juvenile Sex Offender*, pp. 84–103 (New York: Guilford Press, 1993), p. 86.

40. Ibid., p. 91.

41. Ibid., p. 91.

42. Craig S. Cashwell and Michele E. Caruso, "Adolescent sex offenders: identification and intervention strategies," *Journal of Mental Health Counseling, 19* (October 1997): 338.

43. Veneziano, Veneziano, and LeGrand, p. 363.

44. Ibid., p. 365.

45. Lana Stermac and Peter Sheridan, "The developmentally disabled adolescent sex offender," in Howard E. Barbaree, William L. Marshall, and Stephen M. Hudson, eds., *The Juvenile Sex Offender,* pp. 235–242 (New York: Guilford Press, 1993), p. 235.

46. Ibid., p. 236.

47. Ritsaert Lieverse, Louis J. G. Gooren, and Johanna Assies, "The psychoneuroendocrinology of (sexual) aggression," *Journal of Psychology and Human Sexuality, 11* (Internet Edition), www.haworthpressinc.com/store/Toc/J056v11n03_TOC .pdf, July 2002.

48. John McCarthy and Ian Lamble, "The nature of adolescent sexual offending: Part one. An overview of the problem and initial assessment," *Social Work Review* (Internet Edition), March 1995.

49. Cashwell and Caruso, "Adolescent sex offenders," p. 336.

50. Natalie Valios, "Damaged beyond repair?" *Community Care* (Internet Edition), January 17, 2002.

51. McCarthy and Lamble, "The nature of adolescent sexual offending."

52. "Sexual offenders," p. 94.

53. Burke, "Empathy in sexually offending and nonoffending adolescent males," p. 227.

54. Howard E. Barbaree and Franca A. Cortoni, "Treatment of the juvenile sex offender within the criminal justice and mental health systems," in Howard E. Barbaree, William L. Marshall, and Stephen M. Hudson, eds., *The Juvenile Sex Offender,* pp. 243–263 (New York: Guilford Press, 1993), p. 245.

55. Ibid.

56. Ibid., p. 246.

57. Ibid.

58. Ibid., p. 249.

59. Burke, "Empathy in sexually offending and nonoffending adolescent males," p. 224.

60. Ibid.

61. Karyn G. France and Stephen M. Hudson, "The conduct disorders and the juvenile sex offender," in Howard E. Barbaree, William L. Marshall, and Stephen M. Hudson, eds., *The Juvenile Sex Offender,* pp. 225–234 (New York: Guilford Press, 1993), p. 227.

62. Barbaree and Cortoni, "Treatment of the juvenille sex offender," p. 256.

63. Lakey.

64. Burke, "Empathy in sexually offending and nonoffending adolescent males," p. 224.

65. "Treatment," *Sexual Deviancy,* www.sexualdeviancy.com/New_Folder /TreatmentPage.htm, June 2002.

66. Lakey.

67. Barbaree and Cortoni, "Treatment of the juvenile sex offender," p. 253.

68. Bukowski, Sippola, and Brender, "Where does sexuality come?," p. 98.

CHAPTER 10

Vandalism

To regard the lion and the water rats and our fellow men as equals is a magnificent act of a warrior's spirit. It takes power to do that.
—Carlos Castaneda, *Journey to Ixtlan: The Lessons of Don Juan*

The resentment of the weak does not spring from any injustice done to them, but from the sense of their inadequacy and impotence. They hate not wickedness, but weakness. When it is in their power to do so, the weak destroy weakness wherever they see it.
—Eric Hoffer, *Reflections on the Human Condition*

The ability to destroy has an uncanny knack for making one feel powerful. Build a sand castle on the beach and leave it alone for a bit and see how long it takes someone—adult or child—to purposefully step on it. Someone sets up dominoes—you feel the urge to set them in motion. Someone builds a house of cards—you want to knock it down. Even though most of us have either thought about these very things or actually done them, think about what unusual behavior this is. Why would we want to destroy something that someone else has worked hard to create? We even find satisfaction in destroying our own sand castles. The answer lies in the power we derive from destruction. When a skyscraper is built, it draws few spectators, but when one is razed, not only do hundreds gather to watch, but the media preserves the event on film for replay on the evening news. Gossip, a verbal form of destruction, provides us with the same sense of power. Think of the last time you heard something really eyebrow-raising about someone. One of the first things that passed through your mind was who you would tell. "So-and-so will just die when he hears this," you might have said to yourself. Telling the story to someone else, hoping they haven't already heard it, gives you a sense of power. Destruction not only proves our power to others, but perhaps even more so, it demonstrates our power to ourselves.

Nietzsche said that we all have a drive to seek power. Perhaps it is for this reason that awe-inspiring images and events—the Grand Canyon, a powerful storm, and tragedies like the September 11 terrorist attacks—are so humbling. At moments like these, we realize how truly small and powerless we really are. Even though we all seek power, not all of us choose the same path to achieve that power. Some acquire a sense of power through their jobs, others seek power through political position, and still others find power and meaning in the things they create—art, raising children, writing books. People can also gain power by tearing down other people. One of the most common forms of humor in American culture is the put-down. Put-downs make us laugh because even when they are not meant to be harmful, demeaning jokes put people "in their place"—a place below us. Whether we are the joke tellers or the listeners, the put-down is one way of saying "You (the target) aren't as good as we are." While this may not be our intention, it communicates this message nonetheless. Other times, verbal attacks clearly are intended to demean another person. No matter how you look at it, one's purpose in demeaning another is to gain power. Saying hurtful things about someone else's appearance, performance, or whatever is another way of saying, "You are not as good as me. Let me show you why." Whether by jest or intention, insults and put-downs place the target below the speaker. This is one reason put-downs are so common among adolescents. At a time when they are the most unsure of who they are, putting someone else down allows them to feel like they are of value or at least better than the person being demeaned. This also explains why it is so hard for people to step back and allow others to take credit for something well done. Just as put-downs automatically place the speaker higher than the target, verbally building someone else up does the reverse. It places the speaker below the target. It says, "Look at how important you are" rather than "Look how good I am." It takes far more maturity and ego strength to build someone up than to tear someone down.

Bullies gain power by defeating all potential enemies before they can strike or even before they have a chance to be an enemy at all. Rapists seek power over their victims. You have heard it said that rape is a crime of power, not sex. In most cases, this is true. Rape is a medium through which a powerless perpetrator can prove to himself that he can be "in charge." This is why rapists will attack very small children, very old women, and even men. Their primary objective is not sex. They only use sex as a means to demean and humiliate another person, thus elevating themselves. Hate-mongers, racists, and bigots derive power by elevating themselves above entire groups of people based on race, religion, gender, or some other attribute.

Gaining power through destructive means is immature and demonstrative of a weak ego. Destructive behavior, whether it is vandalism or verbal abuse like gossip, vindictiveness, and hateful speech—power-seeking forms of verbal vandalism—are means through which weak people seek power. People who engage in these behaviors destroy other people for their own gain. Oddly, it takes more power to create than to destroy. Restraint takes more power than it takes to be quick tempered. It takes more courage and internal self-assurance to build someone else up than to build up one's self. Immature people do not see the value in these traits. Instead, their fear of their powerlessness drives them to seek ways to gain power. Henry Kissinger once said that power was the ultimate aphrodisiac. I think he was right.

VANDALISM

A college student who was suspended for vandalism sued his former college under the 1990 Americans with Disabilities Act. He said that he was a member of a protected class because the college knew he had bipolar disorder and it was that disorder that drove him to vandalize. Thankfully, the court did not accept this argument and it upheld his suspension. Vandalism, even though it may be related to diagnosable mental disorders, is not caused by mental disorder. Vandalism is a way for a powerless person to feel powerful. Unable to direct his frustration and anger toward the real object of his aggression, he redirects it onto another object. This is called *displacement*. He does not have the courage to hit the person whom he loathes nor does he feel it is safe to say, "I hate you." Instead he will communicate the same messages through vandalism. Children frustrated with their schools (actually more likely they are frustrated with themselves because of their academic inadequacies) displace their frustrations and anger on the building by defacing it, on classrooms by damaging them, or on equipment by destroying it. "See! I'm better than you and you can't control me! I'm too powerful!" their behavior screams. When my son was five years old, he and I would often wrestle together. I usually let him win, but in his mind, he won through his superior strength and strategy. After "beating me up" he would stand tall, flex his muscles, and say, "I'm strong." Vandals are very much like my little boy. They flex their scrawny little muscles through their destructive activities and then stand back and say, "Look how strong I am!"

Vandals sometimes videotape their activities. In fact, many times vandals have been arrested and convicted largely because the videotaped images of their behavior found their way into the hands of police. For most of us, it seems ridiculous that people would videotape themselves committing illegal acts. If we were planning to do something illegal, we would do everything possible to conceal our involvement, but for a vandal, recording the behavior is symptomatic of what drives the vandalism in the first place. Vandals want to be noticed. If others cannot see how "powerful" they are, the behavior does nothing to serve them. Not only do they want their friends to know that they have the power to destroy, they require it—otherwise, there would be no need to vandalize. A videotape proves to themselves and their peers that they are powerful. They can watch their destructive activities over and over, reliving the event much like serial killers who will relive their crimes by retaining an object that belongs to the victim in order to repeatedly relive the event.

Vandals attack residences, residences under construction, stores, trains and buses, and public parks. One of the most common targets of vandals is the public school. They damage drinking fountains, vending machines, and laboratory equipment. They destroy office equipment, damage lockers, televisions, and computer equipment, break windows, they discharge fire extinguishers in hallways and classrooms.

School bathrooms are frequent targets of vandals. They clog toilets and sinks with paper towels, break porcelain and mirrors with hammers, and drain the soap dispensers, leaving a coating of liquid soap all over the floors and walls. One writer made the statement that "No one has yet solved the age-old puzzle of what makes restroom vandalism so appealing to students."[1] This seems rather naïve. Any public restroom is an easy target for vandalism because it provides privacy, easy access, and many of the materials for vandalism. Paper towels are provided for clogging toilets and sinks. Toilet paper is provided for unrolling and littering the floors. Soap is provided for smearing mirrors, floors, and countertops. Thus, a vandal doesn't have to bring anything with him. Not only does the bathroom provide the materials, but groups of children congregate together in these secluded rooms, making group persuasion more likely. Finally, everyone has to go to the bathroom, so vandals have a ready excuse for their presence. Since they have a legitimate reason for being there, the easy access to the bathroom makes it a more likely target than some other location where the person would have to sneak in covertly.

Writer Wilbert L. Sadler identifies six different types of vandals. They are vindictive, malicious, ideological, bored, and frustrated vandals, and acquisitive vandals whose primary motive is to steal, but who vandalize in the process.[2] All six types of vandals are driven by the same need to destroy in order to boost their own feelings of power and control. Take acquisitive vandals, for example. If the person's primary motive is to steal, why destroy property in the process? Property destruction takes extra time and it leaves more clues for police. Taking the extra time to spray-paint walls, defecate on furniture, or perform some other act of destruction is most likely the real message the thief wants to communicate. The thief has already told the victim, "I can break into your house and steal your possessions." The vandalism adds emphasis to the statement, saying, "Not only will I take what I want, but I'll destroy what I don't want so you can't have it. I have more power than you."

Vandalism isn't just a city problem. People who live in rural areas are no strangers to vandalism, either. A practice known as mailbox bashing is not an uncommon nuisance. Groups of young people ride around at night in their vehicles and destroy mailboxes, either by running over them or more likely by swinging at them with baseball bats as they drive by. I find it very interesting that one would find pleasure in destroying the property of random victims. Victims of mailbox bashings are not ordinarily people who are known by the perpetrators. Their mailboxes just happen to be on a conveniently isolated road where the perpetrators believe they can do their damage without getting caught. I have talked with a number of juvenile delinquents who have been caught doing this behavior. When I ask them why they did it, they either say, "Because it is fun," or more likely, "I don't know." I know why they do it. The satisfaction of destroying property is bred by insecurity and a need to feel powerful. If it weren't for this need, the activity wouldn't be fun. Likewise, these teens rarely go mailbox bashing by themselves. It is a group activity. Insecurity feeds the need to show one another how powerful they are.

Statistics

Damage to property due to vandalism costs millions of dollars every year. Insurance companies absorb much of the cost of vandalism to private property, but individuals must pay several hundred dollars in deductibles, plus, the actual expense of the vandalism comes back to owners in the form of higher insurance premiums. It is estimated that the annual cost of vandalism to public schools alone, in damage to the facilities, furnishings, and equipment, is $500 million.[3] Even relatively minor incidents may cost thousands of dollars in repairs and replacement of computers and other damaged equipment. One school near Atlanta was vandalized and, despite the fact that the school had an active alarm system, the perpetrators were able to destroy computers, overhead projectors, video equipment, copy machines, overhead lighting, and they even tore the wiring from the ceiling. When the final bill was totaled, the cost was over $300,000. Other incidents of vandalism are not as dramatic, but budget busting just the same. One incident cost a school $7,000, another school spent $12,000 repairing damage due to an incident of vandalism, another $20,000, and yet another $50,000. A report in *Education Weekly* noted that there were almost 99,000 incidents of school vandalism reported in the 1996–97 school year alone; the majority of these incidents occurred in urban schools (33 percent) while rural schools accounted for only 17 percent of all incidents.[4] The remaining incidents occurred in either suburban schools or schools in smaller towns. Even the most conservative estimates of the costs related to vandalism are very high, but what these numbers cannot tell us is the level of anguish, anger, and fear experienced by victims. Students, teachers, and administrators alike experience a host of emotional reactions when a school is damaged by vandalism. Homeowners whose houses are under construction, business owners and employees whose display cases are smashed and merchandise destroyed, and family members whose homes are damaged and defaced all feel violated and angry, and their sense of security is compromised.

Graffiti

When I was an undergraduate student, one of my classmates was a very arrogant young man. He came to our college as a seventeen-year-old freshman. He was loud, obnoxious, and always verbally cutting others down. During that time, in the late '70s and early '80s, huge radios known as boom boxes were becoming popular. The larger one's "portable" stereo, the more impressive it was. One day while I was walking near the dormitory where this guy lived, I saw him leave the building. On his shoulder was the largest boom box I had ever seen. The moment he stepped on the sidewalk outside the dormitory, he turned the stereo up as loud as it would go. As clear as yesterday, I can still see the look on his face as the radio blared across our mountainside campus in East Tennessee. He scanned the campus, obviously looking to see who was looking at him. I am confident he was not all that interested in loud music. What he really wanted was, as loudly as possible and without actually saying the words, to yell, "Look at me! I am somebody!!" His behavior was, in essence, noise graffiti.

In a way, we all produce graffiti. My classmate's obnoxious behavior was noise graffiti, but we do similar things in more subtle ways. The clothes we wear, the cars we drive, and the jewelry that adorns us communicates a message to observers, and each of these things says something about who we are. A wedding ring tells us and those who see it that we are married. A suit and tie purposefully communicates a different message than blue jeans and a T-shirt. One says "professional" while the other says "casual." I rarely wear a suit and I almost never wear a tie. Even though comfort is part of the reason, most certainly the way I dress says something about my personality and how I want people to see me. My family spent some time in Europe recently. I bought a sweatshirt with a small British flag and the word "London" on the front. Why? Why not a sweatshirt that said "Florida"? The obvious reason any of us buys an article of clothing with writing on it is that the writing is not meant for ourselves, exactly. Rather it is meant for the observer and what thoughts we believe that the message invokes about us in the observer. When people see my sweatshirt, they ask, "Have you been to London?" Even though when I bought the sweatshirt I did not consciously think about telling people I had been to London, this is obviously what it communicates. Equally important is what I believe the knowledge that I have been to London makes the observer think about me. Even though I may argue that I bought it because I liked the color or it is comfortable, the message that I believe it communicates about me is the real reason I bought it.

The private college where I am professor of psychology, Atlanta Christian College, is supported in part by a religious body. Among our offered majors is an undergraduate program for students who wish to pursue the professional ministry, and all of our students take basic biblical studies courses as a part of their core curriculum. Therefore, nearly all of our students have some religious background. It is not uncommon for students to wear T-shirts with spiritual sayings or scripture verses. What purpose do these words serve? Just as the purpose of my sweatshirt communicates a message for the observer and what I believe it will make the observer think about me, these students are hoping that the message on their T-shirts communicates something about them, who they are, and what is important to them. It is an attempt to force the observer to see the wearer in a certain way. Graffiti does the same thing. It is an attempt by the artist to communicate something about him/herself and an attempt to force observers to think about the artist in a certain way.

All of us have seen graffiti. On overpasses, vacant buildings, subway cars, bathroom stalls, and even in the middle of the street, vandals draw obscene images, scribble personal messages, and write their names in elaborate script. "Andy loves Whitney," someone etched into an oak tree in a park where my children have played. Why does anyone feel the need to permanently advertise this relationship that probably ended long before I ever read the message? The trail to the top of Stone Mountain, a solid granite mountain at Stone Mountain State Park east of Atlanta that rises to a height of 825 feet, bears the scars of years of vandalism. People have etched their names into the granite path—damage that can never be corrected. Why does a person feel the need to etch his name on a rock? If you can accept the premise that I have maintained throughout this book that all of our behaviors have meaning, then it seems obvious that scrawling one's name in a public place is a way of saying, "I am somebody!" The message carved into a tree as well as those carved into the trail at Stone Mountain are ways of proving oneself immortal—powerful—and these emotionally weak people want to make sure everyone knows who they are.

Graffiti has an interesting history. Workers in airplane factories during World War II painted cartoons on the products they produced. This practice gave rise to the slogan "Kilroy was here." Spray-painting subway cars and buildings in large cities initially began with the writing of one's name. From there, more elaborate and decorative signatures, called "tags," were created. Author Lynn Powers notes that eventually this led to the full-scale murals on buildings or entire subway cars.[5] "Tagging" was competitive among those who practiced it and quantity was as important as quality. Taggers wrote their names and created their artwork in as many places as possible. Powers relates that graffiti artists who were good at the art had apprentices and were sometimes commissioned by street gangs to tag on behalf of the gang.[6] Tagging of subway cars and buses allowed some graffiti artists to gain recognition beyond their own neighborhoods—spreading their message about themselves even further.

Today, the Internet has given rise to a new type of graffiti. Hackers deface Web sites with their own "tags" without the use of spray paint and without ever leaving home. After breaking into a Web site, they post their own messages on other people's Web pages, sometimes in a font that even mimics spray-painted graffiti. One seventeen-year-old hacker arrested by the FBI claims to have hit more than 200 Web sites with digital graffiti in just one year. Even though these vandals may appear to be different than those who clog up toilets in school bathrooms or spray-paint subway cars, their motive is usually the same. They want people to notice them. Even though some hackers attack strategic Web sites in order to make political statements, their egos still drive them to publicize who they are (at least among fellow hackers) and what they have done—just like children with spray-paint cans. Some of these hackers, like this seventeen-year-old, even write to the media and make their identities known. The graffiti generates no power if people do not know who did it.

Solutions

To combat bathroom vandalism, many public facilities have warm-air hand dryers instead of paper towel dispensers. This equipment is more expensive to purchase and costs more to operate, but advocates say it pays for itself in less than one year and some dryers made of cast iron are almost indestructible. Even though it is unlikely, warm-air dryers can be clogged, leading to possible fire, but automatic start and stop functions can prevent fire and also save energy. Yet many schools and parks still use paper towels because companies will provide the dispensers and maintain them for free in exchange for contracts to purchase supplies. Other attempts by schools to reduce bathroom vandalism have included moving sinks to public hallways and removing doors from the stalls, and in some cases even the doors from bathrooms.[7] The development of solvents that easily remove paint as well as surfaces that are do not hold paint very easily, making graffiti removal quick and easy, have reduced the problem of graffiti on trains and in public rest rooms as well.

A store owner in Wisconsin has chosen to protect the 30-by-15-foot wall of his business, an easy target for graffiti, by commissioning taggers to paint it, and he even provided them with the paint. The only instruction he gave them was that the business's name had to appear in the artwork. This sounds like a great idea and it will probably reduce graffiti on his personal building, but it will not solve the problem of graffiti in the community. The purpose of graffiti is not just artistic expression. If it were, there are much easier and legal ways to get one's artwork noticed. Those who are driven to deface property will not be satisfied with this "acceptable graffiti." They may take advantage of opportunities like this when they arise, but they will still deface other property. Part of the purpose of graffiti is that the vandal wants others to know not only the written message, but also that the artist can put it anywhere he wants—on a water tower, a bridge, or a business—and there is nothing the law can do about it.

Smyrna, Georgia, a suburb of Atlanta, joined other cities like New York in banning the sale of "graffiti tools." This law bans the sale of spray paint, felt-tip pens, and the like to anyone under eighteen years of age and those items are kept behind the counter and treated like pornographic magazines.[8] The city of Chicago started a $3.5 million program in 1993 called "Graffiti Blasters" that attempts to remove graffiti as quickly as possible.[9] This program has been successful so far.

Other solutions to address graffiti and other forms of vandalism include more aggressive police patrols and the hiring of night watchmen at schools, businesses, construction sites, and parks. Some schools have hired third-shift custodians, hoping that having activity in the building at all hours will reduce the chance of vandalism. Electronic surveillance via video cameras as well as alarm systems also provide some level of protection, but a number of schools have been vandalized despite expensive security systems. The floor plan of the building can provide many hiding places for vandals out of sight of video cameras and it is often cost-prohibitive to install video cameras that cover every inch of a facility. Alarm systems alone can be very expensive, costing $25,000 or more for basic systems, but advocates for alarm systems say they quickly pay for themselves because some schools spend as much or more each year on repairs due to vandalism as they would on an alarm system. Where alarming the entire building is cost-prohibitive, experts suggest video cameras or alarm devices in the areas that are most vulnerable to vandalism—computer labs, band rooms, chemistry labs, media centers, administrative offices.[10] Even with alarms and a quick response from law enforcement, vandals can spray-paint the outside of the building or even break in and do a great deal of damage in minutes, leaving the scene before law enforcement has time to arrive.

Getting help from the students themselves is an approach some schools have chosen. After their women's basketball team lost a championship game, students at Purdue University caused $75,000 in damage in postgame demonstrations. Offering rewards for information, the school was able to arrest many of the most serious offenders. Even though rewards cost money up front, $23,000 in Purdue's case, it is hoped that over time the fear of being turned in by a peer will reduce both vandalism and the need for payouts in the form of rewards. Other schools have chosen to approach the problem of vandalism through peer assistance, but not by offering rewards. They have targeted vandalism through character training programs. These programs teach young people values and encourage them to maintain a high level of decorum among their peers. Advocates of this approach note that these programs make it more likely that when students know of misconduct by their peers, they will turn them in to administrators. Vandalism is a crime that perpetrators make public—especially among their peers. If peers are likely to turn them in, vandalism is less likely since there would be no one to brag to without the risk of getting caught.

Perhaps the most effective approach is dealing with the underlying cause of vandalism. These young people are trying to communicate a message about themselves. If mental health workers, teachers, law enforcement officials, and parents can find a more productive way for these children to express themselves and to feel powerful, they will no longer have any need to vandalize.

ARSON

Almost all children are fascinated by fire. Fire is a "powerful magical force" that is hard to ignore.[11] Beginning around age three, children are enraptured by the power and mystery of fire and they are drawn to it when they are allowed. The American Red Cross reports that over half of all children have played with fire by age thirteen.[12] Fascination with fire does not go away when we enter adulthood. Even as an adult, you have probably found yourself staring into a blazing fire in your fireplace or on a camping trip, mesmerized by the dancing flames. Normal interest in fire involves its "sensory qualities"—visual, auditory, and tactile. Most of us enjoy the warm feel of a fire as well as the affective warmth a fire provides. We enjoy watching its flames and hearing the crackling sound of burning logs on a cold winter evening. Structure fires, brush fires, and automobile fires attract us as well. Even though we are stunned by the intensity and destructive force of a fire, we are also awed by its power. Deliberate fire-setting goes beyond this normal fascination with fire. Arson is destructive and dysfunctional in nature and is directly related to a child's need for power and attention. Arson is no small problem, as you will see.

Statistics

Over half of all arson fires in the United States are committed by someone eighteen years of age or younger and between 60 percent and 80 percent of all arsonists arrested are juveniles.[13] Six percent of arson fires are committed by children under age ten.[14] These numbers may not fully tell the story because the perpetrators of 80 percent or more of all deliberately set fires are never caught and of those fires where arrests are made, only between 2 and 6 percent end in convictions. The rates of juvenile involvement in fire-setting are high, but these numbers also include many accidental fires set by children. These tots playing with fire do not know what they are doing and have no intent to be destructive. However, even if we don't count this group, juvenile arson rates are still high. When juvenile rates for intentional fire-setting are calculated, excluding arson due to children playing with fire, still fully one-third of all arson arrests are juveniles under the age of fifteen.[15] The problem of juvenile fire-setting isn't isolated to the United States. Other countries experience juvenile arson rates similar to those in the United States. For example, in the United Kingdom, individuals under eighteen are responsible for 40 percent of fires set in private homes and this does not include fires set in automobiles, abandoned buildings, businesses, and schools. Most professionals agree with the FBI, whose researchers claim that arson is the number one crime committed by male juveniles.[16]

More than 25,000 fires occur each year as a result of children playing with matches or some other flammable material, and the number of fires deliberately set by arsonists is much higher. According to the National Fire Protection Association, there were 72,000 suspicious structure fires in 1999 alone.[17] Costs related to property damage from arson totals more than $3 billion a year and the average cost of a fire caused by arson is more than $11,000. Even more devastating, several hundred people die each year in arson fires and thousands are injured, including family members, rescue workers, and sometimes even the arsonists themselves. In 1995, there were 535 deaths and 3,400 injuries caused by arson fires.[18]

Origins

The motives for arson vary with age. Adults may set fires to conceal a crime or to commit fraud, such as burning one's own house or business to collect the insurance money. Adult arsonists may also set fires to make a social statement. Animal rights groups, for example, have been accused of burning down research laboratories in order to condemn animal research. Juveniles, however, rarely set fires for these reasons. With the exception of curiosity seekers and children who set fires by accident, juvenile arsonists almost always suffer from some psychosocial dysfunction. Fire-setting is almost never the problem; rather, it is a symptom of the real problem. At the very least, fire-setting is a compulsive behavior, but the compulsion to set fires does not pop up out of thin air. Arson has its roots most often in psychological problems that are the result of family issues and/or psychological disorders. One small study, for example, demonstrated the relationship between home life and delinquent behavior. In-depth interviews with two dozen delinquent children in prison demonstrated that 28.5 percent had been emotionally abused, 29 percent had been sexually abused, and 40 percent had been physically abused.[19] In this same population, almost half had experienced the loss of someone important in their lives: a parent, grandparent, relative, or friend.[20] Many other studies have also correlated broken homes, especially the absence of a father, with arson. Most arsonists live in a single-parent home, usually with the mother, and many have a psychiatric history, although a psychiatric history is most common among older juvenile fire-setters. According to the FBI, most juvenile arsonists are Caucasian (76%) males in their teens or early 20s.[21] Almost 90 percent of all juvenile arsonists are male. Even though some research suggests that some older adolescent and adult arsonists are above average in intelligence, the most reliable research indicates that across all age groups, arsonists tend to be below average in intelligence.

Fire safety experts classify juvenile fire-setters into three broad age categories. The first category, called *curiosity seekers,* identifies children under the age of seven or eight. The fires these children set are usually set by accident and are the result of playing with matches or flammables. Curiosity seekers set fires most often in the morning hours and their fires are usually set at home or in the home of a relative where they are left unsupervised. These children do not realize how easily a fire can spread from a small flame to a massive blaze. In less than a minute a small flame can ignite curtains or bedding and within five minutes can fully engulf a home.

The second group includes children between eight and age twelve or thirteen. These children set fires as a *cry for help* and demonstrate the beginnings of a serious problem with arson. One eleven-year-old child who was angry about his parents' divorce said fire made him feel in control. "I wanted to stop, but the urge was so strong that I couldn't and I just had to keep on doing it," he said.[22] These children may set fires out of revenge or, like the boy just mentioned, in an attempt to gain the attention of some significant person in one's life. These deliberate fires may be set at home, but may also involve automobiles, barns, or vacant buildings. These children almost always set fires alone and burn something of personal significance to them—a parent's car or a school classroom—and there is usually a precipitating crisis like a divorce or a move.[23]

The third category represents the most *severely disturbed* and the highest-risk juvenile arsonists. These children, ages thirteen and older, are more likely to set fires in groups or as a part of gang-related behavior. Their targets are more likely to be random and have less personal significance than those of their younger peers, although some researchers have found that juvenile arsonists between ages thirteen and sixteen often target schools or structures related to school activities.[24] This age group is more likely to set fires in conjunction with a burglary or vandalism than younger children.[25]

A list of risk factors is listed in Table 10.1. Because most fire-setters under the age of eight are most at risk for setting accidental fires, the primary risk factors for this age group are lack of supervision and access to flammables. Therefore, the risk factors in Table 10.1 generally apply more appropriately to children eight years of age or older.

Most of the items in the table need no explanation, but a few require some elaboration. Bed-wetting and cruelty to animals constitute two of the three parts of the *terrible triad*—arson being the third. These three behaviors are almost always symptoms of serious mental disorder and are often found together. A number of serial killers have engaged in all three of these behaviors. These behaviors have previously been thought to decrease in frequency with age, but some researchers argue that, rather than decreasing in frequency, older children simply are better at concealing their bedwetting and cruel behaviors.[26] Beyond these two specific behaviors, "history of behavioral problems" would include a history of criminal behavior (stealing, burglary, other forms of vandalism, etc.), frequent fighting, bullying, truancy, and lying.

Table 10.1
Risk Factors Associated with Juvenile Fire-Setting

- Bedwetting
- Cruelty to animals
- History of behavioral problems
- History of fire-setting
- Fascination with fire and fire products
- Family turmoil/severely disturbed home
- History of abuse (physical, emotional, sexual or neglect)
- Change in family constellation
- Drug use/abuse
- Mental illness
- Difficulty making friends/poor peer relationships
- Antisocial behavior
- Delinquent friends/gang affiliation
- Lack of empathy
- Failure to accept responsibility
- Low self-esteem
- Accident prone
- Substandard school performance
- Is easily manipulated
- Lacks assertiveness
- Physical or cognitive impairments/disabilities
- Increased risk with age
- Hyperactivity/impulse control problems

"Fascination with fire and fire products" goes beyond the normal curiosity and interest in fire. Included here would be playing with matches or lighters, trying to burn items, carrying fire-starting materials in pockets or keeping them in rooms, talking about fire, and asking how particular materials will burn.[27] Also included would be children who seem mesmerized by fires.

"Family turmoil/severely disturbed home" relates to domestic violence of any kind as well as sexual, physical, or emotional abuse. This would also include neglect, emotional "coolness" or distance from the father or mother, and parents who are rejecting toward their children. Children in single-parent homes are also at greater risk. Also included would be haphazard parenting practices where children do not know what to expect from one moment to the next. These are parents who are moody, irregular in discipline, who provide poor modeling, and who provide mixed messages regarding appropriate displays of emotion. An interesting study in 1999 compared a group of 75 children who set fires to a group of 105 children who were not fire-setters. These researchers noted a high incidence of family dysfunction, including alcoholism, psychosis, criminality, and illegitimacy among the fire-setting group.[28] In further comparisons of the two groups, the following variables were found to be statistically correlated with fire-setting (in order of prevalence/weight): excitement at fires, revenge fantasies, history of playing with fires, cruelty to animals or people, poor social judgment, rage at insults, inadequate superego development, severe maternal rejection, sexual conflicts, obsessive-compulsive features, lack of empathy, history of physical aggression, and anger at a paternal figure.[29] "Change in family constellation" would include the death of a family member, the birth of a sibling, separation or divorce of the parents, abandonment, unemployment of a parent, or even a move to a new home or city.

Two final items that bear elaboration are "mental illness" and "increased risk with age." Mental illnesses associated with arson include depression, psychosis, suicidal behavior, attachment disorder, neurosis, and obsessive-compulsive disorder. Although arsonists may have other mental health diagnoses (i.e., attention deficit/hyperactivity disorder), one or more of these diagnoses does not increase the risk of arson in the absence of other risk factors. In other words, mental illness alone is not highly correlated with arson. "Increased risk with age" addresses the fact that "in all juvenile arsonists, the intensity and enormity of the fire tends to escalate with age."[30] In short, as the list of risk factors related to a given child increases, his age is a critical variable. The older the child, the higher the risk he presents.

Prevention/Treatment

One of the first tasks in treatment is to determine the current level of risk that the child will set another fire. Younger children are less at risk for setting a fire than one who is older, and a child who has a history of setting fires is a significantly higher risk for setting future fires than a child who has set a fire only once. Evaluating risk is imperative because lives may be lost if treatment begins without first ensuring that the child is not a threat to people or property. Psychologist Jessica Gaynor, through grants from the Federal Emergency Management Agency and the United States Fire Administration, published an exceptional volume in 2002 that can assist professionals in evaluating risk for arson. She suggests that assessing fire-setting behavior requires evaluating whether the behavior was a single episode or repeated, a conscious act or an accident, or if it was preplanned or spontaneous.[31] Gaynor notes that between 30 percent and 40 percent of juveniles are a definite risk for arson while less than 1 percent are an extreme risk.[32] The detailed program, weighted checklists, and question-naires for risk assessment are available through the Internet. (See bibliog-raphy for more information.)

All types of juvenile arsonists can be treated with a combination of edu-cation and psychological counseling. By ten years of age, most children are aware of the damage fire can cause and the danger of fire to people and property. Education about fire, its dangers, and the physical and punitive consequences of fire and arson is the most effective way to treat curiosity arsonists. It is important to interrupt fire-setting behavior as soon as it starts. Research shows that once a child sets a fire, there is a 35 percent chance that he will ignite another fire within a year.[33] Likewise, once a fire-setter has been active for several months or years, especially if he is in his mid- to late teens, treatment is very difficult and the recidivism rate is near 50 percent. Generally, younger arsonists are easier to treat than older ones and treatment is also easier if it is administered early in one's fire-setting career.

Effective treatment of all individuals, whether they are minimum, mod-erate, or extreme risks, involves a cooperative effort between social ser-vices, fire-safety educators, the judicial system, mental health counselors, and parents. The research indicates that, even with therapy, one in four fire-setters will repeat his fire-setting behavior.[34] The Arson Prevention Program for Children (TAPP-C) is a collaborative model involving fire ser-vice and mental health professionals in assessment, intervention, and treatment of child arsonists and is usually offered free of charge to chil-dren ages two to seventeen. This program has been shown to be very effective. In a follow-up study of over 1,000 children who had participated in a TAPP-C program, it was found that 70 percent of them had set no fires since leaving the program.[35]

Arson is an especially deadly form of vandalism. Playing with fire is the leading cause of death among preschoolers.[36] It has been shown that some fires are started by children because they have easy access to flam-mables (matches, fireplace starters, etc.) and they are not carefully super-vised. In fact, many children have died in fires started by curious four- or five-year-old children because their mother or father left them alone while they went shopping, to work, or out with friends. Part of any arson treatment and prevention program, according to the United States Fire Administration, is "raising the awareness of parents regarding their own behavior and what they can do to create a fire-safe home environment."[37] Parents need to participate in the correction process, learning how they can prevent curiosity arson as well as the other forms of arson mentioned above. Supervision, modeling proper safety behaviors with fire and flammables, and limiting a child's access to flammables are huge steps toward prevention.

Counselors play an important role in prevention as well as correcting arson behaviors. First of all, they can help parents by teaching them how to responsibly supervise their children. Second, counselors must address the underlying psychological causes that drive arson behaviors. George A. Sakheim and Elizabeth Osborn write that fire-setting "rarely occurs as an isolated symptom, but rather in constellation with a variety of other delinquent-related behaviors."[38] Therefore, counselors must address other delinquent behaviors and their causes. There are at least three psychotherapeutic issues with arsonists, especially older juvenile arsonists. First, counselors must teach the child to empathize, to take another's perspective, and to consider the consequences of his actions. Most of us realize that setting fire to a building puts potential occupants as well as firefighters at risk. Even though arsonists ordinarily do not want to hurt people, arsonists have little empathy for the victims of their fires and they do not consider all the possible outcomes of their behavior—their own incarceration or the injury or death of innocent people. They also have little empathy for the physical and emotional loss suffered by victims whose houses, businesses, or other properties are destroyed.

A second part of counseling involves teaching the perpetrator to productively deal with his anger, frustration, and other emotions. Burning buildings is obviously a dysfunctional way to communicate one's thoughts as well as a dysfunctional coping strategy. As is true with many types of perpetrators, learning more productive coping strategies can greatly reduce their risk of repeating the destructive behavior.

Finally, counselors must deal with the perpetrator's feelings of inadequacy. Arson is a type of vandalism and all vandalism is driven, at least in part, by feelings of inadequacy. The counselor must discover the source of this inadequacy and help the client resolve these issues. Behavioral counseling can be helpful, but without cognitive-insight therapy, these issues will not be resolved.

Other possible therapeutic interventions may include treatment of other mental health problems. For example, some arsonists suffer from mental disorders that must also be treated. Depression, psychosis, and suicide risk are the mental health issues most closely associated with arson.[39]

Attachment disorder, obsessive-compulsive disorder, and neurosis are also linked to fire-setting, and each of these disorders has its own preferred treatment(s). Some of these disorders, in conjunction with cognitive and/or behavioral treatments, may also be effectively treated with medication. Also, as noted earlier in Table 10.1, some adolescent arsonists also suffer from physical disabilities. Rehabilitation therapy may be necessary as well as teaching cognitive strategies for dealing with one's limitations.

CONCLUDING REMARKS

The destruction of property is a symptom of a bigger problem—the child's need to demonstrate his power. This need is often the result of poor parenting practices, poor supervision, and abuse. After twenty years of clinical practice, I am confident that many adolescent problems could be avoided if these children had loving parents who invested time and energy in their children. My friend and I met in a restaurant one afternoon for a business meeting. During the time we were meeting, a local high school dismissed for the day. Over the next two hours, a group of a dozen or more teens crowded into several booths adjacent to ours. They smoked cigarettes, told obnoxious jokes, and loitered for more than two hours. This kind of behavior is even more prevalent on weekend nights. My guess is that the homes where most of these children live were empty after school. Some of their parents were working so they could buy new cars and take nice vacations while others had parents who really didn't care what their children did and who did not want to be bothered by them. Parents who bring their children into my office are often good people but, even then, they have waited until the problems were so bad that they could no longer ignore them before they sought out help. Often, as I make suggestions that would improve the child's home situation, they sit quietly, nodding, knowing all along what they should have been doing, but they were either too busy or they just didn't want to do what they knew they should.

Of course, children can fall into the wrong crowd despite the efforts of their parents. I have several very close friends whose children have taken paths that perplex me, knowing their upbringing, but these children are the exception, not the rule. It is very rare that I see a child who has been arrested for vandalism, arson, or some other crime whose parents were committed first and foremost to parenting. I don't think that is a coincidence.

NOTES

1. Mike Kennedy, "Discouraging restroom vandalism," *American School & University*, 73 (July 2001): 32.

2. Wilbert L. Sadler, "Vandalism in our schools: A study concerning children who destroy property and what to do about it," *Education, 108* (2001): 556–560.

3. Ibid.

4. Darcia Harris Bowman, "Vandals target school technology items," *Education Week, 21* (Internet Edition), February 20, 2002.

5. Lynn A. Powers, "Whatever happened to the graffiti art movement?" *Journal of Popular Culture, 29* (Internet Edition), 1996.

6. Ibid.

7. Kennedy, "Discouraging restroom vandalism," p. 32.

8. Janet Ward, "The writing's on the wall, and we want it off," *American City & County, 116* (June 2001): 4.

9. Ibid.

10. Bowman, "Vandals target school technology items."

11. George A. Sakheim and Elizabeth Osborn, "Severe vs. nonsevere firesetters revisited," *Child Welfare League of America, 78* (1999): 428.

12. "Juvenile fire play," The American Red Cross, www.stjoe-redcross.org /safety-tips/juv-fires.html, February 15, 2002.

13. Ibid.

14. "National arson forum campaign to focus on juvenile firesetters," *Fire Engineering, 149* (January 1996): 63.

15. "NFPA releases arson statistics," *Fire Engineering, 148* (Internet Edition), March 1995.

16. "The need is clear," Burn Children Recovery Foundation, www.burn childrenrecovery.org/index2.htm, 2002.

17. "Arson," Santa Monica Fire Department, santamonicafire.org/firesafety /arson.htm, November 7, 2001.

18. Debra Schneider, "Arson," The American Prosecutors Research Institute, www.ndaa.org/pdf/Arson.pdf, 2001.

19. Gwyneth R. Boswell, "Criminal justice and violent young offenders," *The Howard Journal, 37* (May 1998): 153.

20. Ibid., p. 155.

21. Ellen Emmerson White, "Profiling arsonists and their motives: An update," *Fire Engineering, 149* (Internet Edition), March 1996.

22. John Quinones, "When kids start fires," *ABC News,* www.abcnews .go.com/sections/living/DailyNews/arson_promo_feature.html, April 12, 1999.

23. Peggy Little, "Juveniles & arson," Paralegals.com, www.paralegals.org /Reporter/Summer98/arson.htm, 1998.

24. Ibid.

25. White, "Profiling arsonists."

26. Little, "Juveniles & arson."

27. Katherine M. Price, "Juvenile firesetters," *The Online Educator,* www.geocities .com/Athens/Troy/4383/firesetters.html, 1999.

28. Sakheim and Osborn, "Severe vs. nonsevere firesetters," p. 414.

29. Ibid., p. 426.

30. Little, "Juveniles & arson."

31. Jessica Gaynor, "Juvenile firesetter intervention handbook," United States Fire Administration (Emmitsburg, MD: Federal Emergency Management Agency, 2002), p. 2.

32. Ibid., p. 4.

33. Quinones, "When kids start fires."

34. Sakheim and Osborn, "Severe vs. nonsevere firesetters," p. 412.

35. "The Arson Prevention Program for Children," Fire Marshal's Public Fire Safety Council, www.gov.on.ca/OFM/fmpfsc/english/tapp-c.htm, October 15, 1999.

36. David Holmstrom, "Alarms ring over juvenile fire setting," *Christian Science Monitor, 89* (November 19, 1997): 1.

37. Gaynor, "Juvenile firesetter intervention handbook," p. 36.

38. Sakheim and Osborn, "Severe vs. nonsevere firesetters," p. 413.

39. Gaynor, "Juvenile firesetter intervention handbook," p. 21.

CHAPTER 11

Treating Violent Children

"What is REAL?" asked the Rabbit one day, when they were lying side by side near the nursery fender, before Nana came to tidy the room. "Real isn't how you are made," said the Skin Horse. "It's a thing that happens to you. When a child loves you for a long, long time, not just to play with, but really loves you, then you become Real.... generally, by the time you are Real, most of your hair has been loved off, and your eyes drop out and you get loose in the joints and very shabby. But these things don't matter at all because once you are Real you can't be ugly, except to people who don't understand."

—Margery Williams, *The Velveteen Rabbit*

Not only is Margery Williams' classic tale *The Velveteen Rabbit* a wonderful children's story, it is a wonderful grown-up story as well. This conversation between the Velveteen Rabbit and the Skin Horse one night in the nursery was reflective of Rabbit's feelings of inferiority because he wasn't shiny like some toys, he didn't have any fancy clockwork to make him move or talk like some others, and his hindquarters were made "all in one piece" so that he had no distinct legs. By the end of the story, though, the Skin Horse's prophecy comes true. Rabbit's skin is loved off, his joints are loose, and his eyes are missing, but he becomes Real. There are many important lessons in children's literature and this story is one of my favorites. As with Dr. Seuss' *Star-Bellied Sneetches*, the moral of the story is that it doesn't matter what you look like. It may seem an odd segue from children's literature to the treatment of aggressive children, but this lesson from a conversation between two toys is my foundation for treating aggressive children. It pains me to hear hateful words from people when a child commits a crime.

To the distant observer, these are "broken" children with no redeeming value. Their crimes give the public permission to despise them. Spectators yell insults at them as they walk to and from trial, some accused of killing, others accused of raping, molesting, or injuring. They seem ugly because of what they have done, but only to those who don't understand. In many cases, their difficult lives have rubbed off their skin, made their joints shabby, and their bad condition makes people wonder if they really need them around anymore, but I petition that there is something deeper here—something lovely for those who choose to understand. Through therapy, I can help these children see something beautiful in themselves, a prerequisite for overcoming their hurt and dysfunction.

When I am asked how I can sleep at night after a day working with children who have done some of the horrifying things that I have described in this book, I get the chance to help them see what I see when a child comes into therapy with me. I don't see the crime or the violation. Instead, I see possibilities, opportunity, and a chance for healing. Like remodeling an old house or restoring a classic car, I see my work as a chance not only to help others see what lies beneath the issues that brought the child to therapy, but also a chance to help the child see previously untapped possibilities in himself.

VIOLENT CHILDREN

Treatment of aggressive children begins with securing the environment. The therapist must ensure that the aggressive child does not have access to any more potential victims. Measures need to be taken in conjunction with the parent or guardian to protect siblings, stepsiblings, neighbors, classmates, or other children in the environment as well as any adults who may be at risk. If there is any indication that the child's behavior is a response to abuse, the therapist also has to ensure that the child is protected from further abuse. Children who have been repeatedly molested or physically abused eventually give up hope that they can be helped. Intervention may have been attempted through social services or the child may have asked for help directly or indirectly, but when intervention brings no relief from his situation, he assumes that he will always be mistreated because intervention has been ineffective. Oftentimes, the therapist is not the first person to attempt intervention. The child has seen interventions fail in the past and has no reason to suppose that this new attempt will be any different. Therefore, the clinician must do everything possible to protect the child.

Intake and Treatment Planning

Following assessment of any immediate risk to the child or people in the child's environment, intake procedures include a preliminary assessment of the antecedents to the child's behavior, an evaluation of the child's family system, an assessment of the child's physical well-being and potential for psychotropic intervention, and the establishment of a treatment plan and treatment goals.

When the therapist is working with aggressive children, she should always look for the antecedents of the behavior. Does the behavior occur only when certain circumstances precede it, such as parental arguments, a move, or testing at school? Also, are there specific situations, such as school, home, or with certain people, where the behavior is more likely to occur? Answering these questions leads the therapist toward a cause and eventually to a treatment plan.

The therapist should always evaluate the family system. Many intake protocols are available to assist therapists both with the parental interview and the interview of the child so that the therapist can be certain that he has a full understanding of the family system and interactions within that system. Other important individuals in the child's life may also be an important part of this component of assessment. For example, an understanding of the child's school behavior may be important and teacher participation in the treatment plan is often helpful. With the parent's permission, I often talk with the child's teachers and let them know what can be done at school to help the child move toward successful achievement of therapeutic goals.

Information concerning the child's physical health is important. The child's diet, sleep patterns, and exercise habits can give the therapist valuable information when constructing the treatment plan. Pediatric records or conversations with the child's pediatrician can provide further information that may have a bearing on the clinical diagnosis. When necessary, the therapist may need to refer the child to a specialist for a neurological assessment to ensure there is no physiological issue that would inhibit therapy. However, psychotropic intervention should not be used by itself. When a physician prescribes medication as a part of treatment, it should be used in conjunction with individual therapy, group therapy, and/or family therapy. For example, the main problem with medications prescribed for attention deficit/hyperactivity disorder (ADHD) is that many parents address the impulsivity of the child only with medication, assuming that is all they need to do. Yet there are other social and behavioral precursors to the child's disruptive behavior that also need to be addressed for the most complete treatment of the disorder. Otherwise, when the child stops taking medication, when the medication becomes ineffective, or when the medication is inappropriately prescribed, minimal change in behavior, if any, will result.

Once the intake has been conducted, a treatment plan, including measurable goals and objectives of therapy, who will be involved, and frequency of visits, can be established. The treatment plan may involve other professionals, such as a pediatrician for a physical, a psychiatrist for medication, or a psychometrist for testing. In developing the treatment plan, the therapist should take into consideration the logistical and financial burdens that the plan will place on the parent or guardian and negotiate any necessary alternatives to ensure that the parent will follow through with the plan. A treatment plan is of no value if the parent will not participate because of affordability and time or distance constraints.

Explosive Children

More often than not, children who exhibit violent tantrums, sometimes called "explosive" children, are aggressive because of poor parenting practices rather than because of abuse or physiological abnormalities. The clinician must be able to distinguish between inadequate or inconsistent disciplinary practices or the modeling of aggression by adults and true explosive rage. The purpose of tantrums is to coerce adults and to get their way. When these tantrums are the result of inadequate disciplinary practices, for example, they will abate when ineffective discipline is replaced with effective discipline. When the cost gets too high, the poorly disciplined child's behavior will change. However, with truly explosive rage, due to abuse, physiological problems, or other serious dysfunction, the explosive behavior will continue even when it is self-destructive.

The clinician must also distinguish between controlled and impulsive aggression. If the child is uncontrolled and impulsive, the problem may be corrected through behavioral training and possibly medication. The child may have poor social skills, inadequate coping skills, or simply weak impulse control. Teaching these skills may resolve the aggressive behavior. A child who is controlled and deliberate in his anger knows what he is doing, especially if he is being deliberately cruel to people or to animals. He has considered his options and picked aggression as the most desirable option. Just as in treating impulsive children, treatment of controlled aggression must include social skills and coping skills training, but it must also address the underlying reasons why the child believes aggression will solve his problems. In both cases, the underlying causes of aggression, whether inadequate parenting, social skills problems, or more serious issues like abuse or attachment issues, must be addressed.

Signs of Serious Trouble

There are very few symptoms that are always signs of a serious problem. The terrible triad—enuresis, fire-setting, and cruelty to animals and/or people—that I have mentioned in previous chapters almost always constitutes troubling symptoms. Enuresis is obviously normal up to a certain age. All babies and toddlers have difficulty maintaining bladder control during the day, and some children have difficulty controlling their bladders at night even well into their grade school years. Enuresis is a sign of serious dysfunction only when the child has successfully completed potty training and has gone many months without accidents. For example, a child who has an occasional accident at night, even if the child is nine or ten years of age, but has never gone more than a few weeks without an accident is not demonstrating enuresis as it pertains to the terrible triad. On the other hand, a child who is five or six and hasn't had an accident in the daytime for two years, yet all of a sudden is having accidents every few days, is exhibiting enuresis as it pertains to the terrible triad. (There are also physical issues that can cause enuresis and consultation with a physician may be necessary.) Evaluation of fire-setting should distinguish between normal interest in fire and deliberate setting of fires. Cruelty to animals and/or people involves a broad range of behaviors, but includes physically harming or torturing an animal or person and may also include relentless psychological torture of a sibling or acquaintance.

Another behavior that should give the therapist reason to be concerned is dehumanization of people. Disturbed individuals dehumanize people in order to cope with the inhumane way they have been treated. This behavior is especially risky if the therapist determines that there is a sadistic or emotionally detached mother/parent at home because this type of home situation has been correlated with violent children.

Gradual increase in use of pornography should be addressed, especially if it escalates to acting-out behavior. In cases where the child seeks out pornography—in print, on the Internet, or in film—the therapist should ask about the child's fantasies. If the child is increasing his use of pornography and at the same time has violent fantasies, the child poses a risk to others. Addressing violent fantasies, especially those with sexual content, must always be a part of therapy. Janet Rulo-Pierson writes that, "Fantasy offers the abused lonely child an escape from reality, a sense of control, a source of self-stimulation, and a safe place to express his pent-up emotions, fears, and desires" and that fantasy allows the child to "construct his own psychological amusement park."[1] Researchers have found that about half of adult murderers and 80 percent of sadistic killers began fantasizing about deviant, violent, sexual encounters in their preteens and some as early as age five.[2] Experts in serial rape and murder have found that adult perpetrators often begin their violent careers as adolescents, practicing their techniques with animals and eventually with people, as they refine their methods of rape and torture. In other words, aggression toward animals and people, as well as violent sexual crimes committed in adolescence, can become the training ground for future serial killers and serial rapists.

One last note is important with regard to serious problems in childhood. Often parents choose to "wait it out" when they see disturbing symptoms in their children. They either ignore signs of disturbance or they just hope the symptoms that they see will go away by themselves. Sometimes children do outgrow some problems and the child adjusts in later life, but this is a risky assumption. Operating on the assumption that the child will heal himself not only places the child's healthy adjustment at risk but also places others in the aggressive child's environment at risk.

If a child experiences some specific trauma, such as physical abuse, sexual abuse, or some other issue that is closely related to aggression, the parent should have the child evaluated by a professional even if no troubling symptoms are present. Some research indicates that children who have the potential for homicide may function well until their adolescent years, at which time they commit aggressive acts.[3] The child specialist must be the one to make the determination regarding the child's adjustment; haphazard and ill-informed assessments from pediatricians, teachers, or others who are unqualified to make these assessments should be avoided.

SCHOOL VIOLENCE

Perhaps of utmost interest to the general public in the past few years is school violence. Between 1992 and 1994, 105 people, including 76 students, died on school grounds or on the way to or from school, and 81 percent of those deaths were homicides.[4] Furthermore, a study of school killings between 1994 and 1999 showed that even though the number of violent deaths at schools is dropping, murders with multiple victims are increasing.[5] On average, there is roughly one school-related killing somewhere in America every seven days.[6] Despite these numbers, the chance of a child being murdered at school is very small—less than one in a million, according to the Centers for Disease Control and Prevention.[7] But even though mass shootings at schools are rare, they capture our attention and force us to realize that schools are not the sanctuaries we may have thought them to be. Here are a few cases in recent history:

- A thirteen-year-old boy shot four classmates at an Oklahoma middle school in December 1999. Just minutes after he was dropped off at school, he pulled out a 9mm handgun and began firing at the students. He emptied the weapon and then was taken into custody by the school's resource officer. When questioned by the sheriff, the boy said he didn't know why he had shot the four students. None of the injuries were serious.

- The father of a seventeen-year-old high school senior in Ohio in 2002 called police when he discovered that his gun was missing and he feared that his son had taken it to school. The principal saw the boy carrying a coat and detained him. The boy acted evasively and tried to make excuses to get away, but the principal kept him from leaving until police arrived. When they did, they found that the boy had two sticks of dynamite and two blasting caps in his possession. There was no motive disclosed.

- Almost two dozen grade school children, ranging in age from ten to fourteen in Chicago in 2002, were arrested when they attacked a group of students from another grade school as they walked to school. Police confiscated a baseball bat and a two-inch-thick stick that they believed were used in the attacks. Most of the injured children received minor injuries, but two children were treated for blunt trauma to the head. The attack was in retaliation for an altercation that had occurred the day before.

- Two seventeen-year-old California high school students were arrested on conspiracy charges in April 2000 for planning a massive attack on their school. Police confiscated knives, swords, and other weapons that were to be used in the attack they had planned for over a year, planning that began even before the Columbine attack. Police did not disclose their motive.

- In March 2001, a high school student in California injured five people. He pled guilty to attempted murder, but later hanged himself in jail.

- In Meissen, Germany, in 1999, a fifteen-year-old boy stabbed a teacher to death because friends dared him to do it. He was sentenced to seven years in jail.

- A fifteen-year-old freshman at a high school in California in 2001 used weapons from home to shoot two adults and thirteen students, two of whom died, at his high school. It was reported that he had been victimized repeatedly by bullies in the school he had only attended for a few months. The teen pled guilty to two counts of murder and thirteen counts of attempted murder.

- A fifteen-year-old student was arrested for allegedly plotting to poison the punch at his high school prom in Iowa in 2002. After his arrest, the boy claimed it was a joke, but friends in whom he had confided believed him and notified police. No one was injured.

The U.S. Secret Service produced a training manual in 2002 that addressed school violence. It proposed that most school shooters shared a few similarities. All the perpetrators in their study were male and they often were bullied or felt neglected and alone. Prior to their attacks, they were rejected by girlfriends or threatened by someone else. When the report was first released, the press headlined the story by saying that school shootings are preventable. Around that same time, the FBI also published a list of risk factors that contribute to school violence. The public interpretation of these studies was overstated. In reality, almost all adolescents feel rejected at one time or another and many young people are victims of bullies, not to mention the fact that many boys have been rejected by a girlfriend at some time during junior high and high school years.

The fact is that school shootings are as different as they are similar. The Secret Service study found that half of all the shootings occurred in the middle of the school day.[8] However, there is ample evidence that the beginning and end of the school day are also risky periods because these are times when students congregate in groups but are under limited supervision. Schools are most at risk for violence immediately following long breaks. A study conducted by the Centers for Disease Control and Prevention noted that most shootings occurred right after the return from summer or winter breaks, and the researchers concluded this was due, in part, to the change and stress related to the start of a semester.[9] In this study, researchers found that rates for homicide at school decline over the course of each semester.[10] No location is any more likely to be a target than another. Homicides in general are nine times more likely to occur in urban schools than in rural or suburban schools.[11] However, this number includes all forms of homicide. Mass shootings, like the ones in Littleton, Colorado, Springfield, Oregon, Paducah, Kentucky, and others are no more likely at urban schools than rural ones. The only thing that seems consistent among perpetrators of school shootings is gender. Nearly all of these perpetrators are male.

Even though many researchers have tried to formulate a profile of school shooters, because of the heterogeneity of these perpetrators, there is no effective profile at this time either for identifying high-risk students or for assessing risk once a student has been identified as a risk. In 2001, Marisa Reddy and her colleagues, several of whom also participated in the development of the Secret Service study, unequivocally stated, "the use of profiles is ineffective and inefficient."[12] Likewise, the research indicates that there is no "useful relationship between the results of standard psychological tests and instruments and the risk of targeted violence in schools."[13] Instead of a profile or testing, the U. S. Secret Service, based on their research in thirty-seven school shootings and forty-one attackers, suggests that assessment of risk once a potential threat has been identified should be made based on the behaviors that a given individual exhibits and the messages that are communicated verbally, through writing, and through one's behavior.[14]

When attempting to evaluate the risk for school violence, one should not expect a direct threat, although research has indicated that in one-third of all cases the perpetrator made a direct threat.[15] Yet for the careful observer, there will be indications of the perpetrator's intent prior to a school shooting. In one study presented in the *Journal of the American Medical Association*, researchers found that over half of all school shootings were preceded by "some action that indicated potential for the coming event."[16] These researchers also found that most perpetrators left some clue to their intentions, either through a note, a direct threat, a journal entry, or some similar action.[17] The U.S. Secret Service study on school homicide found that even though less than 25 percent of school shooters directly communicated a threat to their targeted victim(s), at least 75 percent communicated their intentions to someone before the attack and "that person was almost always a friend or sibling, but they almost never told an adult."[18] Of similar significance is the fact that even though these perpetrators rarely told an adult about their intentions, in over 75 percent of the cases, an adult expressed concern about the attacker.[19] Reddy and her colleagues found that almost all perpetrators of school shootings selected a target prior to the violent incident.[20] These young people will leave clues, either by directly communicating their intentions to harm a specific target or by communicating their intentions in more subtle ways. The authors of the Secret Service study record that attackers developed an idea and eventually planned their attack, half because of revenge and 75 percent because of revenge and/or some other grievance.[21] In approximately two-thirds of these cases, attackers also felt persecuted, bullied, or threatened.[22] The longer the perpetrator plans an attack, the more likely he is to exhibit some behavior that reflects his intentions.

Drawing on data from the U.S. Secret Service's research, the FBI's study of eighteen school shootings, and other research, Table 11.1 lists the variables that have been correlated with individuals who have committed shootings at schools.[23] These variables do not represent a profile;

Table 11.1
Variables Associated with Perpetrators of School Shootings

- ☐ Exposure to violence
- ☐ Cognitive dysfunction
- ☐ Inferiority
- ☐ Exhibits pleasure at the suffering of people or animals
- ☐ Obsession with violent movies, video games, weapons, or literature
- ☐ Family violence
- ☐ Parental drug abuse
- ☐ Poor social skills
- ☐ Transient relationships
- ☐ Impulsivity
- ☐ Poor attachment
- ☐ Promiscuity
- ☐ Fatalistic attitude
- ☐ Inferiority
- ☐ Loneliness/alienation
- ☐ Difficulty expressing anger
- ☐ Poor coping skills
- ☐ Abandonment or betrayal/personal grievances with students/teachers/administrators
- ☐ Depression
- ☐ Narcissism
- ☐ Inappropriate humor
- ☐ Drug/alcohol use
- ☐ Direct threats or implication of threats through journals or other sources
- ☐ Victim of bullying or threats
- ☐ Identifiable target(s)
- ☐ Access to weapons
- ☐ Male gender

rather, they represent issues correlated with perpetrators of school shootings. With further research, these variables could lead to an effective profile.

Unlike many other forms of violent crime, including most of the aggressive behaviors detailed in previous chapters, the research indicates that neither a history of mental illness nor a history of criminal behavior is correlated with school shootings. D.C. Cornell found that, compared with juveniles who were referred for evaluation after committing larceny, juveniles who were referred for evaluation after committing homicide were *less* likely to have mental illness history, *less* likely to have school adjustment problems, and *less* likely to have exhibited prior violent behavior.[24] However, it cannot be inferred from this statistic that the lack of a diagnosed mental illness makes one *more* likely to commit a violent act. In actuality, it is reasonable to suppose that these perpetrators may very likely have had a diagnosable mental disorder (anxiety, depression, etc.) prior to the incident, but for one reason or another it was never diagnosed by a mental health professional. Likewise, the absence of a criminal record does not mean that the perpetrator had not committed any crimes in his past. This only means that prior to a shooting the perpetrator had never been caught in any criminal act. I reject the assumption that any violent individual "snaps" all at once and commits a violent crime. Of the hundreds of homicides I have researched, I have never come across a homicide where there was not some symptomatology of mental illness prior to the episode, whether or not it had been diagnosed prior to the episode, and where there was not some symptom of aggression prior to the homicide. The U.S. Secret Service found that nearly all the perpetrators of school attacks in its study had planned their behavior for some time and that the attacks were the "end result" of a long period in which the perpetrator attempted to cope with his grievances, anger, jealousy, or frustration. Prior to committing homicide, they will almost always show their homicidal potential in some way.

Treatment both of the individual at risk for violence as well as those who have already committed an act of aggression must address coping skills. As with all of us, these individuals use the coping skills that they believe to be effective, whether or not they actually are effective. When they decide that the coping strategies they have used in the past are no longer working, they pick new ones. Aggression is only one option among many. Most of us choose other options first, but for people with minimal coping skills, high levels of frustration, an externalized attribution of one's situation, and minimal perceived control over their circumstances, aggression quickly moves onto the short list of possible coping strategies. This explains why some perpetrators, although very few, may not have exhibited violent behavior in the past. Prior to their violent outburst they used other coping strategies, but when they came to a point where those strategies were no longer effective, they believed that they had no other choices available to them.

Social skills training can also help them avoid confrontations, deal with bullying behavior, and build a support system that can reduce the need to act out. Finally, anger management is imperative. Learning appropriate outlets for one's anger can defuse the drive for violent outbursts and the need to seek revenge.

Prevention

Threats of violence should be taken seriously and aggressive behavior of any kind should be considered a dangerous symptom of one's potential for future violence, but knee-jerk responses that involve profiles and sweeping policies that have not been proven effective should be avoided. The "vexing" nature of these incidents creates fear that can "drive radical policy change, in some cases leading to the implementation of bad policy."[25] Reddy and her colleagues maintain that, rather than profiling and attempting to assess risk, the most effective measure is prevention.[26] Programs that deal with the issues that correlate with aggressive behavior (i.e., loneliness, isolation, bullying, etc.) can decrease the likelihood of an aggressive attack. Students considering violence at school are very likely to talk to their friends or siblings about their plans, but these children do not always tell an adult, so programs that encourage children to talk to someone in authority should be put in place. In fact, in the years since the Columbine shooting, many potential attacks around the country have been thwarted when classmates did this very thing.

Gun control advocates argue that gun control changes are necessary because two-thirds of all school shootings and nearly all suicides are committed with firearms—mostly handguns. As I have mentioned previously, in lieu of new gun control laws, gun owners should be more diligent in safely storing their firearms. Even when a firearm is present in a home, if the weapon is securely stored, the child should not be able to access it, thus removing the possibility that it can be used for suicide or to perpetrate a crime.

In summary, at this time, profiling is ineffective for assessing risk for school violence. Instead, administrators, counselors, social workers, and law enforcement officials should deal with specific behaviors as they arise, at the same time considering the possible escalation of those behaviors to more dramatic forms of violence. Being aware of clues that indicate one's intention to commit a violent act is also important and not beyond the layperson's ability. Treating potentially violent individuals must involve social skills training, the teaching of coping strategies, and anger management.

TREATING SUICIDAL CHILDREN

When suicidal ideation is suspected or when clients make direct statements about suicide, it is the counselor's obligation to address the possibility of suicide. Whenever a client implies suicide in any way, a direct question is most efficient. With my own clients, regardless of what we are talking about, I will almost always interrupt the session and address the suicidal implication directly with a statement like, "You said something that worries me. Your comment makes me think you may have thought of harming yourself. What do you think?" In twenty years of therapy, I have never been wrong when I suspected suicidal ideation and my questions have never been received in anything less than a receptive manner. The reason I have never been wrong is that suicidal clients want to talk about their thoughts and their troubles. That is why they give us clues about their suicidal thoughts. In fact, they are disappointed if the counselor or confidant doesn't pick up on those clues. For one reason or another, they often do not want to explicitly say, "I've thought about killing myself," so they drop hints instead.

Once she has admitted their ideation, the client should be asked by the counselor to elaborate on her thoughts about suicide. The more detailed the client is about method, timing, and so forth, the higher she is at risk for impending suicide. In assessing the potential for suicide, Holinger and his colleagues have outlined three areas to consider—prior attempts, current ideation, and environmental supports. If there have been prior attempts, the counselor should assess what the precipitating events were, how lethal was the method employed, and whether or not the patient followed up on any treatment plan that may have resulted from that prior attempt.[27] Second, current ideation should be evaluated for planning and method as well as one's sense of hopelessness and loss of esteem.[28] Finally, these researchers suggest that the clinician evaluate the support system, looking for the level of stability in the child's parents and other available adults in the child's life and the level of stress in the home.[29] Based on this three-step assessment, the clinician can judge the likelihood of any future attempt and assess the potential need for hospitalization or some other intervention to ensure the safety of the client.

Contracts are a basic part of suicide treatment. With young children, verbal contracts may be sufficient, but with older children and adolescents, a written contract is psychologically more binding. Contracts include a statement that the client will not make any suicide attempts until the next meeting and that, at the very least, if she is having suicidal urges, she will contact the counselor to talk about it.

The treatment plan for suicidal clients must include some form of follow-up evaluation and support. Short-term changes may indicate to the suicidal person that he is "cured." However, one should expect relapse as the "cure" is overshadowed by disappointment when life's problems inevitably return. Clients often believe that when they start feeling better they will not return to their former depressive moods. This is an unrealistic belief and when depression and disappointment return, these clients may quickly fall back into their prior hopeless, suicidal situation. Clients should be prepared for this kind of relapse and during the process be informed that counseling does not remove the problems; rather, it provides a means for coping with the problems we have.

Suicide prevention programs in schools that are directed to all the children are ineffective at preventing suicide. They present broad, general messages to the population at large rather than specific information aimed at the specific needs of varied individuals. Some evidence exists that these programs may actually increase the risk for suicide. Unfortunately, young people may be unwilling to tell an adult if they fear that a friend is considering suicide. When a young person tells a friend about her intentions or thoughts about harming herself, the friend inappropriately believes that she cannot violate the confidence of that conversation. One survey found that the majority of young people believed in protecting the suicidal secrets of their friends.[30] Therefore, adults must be alert to symptoms of suicidal thoughts and be proactive in intervening. Effective suicide prevention plans in schools involve suicide prevention training for staff and teachers, rather than students, training these adults to recognize the warning signs for suicide. Alert teachers and staff can then use their skills to intervene directly or to refer students to a mental health professional when they recognize signs of potential suicidal ideation.

In settings where a person has attempted suicide, one first must secure the area. The suicidal person should not have any object in his possession that could further assist him in harming himself. Knives, sharp objects, firearms, medications, and so forth should be removed from the immediate area. Second, after calling for medical assistance, one should ensure that the patient has fully disclosed all necessary information regarding everything that he has done in his attempt to take his own life. For example, it may appear that he has cut his wrists, but he may only have minimal damage to his wrists and he may look fine. Yet unless asked, he may not tell the counselor that he also has taken an overdose of medication. Even though the wrist damage may be minimal, the medications may cause him to lose consciousness or die. When medical assistance arrives, they will be at a distinct disadvantage to render aid without this added information.

In summary, counselors must recognize that every suicidal statement or attempt, no matter how feeble, is a cry for help and should be taken seriously. These patients do not want to die. They want relief from their distress and the counselor's role is to help them find that relief.

INCARCERATION

As much as I may occasionally appear unrealistically hopeful, I recognize that some children either can't be treated or will refuse to be helped. For those children, some form of detention is necessary. Other children, for whom treatment *is* a realistic option, may need to be detained during their treatment because of the risks they pose to society. Children can be just as dangerous as adults, if not more so, and the community needs to be protected from them, but jail is not the only option. I do not believe it is ever appropriate to put children or adolescents in an adult prison population. They are totally incapable of defending themselves. Even many adults are unable to defend themselves against stronger inmates or gangs within prison walls. Sending an adolescent into an adult prison population is like throwing him to the wolves. Juvenile prisons most often are miniature reproductions of the adult prison system. Therapy is a minimal part of the program and the assumption of these prisons, regardless of their public relations claims, is that the children are there to be punished, not rehabilitated. Housing delinquent children with other delinquent children with no therapeutic intervention only produces more savvy delinquents. Negative peer influence in these facilities far outweighs therapy and rehabilitation programs.

Alternatives to prison include boot camps, juvenile detention and rehabilitation programs, foster care, and private therapeutic facilities. Boot camps were established for youth offenders on the theory that rigid discipline would instill respect for authority and for self. These programs have sparked great controversy. Some children have even died in these programs, most often from dehydration during exhausting exercise programs, and allegations of abuse or misconduct by staff personnel is widespread. The data that is available on these programs appears to indicate that programs where abuse is taking place are the result of poorly trained staff rather than problems with the underlying premise of the program. In theory, these programs should work, but in practice it appears they may create as many problems as they solve.

My home state of Georgia has replaced its boot camp programs with educational-therapeutic programs. One such program is the Savannah River Challenge Program for first-time offenders. In this highly structured program, positive behavior is encouraged by rewarding appropriate behavior rather than punishing misbehavior. Inmates attend school seven days a week and teachers provide mentoring in addition to education. The educational program helps inmates pursue a high school diploma or GED. Even though the average stay in these programs is only ninety days—too short a time, some critics argue, for meaningful rehabilitation—those who want to change their ways have every opportunity in a setting like this one. One father rued that his son, upon completion of his sentence in the program, said he "enjoyed" the program. "When you get in trouble, you are supposed to be in trouble," the father said.[31] Yet this father supposed that change could only happen if it was unpleasant—a flawed belief. Therapy is a part of these programs, which assume these first-time offenders can be rehabilitated. Education and change don't have to hurt. The most obvious problem with these programs is that they do nothing to address the home situation. Once released, there is no follow-up program or family therapy; therefore, the likelihood of offenders returning to their old ways is very high.

Foster care can provide a number of benefits to the aggressive child. First, foster care removes the child from negative influences at home or in the home culture. Second, when foster parents are adequately trained and when they invest adequate attention on their charges, the highest probability of positive change exists. Foster care also provides these children with more individualized attention than they could receive in any other program. Where foster parents have more than one foster child, the children in that home are still in a smaller, more focused environment than they would be in juvenile detention, a boot camp, or a group treatment home. Foster care is not always appropriate, especially if the child is violent or if the foster parents have small children who could become victims, but foster parents can supervise all programs necessary for the child by seeking professional counselors, medical attention, and educational opportunities, as necessary.

There are numerous private facilities around the country that provide both inpatient and outpatient programs for disorders ranging from sexual misconduct to attachment disorders. These programs are therapeutically intensive, and the success rates from these programs tend to be higher than other alternatives. Some juvenile courts are willing to defer sentencing in state-run juvenile homes and allow youths to serve their sentences in these privately funded facilities. I worked in one such facility for several months and found it to be warm, appropriately structured, and well rounded, providing the youthful offenders with a variety of recreational, educational, emotional, and therapeutic opportunities. However, these programs are very expensive and without insurance or financial assistance, often beyond the reach of the parents of many aggressive children.

PARENTS, CLINICIANS, AND THE COMMUNITY

Intervention and prevention are most effective when a cross-section of the people in the child's life are participating. Treating one part of the system while neglecting other parts that clearly contribute to the problem is irresponsible. Effective treatment must include participation of parents, clinicians, social services personnel, when necessary, and perhaps other segments of the community.

Parents

There is no doubt that parents, especially when children are preadolescent, have a greater ability to influence their children—in either a positive or negative way—than any video game, television show, peer group, or counselor. Parents must take their responsibility seriously and realize how their behavior affects their children. Proper supervision, at the very least, is important. I am still amazed that the boys from Columbine could have planned their attack for over a year, collecting weapons, producing Internet Web sites, consuming alcohol, and filming hate-filled videos, while their parents were unaware of what they were doing. Ideally, if adults choose to have children, they should see their role as a teacher and mentor to their child—every day. If they do not want this responsibility, they should choose to remain childless. Mentoring and teaching children involves being actively involved in their lives, knowing their friends, where they go, what their troubles are, what they read, and what interests them. In the few cases where young men who have been involved in school shootings had very responsible and involved parents, those parents were not surprised by their behavior and, in fact, had taken proactive steps in an attempt to head off the very kind of aggression their children exhibited. One has to wonder about how involved with their child parents are when the child kills or rapes someone and the parents say, "I never would have imagined he could do such a thing." This type of parent is either in total denial or more likely completely disengaged from the child's life. There is a reasonable level of trust and responsibility that children should earn as they get older, but parents should not mistakenly assume that trusting their children means they should not still remain involved with them and also maintain a supervisory role.

The Media

There is no question that violent television shows have an effect on children. In fact, a recent study of 700 males and females over a seventeen-year period showed that three hours of television a day—any television—increases the likelihood of aggression in children.[32] Parents need to monitor the programs that their children view on television as well as the music to which they listen and the movies they watch. Programming that encourages violence, degrades women, or glorifies promiscuous sexual behavior serves no productive purpose for children. It is perhaps unfair to isolate a single medium, but rap music, apart from almost all other forms of entertainment, more often than not tends to do all three of these. If adults wish to listen to rap or even promote the violent and sexist messages of rap music, they are free to do so, but children should not be exposed to the filth that masquerades as an art form in the work of so many rap performers.

Video games can be fun and entertain children for hours. It is not a good idea for children to spend hours in their rooms playing video games, but if they play them, violent games should be avoided. There is nothing productive to be gained from games that rely heavily on gore and mayhem. Just like television and movies, these games breed aggression. A number of children who have killed their classmates at school were heavily involved in violent home video games—most notably, the Columbine killers. There are plenty of nonviolent, exciting, entertaining video games available so it is not necessary to buy violent games.

The Internet is a haven for predators. Child predators have the luxury of hunting for children without ever leaving home through the convenience of Internet chat rooms. For example, in May 2002, authorities in Connecticut found the body of a thirteen-year-old girl who had been missing for three days. A twenty-five-year-old Brazilian man was arrested for the crime and allegedly confessed to killing the girl, who medical examiners said died from strangulation. After his alleged confession, he led police to the girl's body. Police first became aware of the man after they found his name on the child's computer. He allegedly met the girl in an Internet chat room. Parents, schoolteachers, and librarians must closely monitor a child's activity on the computer. I am amazed at how many parents allow their children unrestricted and unsupervised access to the Internet. I recommend that parents monitor all their child's Internet activities. Computers should be placed in public areas in the home, thus making it more difficult for a child to slip onto a prohibited Internet site or chat room.

Clinicians

In addition to serving their clients as therapists, clinicians can assist in intervention and prevention in many other ways. With the benefit of their expertise in development and psychological issues, the clinician can take the lead in the community, providing training for parents, pastors, law enforcement officials, social workers, and teachers. Utilizing their knowledge and experience, counselors can extend their influence in the prevention of child aggression, as well as in addressing the issues that increase the probability of delinquent behavior.

Hope

In my book *Blind-Sided: Homicide Where It Is Least Expected*, I described the HOME-Safe Project—a program I have developed that addresses violence, aggression, and safety in schools, businesses, and other organizations. "HOME" is an acronym that stands for *h*ope, *o*bservation, mentoring, and empowerment. *Hope*, the first component, is a vital part of any treatment plan with aggressive children. They must have some reason to hope that things should be and can be better than they are, giving them reason to change. Especially with suicidal individuals, provision of a sense of hope is critical. As children lose hope that their lives will improve, that their problems can be solved, and that they can ever find happiness, they become more desperate. Providing hope involves finding something that has meaning to the individual and developing it. Many times when children are suicidal, they focus all of their energies on a single issue to the exclusion of everything else in their lives. They see only the problem and none of the positive aspects of life. Therefore, providing hope not only involves helping clients find solutions to the problems they face, but also accentuating the other parts of their lives, thus bringing their focus into balance.

Providing hope also includes believing in these children—believing they can be more than they are. My life took a noticeable turn in the sixth grade almost exclusively because of my sixth-grade teacher, Mr. Rouse. Early in the first semester that year, I had performed rather poorly on a test. Mr. Rouse said one thing to me that changed the way I saw myself and my future. "You are too bright to be satisfied with a grade like that," he told me. I never had seen myself as "bright" and I assumed when I got bad grades it was because I wasn't very smart. I was always satisfied with "a grade like that," but his words made me think that I could do better— that I wasn't as dense as I thought I was. I began to work harder and even though I was never a straight-A student through my middle school and high school years, I was nearly a straight-A student for Mr. Rouse. I earned those grades because I believed I could and he had made me realize I could dream dreams and maybe even achieve them some day. The way he saw me that year changed the way I saw myself and affected me for the rest of my life, all because he took the time to give me something to strive for—because he believed in me.

Because of Mr. Rouse, I always take time with the children in my practice as well as children I tutor or mentor in other environments to talk to them about their future—to help them see what I see in them. I believe in them and I let them know it. Cynics will argue that a few words won't make a difference, and perhaps they are right in some or perhaps even many cases, but I know it can make a difference for at least some children; therefore, I've made it a part of my therapeutic lifestyle.

The Role of the Religious Community

For families who elect to engage in religious practices, religion offers many things that can prevent aggression. Religious teachings provide a sense of responsibility, a moral or ethical grounding, and a code of conduct. If the religion is not overly dogmatic or punitive, it can help children develop appropriate guilt when they misbehave. Many religions have pastors responsible exclusively for the youth in their parish, church, or synagogue. These youth pastors specialize in the developmental issues related to adolescents and can provide guidance, especially for children whose parents are uninvolved in their lives. Religion helps children focus on something beyond themselves, especially during adolescence, a time of increased egocentrism, and religion provides hope and coping resources through prayer, petition, penance, absolution, and other spiritual rituals. A number of studies indicate that families with an active religious life have a better chance at dealing with conflict and difficulties.[33]

For some reason, however, counselors are reluctant to encourage religious involvement. Freud believed religion was only for the feeble-minded and it seems that many psychologists have adopted that philosophy. I once led an ethics seminar for counselors and posed a question to them concerning religion and its place in therapy. "If the client was of the same religion as the counselor," I said, "and the client brought up religious issues in the session, would it be acceptable to discuss how that religion could help the client?" About half the audience of counselors and psychologists said "no," even though there is nothing in any ethical code of conduct for psychologists or counselors that justified their response. Training programs emphasize the separation of one's personal beliefs from the counseling process to such a degree that they assert that religion should never be used in therapy. Many of these counselors who said one should not discuss religion would have no difficulty discussing abortion, homosexuality, premarital sex, birth control, or other issues that have a moral component. In fact, some therapists are overtly proactive in encouraging their clients to pursue a sexual lifestyle that is compatible with the world view of the therapist. This is equally as unethical as pushing a religious teaching on a client against the client's will. However, the cautious therapist will use any and all options available, including discussion of religion, when it is appropriate.

Social Services

Social services investigators must be willing to remove children from environments that perpetuate their dysfunction. The recidivism rates for treatment programs, juvenile detention programs, boot camps, therapy, and almost all other forms of intervention are seriously impacted by the home environment. A child who responds well to any of these interventions has a much higher probability of recidivism if he or she is returned to an environment that necessitated their treatment in the first place. In order for these caseworkers to do their jobs, they need funding, smaller caseloads, and more foster care facilities in which to place the children that they are responsible for.

My experience has been that social services is more likely to err by failing to remove a child from a dangerous or dysfunctional setting than the reverse, but even though social services workers need to be willing to remove children from a home, they must also use discretion. While working as a school counselor in Atlanta some years ago, I became aware of a mother whose children were removed by family services. They charged her with neglect because she failed to take her three children to school. What the caseworker failed to consider was this woman's decision in the context of her environment. She was a single mother on welfare and she needed to apply for food stamps. Instead of leaving her children at home alone, as many parents had a habit of doing, she took them with her to stand in line at seven o'clock in the morning, hoping she would be done in time to get them to school at a reasonable hour. The longer she stood in line, the more she realized they would not make it to school. If she got out of line to take them to school, she would have lost her place after waiting for several hours, so she chose to stay in line. It took eight hours for her to be served. The purpose of the entire event was to provide and care for her children, yet her responsible decision making, given her circumstances, was not considered when family services did their evaluation.

A CALL TO PROFESSIONALS

In several chapters I have talked about recovery rates of 50 percent, 70 percent, or more. On the one hand, this sounds good, but as a clinician, I find it unacceptable that the profession has grown satisfied with a 30 percent recidivism rate. I have been to many conferences and read many books that specify the recovery and recidivism rates for specific populations, but in almost twenty years of professional practice, I have never been to a conference where they addressed our contribution to why the recidivism rate is what it is. I fear one of the reasons lies in the way we practice psychotherapy. Even though we cannot realistically expect a recovery rate of 100 percent in all areas of mental disorder, the recovery rate could be higher if we did one thing differently—if we invested more in our clients. My daughters both have had braces and their orthodontist has told my wife how much he "cares" about my children. I don't doubt that he has some compassion for children, but his concern for my children only begins after he has been paid. If he were truly concerned about them, he would treat them regardless of my ability to pay. In mental health, most practitioners operate on a sliding scale, meaning they reduce their rates given certain circumstances so that therapy can be more affordable, and many therapists even see some clients pro bono. The vast majority, however, are willing to let clients go untreated if they cannot pay. It is only fair to acknowledge that nearly all of us could have a full client load made up only of pro bono clients. We would all be bankrupt in a few weeks if we accepted all clients in need, regardless of their ability to pay, but if we really cared about our clients, we would be willing to do more pro bono work than we do.

One of my professors when I was a doctoral student chastised me because I was seeing clients for $25 an hour—a rate far below the normal per hour rate at the time. He said I was doing a disservice to the profession. In my classes, professors told me that it was important for clients to pay for their therapy because that way they work harder and take therapy more seriously than if they were paying nothing for it. Even though this is sometimes true, I wonder how much of this part of our education had to do with justifying our billing practices rather than research-based fact. I also heard a nationally syndicated radio talk show host condescendingly comment about a caller's free therapy: "You get what you pay for." It is this kind of thinking that means only the fiscally solvent can afford therapy. Of course, sometimes therapy is low rate because it is poor quality, but I am not proposing any reduction in quality—only a reduction in cost.

Psychiatrists charge $150 an hour or more and the going rate for counselors usually begins around $75 an hour. My clients pay anywhere from full rate if they can afford it to nothing if they cannot. Only after I agree to see a client do I discuss finances. Privately, I assume the client cannot pay before I agree to accept the case. If the client's parents have the means to pay, then I make money. If they do not, I don't, but either way the child is helped. Some clients have money, but are unwilling to spend it on therapy. It is frustrating to see clients who drive to my office in $40,000 cars but have little money for therapy, but we should expect dysfunction in many areas of a person's life when he or she has a mental illness. Why should her money management be any different? I also know many of these clients driving fancy cars are on the verge of bankruptcy.

Therapists and psychiatrists are not the only ones to blame. Managed health care has created such a labyrinth of paperwork that many therapists have opted to refuse to work with health insurance companies, operating as a cash-only business. In my own practice, I stopped taking insurance for this very reason. HMOs and PPOs required so much paperwork that I would easily spend more time processing the insurance paperwork than I did in therapy with the child. I decided it was actually cheaper for me to reduce my rates than it was to invest the hours involved in filing insurance papers.

No one expects therapists and psychologists to take a vow of poverty. However, ours is called the "helping profession." We pursue this profession because we want to help people, not because we want to get rich. How each therapist handles billing is ultimately a personal choice, but I petition those in the profession to search deep inside and ask whether or not clients are being turned away because of money problems, reasons that fall short of our calling.

CONCLUDING REMARKS

Treatment of aggressive children goes far beyond what I have described in the chapters of Part II and this chapter. As with any professional specialty, not only must the counselor be proficient in the general field of counseling, he must also have training, supervision, and experience in the area of his specialty. Many of the play therapy techniques described in Chapter 5 also apply to treating aggressive children. Depending on their ages, drawing, painting, Play Dough, puppets, dolls, and sand trays are all possible media for therapy. Whether one chooses to specialize as a marriage and family therapist, a play therapist, a group therapist, or in some other area, ongoing supervision and training are imperative. These children can be helped with proper intervention.

Some of my former clients have not changed their ways. They may have come into therapy with too many strikes against them—dysfunctional homes, too many years of abuse, entrenched behaviors, and seriously delinquent friendships. Others simply liked their lifestyles as they were, despite the risks to their lives and freedom, not to mention the risks they posed to others, and they were determined not to change. Therefore, they did not. However, many of them do change. There is little that is more satisfying to me than to hear from a former client or the parent of a former client and to learn how their lives have changed for the better. Occasionally, I will get a letter, a picture, or a wedding invitation. These brief glimpses of positive outcomes encourage me and remind me that my work as a therapist makes a difference. Children who might have ended up in prison as adults, instead become adults who marry, finish their educations, have children, pursue careers, and become good mothers and fathers. They become Real, I guess.

NOTES

1. Janet S. Rulo-Pierson, "Etiology of stalking and violence in troubled youth," *The Forensic Examiner* (December 2001): 15.

2. Ibid.

3. José Alejandro Silberstein, "Matricide: A paradigmatic case in family violence," *International Journal of Offender Therapy and Comparative Criminology, 42* (1998): 218.

4. David Ciampi, "Perpetrators of violence: Adolescents in America," *The Forensic Examiner* (September/October 2001): 31.

5. Mark Anderson, Joanne Kaufman, Thomas R. Simon, Lisa Barrios, Len Paulozzi, George Ryan, Rodney Hammond, William Modzeleski, Thomas Feucht, and Lloyd Potter, "School-associated violent deaths in the United States, 1994–1999," *Journal of the American Medical Association, 286* (December 5, 2001): 2699.

6. "School homicide rates highest after breaks," *CNN On-Line*, fyi.cnn.com /2001/fyi/teachers.ednews/08/10/school.violence.ap/index.html, August 10, 2001.

7. "Study: School violence rare but multiple killings increasing," *CNN On-Line*, fyi.cnn.com/2001/fyi/teachers.ednews/12/05/school.violence.ap/index.html, December 5, 2001.

8. Bryan Vossekuil, Marisa Reddy, Robert Fein, Randy Borum, and William Modzeleski, "U.S.S.S. safe school initiative: An interim report on the prevention of targeted violence in schools," United States Secret Service National Threat Assessment Center (Washington, DC: National Threat Assessment Center, October 2000), p. 3.

9. "School homicide rates highest after breaks."

10. Ibid.

11. Ciampi, "Perpetrators of violence," p. 31.

12. Marisa Reddy, Randy Borum, John Berglund, Bryan Vossekuil, Robert Fein, and William Modzeleski, "Evaluating risk for targeted violence in schools: Comparing risk assessment, threat assessment, and other approaches," *Psychology in the Schools, 38* (2001): 169.

13. Ibid., p. 165.

14. Vossekuil et al., "U.S.S.S. safe school initiative," p. 5.

15. "Study: School violence rare."

16. Anderson et al., "School associated violent deaths," p. 2700.

17. Ibid., p. 2701.

18. Vossekuil et al., "U.S.S.S. safe school initiative," p. 4.

19. Ibid., p. 7.

20. Reddy et al., "Evaluating risk," p. 158.

21. Vossekuil et al., "U.S.S.S. safe school initiative," p. 3.

22. Ibid., p. 7.

23. Vossekuil et al.; "Risk factors for school violence," *CNN On-Line*, www.cnn.com/2001/US/03/05/fbi.shooter.profile/index.html, March 5, 2001; Ciampi.

24. Cornell, D.G., Prior adjustment of violent juvenile offenders, *Law and Human Behavior, 14* (1990), 569–577. Quoted in Reddy et al., p. 160.

25. Reddy et al., "Evaluating risk," p. 159.

26. Ibid., p. 169.

27. Paul C. Holinger, Daniel Offer, James T. Barter, and Carl C. Bell, *Suicide and homicide among adolescents* (New York: Guilford Press, 1994), p. 116.

28. Ibid.

29. Ibid.

30. Katharine Davis Fishman, *Behind the one-way mirror: Psychotherapy with children* (New York: Bantam, 1995), p. 11.

31. Patti Ghezzi, "Books, not bars: Juvenile offenders test a reform plan," *Atlanta Journal/Constitution* (January 13, 2002): B1/B4.

32. "Study links TV viewing among kids to later violence," *CNN On-Line*, www.cnn.com/2002/HEALTH/parenting/03/28/kids.tv.violence/index.html, March 28, 2002.

33. Doug Fox, "Lewisville case latest in rising number of juvenile killings," *WFAA.com*, www.wfaa.com/dfox/stories/wfaa020416_am_lewisvillefolo.80d45e 6a.html, April 17, 2002.

CHAPTER 12

Epilog

He who passively accepts evil is as much involved in it as he who helps to perpetrate it.

—Martin Luther King, Jr.

I know not what the world will think of my labours, but to myself it seems that I have been but as a child playing on the seashore; now and then finding a smoother pebble or a prettier shell than ordinary, whilst the immense ocean of truth extended unexplored before me.

—Isaac Newton

Evil takes many forms—terrorism, racism, anti-Semitism, ageism. It is easy to see Jeffrey Dahmer, Timothy McVeigh, or al Qaeda terrorists as evil, but evil also resides closer to home in the form of abusive and neglectful parents like the woman in Enid, Oklahoma, who tried to trade her seven-month-old daughter to a neighbor in exchange for a puppy or the man in Phoenix, Arizona, who bit the thumb off his two-year-old son's hand while in a drug-induced frenzy (he still had the appendage in his mouth when he was arrested several hours later). But evil also resides in the form of distant and uninvolved educators, ill-prepared or thoughtless teachers, lazy police officers or social workers, and counselors who prefer to work with pretty and easy clients rather than difficult, ungrateful, and unlovely clients. I am often criticized for some things that I write, especially on sensitive topics like homosexuality, abortion, and parents who abandon their children at day care not out of necessity, but so they can buy more toys for themselves. I don't like hate mail, but I am not afraid to say what I believe needs to be said. I do not deliberately insult people or use politically incorrect language for its own sake, but I am in a position to make changes and that position carries with it great responsibility. Through my seminars, classroom lectures, newspaper column, books, and articles, I have the opportunity to call people to responsibility—especially with regard to protecting our children. I don't take that responsibility lightly and I will not shrink from it for fear of being labeled, condemned, or chastised. One of the many lessons my American idol Martin Luther King, Jr. has taught me is to have the courage to sacrifice and to do what I believe to be right even if it costs me financially, emotionally, or physically. I call upon all who work with children to take this same lesson to heart. Perhaps the biggest sacrifice that could be made in American homes today is for one parent to stay home and raise the children they have chosen to have. These children do not care about fancy vacations, nice cars, or big houses nearly as much as they want a loving parent at home. More often those are things that the parents want, but they rationalize abandoning their children to justify pursuing their own desires. A child would rather have a parent at home, teaching, mentoring, and nurturing, than anything a second salary could buy.

ANTECEDENTS OF BEHAVIOR

We all want to see ourselves as blameless and righteous in what we do. We tend to justify our actions, no matter what they are, using the defense mechanisms (justification, rationalization, etc.) that we have discussed in previous chapters. Whether taking sexual advantage of another person, damaging someone's property, lying to cover up one's misdeeds, or cheating on taxes, the processes that allow us to justify the behavior are the same. Every behavior has an antecedent, something that prompts it. As a counselor, I have several goals with clients. First, I attempt to find out what the problem is. Then I look for the antecedent—what prompts this feeling or behavior? Next I try to find out why the person continues to behave in the way he/she does, even though he/she finds the results of those behaviors undesirable. This is the defense mechanism. Once I've done those things, I can then help them reprogram their thinking so that they can reach their goals. Antecedents and motives drive all our behaviors. If I can identify motive, I can understand behavior. Once I understand motive and behavior, I can search for more productive ways for people to achieve their goals.

Interpreting motive is not just a counseling skill. Whether you realize it or not, you are looking for meaning and interpreting behavior all the time. We interpret a friend or colleague's words based on the intention behind those words. We rarely take things at face value without first considering motive. For example, if someone does something nice for you, it is hard to accept it at face value—they just wanted to be nice. Instead, we think,

"Now why did they do that?" Even children look for motive. For example, my family spent some time in France in 2001. As my children and I toured Notre Dame cathedral, my nine-year-old said, "That sure is a fancy building." I asked her why she thought they built such a fabulous building. "I guess they wanted to make something nice for God," she said. Even at nine, she is able to recognize the motive of the builders by a cursory overview of the building.

One of my adult clients had body piercing in his eyebrows, nose, ears, lips, and tongue. He wore very unusual clothing, colored his hair a bright orange, and had several tattoos. During our two months of therapy, it became obvious that he had always felt rejected by peers and, more importantly, by his father. During one of our sessions I asked him about the body piercing and orange hair. "Why do you think you like body piercing?" I asked him. I wanted to him to know the meaning of his own behavior. "I don't know," he said. "I just like it."

I told him I that I thought that deep inside he really did know the answer to my question. I explained that our behaviors are what they are because they serve us in some way. "How do body piercing and orange hair serve you?" I asked. He told me he understood my point, but he said he still didn't know.

"May I venture a guess?" I asked. When he said I could, I posited this: "I think that you have always felt rejected and that you never have felt good enough. Body piercing, even though it is becoming accepted, is still unusual in our culture. I think that you anticipate that people won't like you or that they will think you are weird so you have given them a very easy way to do that. This way you can say, 'They just don't understand me.' It is easier to talk about them misunderstanding you—more importantly your father misunderstanding you—because of a nose ring or hair color than it is to admit how much it hurts that you don't feel good enough for your father. What do you think?"

He sat very quietly for a few minutes and then began to smile. "You know," he said, "I never thought of it that way, but I know you are right."

My point with this client wasn't that there was anything wrong with body piercing. If he liked it, fine. The point, rather, was to help him see the meaning behind his behavior, the antecedent that drove that behavior so that he could address the real issues if he chose.

A SEARCH FOR CHARACTER

Character is just one antecedent of behavior, but it is a powerful one. What we are deep inside will eventually show up in our behavior. People communicate their character by what they do. Not only will it be there, but it *must* be there; otherwise, we would not do what we do. As I have described in these pages, many things contribute to who we are and how we behave. I have addressed mental illness, physiology, social dynamics, psychological issues, and family of origin. One thing that I have yet to address is character. Our character is the collective qualities that distinguish one person from another; it is during childhood that the foundations for character are established. A child who learns that he does not have to be accountable for his behavior will develop a selfish character that seeks self-gratification at the expense of others. On the other hand, a child who learns that she is responsible for her own behavior will not only develop a responsible character, but she will also be self-motivated to succeed because she sees the consequences of her actions, both good and bad. There is no doubt that character is learned.

I had the unusual opportunity to interact with a young man named Leon from his childhood all the way into his adult years. He was very talented, funny, and handsome and he was raised in a loving family. One flaw that became obvious in his upbringing, however, was that no matter what he did, his parents would excuse his behavior. If he had trouble with grades at school, it was the teacher's fault. One time he was caught shoplifting with two other boys. His father blamed the other two boys and said their influence caused his son's actions. As Leon reached adolescence he found himself in trouble more frequently—at school, at band camp, and in church. Each time, his father bailed him out and made excuses for his behavior and Leon was never held accountable at home for any of his behaviors. Where he could, his father would intervene, making sure he did not have to pay for his behavior anywhere else either. When he went to college, Leon quickly found himself in front of the university tribunal for a relatively minor infraction. He and his accomplices were given a second chance, but it was only a matter of weeks before he was in front of the tribunal again, this time for a much more serious infraction. The tribunal was about to suspend him, but Leon's father intervened and the tribunal decided to give him one more chance. Leon was required to fulfill four specific obligations during the following weeks and he was told that if he failed to do any of them, he would again be called before the tribunal and would likely be suspended. As I could have predicted, not only did Leon fail to fulfill one of his four obligations, he didn't fulfill any of them. Subsequently, he was suspended. His father, again, blamed the university for not being lenient enough with his son and he threatened the university financially, although in the end he failed to get his way.

Two years later, Leon was twenty-one years old and living on his own. He hosted a party and because of a seriously negligent, not to mention illegal, act on his part, a sixteen-year-old boy died in Leon's home. Leon was charged with manslaughter and eventually convicted. His father was powerless to rescue him from this mess and one would have thought that this episode would have taught Leon a lesson, but it did not. After his release from prison on probation, Leon was required to perform community service. Failure to do so would result in revocation of his probation. Again, Leon failed in his responsibility, just as he had his entire life, and found himself back behind bars. Leon learned very early in life that he did not have to be accountable for his behavior. He could do what he wanted with impunity because his father, who was a very sincere and likable man, would always cover for him. This led him to develop a selfish character. It wasn't such a big deal at band camp or in the classroom. It was irritating, but his teachers and counselors probably don't even remember him. It was a big deal, though, once he reached adulthood. His character was set, but the stakes were much higher and his character flaw led to the death of a teenager.

In one large U.S. city, state employees were caught calling in sick for their state jobs so they could work a second job for another state agency. In this state, state employee contracts clearly state that government workers cannot collect paychecks during the same working hours from two different government jobs. When supervisors discovered what the employees were doing, the employees were fired, but instead of being embarrassed by the fact that they were caught, these employees sued the state. Attorneys for several of the fired workers said it was merely a "misunderstanding." I find it hard to imagine how people could lie about being ill so that they could work a second job when they had been expressly told that they could not draw a paycheck from two government agencies, and yet call it a misunderstanding. I presented the scenario to my nine-year-old daughter and asked her whether it would or would not be acceptable to behave in this way. She did not have any difficulty realizing that it would be a violation of the rules to do this, but for these "adults," it was a "misunderstanding." There was no misunderstanding. These were dishonest people who simply refused to admit they were dishonest.

In 2000, after a night of drinking and taking drugs, a woman in Texas drove home. On her way, she struck a homeless man with her car. The accident nearly severed his leg and when his body flew into the windshield his head broke through the glass and he became lodged with his head inside the vehicle and his body outside. Instead of stopping to help the man, she drove home, his body dangling outside her car, and parked her car in her garage. For the next two days, this woman's character was demonstrated by her repeated decisions to look out for her own interests at the expense of another human being—decisions that prosecutors said cost this man his life. Her first missed opportunity to be responsible was when she decided to get behind the wheel of her car after she had been drinking and taking drugs that October night. Her attorney said she was not intoxicated, but quite frankly her subsequent decisions would be easier to understand if she had been. Next, when she struck a pedestrian, instead of accepting responsibility for the accident and rendering any aid that she could, she decided to hide the evidence of the accident, driving home with an injured man impaled in her windshield, begging her for mercy. Yet his pleas did not move her to help him. She didn't even free him so someone else could help him. Instead, she parked her car in her garage and went inside, allegedly making love to her boyfriend before going back to the garage to check on the man. She claims that she apologized to the dying man, but her apologies did not stop his bleeding or ease his agony. Friends encouraged her not to call authorities and she followed their advice. According to the coroner, the man probably died within twenty-four hours due to blood loss from the severed leg. Even though he died, she still could have made a decision to accept responsibility for her behavior, but she did not. She called on a friend who then helped her to dump the man's body in a park. Some time afterward, she removed the windshield from the car and also removed the seats and burned them, all in an attempt to hide evidence. She later told police that she had also planned to burn the entire car when she got her income tax refund and could afford another car.[1] Five months went by. During that time, she allegedly laughed about the incident while at a party.[2] Someone who overheard her horrifying story told police and the woman was arrested.

I suppose that I should never be surprised by excuses made by defense attorneys, but the excuses her attorney made were so outrageous to me that I laughed out loud when I heard them. Initially, he argued that she wasn't the "monster" that she was being made out to be. In response to this I must ask what one has to do to be considered monstrous? I would think that driving while under the influence of not one, but two, drugs hitting a pedestrian, impaling him in one's windshield, ignoring his pleas for help, parking him and the damaged car in one's garage, watching the man slowly bleed to death over several hours, irreverently dumping the man's body in a park, and destroying evidence to cover up the crime would qualify as monstrous behavior. Yet this wasn't the end of his commentary. Several days after her arrest, the attorney disputed several claims by the prosecution. He disputed claims by police that the man was alive for two or three days and he disputed claims that the man talked to her. His body was not in her garage more than twenty-four hours, the attorney said, before she dumped it in the park. He said that the man "died maybe a couple of hours after the accident and he initially moaned and groaned, but she couldn't tell what he was saying."[3] He also said she apologized to him, but he only groaned and did not exchange any clear words with her. It appeared that the attorney was making the case that, since the man couldn't clearly articulate his words and since he died within twenty-four hours, her behavior wasn't really that bad. Unbelievable! He also said she shouldn't be charged with murder, even though the coroner said the man probably would have lived if he had received medical attention immediately.

I can understand making a bad decision at the point of the accident. Striking a pedestrian with one's car would be traumatic, and seeing his head impaled through the windshield would have only made it worse.

However, she somehow found presence of mind to go home, have sex, check on the man, and still go back in and go to sleep. One would suppose that the next day, when the alcohol and drugs were out of her system, that she would have realized what she had done and had some compassion on the man, but she did not. Instead of seeking help for the injured man, she sought accomplices to help her dump the body. I argue that even her selection of friends says something about her character. I doubt that many of you reading this book have friends who would encourage you to hide such a crime and I also doubt that you have many friends who would help you dispose of a corpse. I do not have a single friend who would accept that kind of behavior from me, let alone abet in the crime. Even though I am impassioned when I think about this case, the real point of this case is to demonstrate the way *adults* behave in our culture. Her character was selfish. If this is the way adults behave, we should not be surprised by outrageous behavior from our children. As long as we accept this form of behavior, even making excuses for it, we perpetuate the evil we claim to abhor. Mental illness can account for some dysfunctional behavior; therefore, our actions are not the sole reflection of our character. I find it fascinating that a seriously mentally ill woman like Andrea Yates still had the character to take responsibility for her actions when others whose mental health is supposedly more sound cannot.

Our country has conditioned its citizens to accept what Alan Dershowitz calls the "abuse excuse."[4] Things that happen to us are never of our own doing. They are the results of someone else's irresponsibility. Even in lawsuits, people will settle "while admitting no responsibility ..." What does that mean? I understand the legal implications of admitting responsibility, but failure to accept any responsibility under any circumstance has become the norm rather than the exception. As long as we teach our children that they can do what they want without consequences—that they can act and then blame others, that they can make a choice and then, if they're unhappy with the outcome, demand a second choice—we will continue to see aggressiveness in both childhood and adulthood. Why wouldn't we?

SEEKING THE TRUTH

The study of children, aggression, and its short- and long-term effects on them is in its infancy. Just one hundred short years ago, there were no laws that addressed child abuse. A parent could do whatever he wanted with impunity. At that time, a social worker who was attempting to protect an abused child found the courts to be of no help. Then she discovered that there were laws that protected farm animals from abuse. She proceeded to have the child declared an animal so that the law would protect her. She won her case.

Even though child labor laws were initially enacted to open the job market up for adults who needed them, the creation of this legislation was the beginning of a national recognition that children were at the mercy of adults and needed protection. In the last fifty years, psychologists have joined the battle to protect children, learning more and getting better at it every year. We have come a long way in recognizing the biological and psychological makeup of children and, perhaps equally as important, the effects the environment has on those components. There is clearly a genetic root to many of our behaviors and much of our way of thinking is driven by our genetics as well. But we also know that regardless of one's genetics, environmental factors—family, peers, cultural rules of conduct— have immeasurable influence on the organism. However, the fascinating and mystical thing that makes human beings more complex than any other creatures on earth is our vast diversity, given relatively similar ingredients. Two children, perhaps even twins, can be raised in the same home. One may become a physician, a college professor, or some other educated professional, while the other may opt for a strikingly different path. This variability goes beyond personal choice, but *choice* of behaviors is certainly part of the equation. These stark differences are a product of the symphony of influences under which we all exist. Coping skills, peer influence, resiliency, personality type, intellectual ability, parental influence, and many other factors join to create a unique creature. No single variable is to blame and no variable is without influence.

I once attended a conference where a psychologist told the room of three hundred or so psychologists that a research study that nearly all of us had used to support our ideas regarding gender and learning was seriously flawed. After she finished her talk, it was apparent to all of us that we had been teaching something—some of us for decades—that was untrue. When I returned to my own students after the conference I told them about this new finding. One of my students asked me if it bothered me that I had been teaching something that was incorrect for all these years. It didn't bother me at all, I told her. I communicate the very best information that I have at the time that I have it. There is an interesting difference among researchers. Some are very compulsive and want to have absolutely all of the facts before they make any statement and even then they are very hesitant, making carefully worded statements full of conditions. Others, like me, are ready to do something with what we have. We are willing to take measured risks. If I waited until I knew all there was to know about child abuse and child aggression, in my lifetime I would never be able to make any assessments or statements about children, aggression, motive, or behavior. Instead, I work with the data that is available, carefully laying out what appears to be true, what is almost certainly true, and what may be true, but is still open to question. I know I may be wrong—perhaps about many things. Christopher Columbus was wrong when he thought he landed in India, but look where he was right! He was correct in his general theory that the world was round instead of flat and because of him (and his mistake), great progress was made. Aristotle believed the brain cooled the blood. Albert Einstein once averred that there was not the "slightest indication that energy will ever be obtainable from the atom." Euclid's plane geometry was later eclipsed by the work of Lobachevsky and Riemann, who provided theories of geometry based on four dimensions instead of three. Interestingly, even though Riemannian geometry is more effective for answering questions regarding space and time, the very tool Einstein needed to develop his first general theory of relativity, nearly all schools still teach Euclidian geometry almost exclusively, even at the graduate level. Other great thinkers like Leonardo da Vinci, Plato, and others made many mistakes in their assumptions about life and science, yet they are still known for their brilliance.

I have a quote on the bulletin board in my office that says, "If you wait until you have all the facts before you make a decision, it isn't a decision. It is a conclusion." Life is full of turning points where we must act on what we think we know—fully aware that our decision could be based on errors, yet a decision is required. Children need our attention today, not fifty or a hundred years from now. If any of my work is even a part of the equation in fifty years, surely there are parts of it that some educator or researcher will be teaching differently, pointing out to students why I was naïve and obviously wrong. That is OK with me. I am not so arrogant to assume I haven't made mistakes in my evaluations and assessments. I don't make statements of "fact" haphazardly, but I am not afraid to take a risk. In fact, I have little patience with researchers who are so afraid of being wrong that they never actually say anything useful. I make the best decision I can with the data I have available at the time. When new data become available and if I find that I have been wrong, I will admit it, correct myself, and adjust what I teach. Until that time, I'll press on with what I believe to be true as my guide.

These are the early days of this science and there are more questions that remain unanswered than there are questions resolved. Around 300 B.C., the great mathematician Euclid once said there were two kinds of roads—"the hard road for the common people and the easy road for royalty. Unfortunately, there is no royal road to geometry." As Euclid said of geometry, there is no royal road to this study. Progress requires the prodding dedication and combined energies of social workers, psychologists, researchers, parents, educators, and others concerned with children and their welfare. What I have provided for you in the preceding pages is my best effort to demonstrate what we think we know. I have provided very few definitive answers—only tentative ones that we can work with at this point in time—and in some cases I have only provided enough information to help us to begin forming good questions. However, as a researcher, writer, teacher, and father, I can't be satisfied with where we are in our knowledge. There must be many more books, articles, research studies, and even anecdotal experience (all of which I have provided for you in these pages) that will contribute to this most important part of our future—the raising of our children.

NOTES

1. "Police: hit-run victim left to die in car windshield," *CNN On-Line*, www .cnn.com/2002/LAW/03/08/hit.and.rundeath.ap/index.html, March 8, 2002.

2. "Man charged with removing body from windshield," *CNN On-Line*, www.cnn.com/2002/LAW/07/02/windshield.death.ap/index.html, July 2, 2002.

3. "Attorney claims hit-run victim died in 24 hours," *Atlanta Journal/Constitution* (March 10, 2002): B4.

4. Alan M. Dershowitz, *The abuse excuse and other cop-outs, sob stories, and evasions of responsibility* (New York: Little Brown, 1994).

Bibliography

"Adolescent sexual offenders." The National Clearinghouse on Family Violence. Ottawa, Ontario: Family Violence Prevention Division, January 1990.

Alessi, Hunter Downing. "Memory development in children: Implications for children as witnesses in situations of possible abuse," *Journal of Counseling & Development, 79* (2001): 398–405.

Alexander, Bill. "Whistleblower: 'My life ruined.'" *Youth Today*, www.psrn.org /News%20articles/school%20climate%202-10-02.html, February 10, 2002.

American Psychiatric Association. *Diagnostic and Statistical Manual of Mental Disorders, 4th ed., text revision*. Washington, DC: American Psychiatric Press, 2000.

Anderson, Craig A., and Bushman, Brad J. "The effects of media violence on society." *Science, 295* (March 29, 2002): 2377–2379.

Anderson, Mark; Kaufman, Joanne; Simon, Thomas R.; Barrios, Lisa; Paulozzi, Len; Ryan, George; Hammond, Rodney; Modzeleski, William; Feucht, Thomas; and Potter, Lloyd. "School-associated violent deaths in the United States, 1994–1999." *Journal of the American Medical Association, 286* (December 5, 2001): 2695–2702.

Artingstall, Kathryn A. "Munchausen syndrome by proxy." *FBI Law Enforcement Bulletin,* 198.252.9.108/govper/fbi.law.enforcement.bulletin/www.fbi.gov /library/leb/1995/Aug/95AUG002.TXT. August 1995.

Barbaree, Howard E., and Cortoni, Franca A. "Treatment of the juvenile sex offender within the criminal justice and mental health systems." In Howard E. Barbaree, William L. Marshall, and Stephen M. Hudson, eds., *The Juvenile Sex Offender*, pp. 243–263. New York: Guilford Press, 1993.

Batterman-Faunce, Jennifer Marie, and Goodman, Gail S. "Effects of context on the accuracy and suggestibility of child witnesses." In Gail S. Goodman and Bette L. Bottoms, eds., *Child Victims, Child Witnesses: Understanding and Improving Testimony*, pp. 301–330. New York: Guilford Press, 1993.

Blutchic, Robert, and Van Praag, Herman M. "Suicide, impulsivity, and antisocial behavior." In David M. Stroff, James Breiling, and Jack D. Maser, eds., *The Handbook of Antisocial Behavior*, pp. 101–108. New York: John Wiley & Sons, Inc, 1997.

Brahams, Diana. "'Repressed memories' and the law." *Lancet, 356* (July 29, 2000): 358–360.

Bukowski, William M.; Sippola, Lorrie; and Brender, William Brender. "Where does sexuality come from?: Normative sexuality from a developmental perspective." In Howard E. Barbaree, William L. Marshall, and Stephen M. Hudson, eds., *The Juvenile Sex Offender* pp. 84–103. New York: Guilford Press, 1993.

"Bullies and their victims." *Harvard Mental Health Letter, 18* (November 2001): 4–6.

"A bully apologizes." *Scholastic Choices, 17* (October 2001): 14.

Burke, David M. "Empathy in sexually offending and nonoffending adolescent males." *Journal of Interpersonal Violence, 16* (March 2001): 222–233.

Carlson, Margaret. "Daddy's little girl." *Time* (June 4, 1990): 2C.

Cashwell, Craig S. Cashwell, and Caruso, Michele E. "Adolescent sex offenders: Identification and intervention strategies." *Journal of Mental Health Counseling, 19* (October 1997): 336–349.

Charles, Nick; Morrissey, Siobhan; Trischitta, Linda; and Eunick, Deweese. "Judging Lionel." *People* (February 12, 2001): 87–88.

Christoffel, Katherine Kaufer. "Firearm injuries affecting U.S. children and adolescents." In Joy D. Osofsky, ed., *Children in a Violent Society,* pp. 42–71. New York: Guilford Press, 1997.

Ciampi, David. "Perpetrators of violence: Adolescents in America." *The Forensic Examiner,* (September/October 2001): 31–34.

Coeyman, Marjorie. "Schools still working to rein in bullies." *Christian Science Monitor* (December 4, 2001): 14.

"Crisis intervention assessment." National Clearinghouse on Child Abuse and Neglect Information, Washington, DC, www.calib.com/nccanch/pubs /usermanuals/crisis/assess.cfm, April 6, 2001.

Daly, Martin, and Wilson, Margo. "Child abuse and other risks of not living with both parents," *Ethnology and Sociobiology, 6* (1985), 197–210.

"Depression and suicide in children and adolescents." Surgeon General, www.surgeongeneral.gov/library/mentalhealth/chapter3/sec5.html, June 6, 2002.

Dershowitz, Alan M. *The Abuse Excuse and other cop-outs, sob stories, and evasions of responsibility.* New York: Little, Brown and Company, 1994.

Eke, N. "Genital self-mutilation: There is no method in this madness." *BJU International, 85* (2000): 295–298.

Faulconer, Elizabeth, and House, Matt. "Arterial blood gas: A rare form of self-mutilation and a review of its psychological functions." *American Journal of Psychotherapy, 55* (2001): 406–413.

Ferrara, F. Felicia. *Childhood Sexual Abuse.* Pacific Grove, CA: Brooks/Cole, 2002.

Finkelhor, D.; Hotaling, G.; Lewis, I. A.; and Smith, C. "Sexual abuse in a national survey of adult men and women: Prevalence, characteristics, and risk factors." *Child Abuse and Neglect, 14* (1990): 385–401.

Firstman, Richard, and Talan, Jamie. *The Death of Innocents.* New York: Bantam Books, 1997.

Fishman, Katharine Davis. *Behind the One-Way Mirror: Psychotherapy with Children.* New York: Bantam, 1995.

Fowler, J. Christopher; Hilsenroth, Mark J.; and Nolan, Eric. "Exploring the inner world of self-mutilating borderline patients: A Rorschach investigation." *Bulletin of the Menninger Clinic, 64* (Summer 2000): 365–385.

France, Karyn G., and Hudson, Stephen M. "The conduct disorders and the juvenile sex offender." In Howard E. Barbaree, William L. Marshall, and Stephen M. Hudson, eds., *The Juvenile Sex Offender,* pp. 225–234. New York: Guilford Press, 1993.

Gesalman, Anne Belli. "In medical records, hints of a tragedy." *Newsweek* (September 17, 2001): 6.

————. "Signs of a family feud." *Newsweek* (January 21, 2002): 41.

Given, David M. "Interview with Frank Zappa." *The Entertainment and Sports Lawyer, 9* (Summer 1999): 9–12, 32.

Holinger, Paul C.; Offer, Daniel; Barter, James T.; and Bell, Carl C. *Suicide and Homicide among Adolescents.* New York: Guilford Press, 1994.

"International child abduction Remedies Act (ICARA)." Section 11601a.4., travel.state.gov/icara.html, April 18, 2002.

"International child abductions." U.S. Department of State, Bureau of Consular Affairs, dosfan.lib.uic.edu/ERC/population/children/9501.html, January 1995.

Kantrowitz, Barbara, and Joseph, Nadine. "Forgetting to remember." *Newsweek* (February 11, 1991): 58–60.

Kerik, Bernard. *The Lost Son: A Life in Pursuit of Justice.* New York: Regan Books, 2001.

Knight, Raymond A., and Prentky, Robert A. "Exploring characteristics for classifying juvenile sexual offenders." In Howard E. Barbaree, William L. Marshall, and Stephen M. Hudson, eds., *The Juvenile Sex Offender,* pp. 45–83. New York: Guilford Press, 1993.

Lakey, Joyce F. "The profile and treatment of male adolescent sexual offenders." *Adolescence, 29* (Winter 1994): 755–782.

Lawson, Aaron R. "False accusations of abuse." *Expert Law,* www.expertlaw .com/larson/articles/false.html, March 2002.

Leder, Ranee M.; Knight, John R.; and Emans, Jean S. "Sexual abuse: When to suspect it, how to assess for it, part 1." *Contemporary Pediatrics* (May 2001): 59–68.

————. "Sexual abuse: Management strategies and legal issues, part 2." *Contemporary Pediatrics* (May 2001): 77–85.

Lemonick, Michael D., and Wallace, Charles P. "Germany's Columbine." *Time* (May 6, 2002): 36.

Levine, Madeline. *Viewing Violence: How media violence affects your child's and your adolescent's development.* New York: Doubleday, 1996.

Madu, S. N. "The prevalence and patterns of childhood sexual abuse and victim-perpetrator relationship among a sample of college students." *South African Journal of Psychology, 31* (2001): 32–38.

"Man jailed in repressed memory case is finally free." *Skeptic* (1996): 14–15.

Marr, Neil, and Field, Tim. *Bullycide: Death at Playtime.* London: Success Unlimited, 2000.

Mart, Eric G. "Problems with the diagnosis of factitious disorder by proxy in foren-
    sic settings." *American Journal of Forensic Psychology* (Internet Edition),
    www.msbp.com/ericmart.htm, 1999.

McCarthy, John, and Lamble, Ian. "The nature of adolescent sexual offending: Part
    one. An overview of the problem and initial assessment." *Social Work
    Review* (Internet Edition), March 1995.

Milia, Diana. "Art therapy with a self-mutilating adolescent girl." *American Journal
    of Art Therapy, 34* (May 1996): 98–107.

Moffatt, Gregory K. *Blind-Sided: Homicide Where It Is Least Expected.* Westport, CT:
    Praeger, 2000.

———. *A Violent Heart: Understanding Aggressive Behavior.* Westport, CT: Praeger,
    2002.

"New plan to put bullies behind bars." *Christian Science Monitor* (February 26,
    2002): 64.

O'Grady, Ron. "Eradicating pedophilia: Toward the humanization of society."
    Journal of International Affairs, 55 (2001): 123–131.

"Parricide mostly committed by adult offspring." *Brown University Child and Ado-
    lescent Behavior Letter, 10* (February 1994): 4.

Peretti, Frank. *The Wounded Spirit.* Nashville, TN: Word Publishing, 2000.

"Preventing bullying: A manual for schools and communities." U.S. Department
    of Education, www.cde.ca.gov/spbranch/ssp/bullymanual.htm, Novem-
    ber 3, 1998.

Reddy, Marisa; Borum, Randy; Berglund, John; Vossekuil, Bryan; Fein, Robert; and
    Modzeleski, William. "Evaluating risk for targeted violence in schools:
    Comparing risk assessment, threat assessment, and other approaches." *Psy-
    chology in the Schools, 38* (2001): 157–172.

Richardson, Darrell W. "The effects of a false allegation of child sexual abuse on an
    intact middle class family." *Institute for Psychological Theories Journal* (Inter-
    net Edition), www.ipt-forensics.com/journal/volume2/j2_4_7.htm, March
    8, 2001.

Rinaldo, Denise. "What's a bully?" *Scholastic Choices, 17* (October 2001): 12–15.

Rind, Bruce, Tromovitch, Philip, and Bauserman, Robert, "A meta-analysis exami-
    nation of assumed properties of child sexual abuse using college samples."
    Psychological Bulletin, 124 (July 1998): 22–53.

Ripley, Amanda; Fowler, Deborah; and Park, Alice. "A mother no more." *Time*
    (July 2, 2001): 30.

Ripley, Amanda, and Jackson, David S. "Throwing the book at kids." *Time* (March
    19, 2001): 34.

Rulo-Pierson, Janet S. "Etiology of stalking and violence in troubled youth." *The
    Forensic Examiner* (December 2001): 15–17.

Schindehette, Susan; Cosgriff, Gabrielle; Stewart, Bob; Weinstein, Fannie; Sim-
    mons, Melody; Sider, Don; Keel, Beverly; and Biddle, Nina. "Nightmare."
    People (Internet Edition), July 9, 2001.

Schreier, Herbert A., and Libow, Judith A. *Hurting for Love: Munchausen by Proxy
    Syndrome.* New York: Guilford Press, 1993.

"Sexual abuse by priests." *America* (February 18, 2002): 3.

Shapiro, Shanti. "Self-mutilation and self-blame in incest victims." *American Jour-
    nal of Psychotherapy, 16* (January 1987): 46–54.

"Signs of the times." *America* (March 4, 2002): 4–5.

Silberstein, José Alejandro. "Matricide: A paradigmatic case in family violence." *International Journal of Offender Therapy and Comparative Criminology*, 42 (1998): 210–223.

Skelly, Richard. "Massacre at Buffalo Creek." *Alberta Report/Newsmagazine* (February 24, 1997): 20–22.

Stermac, Lana, and Sheridan, Peter. "The developmentally disabled adolescent sex offender." In Howard E. Barbaree, William L. Marshall, and Stephen M. Hudson, eds., *The Juvenile Sex Offender*, pp. 235–242. New York: Guilford Press, 1993.

Straus, M. A., and Gelles, R. J. "Societal change and change in family violence from 1975 to 1985 as revealed by two national surveys." *Journal of Marriage and the Family, 48* (1986): 455–467.

"Suicide facts." National Institute of Mental Health, www.nimh.nih.gov /research/suifact.htm, March 25, 2002.

"Teen suicide." American Academy of Child and Adolescent Psychiatry, www .aacap.org/publications/factsfam/suicide.htm, November 1998.

Terr, Lenore. *Unchained Memories: True Stories of Traumatic Memories, Lost and Found.* New York: Basic Books, 1994.

Terry, S., and Kunz, A. "Sins of the innocent." *Rolling Stone* (October 31, 1991): 67–71.

Thomas, Evan; Johnson, Dirk; Gesalman, Anne; Smith, Vern E.; Pierce, Ellise; Peraino, Devin; and Murr, Andrew. "Motherhood and murder." *Newsweek* (July 2, 2001): 20–25.

Thompson, Charles, and Rudolph, Linda B. *Counseling with Children*, 4th ed. New York: Brooks/Cole Publishing Company, 1996.

"Understanding special family situations." National Clearinghouse on Child Abuse and Neglect Information, www.calib.com/nccanch/pubs/usermanuals /crisis/family.cfm, April 6, 2001.

Vaisman-Tzachor, Reuben. "Could family dog bites raise suspicions of child abuse?" *The Forensic Examiner* (September/October 2001): 18–25.

Valios, Natalie. "Damaged beyond repair?" *Community Care* (January 17, 2002): 32–33.

Veneziano, Carol; Veneziano, Louis; and LeGrand, Scott. "The relationship between adolescent sex offender behaviors and victim characteristics with prior victimization." *Journal of Interpersonal Violence, 15* (April 2000): 363–374.

Vossekuil, Bryan; Reddy, Marisa; Fein, Robert; Borum, Randy; and Modzeleski, William. "U.S.S.S. safe school initiative: An interim report on the prevention of targeted violence in schools." United States Secret Service National Threat Assessment Center. Washington, DC: National Threat Assessment Center, October 2000.

Wainwright, Martin. "Care muddle let teenage sex abuser slip through net to kill boy." *The Guardian*, www.guardian.co.uk/child/story/0,7369,593590,00 .html, November 15, 2001.

Wallace, Charles P. "Massacre in Erfurt." *Time Atlantic* (May 6, 2002): 24–29.

Wecht, Cyril H. "Sudden infant death." *Journal of the American Medical Association, 279* (1998): 85–86.

Weir, Erica. "The health impact of bullying." *Canadian Medical Association Journal,* 165 (October 30, 2001): 1249.

Wolke, Dieter; Woods, Sarah; Stanford, Katherine; and Schulz, Henrike. "Bullying and victimization of primary school children in England and Germany: Prevalence and school factors." *British Journal of Psychology, 92* (November 2001): 673–697.

Yuille, John C.; Hunter, Robin; Joffe, Risha; and Zaparniuk, Judy. "Interviewing children in sexual abuse cases." In Gail S. Goodman and Bette L. Bottoms, eds., *Child victims, child witnesses: Understanding and improving testimony,* pp. 95–115. New York: Guilford Press, 1993.

Zaslow, Jeffrey. "Tough kids, tough calls." *Time* (April 22, 2002): 76–79.

Zigler, Edward F., and Stevenson, Matia Finn. *Children in a Changing World: Development and Social Issues,* 2nd edition. New York: Brooks/Cole Publishing Company, 1993.

Zila, Laurie MacAniff, and Kiselica, Mark S. "Understanding and counseling self-mutilation in female adolescents and young adults." *Journal of Counseling and Development, 79* (Winter 2001): 46–52.

Index

About the Author

GREGORY K. MOFFATT has been a college professor for nineteen years and a private practice therapist, specializing in children, since 1987. He regularly lectures at the FBI Academy in Quantico, Virginia, and has addressed hundreds of audiences, including law enforcement professionals, parenting groups, and schools, on the topic of homicide risk assessment. He is a diplomat with the American College of Forensic Examiners. He writes a regular newspaper column addressing families and children and consults with businesses on violence risk assessment and prevention.